Local Governance and Rural Empowerment

BY THE SAME AUTHOR

- Development Issues in Contemporary India,
- Rural Development Governance and Participation,
- Rural Development under Decentralised Governance

About the Editor

Dr. M.R. Biju, (b. 1965) Editor of *South Asian Journal of Socio-Political Studies* (SAJOSPS) and Editor-in-Chief of *International Journal of Political Science* (IJOPS) is a prolific writer on socio-political and developmental issues. He has published 24 books and 115 research papers in the prestigious journals viz., *Economic and Political Weekly, Mainstream, The Atlantic Journal of World Affairs, South Asia Politics, The Indian Journal of Political Science, Journal of Political Studies, The Indian Journal of Political Studies, South Asian Journal of Socio-Political Studies, International Journal for Research and Business Innovation, Indian Journal of Current Research (Quarterly International), Grassroots Governance Journal, Punjab Journal of Politics, Meerut Journal of Politics and Public Administration, Journal of the Institute for the Study of Developing Areas, Kurukshetra, Yojana, Social Science in Perspective* etc. Some of these have been abstracted in the International Political Science Abstracts, Paris. He is also working as Member, Associate Board of the renowned *Management Journal Economics and Management* (E+M) published by the Technical University of Liberce, Czech Republic. He is also working as Member Editorial Advisory Board of the International Journal of Business and Innovation. He has reviewed over Seven Hundred books for *South Asian Journal of Socio-Political Studies*. He has contributed 14 chapters in Edited volumes and published over a dozen papers in the proceedings of National and International conferences.

He was conferred with Post Doctoral Research Award by the University Grants Commission in 2004-2007. He has successfully completed three major research projects on Panchayati Raj founded by Ministry of Panchayati Raj, Government of India and University Grants Commission.

Dr. Biju has successfully guided doctoral students of University of Kerala and also been serving with over a dozen of professional, academic, organizations of National and Global repute. He has presented papers and chaired sessions of a number of national and international seminars and conferences. He is also working as Director and Member Secretary of the Asian Institute of Development Research (AIDR) since 2007. Dr. Biju is currently working as Associate Professor, PG & Research and Department of Political Science, Sree Narayana College. Kollam affiliated to University of Kerala. He is a Member in the PG Board of Studies in Political Science and Public Administration, University of Kerala.

Local Governance and Rural Empowerment

TRENDS AND CHALLENGES

Edited by
M.R. BIJU
Associate Professor,
P.G. and Research Department of Political Science,
Sree Narayana College, Kollam, Kerala (INDIA)

CONCEPT PUBLISHING COMPANY PVT. LTD.
NEW DELHI-110059

ISBN-13: 978-93-5125-182-8

First Published 2015

Published and Printed by

Concept
Since 1974

Concept Publishing Company Pvt. Ltd.
A/15-16, Commercial Block, Mohan Garden
New Delhi-110059 (India)
T: 25351460, 25351794, *F*: 091-11-25357109
E: publishing@conceptpub.com, W: www.conceptpub.com
Editorial Office: H-13, Bali Nagar, New Delhi-110 015, India.

Cataloging in Publication Data--Courtesy: D.K. Agencies (P) Ltd. <docinfo@dkagencies.com>

Local governance and rural empowerment : trends and challenges / edited by M.R.Biju.
pages cm
Contributed articles.
Includes bibliographical references and index.
ISBN 9789351251828

1. Local government--India, South. 2. Local government--India, Northeastern. 3. Rural development--India, South. 4. Rural development--India, Northeastern. I. Biju, M. R., 1965- editor.

JS7025.I53L63 2015 DDC 320.809548 23

Dedicated to
the everloving and everlasting memory
of my beloved wife
JAYA BIJU
(7th September, 1969–31st August, 2012)

Preface

The Constitution of India provides a clear mandate for democratic decentralisation not only through the Directive Principles of State Policy which exhorts the State to promote Panchayati Raj Institutions but more specifically now through the 73rd and 74th Amendments of the Constitution which seek to create an institutional framework for ushering in grassroots democracy through the medium of genuinely self-governing local bodies in both urban and rural areas of the country. However, despite the constitutional mandate, the growth of self-governing local bodies as the third tier of governance in the country has been uneven, halting and slow. Even after the passing of the 73rd and 74th Constitutional Amendments, the transfer of funds, functions and functionaries has been nominal in most States with notable exceptions such as Kerala. Throughout the seventies and eighties, a process of centralisation of even basic municipal functions such as water supply and sanitation into the hands of parastatals such as water boards and authorities has led to a massive decline in the role and status of local bodies which is only now sought to be reversed. Such reversal faces inevitable hurdles from the established institutional structures at the State Government and district levels.

Local democracy is sometimes treated as synonymous with 'decentralisation', but the two are in fact quite distinct. In particular, decentralisation is not necessarily conducive to local democracy. In fact, in situations of sharp local inequalities, decentralisation sometimes heightens the concentration of power, and discourages rather than fosters participation among the underprivileged. To illustrate, in some tribal areas where upper caste landlords and traders dominate village affairs, the devolution of power associated with the Panchayati Raj Amendments has consolidated their hold and reinforced existing biases in the local power structure.

It is now well established that the constitutional division of subjects between the Centre and the States has been overdrawn and that what matters is not the subjects but the functions under each subject. These should ideally be performed according to the principle that the central authority should have a subsidiary function performing only those tasks which cannot be performed effectively at the more immediate or local level. That is the decentralisation envisaged in the 73rd and 74th Constitutional Amendments which now needs to be implemented in full.

The world today is poised to leave its rural past behind. With cities being the main beneficiaries of globalisation, millions of people chasing jobs are migrating to cities, both large and small. For the first time in history, more than half the world's population of 3.3 billion is living in these urban complexes. Within the next two decades, five billion people, i.e. 80 per cent of the world's population will be living in cities. By contrast, the world's rural population is expected to decrease by 28 million during this same period. Since most of this demographic growth will be in Asia and Africa, the crucial question is how Nation-States will cope with this demographic transition, especially since most of this urban growth is going to be propelled by the poor. Are our policy-makers and civil society with their ill-equipped managerial capacities equipped to deal with this mounting population growth? Satellite pictures show that together the urban sites now cover more than 2.8 per cent of the earth's landmass, an area slightly smaller than Japan. But because our cities are pulsating with a concentrated mass of people, we tend to see them as being larger than what they actually are. A recent UNFPA report on the status of world population has said that India does not even recognise semi-urban areas within its urban population and so understates the percentage of people who need to be funded in plans for urban areas. Semi-urbanisation refers to rapid unplanned settlement over large tracts of land in the precincts of manufacturing facilities on a city's periphery. Such areas lack clear administration, suffer from sanitation and water problems and are transitional zones between towns and the countryside.

The key question of course is just how sustainable our urban conglomerates are. The answer to this complex question lies in the kind of consumption patterns our city dwellers are going to adopt. If we continue to foolishly dip into our natural resources—to give a few glaring examples, Brazilian Amazon forests are being torn down to export wood to the United States and Europe, or closer home, lakhs of farmers and villagers are being displaced to build dams in order to provide electricity and water to our metropolis—we will have to pay a heavy price. The interaction between urban and rural growth and sustainability is particularly critical for our future. Preventing environmental degradation and reducing vulnerability of the poor are key interventions that will determine the quality of life in our cities. In India, we are having the worst of urban development in the form of unsustainable slum improvement. We are also having the worst of rural development in the form of ill-designed SEZs. We have made a mess in both because we have not asked what the people want; only what we want for ourselves. To treat "rural" and "urban" poverty as somehow separate is to adopt a rather short-sighted view of the problem. Rural development supports urban development and *vice versa.* Another blinkered approach is to regard the urban poor as being a drain on the urban economy. Experts insist that the urban poor are essential to the economy and well-being of our cities. The majority may be working in the informal sector, but this sector is not a messy mix of marginalised activities as it tends to be viewed. Rather, it is a competitive and highly dynamic sector, which is well integrated into the urban and even the global economy.

Over half the urban population in most developing nations is being forced to live in slums, with China and India together having 37 per cent of the world's slums. The 2001 census estimated the number of slum dwellers in India at 40.3 million that is about 14.2 per cent of the population. Yet, India need not have slums. It is less densely populated than England, Japan, Holland and several other countries. If those nations have avoided slums, we should be able to do the same. The majority of those living in these slums are young people below the age of 18. Inter-personal rivalry and insecurity are rising amongst these young people who have been found to be the largest perpetrators of violence. As high prices of urban land affect the poor and the lower middle classes (whose population exceeds 50 per cent of the total) the most, it is incumbent upon government to stop all speculative increases in urban land prices. Towards this end, the Centre/State and Local Self-Governments need to undertake legal and administrative reforms.

The world sees India as potentially the biggest growth story, after China, in the coming decades. Some of the cities like Singapore, Kuala Lumpur and a few cities in China are now taking quantum leaps to become the greatest urban landscapes. Indian cities need to compete with them in a big way. If India is to meet the growing expectations of the global investors, one key test will be how it manages its rapid urbanisation. Everything else will flow from how well this is done. We need to create world class cities big and small which attract people from within and outside to participate in the economic social and cultural activity. In fact, many reckon this to be the most important condition for turning Mumbai into a world financial centre that will act as an aggregator and executor of complex financial transactions from across the world (ARC Report: 2007).

Today, the extent to which decentralisation has actually taken place differs from state to state. Each state enacts its own legislation on decentralisation, which has to conform to the principles of the 73rd and 74th Constitutional Amendments. This leaves considerable scope for States to either devolve substantial powers to the local governance bodies or to limit devolution to the required minimum to meet the constitutional enactment. Recognizing that devolution of powers and responsibilities to local governments is one of the most important challenges in governance reforms, a growing number of state and civil society institutions are engaged in strengthening elected local governments in rural and urban areas. The need for capacity building is of considerable importance in view of the fact that newly elected representatives at all levels in urban and rural bodies have little or no experience of conducting the work in a Panchayat. However, efforts to transfer adequate power and delegate responsibilities are often slowed down by vested interests that have a stake in centralization of powers and authorities.

Keeping this background in view, this book attempts to address the issues pertaining to various aspects of local governance and rural empowerment viz., Development Schemes, Criteria for financing LSGs, Centrally Sponsored Schemes and Centrally Assisted Schemes, Accountability and Transparency in Local Governance, LSG and Excluded Sections, Role of NGO's in Rural Development, Public Opinion on the Performance of LSG, Accounting Procedures in LSG, Women Empowerment through Micro-Enterprises, Impact of MNREGP on Rural Masses, Gandhian Approach to Simple Living and Development, Sustainable and Environmental Development Contract Farming, New Economic Initiatives under Rural Development, etc. The research papers and articles are contributed by senior academics, administrators and rural development activists with rich experience on the core areas of the study. In their submissions, the authors have tried to explore the existing problems faced by local government and rural development sectors in the aforesaid areas and present solid suggestions to revamp India's rural scenario.

New Year Day, 2015 **M.R. Biju**

Acknowledgements

I would like to express my gratitude to those who have been kind enough to help me in the preparation of this book. I wish to express a deep sense of gratitude to the esteemed contributors to this anthology of articles. The views and opinions expressed by the contributors are of immense value for researchers and academics and administrators for framing policies and strategies on Local Governance and Rural Empowerment. I am extremely thankful to Shri Ashok Kumar Mittal of Concept Publishing Company Pvt. Ltd., New Delhi, who brought out the book in an elegant form. I also wish to express my sincere thanks to Dr. M.B. Manoj, Principal, Sree Narayana College, Kollam for his support.

I also express my deep sense of affection, love and gratitude to my beloved wife for her support, care and exceptional sincerity. I lost her on 31st August 2012 at an age of 42. Whatever, little academic activity I had undertaken hitherto was due to her solid support. Jaya came to my life on 14th November 1993. From that day onwards she supported me like a friend and motivator. She inspired me a lot giving a new meaning and dimension to my life. All the prefaces to the book I have published upto 2012 have been concluded by showering petals of love and affection for Jaya and our kids. From the previous book onwards, she turned a fragrant memory. My onward journey and academic mission were in a standstill after the painful departure. From the previous issue onwards, I am making an attempt to carry forward the unfulfilled mission. If not, I may be doing an injustice to Jaya. Moreover, I pray to the Almighty to give her soul eternal peace and guide us—Aishwarya, Ananthapadmanabha and me—to face the days to come.

Finally, I am also grateful to Paul Ambrose, JoySoft Computers, Kollam, for the data entry services.

M.R. Biju

Contents

SECTION-III
WOMEN EMPOWERMENT, SUSTAINABLE DEVELOPMENT AND NEW ECONOMIC INITIATIVES

List of Contributors

A.K. Makar, Faculty member, Department of Rural Development and Planning, School of Agricultural Sciences and Rural Development, Nagaland University, Medziphema Campus, Nagaland.

Anthony Rodrigues, Associate Professor, Department of Commerce, Fr. Angel College of Arts & Commerce, Pilar, Goa-403203.

Ashok S. Anikivi, Assistant Professor, Department of Political Science, KLE's Lingaraj College, (Autonomous) Belgaum-590001, Karnataka.

B. Ananda Naidu, Head and Chairman Board of Studies, Department of Political Science and Public Administration, Sri Krishnadevaraya University, Ananthapuram, A.P.

C. Krishnamurthy, Research Scholar, Department of Political Science and Public Administration, S.V. University, Tirupati, A.P.

Ch. C. Prasad, Assistant Director, Dr. B.R. Ambedkar Open University, Hyderabad, A.P.

D. Indrakumar, Deputy Director, Institute of Applied Manpower Research (IAMR), Plot-25, Sector A-7, Institutional Area, Narela, Delhi-110040.

G. Palanithurai, Professor, Rajiv Gandhi Chair, Department of Political Science and Development Administration, Gandhigram Rural Institute, Dindugal, Tamil Nadu.

John S. Moolakkattu, Professor and Director, School of Gandhian Thought and Development Studies, Mahatma Gandhi University, P.D. Hills P.O., Kottayam, Kerala-686560.

M.R. Biju, Associate Professor, P.G. and Research Department of Political Science, Sree Narayana College, University of Kerala, Kollam, Kerala.

Merensangla Longkumer, Research Scholar, Department of Rural Development and Planning, School of Agricultural Sciences and Rural Development, Nagaland University, Medziphema Campus, Nagaland.

Nisha Velappan Nair, Post-Doctoral Fellow in Economics, School of Gandhian Thought and Development Studies, Mahatma Gandhi University, P.D. Hills, P.O., Kottayam, Kerala-686560.

P. Shreenivas, Project Fellow, UPE-CART-G&D, Osmania University, Hyderabad, A.P.

S. Harsha, Assistant Professor, Department of Political Science, Assam University, Silchar, Assam-788011.

S.K. Sathyaprabha, Lecturer, School of Governance and Public Policy, Rajiv Gandhi National Institute of Youth Development, Chennai-Banglore Highway, Beemanthangal, Sriperumbudur, Tamil Nadu-602105.

T.G. Ramaiah, Associate Professor, Centre for Self-Employment and Rural Enterprises, NIRD, Rajendranagar, Hyderabad, A.P.-30.

V. Ramakrishna, Assistant Professor, Department of Political Science, Tumkur University, Tumkur-572103, Karnataka, INDIA.

V. Saravanan, Assistant Professor, Department of Economics, Sir Theagaraya College, Old Washermenpet, Chennai, Tamil Nadu-600 021.

Y. Gurappa Naidu, Professor, Department of Political Science and Public Administration, S.V. University, Tirupati, A.P.

Introduction

> *"In this structure composed of innumerable villages, there will be ever widening, never ascending, circles. Life will not be a pyramid with the apex sustained by the bottom. But, it will be an oceanic circle, whose centre will be the individual, always ready to perish for the village, the latter ready to perish for the circle of the villages, till at last the whole becomes one life composed of individuals, never aggressive in their arrogance, but ever humble, sharing the majesty of the oceanic circle of which they are integrated units. Therefore, the outermost circumference will not wield power to crush the inner circle, but will give strength to all within and will derive its own strength from it."*
>
> **—Mahatma Gandhi**

The Constitution of India provides a clear mandate for democratic decentralisation not only through the Directive Principles of State Policy which exhorts the State to promote Panchayati Raj Institutions but more specifically now through the 73rd and 74th Amendments of the Constitution which seek to create an institutional framework for ushering in grassroots democracy through the medium of genuinely self-governing local bodies in both urban and rural areas of the country. However, despite the constitutional mandate, the growth of self-governing local bodies as the third tier of governance in the country has been uneven, halting and slow. Even after the passing of the 73rd and 74th Constitutional Amendments, the transfer of funds, functions and functionaries has been nominal in most States with notable exceptions such as Kerala. Throughout the seventies and eighties, a process of centralisation of even basic municipal functions such as water supply and sanitation into the hands of parastatals such as water boards and authorities has led to a massive decline in the role and status of local bodies which is only now sought to be reversed. Such reversal faces inevitable hurdles from the established institutional structures at the State Government and district levels.

Local democracy is sometimes treated as synonymous with 'decentralisation', but the two are in fact quite distinct. In particular, decentralisation is not necessarily conducive to local democracy. In fact, in situations of sharp local inequalities, decentralisation sometimes heightens the concentration of power, and discourages rather than fosters participation among the underprivileged. To illustrate, in some tribal areas where upper caste landlords and traders dominate village affairs, the devolution of power associated with the Panchayati Raj Amendments has consolidated their hold and reinforced existing biases in the local power structure.

It is now well established that the constitutional division of subjects between the Centre and the States has been overdrawn and that what matters is not the subjects but the functions under each subject. These should ideally be performed according to the principle that the central authority should have a subsidiary function performing only those tasks which cannot be performed effectively at the more immediate or local level. That is the decentralisation envisaged in the 73rd and 74th Constitutional Amendments which now needs to be implemented in full.

The world today is poised to leave its rural past behind. With cities being the main beneficiaries of globalisation, millions of people chasing jobs are migrating to cities, both large and small. For the first time in history, more than half the world's population of 3.3 billion is living in these urban complexes. Within the next two decades, five billion people, i.e. 80 per cent of the world's population will be living in cities. By contrast, the world's rural population is expected to decrease by 28 million during this same period. Since most of this demographic growth will be in Asia and Africa, the crucial question is how Nation-States will cope with this demographic transition, especially since most of this urban growth is going to be propelled by the poor. Are our policy-makers and civil society with their ill-equipped managerial capacities equipped to deal with this mounting population growth? Satellite pictures show that together the urban sites now cover more than 2.8 per cent of the earth's landmass, an area slightly smaller than Japan. But because our cities are pulsating with a concentrated mass of people, we tend to see them as being larger than what they actually are. A recent UNFPA report on the status of world population has said that India does not even recognise semi-urban areas within its urban population and so understates the percentage of people who need to be funded in plans for urban areas. semi-urbanisation refers to rapid unplanned settlement over large tracts of land in the precincts of manufacturing facilities on a city's periphery. Such areas lack clear administration, suffer from sanitation and water problems and are transitional zones between towns and the countryside.

The key question of course is just how sustainable our urban conglomerates are. The answer to this complex question lies in the kind of consumption patterns our city dwellers are going to adopt. If we continue to foolishly dip into our natural resources— to give a few glaring examples, Brazilian Amazon forests are being torn down to export wood to the United States and Europe, or closer home, lakhs of farmers and villagers are being displaced to build dams in order to provide electricity and water to our metropolis— we will have to pay a heavy price. The interaction between urban and rural growth and sustainability is particularly critical for our future. Preventing environmental degradation and reducing vulnerability of the poor are key interventions that will determine the quality of life in our cities. In India, we are having the worst of urban development in the form of unsustainable slum improvement. We are also having the worst of rural development in the form of ill-designed SEZs. We have made a mess in both because we have not asked what the people want; only what we want for ourselves. To treat "rural" and "urban" poverty as somehow separate is to adopt a rather short-sighted view of the problem. Rural development supports urban development and *vice versa*. Another blinkered approach is to regard the urban poor as being a drain on the urban economy. Experts insist that the urban poor are essential to the economy and well-being of our cities. The majority may be working in the informal sector, but this sector is not a messy mix of marginalised activities as it tends to be viewed. Rather, it is a competitive and highly dynamic sector, which is well integrated into the urban and even the global economy.

Over half the urban population in most developing nations is being forced to live in slums, with China and India together having 37 per cent of the world's slums. The 2001 census estimated the number of slum dwellers in India at 40.3 million that is about 14.2 per cent of the population. Yet, India need not have slums. It is less densely populated than England, Japan, Holland and several other countries. If those nations have avoided slums, we should be able to do the same. The majority of those living in these slums are young people below the age of 18. Inter-personal rivalry and insecurity are rising amongst these young people who have been found to be the largest perpetrators of violence. As high prices of urban land affect the poor and the lower middle classes (whose population exceeds 50 per cent of the total) the most, it is incumbent upon government to stop all speculative increases in urban land prices. Towards this end, the Centre/State and Local Self-Governments need to undertake legal and administrative reforms.

The world sees India as potentially the biggest growth story, after China, in the coming decades. Some of the cities like Singapore, Kuala Lumpur and a few cities in China are now taking quantum leaps to become the greatest urban landscapes. Indian cities need to compete with them in a big way. If India is to meet the growing expectations of the global investors, one key test will be how it manages its rapid urbanisation. Everything else will flow from how well this is done. We need to create world class cities big and small which attract people from within and outside to participate in the economic social and cultural activity. In fact, many reckon this to be the most important condition for turning Mumbai into a world financial centre that will act as an aggregator and executor of complex financial transactions from across the world (ARC Report, 2007).

Today, the extent to which decentralisation has actually taken place differs from state to state. Each state enacts its own legislation on decentralisation, which has to conform to the principles of the 73rd and 74th Constitutional Amendments. This leaves considerable scope for States to either devolve substantial powers to the local governance bodies or to limit devolution to the required minimum to meet the constitutional enactment. Recognizing that devolution of powers and responsibilities to local governments is one of the most important challenges in governance reforms, a growing number of state and civil society institutions are engaged in strengthening elected local governments in rural and urban areas. The need for capacity building is of considerable importance in view of the fact that newly elected representatives at all levels in urban and rural bodies have little or no experience of conducting the work in a Panchayat. However, efforts to transfer adequate power and delegate responsibilities are often slowed down by vested interests that have a stake in centralization of powers and authorities.

Keeping this background in view, this book attempts to address the issues pertaining to various aspects of local governance and rural empowerment viz., Development Schemes, Criteria for financing LSGs, Centrally Sponsored Schemes and Centrally Assisted Schemes, Accountability and Transparency in Local Governance, LSG and

Excluded Sections, Role of NGO's in Rural Development, Public Opinion on the Performance of LSG, Accounting Procedures in LSG, Women Empowerment through Micro-Enterprises, Impact of MNREGP on Rural Masses, Gandhian Approach to Simple Living and Development, Sustainable and Environmental Development Contract Farming, New Economic Initiatives under Rural Development, etc. The research papers and articles are contributed by senior academics, administrators and rural development activists with rich experience on the core areas of the study. In their submissions, the authors have tried to explore the existing problems faced by local government and rural development sectors in the aforesaid areas and present solid suggestions to revamp India's rural scenario.

Contents of the Book

In the inaugural chapter **G. Palanithurai** examines the faces of development schemes and critically evaluates its application as a means of vote catcher. According to him, the ultimate aim of any government is to enable the people to lead a decent and dignified human life in the society. To achieve the above governments are trying through a combination of actions namely enacting laws, chalking out policies, evolving development programmes and schemes, and allocating resources. To uplift the poor, welfare schemes with different nature are being implemented by the government as a welfare state. Many of the welfare schemes are almost investment in human being. The investment in human being will be viewed as an investment for growth and development. Ultimately, it ends in human growth. But all investments have not brought the expected results as the government expected or targeted. After carrying out plethora of development schemes and programmes, democratic governments in the world have identified the gaps in all those schemes. It was realized that unless the poor, deprived, marginalized are empowered to participate in the process of governance and development it is very difficult to reduce poverty and achieve development for the poor. Hence, it has been decided that governments have to act as a catalyst and the poor should be made as participants. Empowerment and participation are the two factors which are key for transforming the life of the poor in India.

The author further states that, Tamil Nadu is a pioneer in implementing various kinds of welfare schemes. These schemes are viewed differently with different perspectives. Yet the Government of

Tamil Nadu has continuously been implementing series of schemes to transform the life of the poor. The schemes targeted individual, groups and communities. Hence, individual oriented, group oriented and community oriented schemes have been evolved and carried out continuously and relentlessly without paying heed to any of the criticisms against the schemes. Impact of many of the schemes could be seen in the human development index of the State. Many of the social welfare schemes enabled the state to secure higher points to reach nearer to Kerala in terms of Human Development. Both Amartya Sen and Jean Dreez have appreciated the social welfare measures initiated by different governments in Tamil Nadu which enabled the poor to come out from poverty and lead a decent human life. At present Tamil Nadu has been considered as a place for innovative welfare programmes and through which the poor and the lower middle classes have been drawn towards the party in power. Arguments have been projected that Tamil Nadu is known for competitive populism and it has influenced all other provinces which have been ruled by the regional political parties.

According to G. Palanithurai, in the whole of India, Tamil Nadu has got the highest number of development schemes. Some argue that it is a vote catching technique and some argue that the government relies on the support of the poor and hence they wanted to uplift the life of the poor and for which Government of Tamil Nadu had introduced series of schemes. Of the schemes giving laptop to the students who are pursuing studies in government and government aided institutions is considered as unique and important. It was interpreted that by giving such laptop to the youth who are first time voters will be drawn towards the ruling party. Against this background an attempt is made to study the impact of this scheme in the life and life style of the beneficiaries.

Palanithurai further adds that at present Tamil Nadu has been considered as a place for innovative welfare programmes and through which the poor and the lower middle classes have been drawn towards the party in power. Arguments have been projected that Tamil Nadu is known for competitive populism and it has influenced all other provinces which have been ruled by the regional political parties. In the whole of India Tamil Nadu has got the highest number of development schemes. Some argue that it is a vote catching technique and some argue that the government relies on the support of the poor and hence they wanted to uplift the life of the poor and for which Government of Tamil Nadu had introduced series of schemes. Of the schemes giving laptop to the students who are pursuing studies in government and government aided institutions is considered as unique and important. It was interpreted that by giving such laptop to the youth who are first time voters will be drawn towards the ruling party. Against this background an attempt is made to study the impact of this scheme in the life and life style of the beneficiaries. This article tries to analyze to what extent it helps the end user of the scheme and what will be the impact created in the minds and lives of the beneficiaries. The above study has been conducted through a combination of methods. Data have to be generated through focus group discussion and case study method.

He concludes his study by saying that, any decision in any government in a democracy is aimed at keeping the people with the establishment. To reach out the people governments chalk out schemes and programmes which are considered as welfare programmes and schemes. Welfare programmes and schemes will bring many benefits to the beneficiaries. The benefits are of many types. Some are indirect and some are direct. Direct benefit and individual oriented schemes started operating from beginning of 1980 in Tamil Nadu. It has been gradually multiplied. Many of the schemes have created reasonably good impact in the society. Social welfare programmes for the poor will help the poor come out from poverty and hunger. Tamil Nadu is always a pioneer in welfare programmes and schemes. In this context every scheme and its impact has to be evaluated. Now, new methodological nuances are needed for micro-studies. Nuanced focus group discussion would enable us to understand many of the deeper issues in the process of transformation of the society. Giving laptop to students of the government and government aided educational institutions by the Government of Tamil Nadu has been viewed with different perspectives. To understand the deeper implications of the scheme of the government a study has been conducted and that too through a focus group discussion. For the focus group discussion only students from poorest segment of the society had been drawn. In the focus group discussion what have been drawn are given below.

In the second chapter **Nisha Velappan Nair** and **John S. Moolakkattu** have presented a study captioned "Criteria for Financing Rural Local Government in Kerala: Do Recommendations of State Finance Commissions Matter?" Through this paper the authors look at the developmental role of Panchayats in Kerala, the criteria that the Union Finance Commission has evolved for release of grants to the local bodies through the consolidated fund of the state and the record of the four State Finance Commissions in a comparative perspective. It also look at the sources of funding of panchayats and the share of local government allocation and expenditure in the State's plan.

According to Nisha and John, S.M., rural development financing is a major issue in many developing countries. Providing stable sources of funding is necessary if rural development is to take place in a sustainable manner. After the Seventy-Third Amendment to the Constitution, panchayats have emerged as key means of implementation of rural development schemes with varying degrees of freedom to do so. While the Centre acts as a major source of funding for the rural areas through various programmes, the states also now contribute to the development of local areas and people through plan grants. In some states like Kerala, the share of the grants in the total funds available for local development exceeds what is received from the Centre. Having a commission to make recommendations on the modalities of grants and distribution of shared taxes suggests that it will guarantee assured flow to the local bodies and enable them to plan for a longer period. This is the logic behind the creation of State Finance Commissions (SFCs) on the pattern of the Union Finance Commissions (UFCs). The Union Finance Commission (UFC) constituted every five years is for assessing the expenditure requirements of Panchayats and explore their potential to raise revenues from existing and new sources and recommend the amount of grants for performing their assigned functions. The Central Government also gives grants on the recommendation of the Central Finance Commission (CFC). They further states that most states in India have set up such commissions and several of their recommendations have been accepted and implemented either wholly or partly by the governments. However, only few States "have rigorously kept to a time table of setting up SFCs". "The timing of setting SFCs up have also not been synchronised with the CFCs, thus, depriving CFCs of the crucial inputs as envisaged". These inter-governmental transfers are necessary in developing countries because, unlike the developed countries where people migrate from places where the local government offers fewer services to those where more services are offered leading to some kind of horizontal equalization and competition among the local bodies, people in developing countries do not have such mobility option, and it is through these transfers that some kind of inter-panchayat equalization is achieved.

After a detailed presentation, the authors came to the conclusion that Kerala State Finance Commissions have been proactive in adopting a local bodies friendly policy and have recommended transfers that could assure fund flow to the tune of around 20 per cent with recommendations to enhance it further either by making a certain percentage statutory or by gradually enhancing the share with successive years. However, something like flypaper effect exists as far as the own fund is concerned. The assured flow of grants has made the rural local bodies to go slow on own fund mobilisation. The refusal of the government to commit itself to a certain percentage of the state revenue suggests that the development fund devolved as a part of budget could be cut if the plan size is reduced in the course of the year. Given the fact that property tax, the main source of own funds, has only recently been slated for revision after a long period of 20 years could mean higher revenue in the near future with a share of it going for development purposes. Efforts also have been made over the years to achieve horizontal fiscal balance. But these efforts are not enough because development is most needed in those panchayats where own income is low because the poor are mainly located in them. While the threshold level of funds set for these panchayats do contribute to the reduction of horizontal inequalities, there are limitations to what they can accomplish in the long run given the general tendency to adopt a redistributive approach to development by the Gram Panchayats. Unlike in the case of the Union Finance Commission recommendations which have a convention be being accepted by the Union Government, there is no such convention in the case of SFC recommendations.

M.R. Biju in his chapter examines the significance of Centrally Sponsored Schemes and Centrally Assisted Schemes with special focus on the recommendations of M.M. Punchi and B.K. Chaturvedi. This chapter has been organized in the following manner. The introductory part presents the Constitutional provisions and role of Central and State governments in the fiscal federal structure of India. Part two unfolds the evolutionary process of financial assistance from Centre to State. Part three evaluates the major recommendations of M.M. Punchi Commission (2010) and B.K. Chaturvedi Committee (2011) on the relevant aspects of the subject. The concluding part presents briefly the major findings of the study.

According to the author, in India, the Central and State legislatures are responsible for law making, the central and state governments are responsible for the implementation of laws and policies, and the judiciary interprets laws. Subjects are divided between the centre and the states on the basis of the union, state and concurrent lists. The centre is responsible for subjects that fall within the union list, the states for those subjects which fall in the state list and both the centre and the states are jointly responsible for subjects that fall within the concurrent list. There are several subjects such as education and health, which states are responsible for (as they are included in the state list) but might not have the resources to address adequately. The centre can provide additional resources to meet challenges in these sectors. One of the ways it does this is through establishing Centrally Sponsored Schemes (CSS), CSS are schemes that are funded fully or partly by the central government, but implemented by the states. This is because they address subjects that are included in the state list.

After evaluating the key recommendations of all major committees and commissions on CSS and CAS, M.R. Biju concludes his study by stating the following;

- The 73rd and 74th Amendments to the Constitution were game changing developments in the Indian federation and were intended to strengthen self-governance at the grassroots level and to make local bodies important agencies for the delivery of public services. Decentralisation is intended to result in greater efficiency in the delivery of services. Local bodies being closer to people are expected to meet the local needs better than a centralized system of governance. Under Articles 243G and 243W, State legislatures may by law transfer powers and authority to rural and urban local bodies as are necessary to enable them to function as institutions of self-government. Powers and authority include transfer of functional responsibilities and powers to levy and collect taxes as may be assigned to them by the State legislatures.
- Following the 73rd and 74th Amendments to the Constitution, a number of States have notified transfer of functions to local bodies. But there has been limited progress in the direction of transfer of funds and functionaries. The expectation that funds and functionaries will follow functions has remained unfulfilled. Decentralisation is not fiscally neutral. Decentralisation requires empowering local bodies with adequate resources to discharge their assigned responsibilities.
- The 73rd and 74th Amendments to the Constitution do not provide for direct funding of local bodies by the Central Government. The involvement of the Central Government in strengthening the financial position of the local bodies is indirect following the consequential amendment made to Article 280

mandating the Central Finance Commission to make recommendations on the measures needed to augment the Consolidated Fund of a State to supplement the resources of Panchayats and Municipalities in the State on the basis of the recommendations made by the Finance Commission of the State. The purpose of this provision is to find ways and means to meet the financial requirements of local bodies without in any way changing the primary role of States.

Before conclude the author put forward the following suggestions to revamp the CSS and CAS.

- The Centrally Sponsored Schemes carry substantial amounts of grants transferred from the Government of India (GoI) to States to influence expenditure in areas that are Constitutional responsibilities of states and addressing national objective of critical importance. We have seen that the percentage allocation from Central Plan Assistance towards CSS has been increasing at a rapid pace over the years.
- In general, most departments opine that CSS have served an important purpose and therefore must continue. This is despite having problems with some or the other aspect of the specific scheme in many cases. However, a large number of issues and learning emerged through an analysis of the implementation experience of various schemes. Although, the nature, design, purpose, structure, funding patters and mechanisms vary quite largely from one scheme to the other, certain common learning emerged which could act as ready check list for future planning or restructuring of the scheme/s.
- Provision of adequate human resources to plan, implement and monitor the scheme is considered critical. A number of existing schemes are well-placed in this regard whereas many suffer due to lack of adequate provisions. CSS has good record on investing in professional development of human resources, which needs to continue. But the departments also felt that the training and capacity building component is more sustained if the focus is on the respective departmental staff rather than those hired for short-term.
- The consultations with almost all the departments in the state revealed that despite the presence of monitoring structures, formats

and pre-determined frequencies, monitoring is generally weak for a variety of reasons. There is a need to move from filing up and collecting monitoring formats to utilization of the same in decision-making. The use of IT is highly recommended. Keeping the sensitive relationship between the centre and the state, third party monitoring may seem to be an appropriate method.

- There is constant debate on the primary responsibility of providing quality services across departments, and burden sharing between the State and Centre. One of the largest problems with inter-governmental transfer schemes is the overlapping jurisdiction of multiple agencies. While in general the Additional Central Assistance Schemes are 100 per cent Centrally Assisted and CSS have some state contribution ranging from 10 per cent to 50 per cent, the definition of CSS remains unclear. Chaturvedi Committee points out that the distinction between CSS and ACA based schemes is artificial as both are conceptually the same. Greater clarity in such definitions is indeed desirable.
- Flexi funds can be introduced at the Central, State and district level within the scheme, between schemes and between sectors. Flexi funds could help in filling the gaps in regional variations, encourage innovations and reduce procedural delays. The risks associated with the introduction of flexi funds, as identified by the departments, include the possibilities of vested interests influencing the investments at the cost of real priorities, and diversion of funds in paying salaries and financing state sectors schemes. Well-designed and detailed guidelines and monitoring system need to be in place to minimize such risks. We have suggested that 80 per cent of the funds can come through CSS while 20 per cent of the funds should be allotted to flexi fund kitty. Chaturvedi Committee also suggests allotting 20 per cent of funds as flexi funds.
- Flexi funds can also be used an incentive for states that have made greater investments in particular sectors, that are considered priority. For instance, Karnataka and other states who had introduced free text-books before SSA initiation could be given the equivalent amounts as flexi funds to be used for some other purpose within the sector.

S. Harsha in his chapter examines the issues of accountability and transparency in the decentralized governance of Karnataka. According to Harsha Karnataka was the first State to pass the legislation on 7th April, 1993, which included the provisions of 73rd Constitutional Amendment Act and it came into force from 30th April, 1993. The three-tier structure of Panchayati Raj with Zilla Panchayat at the district level, Taluk Panchayat at the taluk level and Grama Panchayat at the village level are given impetus to promote development projects in terms of infrastructure, poverty alleviation, education, health and improvement of living conditions in rural areas. The available literature on the functioning of Panchayats in Karnataka reveals that it has achieved success to some extent in implementing plans and programmes of decentralization.

He further observes that micro-level accountability mechanisms support decentralization, participation and competition allow the public to influence the quality and quantity of the public services. The proponents of good governance like Soren Villidsen and Manor, Heller, argue that decentralization ensures more accountability, transparency and participation and thereby it reduces the extent of corruption. Heller observes that strengthening and empowering local government has been justified not only on the grounds of making government more efficient but also on the grounds of increasing accountability and participation. The advantages of decentralization centre around increased popular involvement and their control over decision-making and access to services. The local people can also put pressure on local authorities to influence public servicing and thereby reducing financial mismanagement. The common opinion of good governance view is that transparency improves the incentives and pressure for public sector performance while lowering the scope for corruption, reducing transaction costs and improving the efficiency.

According to Harsha, accountability, transparency and increased people's participation in governance reduce the scope for corruption. Thus, it is believed that decentralization ensures accountability between the elected representatives and the officials and between the elected representatives and the people. Further, more decentralization tends to produce greater transparency and facilitates more people participation. It also leads to closer contact between the government officials and the local people, which will allow better information, more realistic and effective plans for government and programmes. Notwithstanding, the novel and laudable features of the Karnataka Panchayati Raj Act, there are some aberrations which hinder the effective utilization of transparency and accountability mechanisms.

The pre-requisite of decentralized planning according to Harsha, is the identification of beneficiaries in the Gram Sabha by involving people and their representatives. There are studies which have documented that there instance of Panchayats not holding the ward and Gram Sabha's regularly. In some Panchayats Gram Sabhas are convened to identify the beneficiaries, there were many cases of misidentification of beneficiaries reported in the selected Panchayats.

The new punitive clause of termination of the membership for not convening ward and Gram Sabha has been considered as a draconian legislation by the opposition parties. The state level co-ordination body State Panchayat Council has not been made functional.

In his concluding observation Harsha comments that, *Jamabandhi* is also plagued by several shortcomings. The lack of awareness among the people, officials deputed on *Jamabandhi* duty most often did not undertake field visits along with the affected persons and usually action was initiated only against officials. A field study by Sivanna and Babu revealed that the programme ensured both vertical and horizontal accountability particularly among the officials.

V. Ramakrishna in his chapter examines the welfare and political dimensions of the excluded sections and its linkage with the LSGs. Key areas of his enquiry include:

(1) To analyze the involvement of weaker sections representatives in the institutions of Panchayati Raj in Gulbarga and Afjalpur Taluk of Gulbarga District.
(2) To assess the awareness, commitment, ability and problems of weaker sections representatives in the process of implementing the welfare policies for SC, ST and OBC, historical descriptive and analytical methods have been employed in the present study.
(3) To examine the status of weaker sections in Village Panchayats of Gulbarga and Afjalpur Taluks in Gulbarga District and to compare the status of weaker section's representatives with the representatives of other castes in Panchayati Raj Institutions of Gulbarga District.
(4) To identify the education level of weaker sections representatives in Panchayati Raj Institutions of Gulbarga District. Awareness towards the working of Panchayati Raj Institutions, suggest policy implementations for the effective involvement of weaker section and to implement welfare policies for weaker sections through Panchayati Raj Institutions.

According to Ramakrishna, it is widely believed that the analysis of age, education, caste, family structure, occupation, income, land holding, party affiliation, etc., are important in determining the nature of leadership. The data relating to socio-economic background of elected respondents of Panchayati Raj Institutions were collected in the per cent study to get an insight into the emerging pattern of rural leadership in the Afjalpur Taluk of Gulbarga District. The socio-economic conditions play an important role in characterizing the social life and behaviour of an individual. The socio-economic status of an individual affects the patterns of interaction in the society. It is therefore, essential to analyse the socio-economic background of the relationship between the leader and the environment. In a developing society like ours where forces of caste and kinship influence the social life and acute disparity in the standard of living and sub culture among various groups and regions are existing, a study of the socio-economic conditions of SC, ST and OBCs respondents would help reveal sociologically significant dimensions.

He further adds that the socio-economic, educational and political background of the leaders would also enable us to anticipate as to what they are capable of doing, what we should expect from them and how well they are equipped to discharge the responsibilities developed upon them by the electorate. Knowledge of socio-economic background of a community is an indispensable prerequisite, for the understanding of the thought or behaviours of its members. This holds good for all human communities, and more so in the case of SC, ST and OBC communities, which are intrinsically more traditional in their structure.

Ramakrishna concludes in his study by saying that, social inequalities existed in the villages and these have continued for centuries. Under these circumstances, soon after Independence the concept of social justice figured in the Constitution of India. Thus, the Constitution of India made an attempt to provide equal social opportunities for the development of personality of all the people in the society, without any discrimination on the basis of caste, sex or race. Therefore, after Independence, India was one among the countries which went in for social and economic transformation of the rural population. As a preferred condition, rural development became a definite strategy for the improvement of the living conditions of the rural poor. In this direction the Government of India made efforts to solve problems such as poverty, ill health, illiteracy, and backwardness of varied nature prevailing in rural areas, by giving greater attention to the uplift of the rural poor. By this case study we came to know that the representatives belonging to weaker sections are able to implement welfare policies for the development of SC, ST and OBC in the study area. Due to the illiteracy and ignorance of weaker section's representatives, several welfare policies intended for the welfare of SC's, ST's and OBC's are not implementing properly in the institutions of Panchayati Raj and suggest for effective implementation of these policies for the welfare of weaker sections and bring them to the main stream as well as equal opportunity as stipulated in the Constitution of India.

C. Prasad and **P. Sreenivas** has presented a chapter on the linkage between NGOs in Rural Development. This study is based on Telangana State. According to the authors, civil society is playing an increasingly important social and economic role around the world. One of the more positive moves of the 1980s has been recognition of the essential development role of civil society. People are creating new institutions at both the local levels and national levels to provide for needs that are not being met by either the market place or the public sector. Non-Governmental Organizations (NGOs) are important actors from civil society.

The present study is undertaken in Nalgonda district of newly carved Telangana State. The study selected all the four Revenue Divisions of the district viz., Bhongiri, Nalgonda, Miryalaguda and Suryapet. The study selected one active NGOs from each Revenue Divisions on random basis to examine the activities and programmes that are undertaken in their adopted villages since inception. The factors like year of establishment, nature of activities, composition of members, area of operation are taken into consideration while selecting NGOs for the study.

The major findings of their studying can be summarized as:

- Contextual understanding of rural development has been changing over the years. There is a shift in the emphasis on the discourse on rural development form 'intellectual idealism to techno-bureaucracy', and eventually to the present 'participatory development'. All these changes in the perspectives on rural development have been associated with changing approaches and strategies. There is growing emphasis on such criterion as sustainability, participation and decentralization, while formulating strategies for rural development. These criteria have assumed greater significance in the era of globalization as rural development and requirements of globalization raise a debate.

- Over the last decade there has been a dramatic growth in the number of NGOs involved in development aid, in both developed and developing countries. Today India has a vibrant NGOs sector. India is estimated to have 3.3 million registered NGOs. With rapid deterioration on performance side of the Government agencies, the NGOs role and importance has increased manifold. The reason behind this is that government structures are not geared for integrated development like agriculture, energy, environment, water resources, equity and social justice.
- NGO is one of the interventions in a society to achieve development. It acts as catalyst to enhance development process. Therefore, there is a need to assesses the impact of NGO practices that how they contribute to different facts of development. Measurement of NGO's performance is a very complicated and complex phenomenon due to qualitative nature of its contribution. It is argued that performance of NGO need not be evaluated on the same yardsticks as those for judging the performance of a commercial organization.

The authors conclude their study by stating that the new critical approach to development has shifted focus from structure (state) to actors (civil society). The top-down approach has been displayed by bottom-up community approach. NGOs are now an important part of the civil society and legitimate negotiations on behalf of the people. In most of the third world countries, and also in India, NGOs are now playing an important role in the rural development processes.

The authors also adds that the new economic policies heralded in the early 1990s in India acknowledge the role of NGOs in implementing developmental programmes. A plethora of NGOs operate in Telangana in various fields in general, rural development in particular. The study highlights that rural people have more positive attitude towards significance role of NGOs in rural development. NGOs are not only influencing local administration and institutions involving in rural development, but also inculcating participative culture and attitude to achieve grassroots democracy. They are enlarging the scope of rural development and acting as watchdog to prevent arbitrary exercise of state power. Further, measures like establishment of separate directorate, networking of NGOs in similar field, democratising NGOs management and transparent financial management will go a long way to improve the role of NGOs in rural development. The Telangana State by acknowledging the role of NGOs in rural development, formed an NGO with World Bank assistance i.e., The Society for Elimination of Rural Poverty. Despite the increasing assertiveness of NGOs role in rural development, they cannot be a substitute to states and governments.

S. K. Sathyaprabha evaluates people's opinion on local governments performance in hospitality industry. To her, local governance has significant role in tourism sector as both local government and tourism are interdependent for their development. Local governments are practically acting agents for the conservation of the local area which needs the support of the local people. It is undeniable that the relationships between the environmental conservation, local governments and local people inseparable and inevitable. To have sustainable development of the local area as well as the tourism industry it is essential to involve the local people in all its developmental activities. Studies have examined the involvement and participation of Indigenous people in the tourism development process. A similar idea was put forth by Simmons the relationship between tourism development and indigenes participation indicates that community involvement is, indeed, crucial in order to avoid more likely uncertainties and misunderstandings about tourism development in the area.

In the local governance role in the tourism according to Sathyaprabha is very essential for the development of area infrastructure because the local urban government knows the quality of that area. Local government is a key player in Nainital Urban tourism sector. Local government manages the natural and cultural resources that tourism relies on, provides core infrastructure, attractions and facilities, and often funds regional marketing and visitor information.

In the local government according to the author is responsible for the planning and management of Nainital natural and cultural resources. The local administrative department is very helpful for the local citizen and visitors. The local government is providing attractive facilities for the public and tourism aspect also.

It also provides the core utilities and infrastructure on which the tourism industry is based. This includes district and city roads, lighting, water and sewerage, public transport systems. Local government operates attractions such as museums, art galleries, sports stadium, convention centres, parks, events, tours, and other amenities.

She further adds that local government enables regional marketing and provides visitor information by being the primary source of funding for Regional Tourism Organizations (RTOs) and the Visitor Information Network (VIN). There is very good IT facility for getting information about the Nainital place and other tourist spots, all offices and hotels are attach with the internet facilities for people welfare. Thus the research on linkage between the local governance and Nainital Urban Tourism in the people's point of view would be greatly helpful for both the tourism department and the local government institution to aware about the shortcomings as well as to improve their quality of service.

Major findings of her study includes:

- The role of local governance in Nainital Urban Tourism in the perspective of the local people are satisfactory. The local people participation in all the tourism activities is excepted as most of the people have the tourism as their livelihood and main business.
- Most of the local people families residing in this hilly area are predominantly depend on tourism related business which is leading to expect more from the government sector. Since Local Government Institution has an important responsibility in enhancing tourism in its areas as it will bring in more income, these local people could also be involved in its process which in turn will reflect in the sustainable development of the lives of local people and their area.
- According to the people's view encouraging local people to invest in the tourism sector, to work for the tourism sector, involve in tourism survey are the suitable means of involving local people for tourism development and also they want to take the leading role as entrepreneurs, as workers at all levels so that they have a voice in decision-making process of local tourism development.
- For the betterment of Nainital tourism healthy environment, good and cheap transportation system, developing new attractive tourist sport, improvement in the local infrastructure and sanitation facilities. Modern and stylist boat in the Nainital Lake and keeping the bank of lake clean, Opening Tourism Information Centre working twenty-four hours which gives greater access of information for the tourist are some of the suggestions.

Nisha V. Nair's chapter focuses on the construction-related projects under Women Component Plan (WCP) implemented in Kerala at the local level by selecting five Gram Panchayats randomly from the five taluks in Kottayam District in Kerala. The chapter draws on data relating to a ten-year reference period (1997-2007) collected from each of the five panchayats through field visits as well as through interviews of panchayat representatives (50 males and 50 females). The main objective of study is to understand the nature of construction-related projects under WCP, the increasing tendency to go for such projects and whether such projects are of any benefit to women.

According to Nisha, the shift to more and more construction-oriented projects is a general trend in most Panchayats in Kerala and this not unique to WCP projects. But this encourages many Panchayats to construct buildings in the name of women which could be used later for general purposes. This shift deprives many poor women of the opportunity to tap the WCP funds to earn an income by engaging in productive activities such as agriculture, animal husbandry and so on. Such projects are seen as challenging and cumbersome for elected representatives to implement. In the absence of sustained commitment to the WCP by women representatives themselves, the WCP can only be carried out only in this lacklustre fashion. While some projects like women's houses can be useful for women, the construction of women's industrial units and conference halls for women will not be of much benefit to them. Given the fact that an elected woman representative sees herself as a representative of the entire electorate in a constituency, it is difficult to inculcate in her a special interest in a programme meant for women alone. It is here that women's organisations have to step in and play a major role to sustain interest in gender issues relating to local level development.

Nisha further adds that in Kerala, the whole project of mainstreaming gender was confined to the 10 per cent plan funds alone and no conscious attempt was made for enhancing women's share in the total expenditure over the years. The process dimension that makes planning a form of debate between men and women and among women themselves was absent. Planning should become iterative and process–intensive. At the same time one needs to be aware that participation of poor women can come only if the benefits are in sight in the immediate future. Early emphasis on strategic interests of women such as focusing on the gendered division of labour can scuttle the process. Talking about strategic interests to women whose survival needs are not met can turn out to be a futile exercise.

Anthony Rodrigues examines the accounting procedures and guidelines of DRDA in Goa. According to Rodrigues, poverty alleviation through Self-employment and Wage-employment programme is the theme of rural development. It is District Rural Development Agency (DRDA) at the District level which overseas the implementation of different anti-poverty programme. District Rural Development Agency came into existence with effect from 1.4.1980. Previously, it was known as Marginal Farmer and Agricultural Land Development Agency (MFALDA). Later on it became Small Farmer Development Agency (SFDA). These agencies were only to cater the development of Marginal Farmers and Agricultural Labourers in rural area. Now, District Rural Development Agency has embraced manifold activities for upliftment of rural poor.

District Rural Development Agency has traditionally been the principal organ at the district level to oversee the implementation of anti-poverty programmes of the Ministry of Rural Development. This agency according to Rodrigues was created originally to implement the Integrated Rural Development Programme (IRDP). Subsequently, the District Rural Development Agencies were entrusted with number of programmes of both State and Central Governments. From 1st April, 1989 a separate District Rural Development Agency Administration has been introduced to take care of the administrative costs.

Rural India according to the author, which encompasses three fourths of the Country's population is characterized by low income levels, inadequate to ensure a quality of life compatible with physical well-being. The Ministry of Rural Development, spearheading the frontal attack on rural poverty, through its various programmes endeavoured to reach out to the last and most disadvantaged sections of society, provide them with avenues of employment, be it self-employment or wage-employment, and to improve infrastructure relating to their life support system.

Anthony Rodrigues further adds that in State of Goa this task is entrusted to two District Rural Development Agencies viz., District Rural Development Agency—North Goa and District Rural Development Agency—South Goa. The Agency came into existence when the Government established the Small Farmers Development Agency (SFDA) which has been amalgamated with the then Rural Development Agency on 4th November, 1980. District Rural Development Agencies were established by bifurcating the then Rural Development Agency into District Rural Development Agency, North Goa and District Rural Development Agency, South Goa with the objective to take the administration at the nearest steps to the people. The Agency works at Panaji and Margao. North Goa is having jurisdiction over six development blocks of North Goa District namely, Tiswadi, Bardez, Pernem, Bicholim, Ponda and Sattari and District Rural Development Agency, South Goa is having jurisdiction over five development blocks namely, Sanguem, Quepem, Canarcona, Salcete and Mormugao. These Agencies are implementing the programmes with the assistance of the Block Development Officers at the block level.

Anthony concludes his study by pin-pointing that:

- DRDAs/ZPs and Blocks are responsible for the correct accounting of money distributed to the implementing agencies. They are supposed to supervise and control the whole accounting functions of Blocks/Panchayats. Project Directors/CEOs are supposed to carry out essential checks.
- The accounts of the each District Rural Development Agency (DRDA)/ZP/DLC and Block shall be maintained on accrual basis/double entry system like other commercial organisation.
- DRDAs/ZP/DLC/Block and Panchayats should maintain a consolidated Receipt and Payment Account register common for all schemes on the basis of Pass Book, Cash Transaction as recorded in the Cash Book and posted in Ledger.
- Interest earned on funds of each scheme should be added in the scheme fund. Income and Expenditure Account should depict the same separately.
- Principal of one Bank account for each scheme must be followed by DRDA and line level. Second Bank Account for the same scheme, if at all required could only be opened with the approval of the State Secretary (RD). Multiplicity of Bank Accounts for one scheme is not permissible.
- Funds received both from Central and State Governments should be kept in the Savings Bank Accounts only. Funds in no case be kept in the Fixed Deposits/Term Deposits. All existing FDs/TDs should be encashed and transferred to the respective scheme account.

Women empowerment through micro-enterprises is the topic of discussion in the chapter presented by **Gurappa Naidu** and **Krishnamurthy**. According to the authors the empowerment of women for the last two decades has been widely recognized as a central issue in determining the status of women. It covers aspects such as women's control over material and intellectual resources. Empowerment is a process, but not an event, which challenges traditional power equations and relations. In recent past the two landmark initiatives have become very important for the empowerment of women, one being the reservation of seats in local bodies for women and the other being the Programme for Development of Women and Children in Rural Areas (DWCRA). The DWCRA programme, initiated in 1980s, is based on the concept of Self-Help Group (SHG), and has emerged as the most successful programme in promoting the empowerment of women The State of Andhra Pradesh (AP) has become a role model for other states. The SHGs in AP have recorded a rip-roaring success in eliminating the poverty among the rural women and in empowering them in different spheres. The impact of SHGs in Andhra Pradesh has been appreciated by the World Bank.

Authors further adds that, empowerment is a multi-dimensional process, which should enable the group of individuals to realize their full identity and powers in all spheres of life. It also means equal status to women. Empowering women socio-economically through increased awareness of their rights and duties as well as access to resources is a decisive step towards greater security for them. Empowerment includes higher literacy level and education for women, better health care for women and children, equal ownership of productive resources, increased participation in economic and commercial sectors, awareness of their rights and responsibilities, improved standards of living and acquiring self-reliance, self-esteem and self-confidence.

The authors concludes their studying by highlighting the following:

- Unable to fulfil the security obligations of banks to get financial assistance and very often exploited by rural money-lenders and usurers. The benefits of the antipoverty programmes have not reached the poor as expected. Majority of the rural population is unskilled and asset less and purely depending on wage paid employment. Large scale unemployment of rural artisans is due to dearth of demand for their products. Most of the small and marginal farmers possess low holdings and their low farm income pushes them into debt trap and poverty. Women in rural areas are underemployed and their potentialities are underutilized due to poor financial background. Rural poor are resulting in poor recovery of loans. Micro-credit programmes facilitate the poor women to take up micro-enterprises, generate gainful employment and income with low capital investment. This approach is quite suitable for the rural poor because it generates savings of the group members and the repayment performance is good due to regular generation of income. Good recovery of bank loans facilitates recycling of funds which leads to economic empowerment of women and further to social and political empowerment.

- Micro-financial activities of SHGs are able to provide women a means to overcome the problem of poverty. Micro-finance could be a solution to help them to extend their horizon and offer them social recognition and empowerment. Steps should be taken to increase literacy level of women and making them aware about women rights and entitlements. Literacy and numeric training is needed for the poor women to benefit from the microcredit schemes. The members should be given necessary training and guidance for the successful operation of the micro enterprise. There is a need for establishing a computerized Management Information System for SHGs to monitor their performance on a regular basis.
- Proper marketing support is required to the old SHGs and infrastructure facilities to the newly formed SHGs. Steps should be taken for imparting more training to SHGs on book keeping, leadership, decision-making and organization micro-enterprises. State level federations should be formed by the government for promoting marketing tie up. Marketing facilities for the sale of products of SHG may be created. Periodical exhibitions may be organized where the products of SHG can be displayed. These steps help to improve institutional capacity to handle marketing activities independently.
- The micro-enterprise activities undertaken by the women members through SHGs have improved the socio-economic conditions as well as participation of women in decision-making and contributed for the empowerment of women in the state. It made a silent revolution in the rural womenfolk by enabling them to become self-dependant and self-reliant, providing a forum for members for discussing their socio-economic problems and equipping women with basic skills required for money transaction. On the whole, the micro-enterprise activities undertaken by the members ensure for women empowerment in dimensions which include economic, social and political empowerment and of course in psychological empowerment of women.

B. Ananda Naidu's submission is on "the status and specific impacts of Mahatma Gandhi National Rural Employment Guarantee Programme

(MGNREGP) on rural masses". While tracing the evolution of wage employment programmes since independence, Naidu observes that The Gram Unemployment Situation in India led to the introduction of several wage employment programmes since India's Independence in 1947. The Central and various State Governments introduced several wage employment and self-employment programmes from time to time to mitigate the unemployment situation in India. The erstwhile wage employment programmes suffered with several defects and at the same time the Central and State Governments allocations for the implementations of these programmes are inadequate. Moreover, no wage employment programme guaranteed certain number of days of employment to rural households. So, the MGNREGS is unique in its content as well as statutory status. It is the Scheme which legally guaranteed hundred days of employment to all households irrespective of their social and economic status.

After presenting the evolutionary process Naidu focuses on the NCMP launched by the former UPA's government in 2004. According to him, it is envisaged in the NCMP that the UPA's economic reforms will be oriented primarily to spreading and deepening rural prosperity, to significantly improving the quality of public systems and delivery of public services to bring about a visible and tangible difference in the quality of life of ordinary citizens of the country. To achieve the objectives of spreading and developing of rural prosperity, generation of employment, augmenting and modernization of rural infrastructure, including roads, housing for the weaker sections in the rural areas and providing drinking water to all sections and strengthening of livelihood in rural areas were highlighted.

The key objectives of Naidu's study are:

- To discuss the need, importance and features of MGNREG Programme. To examine the performance angle of the MGNREG Programme in Ananthapuram district. To assess the impact of MGNREG Programme on selected beneficiaries in Ananthapuram district, and
- To evaluate the achievements and failures of the MGNREG Programme and to offer some suggestions for the proper implementation of the programme.

The major findings of his study include—

- The MGNREGP aims at bringing economic equality by giving

large share of access and opportunity to the disadvantaged and economically weaker sections of the society, such as Scheduled Castes, Scheduled Tribes and Below Poverty Line (BPL) households.

- The number of households working under MGNREGP in the state has gradually increased during first-four years of study in case of all social categories except minorities. During the eight years of its implementation the percentage of registered households remained same in case of all social categories. With regard to total wages as well as number of person days more or less same trends could be noticed in case of different social categories.
- *By providing hundred days of work to a rural household, the Act provides an income supplement for poor households. The NREGA wage is critical in this* MGNREGA offered nearly hundred days of work and the Scheme's impact on the labour market was substitutive; it drew a sizeable, mostly female, workforce away from agriculture and to make up, farm wages had to go up 50-70 per cent.
- The households who worked for statutory minimum hundred days are not evenly distributed in the district. The per cent of households which got less than fifty days of employment is gradually decreasing. On the other hand the per cent of households which got hundred days of employment, seventyfive to hundred days of employment and fifty to seventyfive days of employment are gradually increasing in the Anandapuram district. In 2006-07, around 6.07 households got minimum hundred days of employment. The average wage per day is also showing definite improvement in the Ananthapuram district.
- Since India's Independence Minimum Wages Act were passed by the Central Government as well as several State Governments. But in practice, these Acts were confined to papers, especially in rural India. After the launching of MGNREGP the Minimum Wages Act came in to lime light. After the implementation of MGNREGP, the daily wages for agricultural labour was automatically increased. But this increase is not universal. In some areas the old rates are still continuing.
- Nearly half of the year, the agricultural labour left without employment and which forces them to migrate to urban areas for work during unseason. The fundamental motive behind

launching various wage employment programmes is to limit the migration of labour in rural areas.

Naidu concludes his case study by stating that the positive and negative impacts of MGNREGP on rural masses empowerment cannot be ignored on the grounds that these are unintended or not covered under the main objectives of MGNREGP. By addressing these impacts will not only help women's empowerment but it will also help in achieving medium and long term goals of MGNREGP and help in moving towards optimum use of labour in the economy. It will also help in moving towards some desirable national level social policies.

Ashok S. Anikivi has made an analytical survey on three key components of Gandhism—sustainable simple living, sustainable development and rural development. According to the author to the author, Gandhi possesses a unique place among modem world thinkers. He was not merely a thinker but also led popular movements to eliminate evils of social life and to recognize society on the basis of equality and social justice. Gandhi visualized for India an ideal society in which advantages and privileges will not be monopolized by anyone section of society but will be shared by all. He wanted to establish an egalitarian society based on principles of equality and justice.

Sustainability according to the author means making provisions for future while living now. Whatever, we have we should use those resources and handover to the next generation. It also implies give more importance to quality of life rather than higher material standards of living. Simple living covers a number of different voluntary practices to simplify one's life style. For instance, these may include limiting one's possessions or increasing self-sufficiency.

According to Ashok, the modern day economy is spreading consumerism and making-man material oriented. It has led to profiteering, the exploitation of the common people, exploitation of society excessive consumption of resources deterioration of moral standards and, hence, the need for understanding Gandhian way of simple living.

Moreover, according to Ashok, Gandhi wish for an ethical solution to an economic problem. He depreciated the powerful play of psychological factors like human greed and acquisitiveness in the material world. Gandhi seems to apply an ethical framework towards the building up of an equitable economic order based on trusteeship. He took a very simplistic view of group dynamics and group conflicts in a feudal or traditional world order. Gandhi's stress on satisfying fundamental requirements of human beings and the simplicity of life were contrary to the existing social environment which build very heavy importance on a material civilization. So, it must be remembered that "simplicity is also a relative term; it depends upon the circumstance and on surroundings, and in the modem world, where science has made great striking progress and industrialization has taken grip over the whole human society, now to say that we will run away from it would be not only unreal, but it would be giving up good things in order to escape from bad things." (Morarji Desai, 1981). However, beneath such situations acquiescence of trusteeship principle would turn out to be a reversion to industrial primitivism in an age depicted by the scientific and technological revolution.

After making an enquiry on the concepts of simple living as envisaged by Mahatma Gandhi, Ashok further proceeds to two more vital areas—sustainable development and rural development. He underlines the urgency and significance of the Gandhian ideals on these two key areas. To him Gandhi strongly believed that the progress of India lies in the development of majority of its rural villages, develop rural economy, industry and rural skills. Moreover, Gandhi found the only way of bringing hope of good living to the rural people is by making the village the central place in the economic programme. Rural development as outlined by Gandhiji contained self-sufficiency, inter-dependence and other warns and development of village and cottage industries. He wanted to bring about rural reconstruction with sound scientific and spiritual values.

Merensangla Longkumer and **A.K. Makar** presented a chapter captioned on "Sustainable Environmental Project—Nagaland Environmental Protection and Economic Development (NEPED) and its impact on Jhum Cultivation in Nagaland". According to the authors, Jhum or slash and burn cultivation is the traditional farming system of more than 80 per cent of the Naga people who are subsistence farmers. The Naga way of life revolves around this system of cultivation which governs most of their life, culture and tradition. However, the jhum system has been criticized as unsustainable as it was observed that the soil especially in the hill slopes is subject to massive top soil erosion. The Indian Council for Agricultural Research (ICAR) estimated that upto 40 metric tonnes of topsoil per ha per year is eroded in a Naga jhum field. With increasing food demand due to increased in population, the jhum cycle has been reduced leading to decreased in crop yields. Sustainable development of

Nagaland is a high priority. With this viewpoint, the Nagaland Environmental Protection and Economic Development (NEPED) project was implemented in 1994, the first internationally funded development project ever in Nagaland. NEPED aimed to improve jhum from within by planting selected tree species as crops along with regular jhum crops and to improve upon existing soil and water conservation methods. The mainstay of this project has been tree planting. The economic benefits from the trees go hand in hand with environmental benefits. The project has successfully created a source of income for the poor farmers, while simultaneously addressing the larger issue of environmental degradation.

V. Saravanan examines Contract Farming System in India and evaluates the challenges faced by the sector and presents valid solutions to revamp it. In his introductory remarks Saravanan observes that in India, 85 per cent of the farmers are marginal or small, operating less than two acres. In fact, 66 per cent operate less than one acre each. How many will have such land to give for contract crops. It is possible that contract farming can work if there is a collectivisation of small farmers. For instance, ten to fifteen farmers get together, form a group and sign a group contract. It brings down the transaction costs, the farmers are better protected and it is essentially, a win-win situation for both the former and the corporate.

According to him, Contract Farming has been in existence for many years as a means of organizing the commercial agricultural production of both large-scale and small-scale farmers. In an age of market liberalization, globalization and expanding agri-business, there is a danger that small-scale farmers will find difficulty in fully participating in the market economy. The era of globalization, the concept of 'Contract Farming' is an effective way to co-ordinate and promote production and marketing in agriculture. "Contract Farming can be defined as an agreement between farmers and processing or marketing firms for the production and supply of agricultural products under forward agreements, frequently at predetermined prices."

Regarding the issues related to Contract Farming the author states that—

- As with any form of contractual relationship, there are potential disadvantages and risks associated with contract farming. If the terms of the contract are not respected by one of the contracting parties, then the affected party stands to lose. Common contractual problems include farmer sales to a buyer other than the one to whom the farmer is contracted (side selling or extra-contractual marketing), a company's refusal to buy products at the agreed prices, or the downgrading of produce quality by the buyer. Side selling by farmers to competing buyers is perhaps the greatest problem constraining the growth of contract farming. Contractors also may default by failing to pay agreed prices or by buying less than the pre-agreed quantities.

- The existence of an adequate legal framework is thus crucial for the successful implementation and long-term sustainability of contract farming operations. A system of law is essential to assist farmers and their buyers in the negotiation and drafting of contracts. It is also important to protect them from risks that may occur during contractual execution, such as abuse of power by the stronger bargaining party or breach of the contract. Different countries have enacted policies and legislation to ensure fair contractual practices and offer remedies for dispute resolution.
- Another concern about contract farming arrangements is the potential for buyers to take advantage of farmers. Buying firms, which are invariably more powerful than farmers, may use their bargaining clout to their financial advantage. Indeed, if farmers are not well organised or where there are few alternative buyers for the crop or it is not easy to change the crop, there is a danger that farmers may have an unfair deal. Tactics sometimes used are changing pre-agreed standards, downgrading crops on delivery so offering lower prices, or over-pricing for inputs and transport provided. Strengthening farmer organisations to better access appropriate services such as credit, extension services and market information and improving their contract negotiating skills can redress the potential for exploitation of farmers and poorly formulated contracts and their enforcement. There are also proposals for some form of welfare system for contracted farmers akin to the benefits provided in most contractual employment.

He presents the following remedies for revamping the Contract Farming System.

- A typical contract farming agreement is an agreement between two unequal parties involving large number of illiterate farmers on one side and a mighty sponsoring company on the other. These farmers do not have sufficient means to approach the court of law for resolution of disputes, if any, with the company. It is equally difficult for the company to redress the breach of agreement by the farmers through the present mechanism of civil court. Hence, it is necessary to create a dispute resolution mechanism near to the farmers, which can quickly settle the disputes in quasi-judicial manner. The dispute redressal authority should be a body at the sub-divisional level comprising a representative of the sponsoring company, a farmers' representative and the Sub-Divisional Magistrate of the area under whose jurisdiction the contract farming land falls. The party aggrieved by the decision of the prescribed authority as above may prefer an appeal to an Appellant Authority within thirty days from the date of decision.

- The farmers may be required to invest substantial amount of resources to raise the contracted crops and run the risk of incurring huge debt in the event of crop failure, which may result in their displacement from the land, affecting their livelihood. In order to protect the farmers from such displacement, it is considered necessary to prevent, by law, displacement of farmers from their land as consequence of the contract farming agreement.

Saravanan concludes his study by saying that various studies done in India and abroad indicate that the corporate system strongly prefers contract farming system. But the experience of the contract farming system is not very encouraging in different parts of the country, mainly because of corporate tactics such as *post-facto* lowering of prices; delays in payments; defaults on contracts as done by Pepsi in Punjab and mineries in Maharashtra; and improper legislation. The contract system has certain structural characteristics; for instance, the farmer bears the risk even when the decision regarding the choice of crop, input, quality and quantity of crop and schedule of payment rests with the corporate. Morever, contract farming has a strong bias towards large land owners as they have the surplus to invest and can supply the required quantity, a prerequisite for economics of scale.

Moreover, the need of our economy is to take steps to protect, enhance and defined the livelihood of small and marginal farmers and not adopt policies that "take came and promote the profits of super-rich corporates".

If the government feels so concerned about the exploitation of retail by the intermediaries, it should from co-operatives up to the retail level.

Ch. C. Prasad and **P. Shreenivas** presented a chapter titled "Empowering People Through Gram Sabha for Inclusive and Sustainable Rural Development". According to the authors, the Gram Sabha corner stone of the participatory democracy, was not functional prior to the 73rd Constitutional Amendment Act 1992. Realising the importance of this institution at the local level, the Government declared the year 1999-2000 as the "Year of Gram Sabha". The Gram Sabha is an institution which provides an opportunity to participate meaningfully in governance, to all the people willing and capable of participating in the development process. The Gram Sabha is a concept intending to represent ordinary people's needs and wishes which appeals to the general mass of population irrespective of class, caste, gender distinction and political partisanship. It refers to supremacy of the people.

The authors further states that, The Gram Sabha enables each and every voter of the village to participate in decision-making at the local level. It is a constitutional body consisting all persons registered in the electoral rolls of a Village Panchayat. It provides a political forum to people in the village to meet and discuss their common problems and consequently understand the needs and aspirations of the community. It also provides a forum to meet, discuss, debate and analyse the development and administrative actions of elected representatives and thereby ensure transparency and accountability in the functioning of the village panchayat. It act as a watchdog on the working of Gram Panchayats besides facilitating the rural people's participation in the decision-making processes. The Gram Sabha is supposed to play a central role in promoting participatory democracy not only by working as an institutionalised platform to represent each and every section of the community and their needs, but also by functioning as mechanism to monitor and evaluate the development activities carried on by Panchayat.

Gram Sabha according to the authors, has been described as the institution for direct democracy through participation of local community in decision-making, fixing priorities about the development works, analysing and approving the forth coming programmes, Perusing annual reports and conducting social audits of all the works being carried out at village level. It is a corner stone of the entire scheme of democratic decentralisation was non-functional prior to the 73rd Constitutional Amendment Act. The 73rd Constitutional Amendment Act made the establishment of Gram Sabha mandatory. It acts as a watchdog on the working of Gram Panchayats besides facilitating the rural people's participation in the decision-making processes.

The authors concludes their studying by stating that the real picture of Gram Sabha functioning at grassroot level is different and mixed. There is no unanimity among the states in implementing the functions devolved. Most of the village panchayats have failed to execute the decisions taken of the Gram Sabha. It is unfortunate that a majority of State Governments could not show seriousness and have failed to conduct Gram Sabha meetings which is mandatory. However, the recent experience reveals that there is growing awareness among rural people particularly marginalised sections about the significances of Gram Sabha functions and meetings. The goals of inclusive growth and sustainable development as envisaged by the Centre and State Governments cannot be achieved without empowering Gram Sabha. Measures like creating awareness among marginalised sections of villagers to use their constitutional rights, increasing active participation of people in Gram Sabha meetings, capacity buildings of villagers, women empowerment, active role of media, etc., will go a long way to empower Gram Sabha and achieve inclusive and sustainable rural development.

In Chapter sixteen **D. Indrakumar** has made an innovative enquiry on the Role of Textile Industry in the rural upliftment and employment generation under the new economic initiatives in India. According to the author, Manufacturing Industry in India has gone through various phases of development over the period of time. Since independence, the Indian manufacturing sector has travelled from the initial phase of building. The industrial foundation was made during in 1950's and early 1960's. It was controlled through the License–Permit Raj in the period of 1965-1980. Finally, the manufacturing industry went to a phase of liberalization in 1990's, emerging into the current phase of global competitiveness. It has grown at a robust rate over the past ten years and has been one of the best performing manufacturing economy. Manufacturing sector contributes about 16 per cent of India's Gross Domestic Product (GDP) and 50 per cent to the country's exports. The sector employed 44 million people in 1999-2000 to 51 million in 2009-10.

He further adds that in the recent years manufacturing has been playing a dominant role on account of an increase in volume of global trade as a result of globalization and dismantling of trade barriers under the World Trade Organization (WTO). The improvement in the growth scenario of the manufacturing sector has been significant due to the improvement in the performance with regard to exports. However, India's strategy for industrial development witnessed a paradigm shift after the introduction of new economic reforms in 1991. Industrial development until then was largely based on product market regulations, with capacity licensing. Though this strategy had successfully created an industrial base, it had encouraged rent seeking to a considerable extent. Economic reforms initiated in 1991 gradually removed licenses. Industrial Policy since 1991 has been more for facilitating the industrial development rather than anchoring it through permits and controls.

Regarding the major challenges faced by the Textile Sector the author adds that,

- India has become one of the fastest growing economies in the world over the last two decades, undoubtedly, aided in this performance by economic reforms. The striking aspect of India's recent growth has been the dynamism of the service sector, while, in contrast, manufacturing has been less robust. The Manufacturing sector's contribution to the GDP has stagnated at 16 per cent, raising questions about India's development model, including its sustainability, especially for generating adequate employment.
- With changing global realities, the manufacturing sector will need to be the safeguard of employment creation over the next decade, in contrast to current employment of only 11 per cent of India's working population. India's long touted demographic dividend can only then be sufficiently exploited through the systematic growth of this sector. These statistics clearly indicate that while manufacturing has not been the engine of growth for the Indian economy, it now needs to grow at a much faster rate.
- Currently, India's manufacturing sector contributes about 16 per cent to the GDP, and India's share in world manufacturing is only 1.8 per cent. This is in stark contrast to China; where manufacturing contributes 34 per cent to the GDP and is 13.7 per cent of world manufacturing-up from 2.9 per cent in 1991. India's growth has been on the back of a booming services sector which contributes 62.5 per cent of the GDP. These statistics clearly indicate that while manufacturing has not been the engine of growth for the Indian economy, it now needs to grow at a much faster rate. With changing global realities, the manufacturing sector will need to be the bulwark of employment

creation over the next decade, in contrast to current employment of only 9 per cent of India's working population. India's long touted demographic dividend can only then be sufficiently exploited through the systematic growth of this sector.

- The history of the textile and clothing industry has been replete with the use of various bilateral quotas, protectionist policies, discriminatory tariffs, etc. by the developed world against the developing countries. The result was a highly distorted structure, which imposed hidden costs on the export sectors of the Third World. Despite the fact that GATT was established way back in 1947, the textile industry, till 1994, remained largely out of its liberalisation agreements. In fact, trade in this sector, until the Uruguay Round, evolved in the opposite direction. Consequently, since 1974 global trade in the textiles and clothing sector had been governed by the Multi-Fibre Agreement (MFA), which was the sequel to an increasingly pervasive quota regime that began with the Short-Term arrangement on cotton products in 1962 and followed by the Long-Term arrangement. After the successful conclusion of the Uruguay Round in 1994, the MFA was replaced by the Agreement on Textiles and Clothing (ATC), which had the same MFA framework in the context of an agreed, ten year phasing out of all quotas by the year 2005. The section that follows takes a brief look at the history of these protectionist regimes as also a more detailed look at the MFA and the ATC.
- Quantitative restrictions to limit international trade in certain goods have existed for a long time already, but in no sector have they been as common and broadly applied as in the textile and clothing industries. Likewise, no other sector has seen such a rigid institutionalization of quantitative restrictions, which in turn have had very wide reaching intended and unintended consequences. In fact, quotas in this sector have been the common denominator that has shaped the development path of this industry, and—many would argue—have been the single most important factor contributing to its worldwide diffusion in recent decades. International trade policy has for many decades utilized quantitative restrictions on imports as a means of achieving specific developmental outcomes. This form of protection provides a limited shield to local industry against foreign competition, competition which would have been the case if foreign goods were to compete freely on the domestic

market. Quotas differ fundamentally from other policy tools, such as tariffs, in that they restrict competition from imports irrespective of any direct price considerations.

- The lackluster growth of manufacturing can also be traced to the low technological depth of the Indian manufacturing sector. In India Research & Development (R&D) has not been sufficiently exploited and needs an overhaul in terms of its focus and its organization. Most Indian manufacturing firms appear to be stuck at the basic or intermediate level of technological capabilities. Creating conducive environments to increase business expenditure on R&D complemented by institutional measures around skill development, regulation and standardisation need to be key areas of emphasis.
- To ensure sustained growth and expansion of the Indian textile industry, it is necessary to maintain healthy export growth momentum, increase production and productivity in cotton yarn, enhance value addition in garmenting and apparel sectors, promote the rich heritage of handlooms and handicrafts, institutional strengthening in the jute sector, and enhance acreages under mulberry production and safeguard employment opportunities. More concerted efforts need to be taken to bridge the skill gap in the textiles industry. Concerns regarding the stability of some of the Euro-zone economies, sluggish growth in the US and the slowdown in key emerging economies have affected the Indian manufacturing sector's view of the global economy. Given this background, a majority of companies participating in our survey saw the world economy as being in a decline. Looking forward over the next twelve months, the outlook does not seem to improve much, with more companies describing it as uncertain or mildly pessimistic.
- Despite numerous plans on paper, manufacturing never took off in a meaningful way. The contribution of the sector to the country's output has remained stagnant at around 15 per cent for about 30 years now. In China, the sector contributes about 34 per cent to that country's GDP. It implies that there is need for strong policy initiatives to boost the growth of the manufacturing sector.
- Clearly, not much has been achieved since, then as the contribution of manufacturing still stands at 15.2 per cent of GDP (Financial Year, 2012-13). Not to be left behind, the Planning Commission now has an ambitious target of ramping

up manufacturing output to 25 per cent of GDP by 2025 and creating 100 million additional jobs. These targets are unlikely to be realized anytime soon. India lacks the ecosystem for developing a robust manufacturing sector. There are a number of issues—ranging from lack of adequate infrastructure, financing, land acquisition and rigid labour laws—that make business in the sector intensely difficult. While infrastructure bottlenecks are well-known, the Land Acquisition, Rehabilitation and Resettlement Bill—cleared by Parliament—is certain to make land acquisition even more difficult. This will further affect the prospects of creating a manufacturing base in the country.

- The other big impediment in the development of manufacturing is the nation's rigid labour laws. As highlighted in the Economic Survey, rigid regulation in the labour market does not allow small and medium size manufacturing units to grow and attain the economies of scale. If anything, after clearing the new land acquisition law, it makes great sense to relax labour laws to enable the easy establishment of small manufacturing units. If large projects seem unviable, rationality demands that smaller ones, which, in fact, have greater employment potential, be encouraged. In India, 84 per cent of the workforce in manufacturing works for micro and small enterprises. The comparable figure is 27.5 per cent in Malaysia and 24.8 per cent in China. There is plenty of room for growth here if only political parties give up their addiction to inflexible labour laws.
- There are solutions, of course. In the short-run, industrial production can be spurred if the government gets the ban in the mining sector lifted and removes hurdles in the power sector. The depreciation of the rupee and better prospects of exports will also help manufacturing. However, in the medium term, a different measure is required. While the development of infrastructure will take its own time, relaxation in labour laws will be a major boost for the sector. It is true that the issue of labour reforms is politically sensitive, but it is also true that forming consensus on economic issues is relatively easier in difficult economic conditions. In order to contain opposition from labour unions, the reforms can be carried out prospectively, which will not affect existing contracts. A robust manufacturing sector will not only help economic growth in a sustainable way, but also create much needed jobs and contain the trade deficit.

In the concluding chapter T.G. Ramaiah has presented a study on Rural Empowerment through Eco-Tourism. It is a case study on Darap Village in Sikkim. According to the researcher eco-tourism of Darap Village undoubtedly shows the immense potential of rural tourism especially in the area of employment generation and economic empowerment. The study has also excelled in how a group of enterprising and enlightened local people can explore the opportunities and it can be utilized for new employment generation, without endangering existing ecology.

Before concluding I would like to express my gratitude to those who have been kind enough to help me in the preparation of this book. I wish to express a deep sense of gratitude to the esteemed contributors to this anthology of articles. The views and opinions expressed by the contributors are of immense value for researchers and academics and administrators for framing policies and strategies on Indian Polity and Governance. I am extremely thankful to Shri Ashok Kumar Mittal of Concept Publishing Company Pvt. Ltd., New Delhi, who brought out the volume in an elegant form. I also wish to express my sincere thanks to Dr. K.B. Manoj, Principal, Sree Narayana College, Kollam for his support.

I also express my deep sense of affection, love and gratitude to my beloved wife for her support, care and exceptional sincerity. I lost her on 31st August, 2012 at an age of 42. Whatever, little academic activity I had undertaken hitherto was due to her solid support. Jaya came to my life on 14th November, 1993. From that day onwards she supported me like a friend and motivator. She inspired me a lot giving a new meaning and dimension to my life. All the prefaces to the books I have published upto 2012 have been concluded by showering petals of love and affection for Jaya and our kids. From the previous book onwards, she turned a fragrant memory. My onward journey and academic mission were in a standstill after the painful departure. From the previous issue onwards, I am making an attempt to carry forward the unfulfilled mission. If not, I may be doing an injustice to Jaya. Moreover, I pray to the Almighty to give her soul eternal peace and guide us—Aishwarya, Ananthapadmanabha and me—to face the days to come.

Finally, I am also grateful to Paul Ambrose, JoySoft Computers, Kollam, for the data entry services.

New Year Day, 2015 **M.R. Biju**

SECTION-I
Development, Accountability and Transperancy

1
Development Scheme or Vote Catcher
An Analysis of a Scheme in Tamil Nadu

G. Palanithurai

Introduction

Any action of a government improves the standard and quality of life of the people that too the poor, the governance of the political regime can be considered fair and good.[1] The ultimate aim of any government is to enable the people to lead a decent and dignified human life in the society. To achieve the above governments are trying through a combination of actions namely enacting laws, chalking out policies, evolving development programmes and schemes, and allocating resources. To uplift the poor, welfare schemes with different nature are being implemented by the government as a welfare state. Many of the welfare schemes are almost investment in human being. The investment in human being will be viewed as an investment for growth and development. Ultimately, it ends in human growth. But all investments have not brought the expected results as the government expected or targeted. After carrying out plethora of development schemes and programmes, democratic governments in the world have identified the gaps in all those schemes.[2] It was realized that unless the poor, deprived, marginalized are empowered to participate in the process of governance and development it is very difficult to reduce poverty and achieve development for the poor. Hence, it has been decided that governments have to act as a catalyst and the poor should be made as participants.[3] Empowerment and participation are the two factors which are key for transforming the life of the poor. In India, Tamil Nadu is a pioneer in implementing various kinds of welfare schemes. These schemes are viewed differently with different perspectives. Yet the Government of Tamil Nadu has continuously been implementing series of schemes to transform the life of the poor. The schemes targeted individual, groups and communities. Hence, individual oriented, group oriented and community oriented schemes have been evolved and carried out continuously and relentlessly without paying heed to any of the criticisms against the schemes.[4] Impact of many of the schemes could be seen in the human development index of the state. Many of the social welfare schemes enabled the state to secure higher points to reach nearer to Kerala in terms of Human Development. Both Amartya Sen and Jean Dreez have appreciated the social welfare measures initiated by different governments in Tamil Nadu which enabled the poor to come out from poverty and lead a decent human life.[5] At present Tamil Nadu has been considered as a place for innovative welfare programmes and through which the poor and the lower middle classes have been drawn towards the party in power. Arguments have been projected that Tamil Nadu is known for competitive populism and it has influenced all other provinces which have been ruled by the regional political parties. In the whole of India, Tamil Nadu has got the highest number of development schemes.[6] Some argue that it is a vote catching technique and some argue that the government relies on the support of the poor and hence they wanted to uplift the life of the poor and for which Government of Tamil Nadu had introduced series of schemes. Of the schemes giving laptop to the students who are pursuing studies in government and government aided institutions is considered as unique and important. It was interpreted that by giving such laptop to the youth who are first time voters will be drawn towards the ruling party. Against this background an attempt is made to study the impact of this scheme in the life and life style of the beneficiaries. This chapter tries to analyze to what extent it helps the end user of the scheme and what will be the impact created in the minds and lives of the beneficiaries. The above study has been conducted through a combination of methods. Data have to be generated through focus group discussion and case study method.

Methodology

It was decided to have a focus group discussion among the beneficiaries in the Gandhigram Rural Institute. The reason for choosing this institute is that this institute has drawn more than 60 per cent of the students from the rural areas and more than 70 per cent of the students belong to marginalized and other backward class groups. Thirteen students have been drawn from different discipline for the discussion. All the students have been drawn from the poorest strata of the society. They were identified and informed that the whole discussion would be on the utility of the laptop supplied by the Government of Tamil Nadu through a scheme. More specifically the changes it created in the mindset of the beneficiaries. Here, it is to be mentioned that the idea for conducting a focus group discussion with the beneficiaries of this scheme came as the author witnessed a number of students from other Departments came to the Department of Political Science with the laptop provided by the Government and used the laptops in the premises of the Department as the Department of Political Science has got Wi-Fi facility created through the ford foundation project. All the time the students sat in open space, classrooms during free hours used the laptops. It has been witnessed that they have been serious while using the laptops. Many times many thought that the students have been using the laptops only for seeing movies. But the reality is not. Many of them were seriously engaged by using the laptops. This made the author to think of probing the utility and its implication in the life of the beneficiaries. The discussion was conducted in the Department of Political Science from 2.30 p.m. to 5.00 p.m. in the seminar hall. The discussion started from their social and economic background of their families. They explained in detail the conditions of their families. Educational background of their parents, income of their families, their perception about the ICT, and its utility, present usage of the laptop given by the Government of Tamil Nadu, hours of usage, purpose of using the laptops, what improvement they have made in the laptops, the details which they stored in the laptops, what they do when their laptop is in disrepair, how they feel by getting the laptop and using the same while they are in their studies, the amount of political influence it wielded, what additional skills acquired to use the laptop, whether it has increased the employability, and what suggestion could be offered to Government of Tamil Nadu to improve this scheme have been discussed while they were engaged in the focus group discussion. All the deliberations have been recorded point wise by the students themselves. Two and half hour discussion went on consciously. It was lively, passionate and absorbing. It was an involved and an inspiring discourse. During the discussion some of the participants were emotional as it touched their life. Their outpourings could not be recorded as they were. Some took time to record their emotions and feelings and they have handed over the same to the author of this article next day.

Socio-economic Background

All the students are from the economically very poor background ranging the monthly income of their parents from minimum of Rs. 3750 to Rs. 20000. Four respondents' fathers were really coolies working in the farms. A few others are drivers. Their educational background was not sound and they went up to only schooling. Only one respondent father was a graduate. Not even a single respondent said that she could study on their own without the assistance of the government. Every one stated that they pursued their studies from first standard to the post graduation only in government institution with minimum of payment. Even to pay the minimum their parents are struggling. Both the respondents and their parents are in struggle for their livelihood and to pursue higher studies. Their parents have determined to enable their wards to pursue higher studies and equally the respondents have determined to pursue higher studies despite difficult conditions. Their economic conditions made them to feel that government has come to their rescue. It is interesting to note that the respondents have informed that their parents are struggling only to enable them to pursue their higher studies and come up in life. Their parents have a clear vision that higher education to their ward means higher opportunity for their wards to come up in life. It is to be mentioned here that the parents and the students have realized the potentials of education in transforming the life of the human being. This understanding and realization has made them to pursue their education and work hard.

Purpose

Whatever may be the assistance provided by the government, they are to be utilized properly to get advantage of the scheme. In rural reconstruction process plethora of schemes have been evolved and implemented by the governments to reduce poverty and enable the people to lead a decent life. The success rate was not high as expected. Many of the occasions we found the schemes are underutilized and misused. Corruption was rampant in those schemes.[7] Because the schemes were in the hands of the officials and the stakeholders were not able to make their claim rightfully. From this perspective, students have been asked to explain how the laptop is being used. All the participants are in one voice recorded that they created email ID only because of the laptop and they have developed a habit of corresponding with others mostly friends only through email. The respondents have unequivocally said that they have developed an

Tables 1.1: Parents Education, Occupation and Monthly Income

Sl. No.	Participants Name	Father Educational Qualification	Occupation of Father	Mother Educational Qualification	Occupation of Mother	Monthly income of the family	Place of birth	District
(1)	(2)	(3)	(4)	(5)	(6)	(7)	(8)	(9)
1.	V. Nandhini	V	Carpenter	VIII	House wife	5000	Manjakuppam (Rural)	Cuddalore
2.	M. Nagajothi	X	Supervisor	V	Tailor	10000	Mogappair (Rural)	Chennai
3.	S. Dinesh	VIII	Coolie	No Education	Housewife	5000	Vedal (Rural)	Kanchipuram
4.	M. Gomathi	—	—		—	—	Mettur Colony (Rural)	Dindigul
5.	G.M. Abinaya	VII	Coolie	X	Tailor	9000	RM Colony (Rural)	Dindigul
6.	A. Sivamurugan	VIII	Driver	No Education	Housewife	3750	Thadicombu (Rural)	Dindigul
7.	A. Shopia Jency Rani	VII	Coolie	No Education	Housewife	10000	Vellodu (Rural)	Dindigul
8.	T. Ramya	XI	Farmer	VIII	Housewife	15000	Combai (Rural)	Dindigul
9.	G. Padmavathi	X	Archagar	X	Housewife	8000	Bharathipuram (Rural)	Dindigul
10.	L. Rajafnisha	B.Sc. Maths	Driver	X	Housewife	20000	Begambur (Rural)	Dindigul
11.	A. Brindha Devi	VI	Driver	VII	Housewife	20000	Nagar Street (Rural)	Tirnalveli
12.	S. Suriya	XII	Farmer	No Education	Housewife	20000	Manjam Patti (Rural)	Dindigul
13.	C. Vouvanathi Kasthuri	No Education	Coolie	No Education	Housewife	20000	Petham Patti (Rural)	Dindigul

Contd....

Table 1.1 (*Contd.*)

Previous Experience in using Laptop	Duration of usage per / Day	Purpose	Improvement	Stored items
(10)	(11)	(12)	(13)	(14)
Yes (others)	4 hrs	Presentations, Movie, Games, Songs, Typing, Download, Photoshop	Presentation, Photoshop, word, Creativity	Photoshop, Game Graphics, VLC Media, Movies, Materials
No	6 hrs	Presentations, Movie, Games, Songs, Typing, Download, Photoshop	MS office, Photoshop, Friendly with system	Movies, Songs, Games, Photos, Materials, Software
No	4 hrs	Presentations, Movie, Games, Songs, Typing, Download, Photoshop, Browsing	Using System, Browsing, PPT	Study Materials, Family Photos, Songs
Yes (others)	4 hrs	Mail check, PPT, Report writings, Download typing	Enable me to prepare PPT, Report Writing, Friendly with system, Opening Mails	Tally, SPSS, Photoshop, Images, Materials Movies
No	4 hrs	Net usage, Facebook, Photoshop, Mail checking, Typing, New songs, New software download.	Typing, PPT, Downloads	Images, Tally, Photoshop, Movies, Dictionary, Materials, Games, Google Talk, Songs, Film
Yes	4 hrs	Education, Jobs, TNPSC, UPSC, Latest News, MS Office		
No	4 hrs	MS Office, HTML, Movies, Songs	Typing Excel	Movies, Songs, Pictures
No	4 hrs	Movie, Song, HTML	Typing, Excel, PPT	Movies, Songs, Pictures
No	4 hrs	PPT Download, Photoshop, Games, Mail checking, MS word, Videos, songs	PPT, Photoshop, Materials	MS office Windows, Adobe Reader Dictionary, Songs, Videos, Games, SKYPE
Yes (others)	6 hrs	Materials Download, Songs, Games, Mail checking, Facebook	Prepare report, PPT, Word, using software	Software, Downloads, Songs, Videos, Films, Photos, Games
No	4 hrs	MS office, Painting, Movies, Games	Computer Knowledge	Photo shine, Photoshop, MS office, Songs
No	4 hrs	MS office, HTML, Movie, Songs	PPT, Typing	Movies, Songs, Images, Photos
No	4 hrs	Games, Typing, Material	To Use system	Materials , Songs

Table 1.1 (*Contd.*)

If any repair occurred	*Is it useful*	*Is it influence your vote*	*What you feel when you are carrying laptop*	*Have you undergone any course after getting laptop*	*Do you feel that you have fine job opportunities*	*If you think they get votes in society because of this scheme*	*What further improvements you want?*
(15)	*(16)*	*(17)*	*(18)*	*(19)*	*(20)*	*(21)*	*(22)*
Nil	Yes	Yes	Proud	No	Yes	Yes	Wi-Fi Software
Nil	Yes	Yes	Proud	No	Yes	Yes	Tablet
Nil	Yes	Yes	Happy	No	Yes	Yes	CD Drive , Net connector
Nil	Yes	Yes	Proud	No	Yes	Yes	Net connector, CD Drive
Nil	Yes	Yes	Proud	No	Yes	Yes	Tablet
Nil	Yes	No	Happy	Yes	Yes	Yes	More quality laptops
Nil	Yes	Yes	Proud	Yes	Yes	Yes	IPAD
Nil	Yes	Yes	Proud	Yes	Yes	Yes	IPAD
Yes	Yes	Yes	Happy	Yes	Yes	Yes	Wi-Fi, CD Drive, Web Camera
Nil	Yes	No	Proud	Yes	Yes	Yes	Wi-Fi, CD Drive
Nil	Yes	Yes	Proud	Yes	Yes	Yes	CD Drive, Net Connector
Nil	Yes	Yes	Happy	Yes	Yes	Yes	IPAD
Nil	Yes	Yes	Proud	Yes	Yes	Yes	CD Drive, net Connector

Source: Computed Purpose.

e-mail culture because of the instrument. It becomes an inseparable instrument in their life. By creating this contact, they are in a group of students. It enabled for peer group interaction among their friends continuously. After the class hours they are in computer exploring new things. They saw a new world. They informed that they are connected with the world. A Wi-Fi connection provided by the university is fully utilized to see hundreds of websites. In the whole process of learning they devoted more attention and time only on laptop. They openly admitted that they have learnt more through computers than the classrooms.

Matters related to their subjects of studies are downloaded from different locations and stored in the laptop. For all the subjects they keep reading material in the laptop. It becomes a culture and practice to go into Google for every new aspect of study. When they are in the university they use the laptop maximum level to visit different websites and download all needed materials and store in their laptop. All the students are having materials which are needed to their studies and for their future. Some of the students openly informed that the best teacher according to them is the laptop. Participants made yet another observation which every teacher has to bear it in his or her mind. They said that on subjects, they keep more relevant and updated material for their studies on the subjects than the teachers. Their expectation from the teacher is learning methodology and not information. They get updated information from the websites. They do not require information now. They have informed that they have learnt the art of getting information.

Almost all the respondents expressed that they got certificate in type writing training. They got the training in order to increase the speed of their typing skill. As it is a practice in Gandhigram Rural Institute that students of any programmes have to undergo a course in basics of computer usage. In some of the P.G. Programmes students use to undergo two courses on computer. Apart from the above the department of computer science is offering different certificate programmes in the evening. Students who are interested in learning more computing nuances can join such courses. The respondents have utilized all the opportunities to equip themselves in computing skills. Further they informed that they down load heavy material from Youtube as in youtube materials are available for learning. Material related to personality development, self-development and skill development are being downloaded and they are being used by them very effectively. It is to be noted here that all the respondents are highly motivated students and hence they have used the instruments very effectively. One can easily witness find for development in them.

All the respondents have used the instrument for seeing movies also. They are seeing best films in the world. They told that the best Western movies and Hindi movies are seen by them. Highly educative movies they have seen. In their life they have not seen such movies as they have seen movies through internet. Laptop is used much for power point presentation. All the subject assignments are being prepared and typed. Apart from the above it is being used for creation of facebook. As utility increases, the students have picked up new skills and nuances. Some of the students picked up animation skills. They informed that while preparing the curriculum vitae, the skills learnt so far will be packed. Some of the students showed their C.V. and they are very rich. In terms of skills, they are far better than some of the teachers. In such a way they have developed skills by using the laptops. All the reports to be submitted to the teacher, Departments and the Universities are being typed by them. They go out for taking only the print out outside the campus. In this context some of the participants said that they save money. Some others informed that they type project for other students and by which they earn money for their expenses. All works are being carried out by themselves with their laptops.

Owning Development

For many of the development schemes, ownership is a problem. The beneficiaries will not take ownership of the programmes and schemes. When government distributes houses to the poor, their maintenance will not be undertaken by the beneficiaries and they expect that they are to be done by the government. Likewise if toilets are being constructed for the poor, maintenance will not be done by them. For many of the development schemes making the poor responsible and as owners become problematic. But this scheme makes the beneficiaries as owners and as a result it is not only maintenance, but also for enriching the instrument by adding newer Programmes and facilities they took responsibilities. They spent money to make the instrument more sophisticated and extensively usable. The beneficiaries have realized the worth of the instrument. Many of the respondents said that if government evolves schemes like this success rate would be hundred per cent. The beneficiary should feel that the scheme is going to benefit him or her. Beneficiary should realize the worth of the scheme and accordingly it would benefit the user or the beneficiary.

Influencing Factor

All populist measures are introduced by different political regimes are intended to attract the voters for the next election. It is being debated extensively on this issue. There is no doubt that the direct benefits to the people will have more probability to draw the beneficiaries towards the benefactor. It means it would draw the people towards the political regimes which deliver such schemes. In this context the question of their loyalty is being asked. Without any reservation all have said unequivocally that they are loyal and inclined to support a leader or a party which was instrumental in bringing such a kind of scheme. Only two respondents said they are not extending their loyalty to the party which has distributed laptops to the students free of cost. It is not the only benefit given by the leader. Along with that many such benefits are being distributed for the poor, women and children. As a result poor are getting series of benefits from this government. When they are asked about their preference, they all said they would support only J. Jayalalitha. Nobody has reservation over this decision. They are explicit in their response. The intensity of their support is directly linked to the magnitude of the benefits they got out of the schemes. In this context there was yet another question posited to them. Their political party affiliation was asked. Every one said they are not members of any political party. Yet their loyalty goes to J. Jayalalitha as she was the creator of this scheme. They further informed that people those who are benefited by this scheme will be certainly loyal to J. Jayalalitha. This is the trend among the youth.

Suggestion to Improve the Scheme

It is one of the best schemes of the Government of Tamil Nadu like providing bicycle to the girl students. The beneficiaries could get benefit out of it. Since, it has got a wider scope, these kinds of schemes have to be improved. The respondents have recommended that while giving laptops best instrument could be selected for this scheme. It should have huge capacity to store data. Otherwise data storage equipment can be given along with the laptop. There are students who carry a library with them through this instrument. Further, they pleaded that a large number of software which is helpful to the students could be loaded in the system before distribution. For effective maintenance of the system service provider could be located and fixed and the service providers address could be given to the beneficiaries and for the services by the services provides, cost could be borne by the beneficiaries. By doing so a computer culture could be created even among the poor families. As cell phone has created a new communication culture, laptop to the poor will create a new computer culture at the grassroots.

Box 1.1: Neo-untouchability

Of the thirteen students, two students in a very subtle way told that computer literacy and English communication played a very important role in keeping one segment of the society as untouchables. They are neountouchables. "If anybody carries with him or her a laptop, his or her position is very high. They carry some respect as they are technologically equipped and they are in a knowledge world. In the same way if an individual is able to communicate in English he or she feels that he or she will be in the knowledge world. A modern untouchability system has been perpetuated only through this technology and communication. People who have no skill to operate computer and do not have English communication skill are treated very badly among the educated segment of the society. Having seen the plight of the people many tried to spend huge money to learn computer and English communication skill. Where will the poor go for such huge money to procure laptop for their sons and daughters if they are needed. Giving laptop to poor to learn not only computer operation, but also to learn communication skill. Hence, it is a path breaking scheme introduced by J. Jayalalitha the Chief Minister of Tamil Nadu. It is almost removing the modern untocuhability. People from the poor segment of the society had an aspiration, but it is fulfilled only through this computer. In our heart J. Jayalalitha has got a special place. She will be in our heart forever as she lit the lamp of transformation in our life."

—Participants observation

Box 1.2: It is a Good Teacher

"I never heard about languages laboratory. After joining in Gandhigram Rural Institute, I have seen the language lab and its utility. I came to know the software to learn English. My friends helped me to get the software to my laptop and offered me the head phone which they have used for some time. With the help of my friends I have downloaded many lessons from you tube and used it for my learning. For about one year I struggled to learn computer operation. Just like elementary school students I did lot of exercises as they were given by my friends. I used to complete all the exercises given regularly by my friends. In the same way my friends gave exercises for communication skills. My friends helped me to correct the exercises. When I realized the fact that I am learning and my communication skill is improving my struggle becomes a joy. Really I feel the development struggle is a joyful one. Thereby, I learnt communication skill. I had the joy of learning when I realize that I am picking up something that is new. It is to be noted that the utility of the instrument depends on the efforts on the part of the beneficiary who got laptop. We have also seen the laptops on the market for sale. Whenever, test papers were given back to me I felt that I have improved. That kind of confidence I gained only through this instrument. Hence I value the scheme of providing laptop to the students. This kind of scheme will make the students more employable". *—Participants observation*

Box 1.3: Influencing Factor

Photograph of the Chief Minister is pasted on the laptop and hence I was tempted to ask a question to them. Hence, I asked "what extent it will influence you while you are in polling booth?" "One of the students informed that whether photograph is pasted or not, as long as the laptop is with me, it reminds me to be loyal to J. Jayalalitha. The laptop connecting me with the world. It brings volume of information to me. It made me to learn English. I gained self confidence through this instrument. Now I got confidence that I will get a decent job. I can live on my own. I can help my father and mother. I cannot forget J. Jayalalitha in my life. When I was in the undergraduate college, I was looking at the behaviour of my friends those who were having laptops. They behave as if they were in a different world which is meant for knowledge. They used some technical jargons which were not known to others. At that point of time I felt that I was deprived of the facility because of my economic status. I never had a clue that I am going to have such a technology in her hand. It was possible because of J. Jayalalitha. I not only now but ever I will be thankful to her. Because she enabled me through laptop to reach a status what I wanted to achieve.

—*Participant observation*

Box 1.4: Emotional Attachment

When the discussion was on, one of the participants vociferously argued that J. Jayalalitha will continue to launch pro women schemes in Tamil Nadu. When she made the above observation, another participant said that since she is a double beneficiary, she expects more from J. Jayalalitha. Someone said she is not a double beneficiary she is a triple beneficiary. When they are asked to explain how she is a double beneficiary and triple beneficiary the beneficiary herself offered to explain. She said "I got bicycle from the Government and that is why I was allowed to join higher secondary school as the school was far away from my house. Had I not received the bicycle from the government my parents would not have allowed me to go to higher secondary school which is far away from native village. It was timely that I got the bicycle. I continued my education in the school up to higher secondary because of the bicycle. Subsequently, I got laptop from the same government led by J. Jayalalitha. Now I am in a higher learning institution with a laptop. Now I am applying for a fellowship through a scheme meant for one girl child in a family. Thus I got triple benefits from the government. Bicycle and laptop I got from the state government and scholarship from the central government. Now, I have a hope that I can come up in my life on my own. I have a skill, and by using the skill I can earn at least Rs. 15000 per month. My confidence level is high now. I have a feeling that I can lead a decent and dignified life in the society. That much of confidence I have gained and for which the bicycle and laptops were responsible. Both instruments had been provided by J. Jayalalitha. I am emotionally attached with J. Jayalalitha because she only enabled me to continue my studies by providing a bicycle. Only because of the bicycle my family allowed me to go to higher secondary school. Since I completed my school with high marks and I got a laptop I was allowed to come to higher studies. In my life transformation started from owning a bicycle given by J. Jayalalitha. When I started using the bicycle and traveled through bicycle what transformation I got I only know. It cannot be explained. I am a beneficiary no doubt but now I will help others to come up in life and for which light was lit by J. Jayalalitha". When she made such observation she was in tears. After hearing the story nobody will say it is a vote catching strategy.

Conclusion

Any decision in any government in a democracy is aimed at keeping the people with the establishment. To reach out the people governments chalk out schemes and programmes which are considered as Welfare Programmes and schemes. Welfare programmes and schemes will bring many benefits to the beneficiaries. The benefits are of many types. Some are indirect and some are direct. Direct benefit and individual oriented schemes started operating from beginning of 1980 in Tamil Nadu. It has been gradually multiplied. Many of the schemes have created reasonably good impact in the society. Social welfare programmes for the poor will help the poor come out from poverty and hunger. Tamil Nadu is always a pioneer in welfare programmes and schemes. In this context every scheme and its impact has to be evaluated. Now, new methodological nuances are needed for micro-studies. Nuanced focus group discussion would enable us to understand many of the deeper issues in the process of transformation of the society.

Giving laptop to students of the government and government aided educational institutions by the Government of Tamil Nadu has been viewed with different perspectives. To understand the deeper implications of the scheme of the government a study has been conducted and that too through a focus group discussion. For the focus group discussion only students from poorest segment of the society had been drawn. In the focus group discussion what have been drawn are given below:

- The increasing deep division between the students who have got access to information technology and English communication skill and the sections of students who are deprived of the above facilities is bridged through this scheme of providing laptop to the students who are in government and government aided educational institutions.
- The students, who have obtained the instrument, have been using the laptop very effectively to develop different types of skills including communication skill.
- The students are totally connected with the world through the facilities available in the educational institutions. The students

have developed self confidence through this instrument that they will make themselves employable.

- Since, the higher learning institutions have provided Wi-Fi facilities, the beneficiaries of the scheme have used the benefits at the maximum level as they do not have such facilities in their houses.
- Their work culture has been changed. The instrument brought hope in their life and it made them to work hard to quip themselves. As a result during the day time after attending the classes they used the instrument to see the mails, browse the materials needed to their studies.
- The students have demonstrated that they fully equipped to the level of the market requirements.
- They have combination of skills to declare themselves fully employable even though they are from the social science stream.
- The scheme demonstrated that this scheme is best instrument to make the students coming from the poor families joining the social science programmes more employable.
- As the scheme provides benefits to the students, their loyalty is unequivocally towards the benefactor.

Notes and References

1. Gerry Stoker. "Governance as Theory: Five Propositions" in *Public Administration: A Reader* (eds.) Bidyut Chakrabarty and Mohit Bhattacharya, New Delhi: Oxford University Press, 2003.
2. David Lawson, David Hulme, Imran Martin and Karen Moore, (eds.) *What Works for the Poorest?* Warwickshive: Practical Action Publishing, 2010, pp. 1-25.
3. Bidyut Chakrabarty and Mohit Bhattacharya, (eds.) *Administrative Change and Innovation: A Reader,* New Delhi: Oxford University Press, 2005, pp. 245-256.
4. G. Palanithurai, *Rural Development Scenario: A Qualitative Assessment for Action in Tamil Nadu* (Monograph) Gandhigram: Rajiv Gandhi Chair for Panchayati Raj Studies, 2010.
5. Jean Dreze and Amartya Sen, *An Uncertain Glory: India and its Contradiction,* New Delhi: Allen Lane and Imprint of Penguin Books, 2013, p. 77.
6. G. Palanithurai, *Panchayati Raj System in Tamil Nadu: Act, Rules, and Schemes (In Tamil)* Chennai: South Vision, 2009.
7. G. Palanithurai, "Corruption at Micro-Level and ways to Contain" in *Corruption at the Grassroots: The Shades and Shadows* (eds.) N. Narayanasamy, M.P. Boraian and M.A. Jayaraju, New Delhi: Concept Publishing Company, 2000, pp. 169-180.

2

Criteria for Financing Rural Local Government in Kerala

Do Recommendations of State Finance Commissions Matter?

Nisha Velappan Nair and John S Moolakkattu

Rural development financing is a major issue in many developing countries. Providing stable sources of funding is necessary if rural development is to take place in a sustainable manner. After the 73rd Constitutional Amendment, Panchayats have emerged as key means of implementation of rural development schemes with varying degrees of freedom to do so. While the Centre Acts as a major source of funding for the rural areas through various programmes, the states also now contribute to the development of local areas and people through plan grants. In some states like Kerala, the share of the grants in the total funds available for local development exceeds what is received from the centre. Having a commission to make recommendations on the modalities of grants and distribution of shared taxes suggests that it will guarantee assured flow to the local bodies and enable them to plan for a longer period. This is the logic behind the creation of State Finance Commissions (SFC) on the pattern of the Union Finance Commissions (UFC). The State Finance Commission constituted every five years is for assessing the expenditure requirements of Panchayats and explore their potential to raise revenues from existing and new sources and recommend the amount of grants for performing their assigned functions. The Central government also gives grants on the recommendation of the Central Finance Commission (CFC). Most states in India have set up such commissions and several of their recommendations have been accepted and implemented either wholly or partly by the governments. However, only few States "have rigorously kept to a time table of setting up SFCs". "The timing of setting SFCs up have also not been synchronised with the CFCs, thus, depriving CFCs of the crucial inputs as envisaged" (Pethe, Mishra and Rakhe, n.d., p. 12). These intergovernmental transfers are necessary in developing countries because, unlike the developed countries where people migrate from places where the local government offers fewer services to those where more services are offered leading to some kind of horizontal equalization and competition among the local bodies, people in developing countries do not have such mobility option, and it is through these transfers that some kind of inter-panchayat equalization is achieved (Govind Rao *et al.*, 2011).

Unlike the UFC's mandate which is restricted to certain specified taxes only, an SFC has the leeway to link the devolution of funds from the state level to the totality of the State revenues (Gulati, 1994). Following the Constitutional Amendment, Article 280 of the Constitution enlarged the Terms of Reference of the UFC to contribute to the resources of local bodies drawing on the recommendations of the State Finance Commissions. The quality of the sub-state level transfer system and the quality of the SFC recommendations are closely related. In view of the fact that decentralization in India postulates the careful fostering of village panchayats, the formula for the transfer system should also be as simple and transparent as possible (Oommen, 2008).

This chapter looks at the developmental role of Panchayats in Kerala, the criteria that the Union Finance Commission has evolved for release of grants to the local bodies through the consolidated fund of the state and the record of the four State Finance Commissions in a comparative perspective. It will also look at the sources of funding of panchayats and the share of local government allocation and expenditure in the state's plan.

Panchayats as Development Institutions

Apart from performing the civic functions by the Gram Panchayats (GPs), they as well as the other two tiers are expected to serve as mechanisms of development in productive, service and infrastructure sectors. In Kerala, the per capita state plan grant has increased from Rs. 12 in 1993-94 to Rs. 207 in 1998-99, an increase of about 15 times in a period of six years. This corresponds to an increase from 3 per cent to about 12 per cent of state revenue. The state shot into prominence by introducing decentralized participatory planning starting from the Gram Sabha. It had a strong developmental thrust, to promote local economic development by increasing production and productivity of agriculture and allied sectors and traditional and small scale industries with focus on employment and poverty reduction, having regard to gender, environment, integration and equity, besides addressing the problems of the social sector and provision of essential services. Ever since the introduction of participatory planning, Kerala is also in the forefront of fiscal decentralization in terms of the quantum of grants devolved to local bodies. The state had the benefit of the recommendations of four finance commissions so far and the fifth is expected to be set up in 2014. Even before the new Panchayat system was introduced, the state had set up a Panchayat Finance Commission under the then Deputy Chief Minister Mr. Avukaderkutty Naha and two municipal finance commissions.

Rural development financing in the state, like the rest of the country, is characterized by a vertical imbalance in funding in the sense that the Block and the District panchayats have to depend solely on state grants with virtually insignificant funds of their own. Even GP's own funds are insufficient to meet the responsibilities assigned to them. The extent to which the share of the State government's grants in the total expenditure of a Gram Panchayat can be brought down is a sign of the degree of autonomy the local bodies have, and thereby obviate the possibility of they being used as mere tools of the state's micro-management.

The introduction of participatory planning with a focus on rejuvenating the productive sectors of the local economy and the mandatory requirement in the initial years that at least 40 per cent of the plan funds should be earmarked for these sectors added to the significance of the three-tier panchayats as key actors in local economic development. Although these goals could not be realized satisfactorily, the Panchayat's investment in the social and infrastructural sectors has been making significant strides in recent years.

Status of Fiscal Decentralisation in Kerala

No two states are identical as far as the criteria for transfer of grants is concerned. Although population criteria is often the main one in most states, states like Karnataka have been according less emphasis on population criteria as evidenced from the report of its First State Finance Commission. Kerala has given special weight for population of SCs and STs and tax effort and less weight on the area of the local bodies unlike most other states.

It has been found that states with high per capita Panchayat revenue collection during the pre-amendment phase are the ones that have shown higher growth in Panchayat revenues after the post-amendment, thereby suggesting that the reports of the finance commissions have not had a significant impact in own collection (Rajaraman, 2002). The own revenue of the local bodies in Kerala as a percentage of the state's and local bodies total in 98-99 was a little over 4 per cent (Oommen, 2008). Even after the introduction of participatory planning, the budget of the Panchayat and the annual financial statement have not been integrated for several years. The state's Expenditure Review Committee in its second report in December 2013 observed that there was a decline in the share of the expenditure of local government since 2004-05 although there was increase in absolute terms suggesting a decline in the availability of resources for local bodies at a time of increasing civic, administrative and development functions of LSGIs. It was 9.88 per cent of the total expenditure of the state in 2004-05 and it came down to less than 8 per cent from 2008-09 onwards (*Government of Kerala*, 2013: pp. 85-86). Against a norm of plan expenditure by local bodies to the tune of 10, 30, 30 and 30 per cent in the first, second, third and fourth quarters respectively, what could be achieved was 4.86, 12.09, 26.98 and 56.07 respectively, making the last quarter characterized by rush of expenditure (*Ibid.*, p.97).

One method to estimate the level of fiscal decentralization is to look at the proportion of funds set apart as a share of the total funds available and the proportion of the expenditure. This is a more objective kind of measurement than political and administrative decentralization and Kerala has an edge on this front particularly from the Ninth Plan period onwards. Further, the commitment to transfer considerable funds has been stable and has not been largely affected by change of governments. The Table 2.1 shows the share of LSG in state plan outlay and expenditure.

It can be seen from the above that, of the 15 years data available on allocation of development funds, only in three years it was above 30 per cent of the state total and never reaching the promised 35 per cent. Of the eleven years for which expenditure data are available, two years witnessed the share of the local bodies in the total plan expenditure of the state falling below 18 per cent. It was only in one year that it could reach a respectable share of 37 per cent.

It is clear from the Table 2.2 that an average of 25 per cent is the share of the state's total both in plan allocation and expenditure. The bulk of the plan grants have gone to the Gram Panchayats. In absolute

Table 2.1: Share of LSGs in state plan outlay and expenditure

Year	*Allocation of LSGS % to State outlay*	*Expenditure of LSG % to State plan expenditure*
1997-98	26.23	24.49
1998-99	30.65	17.56
1999-00	31.38	31.94
2000-01	29.56	24.79
2001-02	28.19	20.31
2002-03	33.33	15.27
2003-04	29.73	#37.32
2004-05	28.13	26.05
2005-06	25.61	25.43
2006-07	20.96	26.54
*2007-08	22.13	27.09
2008-09	21.69	23.68
2009-10	20.65	NA
2010-11	22.72	NA
2011-12	23.24	NA
2012-13	21.00	NA
Total	24.31	23.68

Note: # during 2003-04 Rs.335 crore was re-allocated to LSGs consequent to the closure of the PD account on 09/07/2003.

Source: RBI State Finance, Economic Reviews and *CAG report.

Table 2.2: Share of allocation and expenditure percentage to State plan outlay and expenditure under different Five Year Plans

Plan	*Allocation of LSGs % to State outlay*	*Expenditure of LSGs % to State plan expenditure*
Ninth Plan	29.29	23.77
Tenth Plan	26.81	25.95
Eleventh Plan	22.17	NA
Total	24.85	25

Source: Economic reviews of various years and CAG report 2012.

terms, it now comes to not less than 7 million rupees, which are the strongest in the country and the backbone of Kerala's Panchayat system. The minimum allocation to a GP was raised from Rs. 51 to Rs. 70 lakh by the fourth SFC. In addition a sum of Rs. 25 lakh each to the Gram panchayats that were found to be very vulnerable and 15 lakh each for those moderately vulnerable was provided on the recommendations of the fourth SFC which identified them.

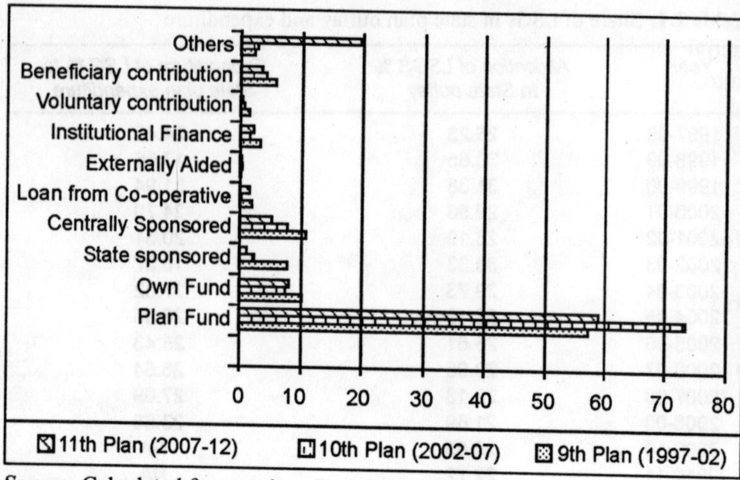

Source: Calculated from various Economic Reviews.

Fig. 2.1: Source-wise funding of LSGS under different plan periods.

The Fig. 2.1 shows that the share of centrally sponsored schemes in the total plan expenditure has come down over the years. The plan fund now known as development fund remains the main source of development financing in the local bodies. The fourth SFC found that there is mismatch of fund function matrix. In other words, the functional responsibilities of the various local bodies overlapped with agencies performing similar

Table 2.3: Criteria for *inter-se* distribution by various UFCs

Criteria	*Eleventh Finance Commission*	*Twelfth Finance Commission*	*Thirteen Finance Commission*	
			Rural	*Urban*
Population	40	40	50	50
Area	10	10	10	10
Distance from highest per capita Income	20	20	10	20
Index of Decentralisation	20	—	—	—
Revenue Effort	10	20	—	—
Index of Devolution	—	—	15	15
Index of Deprivation	—	10	—	—
SC/ST Population	—	—	10	—
Grant Utilisation Finance Commission Local	—	—	5	5
Total	100	100	100	100

Source: Reports of various UFCs.

activities with equally multiple sources of funding. This is an intrusion into the functional domain of the PRIs. The SFC-IV tried to investigate this phenomenon through a micro-level study and strongly recommended that a Committee be constituted to investigate this colossal waste of time, energy and resources due to duplication (4th SFC, Vol. 2).

While the eleventh and twelfth UFCs did not have separate weights for rural and urban local bodies, the 13th went for it adding a weight of 10 for those rural local bodies having SC/ST population. Urban inequality received greater weight than rural. It was only the twelfth UFC that made index of deprivation a criterion of giving grants. However, it was only in the 13th UFC that devolution index was given due weight. While revenue effort received the highest salience in the 12th UFC, it was totally neglected by the 13th SFC. Further, the 13th UFC gave greater weight to population than the earlier two UFCs which had a negative impact for state like Kerala. The share of the Kerala local bodies in the Tenth UFC was 3.96 per cent which increased to 4.54 per cent in Twelfth UFC. There was a sharp decline in the share of the thirteenth UFC to 3.11 per cent. The UFCs assigned heavy weight to population adopting 1991 and 2001 census for calculation and chastised states like Kerala for its reduction in the share of the country's population through family planning measures. The Thirteenth Finance Commission also did not reckon with performance in democratic decentralization as a criterion, which some commentators consider as the most important one (e.g. Oommen, 2013; Oommen, 2010).

State Finance Commission and Plan Fund Devolution

By and large all SFC reports that have so far been available in the public domain expressed their concern over the virtual absence of necessary database at local government level which consequently compeled them to make recommendations in an *ad-hoc* and half-hearted manner. Many SFCs are constituted at times that do not synchronise with the UFC forcing the latter not to factor in the SFC recommendations in their report. There are also other issues like delayed acceptance with the result that the recommendations may hold good for either more than five years or for shorter periods. Reports are also submitted any time ranging between one year and five years. The SFCs are also known to have not conducted studies prior to making their recommendations and seem to rely on impressionistic data. Delay in tabling the report in the state legislative assembly was also noticed. Majority of the members and Chairpersons of SFCs are serving/retired senior level bureaucrats. Reconstitution of

SFCs during its normal tenure and Constitution of it in phases are some of the additional problems noticed in a number of states. While the reports of many states actually do not have a major sway in the way finances are apportioned, there are states like Kerala where they are given greater seriousness (Govind Rao *et al.*, 2011).

The First State Finance Commission had not given any recommendation on the aspect of plan fund devolution. The plan grant-in-aid until then was in the form of a discretionary grant recommended by the State Planning Board (SPB) and approved by the state government. Theoretically, it could be reduced or even abolished at any time by the State government. Institutionalizing the devolution of plan funds to insulate them from arbitrary decisions of the State government was an important challenge for the further advancement of decentralization in the state (Issac, 2000: 208).

The figure 35-40 per cent was originally arrived at through some studies which showed, on the basis of historical data, that the proportion of plan outlay which could in principle fall within the province of district-level planning (including planning by tiers below) was around this per cent. As long as state sponsored schemes existed the outlay on such schemes should not be counted as part of total devolution, but should be treated as an additionality. That is why the Second State Finance Commission recommended that government may devolve to the LSGIs, Plan funds (excluding State Sponsored Schemes) not less than one-third the annual size of the State Plan as fixed by the Planning Commission. The State Government questioned and put off the matter for further examinationon the ground that even though it was not statutory, it has been making substantial allocations anyway (SFC-II).

The Third State Finance Commission had recommended certain reforms on the devolution of grant-in-aid (Plan fund) to LSGs from 2006-07 to 2010-11 and the quantum of funds to be utilized by LSGs from their own revenue for development purpose. As per the recommendation, the grant-in-aid earmarked to LSGs during 2006-07 is Rs. 1400 crore which will be increased at the rate of 10 per cent per annum in each succeeding year. As reckoned by the third SFC, an anticipated amount of Rs. 655.64 crore was earmarked in the state plan budget from 2007-08 to 2009-10 as contribution of LSGs from their own revenue in addition to the plan grant from Government (*Economic Review*, 2009). However, the "actual devolution as per SFC-III has gone down as a percentage to the state's tax revenue from 17.1 per cent in 2006-07 to 14.3 per cent in 2010-11" (Oommen, 2010, p. 44).

The Fourth State Finance Commission recommended an allocation of 25 per cent of the proposed plan size in 2011-12 as Development Fund to LSGs and thereafter increase it in relation to the plan size assumed by SFC based on the historical trends. The recommended Development Fund for the five years of the award period is as shown in Table 2.4. Under no circumstance should any year's allocation be less than 25 per cent of the plan size. But the progressively increasing recommended amounts would be inclusive of the devolution from the Thirteenth Finance Commission (FC-XIII) and the first year of the Fourteenth Finance Commission 2015-16 and the amounts flowing to LSGs from the World Bank supported 'Kerala Local Government Service Delivery Project' as far as the GPs are concerned. The UFC grants have the same conditions as the development fund given to local bodies as far as the state is concerned. The major component of the Kerala Local Government Service Delivery Project allows increases in development spending and discretion in choosing public services including maintenance of infrastructure. Almost 50 per cent of the Performance Grant, the major component of the project, were utilised for construction/maintenance of roads and not to improve GP performance in local governance and public service delivery.

Table 2.4: Development fund to Local Government

Year	*Share of the assumed Plan*	*Size Actual allocation*
2011-12	25	Rs. 2750 crore
2012-13	27.5	Rs. 3388 crore
2013-14	28.5	Rs. 3933 crore
2014-15	29.5	Rs. 4559 crore
2015-16	30	Rs. 5193 crore

Source: Fourth State Finance Commission.

The Record of the SFCs in Kerala

A direct role in planning was sought to be given to local bodies for the first time in 1989-90 when the State government, following the recommendations made by Shri S.B. Sen, decided to provide every village panchayat with an untied plan grant which they could utilize according to their own priorities. The amount set apart for the grant in 1995-96 was Rs 30 crore. During 1996-97 period the state budget set apart 100 crore for village panchayat, 15 crore for block panchayat and 28 crore to the district panchayat (*Economic Review*, 1999). In other words, the criterion for interse distribution was roughly Rs. 10 lakh for each Gram Panchayat and Block Panchayat and 2 crore for each District Panchayat.

The Cabinet Subcommittee set up to examine the First SFC report felt that, instead of the formula recommended by the Commission, plan funds may be distributed according to a simple formula by giving 90 per cent weight to population and 10 per cent to area. The distribution of funds in 1997-98, the year when plan grant-in-aid was greatly increased, was however entirely on the basis of population. The Planning Board set up a working group in October 1997 to look into the matter and evolve a fresh formula for the inter se distribution of plan funds. The first commission introduced the scheme of maintenance grant for transferred institutions such as schools and hospital buildings based on inflation-adjusted costs.

One commentator had this to say about the First State Finance Commission report of Kerala:

> There is an effort in its recommendations to combine selective tax sharing with grants. But inter se distribution is weighted heavily in favour of population both in regard to non-plan and plan grant allocation. The KESFC favours population because it is a neutral criterion. This exactly is its weakness when the need is promotion of territorial equity. KESFC's decision to give more funds to GPs with lower resources has an element of progression about it, but does not adequately reflect financial need (Geetharani, 1999: p. 1637).

The Second SFC wanted the existing devolution formula as well as the distribution formula that emerged after the introduction of decentralized planning to continue. However, up to 10 per cent of non-SCP/TSP funds was proposed to be distributed as an incentive for increase in revenue mobilisation by the village panchayat. The actual percentage to be distributed as incentive grant-in-aid should be the same as the percentage of village panchayats showing an increase in own revenue (*Economic Review*, 2003). And this amount should be shared as per the formula:

$$\theta i = r_i P_i / \Sigma r_i P_i,$$

where θi — share of local government,

r_i — % increase in its revenue and

P_i — population of LSGIs.

The date of effect of the incentive system was to be indicated to LSGIs well in advance. The second FC took the view that its mandate was to devolve funds cutting across the plan-non-plan divide given their inseparability given the fact that an asset created now with plan funds will have to be maintained with non-plan funds. But it did not want to create any confusion in the planning process introduced in a big way with its focus on the plan fund. It, therefore, recommended that not less than one-third of total plan outlay (excluding state-sponsored schemes) should be given to LSGIs, even as the commission confronted the allegation that the transfer of such substantial amounts to the LSGIs had actually slackened the effort to enhance own funds of LSGIs. All important recommendations of the Second SFC have been accepted by government except the recommendation to give statutory basis to the transfer of plan grant to local governments by permanently fixing it as one-third of the state's total plan outlay (*Economic Review*, 2004).

The Third SFC observed that developmental expenditure is an item of great importance in Kerala for which it has gained distinction. However, the expertise available to a Finance Commission is not adequate to judge the quality of performance in this vital area. Nor would the time required for a serious study of this major aspect available to a Finance Commission with a specified tenure. SFC-I did not step into the domain of plan devolution in a big way unlike SFC-II. SFC-II envisaged three components to the vertical share viz., general purpose transfers largely to meet the traditional civic functions, maintenance transfers and plan grants, the share for the first two being fixed at 3.5 per cent and 5.5 per cent of the State tax revenue. SFC-I's recommendations continued until 2003-04 and the SFC-II was made operational only for two years-in 2004-05 and 2005-06. There was no explicit reference to revenue or tax effort in the formula. However, SFC-II recommended to incentivise revenue effort for *inter se* distribution of GP urban local bodies plan funds. Though, this was accepted, it was never operationalised. Since the recommendations of SFC-II were implemented only after the lapse of nearly three years and SFC-III recommended no new formula other than endorsing the SFC-II report without making significant changes. However, from 1998 onwards the item on own income was implemented with a weight of 10 per cent for the *inter se* distribution of GPs. This is done by taking the reciprocal of per capita own income and thereby rewarding those GPs with lower per capita income (OSR). This could be interpreted as having a perverse effect in that it amounts to rewarding poor revenue effort (4th SFC). The most important weakness of the formula was the absence of a deprivation index, which was rectified by the 4th SFC using the data from the BPL survey 2009 of the Government of Kerala having five variables viz., housing status, availability of drinking water, sanitation, electricity and land holding for all the 978 GPs, other PRIs, 60 Municipalities and five Corporations (4th SFC).

SFC-IV felt that the tax effort should be incentivized. While the total expenditure of Gram Panchayats grew at the rate of 15.4 per cent per annum, property tax, the mainstay of Local Government's tax revenue increased only at the rate of 4.5 per cent. This had something like a flypaper effect. The fourth SFC had an additional terms of reference of revisiting the earlier 3 reports and recommending actions on those suggestions accepted by the state but not implemented.

State Finance Commission's (SFCs) Compared

It would be worthwhile to compare the four SFCs of Kerala, two of which were headed by economists. The fourth one is perhaps the more comprehensive of them all in that it tried to evolve a more scientific set of criteria.

Table 2.5: Criteria for *intra-tier* distribution of Plan fund

Criteria	*First SFC Report				Second SFC Report				Third SFC Report				Fourth SFC Report			
	GP	BP	DP	M/C	GP	BP	DP	M/C	GP	BP	DP	M/C	GP	BP	DP	M/C
Population (excluding SC/ST)	65	65	55	75	60	60	50	70	60	60	50	70	50	50	50	50
Tribal Population	—	—	—	—	5	5	5	5	5	5	5	5	—	—	—	—
Geographical Area (Excluding Area under Forests)	5	10	15	5	5	10	15	5	5	10	15	5	10	20	20	10
Area Under Paddy	5	—	—	—	5	—	—	—	5	—	—	—	—	—	—	—
Own Income (GP)	10	—	—	—	10	—	—	—	10	—	—	—	—	—	—	—
Tax effort	—	—	—	—	—	—	—	—	—	—	—	—	10	—	—	10
Composite Index of Agricultural Labourers, Persons Engaged in Livestock, Fisheries etc. and Marginal Workers	15	25	20	—	—	—	—	—	15	25	20	—	—	—	—	—
Composite Index of Backwardness, Houses without Latrines and Houses without Electricity	—	—	10	20	—	—	10	20	—	—	10	20	—	—	—	—
Deprivation Index	—	—	—	—	—	—	—	—	—	—	—	—	30	30	30	30
Total	100				100				100				100			

Source: Various State Finance Commission Reports.
Note: * Criteria were followed from 1998 onwards.

Table 2.5 shows the criteria recommended under all four SFC report. During the 1997-98 criteria for plan fund was only based on population even though area had a 10 per cent weight. The fourth SFC reduced the weight and assigned it equally to all the three tiers and urban local bodies. While the earlier SFCs relied on two composite indices (one on labourers and the other on backwardness) with *inter-tier* variation in assigning weights, the 4th SFC came up with a more scientific deprivation index and assigned the three-tiers not only equal weight, but brought urban bodies also within its purview for the first time. This has led to the reduction of the criteria for grants to just four and removing the distinction between urban and local bodies. This was a departure from the earlier practice. The second and third SFC followed the same criteria with 5 per cent weight to tribal population. The first three SFC had own income criteria which was never implemented due to practical difficulties. Implementation of the recommendation of the 4th SFC to provide ten per cent incentive for tax effort has been thwarted by the inability of the local bodies to furnish precise tax collection data. The details of tax collection of local bodies collected from the Panchayat Directorate in 2009-10 and 2010-11 had several errors and hence the local bodies were informed that the incentive would be released only after analysing and confirming the veracity of the details. The Finance Commission recommendation for reviewing the fees levied for various services, raising the professional tax limit and rationalising the taxes and revenues being collected by the local bodies have not yet been implemented in their true spirit (Nair, 2013).

It has been suggested that a targeted approach is needed to achieve a certain share of Local Government expenditure *vis-à-vis* the country's total public sector expenditure. If the share is high, it can be taken as an indicator of the level of decentralization. Some have even suggested that we should aim at a percentage of 20 per cent by the year 2020, the final year of the FC-XIV's award period, which was the Latin American target for 2008 (Oommen, 2013; p.19). State Finance Commissions have not received the same type of importance as the UFCs have. They are often constituted by people with little knowledge of the subject, and the reports are either not considered or if considered, very few are accepted, and even the few accepted ones are also either not implemented or partially implemented (Alok, 2008). Often acceptance is seen as synonymous with implementation, which is actually not correct. Kerala has quite a good record as far as timely constitution of the SFCs, submission of reports and tabling them in the assembly are concerned with some satisfaction of having many of the recommendations accepted and implemented by the government.

Conclusion

Do State Finance Commission's recommendations actually matter? The answer lies in how strong the priorities of the government are and how stable the state finances are. Kerala State Finance Commissions have been proactive in adopting a local bodies friendly policy and have recommended transfers that could assure fund flow to the tune of around 20 per cent with recommendations to enhance it further either by making a certain percentage statutory or by gradually enhancing the share with successive years. However, something like flypaper effect exists as far as the own fund is concerned. The assured flow of grants has made the rural local bodies to go slow on own fund mobilisation. The refusal of the government to commit itself to a certain percentage of the state revenue suggests that the development fund devolved as a part of budget could be cut if the plan size is reduced in the course of the year. Given the fact that property tax, the main source of own funds, has only recently been slated for revision after a long period of 20 years could mean higher revenue in the near future with a share of it going for development purposes. Efforts also have been made over the years to achieve horizontal fiscal balance. But these efforts are not enough because development is most needed in those panchayats where own income is low because the poor are mainly located in them. While the threshold level of funds set for these panchayats do contribute to the reduction of horizontal inequalities, there are limitations to what they can accomplish in the long run given the general tendency to adopt a redistributive approach to development by the Gram Panchayats. Unlike in the case of the Union Finance Commission recommendations which have a convention be being accepted by the Central Government, there is no such convention in the case of SFC recommendations. Not surprisingly, the recommendations of the SFCs are not taken seriously by the state governments (Govinda Rao, *et al.*, 2011). The Fourteenth Finance Commission should use devolution index as a criterion of grant making and insist that the budget is made an essential element of the local government system. Not giving the District and intermediate tiers any original sources of revenue is also not a fair system and this is likely to make them think of themselves as permanent agencies of the state government. In the memorandum to the 13th Finance Commission Kerala said: "The Finance Commissions have not recognised the role of LSGs in the developmental sphere particularly in bringing about economic development and social justice; they have more or less confined themselves to the traditional view of LSGs as civic bodies whereas the Constitution envisages their transformation into "institutions of self-government" performing predominantly developmental functions". This plea of Kerala, though based on the state's experience in local level development in recent years, is worthy of serious consideration by the 14th UFC.

References

Alok, V.N. (2008). "The Role of State Finance Commissions in Fiscal Decentralisation in India" in M.A. Oommen, *Fiscal Decentralisation to Local Governments in India*, New Castle: Cambridge Scholar Publishing.

Geetha Rani, P. (1999). State Finance Commissions and Rural Local Bodies: Devolution of Resources, *Economic and Political Weekly*, Vol. 34, No. 25. June 19, pp. 1632-39.

Government of Kerala (1996). Report of the First State Finance Commission, Trivandrum, available from: http://sfc.kerala.gov.in/downloads/sfc_I_Report.pdf

_______(2001). Report of the Second State Finance Commission, Trivandrum, available from: http://sfc.kerala.gov.in/downloads/2ndSFCchap1to6.pdf & http://sfc.kerala.gov.in/downloads/2ndSFCchap7to12.pdf

_______(2006). Report of the Second State Finance Commission, Trivandrum, available from: http://sfc.kerala.gov.in/downloads/SFC3reportChap3to10.pdf & http://sfc.kerala.gov.in/downloads/SFC3reportChap11to15.pdf

_______ (2011). "Report of the Fourth State Finance Commission", Vol. I, Trivandrum, available from: http://sfc.kerala.gov.in/downloads/REPORT_PART_I-IVth_SFC.pdf

_______ (2011). "Report of the Fourth State Finance Commission", Vol. II, Trivandrum, available fromhttp://sfc.kerala.gov.in/downloads/SFC_IV_Report_Part-II.pdf

_______*Economic Review* (1999, 2003, 2004), Trivandrum: Kerala State Planning Board.

_______(2013). *Report of the Second Report of Third Public Expenditure Review Committee*, Trivandrum, December.

Government of India (2009). *Report of the Thirteenth Finance Commission of India*, New Delhi, available from: http://fincomindia.nic.in/ShowContentOne.aspx?id=28&Section=1

Govinda Rao, M., T.R. Raghunandan, Manish Gupta, Polly Datta, Pratap Ranjan Jena, Amarnath, H.K. (2011). *Fiscal Decentralization to Rural Local*

Governments in India: Selected Issues and Reform Options, New Delhi: National Institute of Public Finance and Policy.

Gulati, I.S., (1994). "Financial Devolution to Local Bodies: Role of State Finance Commissions", *Economic and Political Weekly*, October 1, pp. 2622-2624.

Issac, Thomas T.M. and Richard Franke. (2000). *Local Democracy and Development*: People's Campaign for Decentralized Planning in Kerala, New Delhi: Left Word Books.

Nair, N.J., (2013). "Kerala's LSGIs lose tax collection incentive", *The Hindu*, October 16.

Oommen, M.A., (2008). "Introduction", in M.A. Oommen (Ed.), *Fiscal Decentralisation to Local Governments in India*, New Castle: Cambridge Scholars Publishing.

_______, (2010). "Have the State Finance Commissions Fulfilled Their Constitutional Mandates?" *Economic and Political Weekly*, Vol. xlv, No. 30, July 24, pp. 39-44.

_______, (2013): "The Third Tier and the Fourteenth Finance Commission", *Economic and Political Weekly*, Vol. XLVIII, No. 45 and 46, November 16.

Pethe, Abhay, B.M. Mishra and Rakhe, P. B., n. d., *Strengthening Decentralisation-Augmenting the Consolidated Fund of the States by the Thirteenth Finance Commission: A Normative Approach*, Mumbai: Department of Economic Analysis and Policy, Reserve Bank of India, Study No. 29.

Rajaraman, Indira, (2002). Growth-Accelerating Fiscal Devolution to the Third Tier, New Delhi: National Institute of Public Finance and Policy, Working Paper No. 2.

3

Centrally Sponsored Schemes (CSS) and Centrally Assisted Schemes (CAS) in India

An Overview

M.R. Biju

"I believe that when Planning Commission was constituted, it was done on the basis of the circumstances and the needs of those times. In recent years, Planning Commission has contributed to the growth of the country in its own way. I respect that, I am proud of that, but the prevalent situation in the country is different, global scenario has also changed, governments are no longer the centre of economic activities, the scope of such activities has broadened. State governments have been at the center of development and I consider this a good indication. If we have to take India forward, it can happen only be taking the states forward. India's federal structure is more important today than in the last 60 years. To strengthen our federal structure, to make our federal structure vibrant, to take our federal structure as a heritage of development, a team of Chief Minister and Prime Minister should be there, a joint team of the Centre and the states should move forward, then to do this job, we will have to think about giving the Planning Commission a look. So, I am saying from the rampart of the Red Fort that it is a very old system and it will have to be rejuvenated, it will have to be changed a lot. Sometimes, it costs more to repair the old house, but, it gives us no satisfaction. Thereafter, we have a feeling that it would be better to construct a new house altogether and, therefore, within a short period, we will replace the planning commission with a new institution having a new design and structure, a new body, a new soul, a new thinking, a new direction, a new faith towards forging a new direction to lead the country based on creative thinking, public-private partnership, optimum utilization of resources, utilization of youth power of the nation, to promote the aspirations of state governments seeking development, to empower the state governments and to empower the federal structure. Very shortly, we are about to move in a direction when this institute would be functioning in place of Planning Commission."

—Prime Minister Narendra Modi
(Speech on 68th Independence day
From the ramparts of the Redfort)

"We will replace the Planning Commission with a new institution having a new design and structure........". This had been talked about since the regime-changed in New Delhi. The idea of rejuvenation is quite different from dismantling as proposed by the Prime Minister. In reality what we need is rejuvenation and strengthening of the planning commission in tune with the challenges. Honest, future oriented and time targeted with the emergence of planning exercises is need of the hour. Against this backdrop an attempt has been made in this paper to examine the significance of Centrally Sponsored Schemes (CSS) and Centrally Assisted Schemes (CAS). This chapter has been organized in the following manner. The introductory part presents the Constitutional provisions and role of Central and State Governments in the fiscal federal structure of India. Part two unfolds the evolutionary process of financial assistance from Centre to State. Part three evaluates the major recommendations of M.M. Punchi Commission (2010) and B.K. Chaturvedi Committee (2011) on the relevant aspects of the subject. The concluding part presents briefly the major findings of the study.

In India, the Central and State legislatures are responsible for law making, the Central and State governments are responsible for the implementation of laws and policies, and the judiciary interprets laws. Subjects are divided between the centre and the states on the basis of the centre, state and concurrent lists. The centre is responsible for subjects that fall within the union list, the states for those subjects which fall in the state list and both the centre and the states are jointly responsible for subjects that fall within the concurrent list. There are several subjects such as education and health, which states are responsible for (as they are included in the state list) but might not have the resources to address adequately. The centre can provide additional resources to meet challenges in these sectors. One of the ways it does this is through establishing Centrally Sponsored Schemes (CSS) CSS are schemes that are funded fully or partly by the Central government, but implemented by the states. This is because they address subjects that are included in the state list.

Constitutional Provisions

The Federal Structure

The Constitution of India clearly defines the role of Central and State Governments in the federal structure. As per the constitutional provision, all activities in Government sphere are categorised as falling in Central List, State List or Concurrent List. While there is no ambiguity with regard to the Central List and State List, activities falling under Concurrent List are subject to overlapping of jurisdiction of the Government of India and the State Governments. States are primarily responsible for major sectors like health, education, employment, etc. which often involve large public expenditures. Since successful implementation of development programme requires availability of adequate funds, appropriate policy framework, and effective delivery machinery, Central Government needs to work with the States to undertake their responsibility in effective manner. Recognising the higher resource requirements of the States relative to their resource raising powers, the Constitution mandates to transfer funds to the State Governments through statutory transfer of tax receipts collected by Centre through the Finance Commission award. In addition, the States access Central plan funds through Centrally Sponsored Schemes (CSS) and Central assistance to State Plans.

Part IV of the Constitution: The Constitution has under Part-IV mentions the Directive Principles of State Policy. These inform the policies of various wings of the Government and act as an overriding philosophical basis. While these are not enforceable in the same way the Fundamental Rights mentioned in the Constitution, they indicate the overall policies which should govern various laws. It is, therefore, important that these are fully kept in mind when the policies for development of the economy are made.

Article 38: These policies specifically mention several areas. Article 38 of the Constitution mentions as follows:

(i) State to secure a social order for the promotion of welfare of the people. The State shall strive to promote the welfare of the people by securing and protecting as effectively as it may a social order in which justice, social, economic and political, shall inform all the institutions of the national life.

(ii) The State shall, in particular, strive to minimizethe inequalities in income, and endeavour to eliminate inequalities in status, facilities and opportunities, not only amongst individuals but also amongst groups of people residing in different areas or engaged in different vocations."

Article 45: It is clear, therefore, that it is important for the national government to make policies to minimize inequalities not only amongst individuals or groups of people living in States but also amongst these people residing in different areas of the country. Similarly, Article 47 of the Constitution mentions that "it is the duty of the State to raise the level of nutrition, standards of living of its people and improve public health. Specifically, under Article 45 of the Constitution mentions, Provision for early childhood care and education to children below the age of six years. The State shall endeavour to provide early childhood care and education for all children until they complete the age of six years." Given the need for employment, the Directive Principles have made a special mention of this. Article 41 mentions Right to work as an important principle which should govern the policies of the States. It states, "Right to work, to education and to public assistance in certain cases. The State shall, within the limits of its economic capacity and development, make effective provision for securing the right to work, to education and to public assistance in cases of unemployment, old age, sickness and disablement, and in other cases of undeserved want." It is, thus, clear that the provisions of the Constitution specifically mandate the governments to ensure provision ofcertain basic services including employment, education, health and raise the level of welfare.

Models from Australia and Canada: Other federations like Australia and Canada make provisions in their Constitutions for equalizing levels of service. The provisions in the Canadian and Australian Constitutions provides for transfer of resources from Central Government to State Governments so that people living in different parts of the federation are given similar level of public services. While the Finance Commission transfers in India, under Articles 275-280 of the Constitution have similar purpose, these are meant to transfer resources to the States to meet their requirements of expenditure. There is no specific mention in our Constitution unlike those of other federations.

The Government of India is involved in a large number of programmes in sectors/area such as education, health, labour, skill development etc. that are in the State List through operation of CSS and provision of Central Assistance to State Governments. These programmes essentially arose from the above national objectives and cut across State boundaries. The CSS are operationalized by Central Ministries based on scheme specific guidelines and are implemented by State Governments or their designated agencies. The Central Assistance to State Plans has two components viz. normal Central Assistance that is based on modified Gadgil Formula; and Additional Central Assistance that consists of Assistance for Externally Aided Projects and Assistance for Special Programmes based on specific criteria and guidelines.

Until the Fourth Five Year Plan, Central Assistance to States for implementation of plan programmes within the States' jurisdiction was given in the form of scheme-wise allocation of funds resulting in rigidities and inefficiencies in the system and inequitable distribution of Central Assistance. The quantum of such assistance depended on the financial position and requirements of both Centre and the States. It was only from the Fourth Plan onwards that a separate classification of schemes as CSS was introduced. These schemes had a national character, and dealt with areas/concerns like family planning, agricultural workers, research and training etc. Since then the number of schemes covered under the Centrally Sponsored category has multiplied.

Historical Perspective

The practice of providing Central Assistance to the States to finance development schemes had been in vogue even before the advent of Five Year Plans. On the termination of the Second World War, the Central and the Provincial Governments had embarked on certain development projects which received Central Assistance in the form of what were known as post-war development grants. Though some of these grants were stopped by 1950-51, grants for schemes like Grow More Food Scheme continued. In the First Five Year Plan, many schemes which should have appropriately found place in the State sector were included in the Central sector because the exact distribution of their financial liability had not been decided upon. Some such schemes/projects taken up in the first Plan were multipurpose river valley schemes like Damodar Valley, Bhakra

Nangal, Hirakud and community development projects and projects for special minor irrigation, local works, etc. However, there was no clear criterion for distribution of Central Assistance to the States.

At the commencement of the Second Five Year Plan, majority of the schemes for which funds were provided in the Central sector and were implemented by the States outside their plan, were transferred to the State and included in the State Plans. As per Second Plan, there were large transfer of resources from Centre to States as the resources of all the States taken together were estimated to be short of the requirement by as much as 60 per cent. Similar was the case in the Third Plan also. However, the Central Assistance in the first three Plans to the States was determined on the basis of needs, problems, past progress, lags in development, contribution to achievement of major national target, potential for growth and contribution in resources by States towards their development programmes, population, area, level of income, etc. The quantum of Central Assistance was decided in the light of gap in resources of each individual State.

(I) Sub-Committee of the NDC constituted in 1967: At the end of the Third Five Year Plan, there were as many as 92 development plans sponsored by Centre, of which 35 were under Agriculture (including cooperation), 16 under General Education and the rest under other heads of development. For most of these schemes, the prescribed patterns were rather complicated. For a number of such schemes the staffing patterns, scales of pay and designs of buildings, equipment etc. were laid down which were often at variance with those prevalent in the States. The matter was considered by sub-committee of the NDC constituted in 1967 which recommended reduction in number of Centre assisted schemes to minimum. The Committee approved the following criteria for the classification of Plan schemes as Centrally Sponsored:

(i) A limited number of important schemes to be implemented as matters of national policy such as Family Planning, Resettlement of landless agricultural workers;
(ii) Schemes such as those for specialized research and training which would benefit more than one State or might be of all-India significance;
(iii) Pilot projects for research and development; and
(iv) New schemes introduced after the Plan has been finalized.

(II) Discussions with Ministries by Planning Commission: The Planning Commission had discussions with the Central Ministries and

36 schemes originally classified as Centrally Sponsored in the Draft Outline of the Fourth Five Year Plan were transferred to the State sector. Accordingly the number of CSS in the Fourth Plan stood at 90, as against 147 included in the Draft Fourth Five Year Plan. The funding pattern for the various schemes differed. Of the total schemes, 59 CSS were eligible for 100 per cent assistance, 12 schemes for 75 per cent, 3 schemes for 60 per cent and 15 schemes for 50 per cent assistance outside the State Plans. Many States observed in the NDC meetings that the pattern of assistance has resulted in inequitable distribution of Central Assistance as better of States were able to get more funds comparedto other States. Accordingly, concept of block assistance for State Plans was introduced.

(III) Recommendations of the NDC, 1968: In 1968, the NDC Committee recommended a cap on the value of the Centrally Sponsored Schemes as 1/6th of the Central Plan assistance to States. However, the Central Ministries continued to introduce new schemes and the financial limit came to be exceeded. The number of CSS increased from 45 in 1969 to 190 at the end of the Fifth Five Year Plan. Considering the criticism voiced by States in the NDC at the time of consideration of Sixth Five Year Plan, large number of CSS (72) were transferred to the State sector as part of the State Plan schemes and the resultant savings of about Rs. 2,000 crore were given to the States as additional block assistance on a formula known as Income Adjusted Total Population Formula. However, the Sixth Five Year Plan also witnessed Draft Restructuring of CSS 8 proliferation of CSS both in terms of number and quantum of funds. The number of CSS increased to 201 at the end of the Sixth Five Year Plan in 1985. The total assistance of Rs. 9,318 crore was allocated to CSS, 35 per cent of total Central Assistance to States. This assistance was provided scheme-wise.

(IV) 32nd Meeting of the NDC: The State Governments again raised the issue of proliferation of CSS in the 32nd Meeting of the NDC while discussing the approach to the Seventh Five Year Plan in July, 1984. In the meeting, the Prime Minister and Chairperson of the NDC opined that "Managing the flexibility in implementing various plan schemes is easier said than done. There could be areas within States which needed special attention but the special problems of such areas should not hold back the overall programme of development. However, with the cooperation of the States, it needs to be seen how this flexibility could be managed."

(V) NDC Expert Group (Chairman: K. Ramamurty): To resolve various issues concerning CSS, NDC constituted an Expert Group under the Chairmanship of Shri K. Ramamurty. The Group looked into various issues relating to CSS particularly need for revision of ceiling in regard to total assistance for CSS and for reducing the number/coverage of schemes as well re-examination of criteria for introducing a CSS. The Expert Group suggested the following criterion for CSS:

(i) It should relate to demonstration, pilot project, survey and research; or
(ii) It should have a regional or inter-state character; or
(iii) It should aim at building an institutional framework for the country as a whole or for a region; or
(iv) It should be in the nature of pace setter with a definite timeframe within the objectives outlined and sought to be realized.

(VI) NDC—Sub-Committee (Chairman: P.V. Narasimha Rao): The Report of the Group was considered by NDC in November, 1985 and it was felt that the criteria suggested by the Expert Group are too broad and that fulfilment of an important national objective as one of the criterion. Accordingly, NDC constituted a Committee under the Chairmanship of Shri P.V. Narasimha Rao, Minister of Human Resource Development, to review the criteria for taking up new CSS; ceiling of 1/6th or 1/7th of Central Plan Assistance for CSS keeping in view the plan objective of poverty alleviation and employment generation; consultation mechanism for starting new CSS; examination of CSS under implementation with a view to drop or transfer some of them with the modalities of transfer of funds involved and suggesting periodical review mechanism for schemes transferred to State Plans etc.

The Committee in its very first meeting in November, 1986 approved a set of modified criteria for the retention of existing and initiation of new CSS as indicated below:

(i) The fulfilment of an important national objective such as poverty alleviation or minimum standards in education; or
(ii) The programme has a regional orinter-State character; or
(iii) The programme or scheme should be in the nature of a pace setter or should relate to demonstration, survey or research.

As for the existing CSS, the Committee felt that schemes of national importance viz., anti-poverty programmes, rural water supply, family welfare and programmes intended to promote human resource development and sustain improvement in quality of life like education which were of national importance may be retained as CSS. Schemes other than those having high national importance could be considered for transfer to the State Plans. As for the new schemes, the Committee recommended that they should be introduced with the approval of the Full Planning Commission.

(VII) Group of Officials Headed by J.S. Baijal: The Committee constituted a Group of officials headed by J.S. Baijal, the then Secretary, Planning Commission to work out the details, in the light of above guidelines, regarding retention of CSS, mode of transfer of schemes to State Plans, allocation of outlays for the scheme proposed to be transferred. After intensive consultation with all stakeholders viz. Central Ministries/ Departments and State Governments, the Group evolved a definition of CSS and decided to exclude the schemes funded by autonomous bodies. The Group felt that area development schemes were in the nature of Special Central Assistance to State Plans and need not be considered as CSS. It decided to omit NEC, Tribal Area Plan, Border Area Development and Hill Area Development Programme, etc. from the scope of CSS. The total CSS after merging, weeding and dropping came to 236. The main recommendations contained in the report of Group of Officials submitted in 1987 are as under:

(i) The total number of CSS under implementation as on 1st April, 1985 is 262. Excluding 24 schemes being implemented by autonomous bodies, the Group recommended the transfer of 113 schemes Draft Restructuring of CSS 11 involving a Seventh Plan outlay of Rs. 1,260.72 crore to the States. 125 schemes with a Seventh Plan outlay of Rs. 14,104.17 crore are to be retained.

(ii) The transfer should be effective from the Eighth Plan. If transfer is desired from an earlier date, it could be from 1st April, 1988 for the remaining two years of the Plan. The updated figure of Rs. 800 crore available for 113 schemes to be transferred could be distributed to the States according to the modified Gadgil Formula.

(iii) Central assistance to the States inrespect of transferred schemes should be governed by the formula applicable to Central assistance to State Plans in the Eight Plan period. The Special Category States should, however, continue to enjoy the special dispensation as here-to-fore.

(iv) All the retained schemes should be critically examined and evaluated with regard to their thrust and content before their inclusion in the Eighth Plan. This examination should be carried out by the administrative Ministries/Departments in consultation with the Ministry of Finance and the Planning Commission.

(v) States should have flexibility in the matter of implementation of schemes to enable them to achieve the objectives in a cost effective manner keeping in view the special conditions and circumstances of each State.

(vi) There should be no mid-plan introduction of schemes. In other words, all the schemes to be implemented in a given Plan period should have been included in the Five Year Plan. In exceptional Draft Restructuring of CSS 12 cases, new schemes may be introduced to meet any emergent situation or to give effect to a new thrust in national policy (e.g. New Education Policy), but these should, as far as possible, be 100 per cent Centrally funded.

(vii) There should be prior consultation with the States not sectoral, but with Finance and Planning Departments before introduction of new schemes and financial arrangements should be carefully worked out if the schemes are not 100 per cent Centrally funded. In order that a broad view may be taken instead of a sectoral one by a particular Ministry, all new schemes should be approved by the full Planning Commission.

(viii) The Group felt that while it is necessary to limit CSS both in terms of number and financial outlays, it may not be practicable to lay down any ceiling. A rigorous procedure for fulfilling the criteria proposed by the NDC Committee, prior consultation with the States and approval of the Full Planning Commission should however, ensure that the propensity for proliferation of schemes is kept in check.

(VIII) The Final Report of the Narasimha Rao Committee: The Final Report of the Narasimha Rao Committee, submitted in 1988, incorporated the above recommendations. The report was considered in NDC meeting in 1990 wherein the Prime Minister and Chairman of NDC stated that the Government was actively considering decentralisation of the CSS but felt that such decentralisation should not be restricted to Centre and State capital alone but percolate down to Panchayat level or at appropriate level associated with a particular scheme for the benefit of the people.

The recommendations of the Narasimha Rao Committee to transfer 113 CSS to States with a combined Seventh Plan outlay of Rs. 1,260.75

crore formed the basis of discussions on Central Assistance through CSS in the 43rd NDC meeting held in December, 1991. NDC decided that the exact pattern of funding for each CSS transferred to the States would be maintained at the 1991-92 level and that the Central share of funds for the transferred scheme would be released to the State outside the formula of Central assistance. The then Deputy Chairman, Planning Commission also indicated that the Commission was willing to transfer more responsibilities to the States provided they are willing to take up the same. It was reaffirmed that only those schemes that have inter-state or regional character or are in the nature of pace setter and ones relating to setting of demonstration or research project would be taken up by Centre.

The issue of provision of Central Assistance to States through CSS and rationalisation of CSS with the objective of providing flexibility to States continued to be discussed in successive NDCs. The NDC in its 46th meeting observed that States did not indicate to the Planning Commission the usefulness or otherwise of the 113 schemes identified for transfer to the States even after lapse of two years. The NDC provided an option to the State Governments to revive defunct schemes in consultation with Planning Commission and observed that all the schemes should be transferred with resources. It was also decided that new CSS would be initiated with the approval of the Full Planning Commission. All the CSS were to be transferred as per the pattern of financing which prevailed before the transfer of these schemes.

The issue of transfer of CSS to the States along with resources again came up for discussion in the 47th NDC meeting held in January, 1997. While discussing the Draft Approach to the Ninth Five Year Plan, several Chief Ministers (Punjab, Delhi, Tripura, UP and Haryana) desired that CSS along with funds may be transferred to the States particularly relating to those sectors which come within the purview of the State List. However, the Central Ministries kept introducing new schemes. The total number of schemes increased to 360 in the last year of Ninth Five Year Plan and accounted for about 60 per cent of Central assistance. NDC observed that the better off States benefit more through the CSS as they have better resource matching and implementation capabilities compared to poor States.

The Planning Commission undertook Zero Based Budgeting (ZBB) exercise in the beginning ofthe Tenth Five Year Plan and recommended weeding out of 48 schemes, merger of 161 schemes into 53 schemes, and retaining the remaining 135 schemes, implying a carrying forward of 188 CSS to the Tenth Plan.

The divergence of opinion on the issue of transfer of CSS was visible in the 48th meeting of NDC in February, 1999. It transpired that this divergence of opinion was not only among the States but also between the States on the one hand and the Central Ministries/Departments on the other. The differences pertained not only to the selection of schemes to be transferred but also to the modalities of transfer e.g. Chief Minister, Andhra Pradesh suggested abolition of all CSS with transfer of funds to the States in true spirit of cooperative federalism. Chief Minister, Arunachal Draft Restructuring of CSS 15 Pradesh proposed that Union Government should finance 100 per cent CSS. Chief Ministers of other NE States suggested retention of few important schemes as CSS and others to be transferred to States with full funding. The issue of providing flexibility in usage of Central Assistance through CSS was raised by Bihar. The NDC decided to constitute a Sub-Committee under the Chairmanship of Deputy Chairman, Planning Commission. The Status Report of Sub-Committee of NDC on transfer of CSS was placed before the NDC in 49th meeting in 2001 wherein NDC directed Planning Commission to take note of suggestions made by Chief Ministers for identifying more schemes for transfer to the States with flexibility.

(IX) Aravind Varma Committee: Subsequently, on the recommendation of the 51st NDC meeting the Planning Commission set up an Expert Group in October 2005 under the Chairmanship of Arvind Varma, ex-Secretary, GoI to develop concrete proposals for restructuring the CSS in consultation with the Ministries/Departments concerned. The Committee in its report submitted in September, 2006 recommended that:

(a) A new CSS should be introduced only with the approval of the Full Planning Commission and in consultation with States.
(b) Planning Commission should undertake ZBB exercise at least once every five years in consultation with the States.
(c) A new CSS should be approved only if annual outlay is more than Rs.300 crore. Existing CSS with less than Rs. 300 crore annual outlay should be wound by 31st March, 2007 and the amount transferred to the States via the Normal Central Assistance route. Draft Restructuring of CSS 16.
(d) Planning Commission should notify terminal dates, targetted outcomes and outcome measurement strategy for all existing CSS. All new CSS should have start and closure dates, and in the absence of a specified date of closure, would come to a close at the end of that Plan period. The issue of terminal liabilities

should be addressed by the Central and State Governments around the time of termination of the CSS.

(e) All CSS funds should be routed through the State Budget. In the interests of practicality, States should make provision in anticipation of the Central releases.

(f) Any funds not transferred via the State budget should be subject to annual expenditure certification by the Indian Audit and Accounts Department like all CSS for which funds are released through the State budget.

The Expert Group Report was considered by the Planning Commission while preparing the Eleventh Five Year Plan. The need for providing adequate flexibility in the design of CSS taking into account the State level realities and priorities was recognised, but the transfer of CSS to States and UTs was not found desirable since CSS are designed to serve specific national objectives cutting across States/UTs. It was felt that the ZBB exercise of reducing CSS from155 in 2006-07 to 82 in 2007-08 would serve the purpose. Planning Commission recommended development of scheme-wise reliable information system with the help of Chief Controller of Accounts attached with each Ministry at CGA level with the objective of monitoring scheme-wise, State-wise releases and expenditure.

(X) M.M. Punchi Commission on Centre-State Relations (2010): The 73rd and 74th Amendments to the Constitution were game changing developments in the Indian federation and were intended to strengthen self-governance at the grassroots level and to make local bodies important agencies for the delivery of public services. Decentralisation is intended to result in greater efficiency in the delivery of services. Local bodies being closer to people are expected to meet the local needs better than a centralized system of governance. Under Articles 243G and 243W, State legislatures may by law transfer powers and authority to rural and urban local bodies as are necessary to enable them to function as institutions of self government. Powers and authority include transfer of functional responsibilities and powers to levy and collect taxes as may be assigned to them by the State legislatures.

Following the 73rd and 74th Amendments to the Constitution, a number of States have notified transfer of functions to local bodies. But there has been limited progress in the direction of transfer of funds and functionaries. The expectation that funds and functionaries will follow functions has remained unfulfilled. Decentralisation is not fiscally neutral.

Decentralisation requires empowering local bodies with adequate resources to discharge their assigned responsibilities.

The 73rd and 74th Amendments of the Constitution do not provide for direct funding of local bodies by the Central Government. The involvement of the Central Government in strengthening the financial position of the local bodies is indirect following the consequential amendment made to Article 280 mandating the Central Finance Commission to make recommendations on the measures needed to augment the Consolidated Fund of a State to supplement the resources of Panchayats and Municipalities in the State on the basis of the recommendations made by the Finance Commission of the State. The purpose of this provision is to find ways and means to meet the financial requirements of local bodies without in any way changing the primary role of States.

Observation made by FC-X

The following observation made by FC-X is very relevant in this context:

(1) The responsibility of sharing taxes with panchayats and assigning grants to them has not been transferred from the States to the Centre. The responsibility for providing panchayats with an independent source of revenue as also grants for specified purposes is very much that of the State Governments. The State Finance Commissions are there to ensure proper allocation of resources as between the State and the Panchayats. If in the process of supplementation of the resources of panchayats a need arises for the augmentation of the State Consolidated Fund, it has to be considered by the Finance Commission.

The above observation was made in the context of the memorandum submitted to the Commission by the Ministry of Rural Development. These observations also represent the views of the Commission on transfers to municipalities. FC-X further observed that in terms of the Constitutional Amendment, many of the functions of the State would have to be transferred to local bodies. The Commission expressed the view that the transfer of functions to local bodies would not result in any extra burden on the State as this would be accompanied by the transfer of the staff already working on these schemes/projects as also the financial allocations budgeted for and envisaged to be spent on the transferred activities.

(2) FC-XI had further clarified the role of the Central Finance Commission in supplementing the resources of the local bodies under Article 280. The Commission stated as follows:

> "If we were to take into account the additional financial burden that falls on a State on account of the acceptance and implementation of the recommendations of the State Finance Commission, such expenditure has to be built into the expenditure stream of the State. Any devolution made by a State for the Panchayats and Municipalities over and above the recommendations of the State Finance Commission is outside the purview of our consideration, as would be evident from the Constitutional provision."

(3) FC-XII had brought further clarity with regard to the role of the Central Finance Commissions. The Commission felt that the purport of the relevant provisions of the Constitution could be two fold. Firstly, there could be a case to augment the Consolidated Fund of the States through additional grants from the Centre keeping in view the special circumstances of the States, which might justify such assistance. Secondly, certain recommendations of the State Finance Commissions for augmenting the revenues of the States might require decision-making by the Central Government. The Commission felt that there was a need to provide an impetus to the decentralization process keeping inview the spirit of the 73rd and 74th Amendments to the Constitution.

(4) The Tenth to Twelfth Finance Commissions recommended ad hoc grants to local bodies and routed them through the respective State Governments. FC-X did not stipulate any conditions for the grants recommended by it to local bodies except that they should be over and above the transfers by States. FC-XI earmarked a portion of the grants recommended by it for the maintenance of accounts and audit and for the development of a database of local bodies and the remaining amount for the maintenance of the core services. FC-XII recommended grants amounting to Rs. 25,000 to local bodies for the five-year period 2005-10. As that Commission mentioned, this was equivalent to 1.24 per cent of the shareable tax revenues and 0.9 per cent of the gross revenue receipts of the Centre as estimated for the period 2005-10. The Commission stipulated that rural local

bodies should utilize the grant for repairs/rejuvenation of water supply schemes and sanitation and that at least 50 per cent of the grants to urban local bodies should be utilized for solid waste management through Public-Private Partnership (PPP).

(5) FC-XIII has observed that there was an undisputed need to improve the finances of the rural and urban local bodies and that they should be supported through a predictable and buoyant source of revenue. It stressed the need to make local bodies more accountable in the discharge of their functions. Taking into account the demands of the local bodies that they be allowed to benefit from the buoyancy of Central taxes, FC-XIII has recommended that local bodies be transferred a percentage share in the divisible pool of Central taxes after converting this share into grant-in-aid under Article 275. The grant eligibility in a year will be related to the size of the divisible in the preceding year. The Commission has recommended grants equivalent to 2.28 per cent of the divisible pool of 2009-14 for the period 2010-15.

(6) The grants recommended by FC-XIII after converting the 2.28 per cent of the divisible pool amount to Rs. 87,519 crore for the period 2010-15. The grant recommended by FC-XIII has two components—a basic component and a performance based component. The basic grant which is equivalent to 1.50 per cent of previous year's divisible pool is available to all the States put together without any conditions. The performance grant effective from 2011-12 will be 0.50 per cent of the divisible pool for the year 2011-12 and 1 per cent thereafter. The release of the performance grant is conditional on meeting certain stipulations. The main stipulations are, putting in place a supplement to budget documents listing out the budget allocations separately for rural and urban local bodies, audit system for local bodies, appointment of an independent ombudsman for local bodies, prescribing through an Act qualification of persons eligible for appointment to SFCs and enabling all local bodies to levy property tax.

(7) For the first time, FC-XIII has linked grants to local bodies to the divisible pool of Central taxes. As the Constitutional provisions do not permit sharing of the divisible pool with the local bodies, FC-XIII recommended grants equivalent to a percentage share of the divisible pool. Like the previous Commissions, FC-XIII too has emphasised that the grants

recommended by it are by way of supplementing the transfers from States.

(8) Though we are in agreement with the approach of the Finance Commissions in recommending grants to local bodies, we are constrained in observing that the assessment of the requirements of the local bodies and the estimation of gap in their resources is ad hoc and is only broadly indicative. In most cases, the assessment of the requirements is based on the estimates submitted by the Central Ministries. The requirements as assessed by the States lack rigour and are gross overestimates based on certain norms which can only be met in the long run and not in the five-year award period of a Central Finance Commission. To address this issue, it is necessary to synchronize the periods covered by the State and Central Finance Commissions and to ensure that the reports of the SFCs are available to the Central Finance Commission well in time. Under the provisions of Articles 243-I and 243-Y, State Finance Commission shall be constituted within one year of the 73rd and 74th Amendments and thereafter after the expiration of every fifth year. Currently, there is no uniformity across States regarding the appointment of Finance Commissions and the periods covered by their reports gives the status of the Constitution of the Third State Finance Commissions. The NCRWC recommended amendment of Article 243-I to provide for the Constitution of SFCs at the expiration of every fifth year or earlier. A similar recommendation was made by the SARC. We strongly endorse this recommendation which will pave the way for the synchronization of the periods of the Central Finance Commission and the SFCS. Since the timing of the appointment of the Central Finance Commission is known, SFCs should be appointed in advance so that their reports are available to the Central Finance Commission well in time to ensure their consideration. It should also be ensured that the reference period of the SFCs should match that of the Central Finance Commission.

(9) Other issues relating to the SFCs are the diversity in their approach, wide variations in the contents of their reports and the undue delay on the part of the States in placing the Action Taken Reports (ATR) on the recommendations of SFCs in State Legislatures. Equally worrisome is the practice of States appointing people not well versed in the affairs of local bodies or their finances as members of the SFCs. The quality of SFCs

reports continues to remain poor. FC-XII recommended that SFCs should collect information in the formats suggested by it to ensure uniformity in their approach across States. The basis with regard to the assessment of needs and determination of grants is also not found to be uniform. FC-XIII has recommended the adoption of a common template by the SFCs for the preparation of their reports. We recommend adoption of a uniform approach by the SFCs and as a first step in this direction, the ToR should mandate the SFCs to adopt the common template recommended by FC-XIII.

(10) FC-XII emphasised the need to appoint people of eminence and competence as members of the SFCs and expressed the desirability of States following the Central legislation and rules which prescribe the qualifications for the chairperson and members of the Finance Commission. Such a need has also been eiterated by FC-XIII. We recommend enactment of a suitable legislation by all States prescribing qualifications of persons to be appointed to the SFCs.

(11) There are numerous instances of States taking their own time in placing the ATRs on the recommendations of SFCs. Even when the SFC reports are available, it would be difficult for the Central Finance Commission to assess the financial implications of the recommendations in the absence of ATRs. We, therefore, recommend that ATRs on the recommendations of the SFCs should be placed in the State Legislature within a period of three months from the date of their submission.

(12) Fiscal autonomy is essential for realizing the benefits of decentralization. Decision-making at the local level will suffer in the absence of fiscal autonomy. The present system of almost total dependence of local bodies on higher levels of government does not promote accountability. As long as local bodies have the pleasure of spending money without the pain of raising it, accountability cannot be ensured in local self-governance. Under Articles 243-H and 243-X of the Constitution, State legislatures are authorized to allow local bodies to levy and collect specified State taxes and to assign the proceeds of specified State taxes to local bodies. These provisions of the Constitution do not seem to have served the purpose of empowering the local bodies financially. While there has been some progress in transferring functions to local bodies, States have been by and large reluctant

to part with financial powers. The present provision of SFCs taking into account the tasks entrusted to the local bodies and assessing the resources available to them does not adequately serve the purpose of financial empowerment. We are of the opinion that there should be some initiatives in the direction of allowing local bodies to levy and collect certain State taxes and assigning the proceeds of some other.

(XI) B.K. Chaturvedi Committee on the restructuring of CSS (2011)

The recommendations of the Chaturvedi Committee on CSS can be broadly classified under four heads (Anita Rath, TISS, 2013):

(a) Restrictive Mandate,
(b) Proliferation of CSS,
(c) Funding Pattern, and
(d) Flexibility in Physical and Financial Norms.

(a) Restrictive Mandate

At the outset, it is important to notice that the mandate given to the Chaturvedi Committee was too narrow. The major Terms of Reference (ToR) related to the restructuring of CSS were:

(1) Rationalisation of Centrally Sponsored Schemes in line with "Challenges for the 12th Plan", such that the total number does not exceed 30.
(2) Determining minimum size for CSS and principles of exceptions, if any.
(3) Consideration of creation of flexi fund under ministries/ departments to experiment/undertake pilot projects on innovative ideas before launch of a scheme.
(4) Considering providing flexibility to states to undertake new initiatives from flexi fund where states would also make a contribution.

There are clear gaps in the Planning Commission's notion, as represented in the mandate, and states' aspirations on these issues. The major concerns raised by the states time and again, and acknowledged by the Chaturvedi Committee have been—

(i) putting a cap on CSS at 1/6th or 1/7th of Central Plan Assistance, (ii) transferring a number of identified schemes to state governments, (iii) consultation with states, particularly if the schemes are not 100 per cent central funded, and (iv) flexibility to states.

A repertoire of other issues were also identified, such as the proliferation of CSS, top-down approaches, provision of flexibility to states to "mould schemes according to local requirements, flow of funds, accountability, enforceability, implementation, and involvement" of Panchayati Raj Institutions (PRIs) etc.

The common issues recognised both by the states and the Chaturvedi Committee are the proliferation of the CSS and flexibility to states. With regard to the CSS/CAS proliferation issue, the states are bothered about the fiscal size of these schemes in terms of their share in GBS. The mandate of the Planning Commission is too narrow and only concerned about the absolute number of CSS. The highly restrictive ToR—with a minimum size for the CSS package to be spelt out first and the rationale for it discovered subsequently—puts the cart before the horse. The articulation of the terms for flexibility to the states in the ToR also has a narrow scope. The mandate is not explicit about the issue of top-down approaches and consultations with states on the gamut of issues related to CSS.

(b) Proliferation of CSS

The Chaturvedi Committee recommended pruning the number of CSS and schemes under Additional Central Assistance (ACA)/central sector (CS). It suggested reduction in the number of CSS, mainly by merging the existing schemes under subsectoral heads (for major departments with many sub-sectors) and umbrella heads (for smaller departments). Existing flagship schemes, 15 in number, could continue into the future. Additional schemes—National Rural Livelihood Mission (NRLM) under CSS and Backward Regions Grant Fund (BRGF) under ACA—were recommended for recognition as flagship schemes.

The Chaturvedi Committee recommended that the maximum number of schemes for a department be limited to Six (applicable to the Departments of Agriculture and Co-operation and School Education and Literacy), reduced from 17 in the existing framework. The criterion for the merger of schemes could be the scheme outlay during the Eleventh Plan period (less than Rs. 500 crore during the plan, with an average annual outlay of Rs. 100 crore, if started late). The Chaturvedi Committee also suggested that new flagships, if considered for introduction during the Twelfth Plan, should have a minimum outlay of Rs. 10,000 crore.

The weeding and merging of schemes has been the most consistent feature of the recommendations of the various committees. Most of them have suggested following simple outlay-based ceilings to prune the number of schemes. A number of CSS are also absorbed under the central plan or ACA. The Chaturvedi Committee suggested that 39 CSS should be merged into schemes and continue as ACA. However, these pruning exercises do not affect centre-state issues in sharing the GBS. This is surprising because the Chaturvedi Committee stated clearly that the "current system of implementing css and ACA separately is artificial. Both are implemented in the same manner".

It has been the practice to transfer a large number of schemes with nominal budgets to the states from time to time so that the css and CAS baskets look neat. But, this exercise will have no effect on the share of CSS in GES because the plethora of small schemes has hardly any fiscal presence. Currently, 44 per cent of total CSS have an annual outlay of less than Rs. 100 crore. The states may not be enthusiastic about accepting and continuing with these schemes, either because they do not meet state requirement or because there is no financial devolution on a long-term basis assured from the centre for managing these schemes.

The transfer of 113 schemes around the Seventh Plan period, following the recommendations of the P.V. Narasimha Rao Committee in 1988 is a case in point. These schemes involved just Rs. 1,260 crore of the Seventh Plan outlay, whereas the 125 schemes retained by the centre as CSS had an outlay of Rs. 14,104 crore. In the deliberations at the 46th meeting of the NDC, it came up that even after two years of the transfer of the schemes, the states had not indicated the usefulness of these 113 schemes. The NDC again provided an option to the states to revive the defunct schemes in consultation with the Planning Commission.

Hence, these transfers are simple number games. Compressing the number of schemes through nominal financial criteria would not alter their significance in the GBS and would not address the general concern regarding growing centralisation of policies and planning. Merging existing schemes and amalgamating small schemes to form mega-schemes may cause implementation issues. Financial and physical flexibility norms are too meagre to have any substantial impact on these trends. The Chaturvedi Committee also made a recommendation regarding NCA, i e, that it should not be reduced below 10 per cent of GBS to enable states to have adequate flexible resources for their plans. However, it did not take a very clear stand regarding the ceiling for the share of the css in GBS.

(c) Funding Pattern

The Chaturvedi Committee's recommendations on several issues related to funding patteins are discussed here under three broad heads: the matching fund to be assured by the states, incentive-based approaches and the procedure for transfer of funds to the states.

Matching Fund: Many schemes sponsored by the centre require counterpart funding by states to avail the centre's contribution. His requirement remains a bone of contention. Such matching requirements vary from scheme to scheme and in certain cases, range to the tune of 50 per cent or even more. There is a dear acknowledgement that such conditions affect the ability of relatively poorer states to access funds. But the conditions are defended on the grounds of accountability and ownership.

While evaluating the success rate of schemes with varying matching requirements, the Chaturvedi Committee acknowledged that "Ownership argument is important but not a critical factor in successful implementation of CSS". It emphasised that the design, monitoring and effective implementation of the schemes had a bearing on their success.

However, the Chaturvedi Committee did not recommend any changes in the funding pattern of the existing css, arguing that it would require large changes for both state and central finances. It suggested that as per the review of the Eleventh Plan, the administering ministry may restructure as necessary based on experience in the light of the relevant steering committee's recommendations. All new CSS, except new flagship schemes, should provide for 100 per cent central funds. The Chaturvedi Committee also recommended that in case of new flagship schemes, counterpart funds from the state government could range to a maximum of 25 per cent (10% for north-east states) "depending upon the interventions planned".

Incentive-Based Approach: Emphasising the need for an incentive-based approach, the Chaturvedi Committee recommended guidelines and an incentive-based structure for certain crucial departments like health, education, urban develop ment, skill development and rural infrastructure. Regarding annual increment in allocation, it suggests that such increase should preferably be given to states which have taken steps to allocate "larger resources of their own" to the "concerned CSS field". A suggestion was made for 50 per cent of the increased allocation under any CSS/ CAS-CS schemes to be distributed proportionately amongst states that have provided larger allocations for the concerned sector in their budgets. This approach could begin with the health, education, urban development, skill development and rural infrastructure sectors.

The leading role taken by the centre in boosting social sector expenditures can result in an appreciable increase in such expenditure only if states also follow suit. The mid-term appraisal of the Eleventh Plan reiterated that states have to substantially increase their health budgets. The centre's health expenditure as percentage of GDP increased from 0.29 in 2005-06 to 0.39 in 2009-10. This is much faster than the states, where the increase was from 0.67 to 0.70 over the same period. This pattern also holds good for health-related expenditure. Total public expenditure on health in India in 2011-12 (BE) has been around 1.3 per cent of GDP. To realise the health spending goal of 2-3 per cent of GDP, as per the estimation by Berman *et al.*, states must increase spending on average by 22-38 per cent per year. The situation remains similar for other social sectors. An incentive structure would be useful if states participate fully in the planning and design procedures and see the policies as meeting their unique requirements.

(d) Flexibility in Physical and Financial Norms

The Chaturvedi Committee suggests incorporating a flexible component into these schemes, to be used for developing specific schemes by the State government consistent with the objectives of CSS. It recommends that ministries should undertake extensive review of the requirements of different regions of the country and prescribe different physical and financial norms for different regions prior to the commencement of the Twelfth Five-Year Plan. Consultation with the State governments and the *modus operandi* for incorporation of these recommendations are discussed in some detail in the report.

It suggests that all sub-sectoral and umbrella schemes must reserve 20 per cent funds as "flexi funds". In flagship schemes, these funds may be to the tune of 10 per cent of the annual outlay. These schemes will be prepared and approved by the State government, while adhering to the broad guidelines for such schemes circulated by the concerned ministries.

While recognising the fact that financial norms are often key to the effective implementation of a programme, the Chaturvedi Committee recommends automatic revisions, after two years of the Plan, in the allocations for all those items that are notified by the Ministry of Finance in consultation with the administering ministry at the beginning of the plan. It recommends that these cost escalations should be accounted for automatically, with the wholesale price index, without any reference from State governments.

This flexibility is restricted in financial terms to 10 to 20 per cent of the amount. Within the larger framework, this implies that only a very minor part of the scheme can be altered by states to suit local needs instead of changing the uniform templates. Alternatively, a particular segment of the programme/process could have been carved out where the states' participation remains crucial.

Conclusions and Suggestions

***Growing Centralisation of Social Sector Policies*:** The above mentioned study of Anitha Rath, undoubtfully shows that there has been growing centralization of social sector policies in India through the proliferation of the CSS and CAS.

The growing centralisation of the social sector can be seen in the changing share of the centre and states in total Social Sector Expenditure (SSE) over the years. During the reform period, a declining trend in expenditure by the states was observed throughout 1990s, while central government expenditure on these sectors was actually increasing. As a result, there were signs of growing centralisation of SSE. The process of centralisation of SSE continued subsequently and has been more rapid in recent times. In the total SSE, i.e., both revenue and capital expenditure on social and community services and rural development jointly by the centre and states, the share of states has fallen from 85 per cent in 1990-91 to less than 70 per cent in the 2009-2010 budget estimate. Some segments like housing and rural development, apart from family welfare, are highly centralised now, with states' share being just about 40 per cent.

Centralisation through the CSS/CAS route affects state policies on social sectors and the general planning process in several ways. First, it squeezes the funds available for supporting state plans. Information on plan transfers from the centre shows that the share of central assistance in aggregate resources for State and Union Territory (UT) plans have gone down from 46 per cent in 1997-98 to 21 per cent in 2011-12. A major concern on this front has been that there is negative growth observed in the proceeds of Normal Central Assistance (NCA), a formula-based transfer for state plans. Correspondingly, there has been a significant and consistent increase in the share of CSS in the centre's support for the plan—i.e., gross budgetary support (GBs) over time. Recent figures suggest that though there is a fall in the number of schemes from the Ninth Plan to the Eleventh Plan period (360 to 147), the share of css to GBS has clearly gone up (31% to 42%).

In India, State governments are entrusted with higher responsibilities by Article 246 of the Seventh Schedule of Constitution with respect to social spending of certain kinds, such as on health, education and family welfare. It is important, therefore, to understand the dynamics of centre-state-shares in total SSE. States' shares also include flows from the centre in the form of normal assistance or other support through State budgets. Hence, it is a conservative estimate, from the point of view of centralisation, because central assistance other than NCA channels comes with certain restrictive conditions.

In 1990-91, the states' share of the total social sector was around 85 per cent. It declined to 80 per cent in 1998-99 and further to 71 per cent in 2007-08. As per the budget estimates of 2009-10, the share of states is expected to further decline to 67.6 per cent. In absolute figures, in 2009-10 (BE), the combined expenditure by centre and states on social sectors is estimated to be Rs. 5,388 billion, out of which states are estimated to spend Rs. 3,645 billion. The share of states declined for most major heads of expenditure during this period. There was a very substantial decline in the share of expenditure of states on rural development. In 1990-91, the states' share of rural development was as high as 90 per cent. At the end of the 1990s, it was only 64 per cent. In 2007-08, states' share in this sector was only 44 per cent. In case of education, art and culture, it has declined from 88 per cent to 79 per cent. Over 1998-99 to 2009-10. In case of health and health-related expenditure (medical, public health, water supply and sanitation), it has declined from 91 to 79 per cent. The family welfare segment is highly centralised now, with states' share falling from 93 per cent to about 44 per cent. The states' share for urban development increased from 1990-91 to 1998-99 and subsequently remained stagnant at that level.

Serious recentralising tendencies as well as curtailing of the fiscal and functional domain of the second-tier governments have been observed in some countries across the world. Such processes are also visible in India with growing intrusion of the union government into many areas which fall in the domain of the states. These developments are attributed, on the one hand, to the forces of globalization.

The growing centralisation of social sector policies has caused apprehension. It upsets states' priorities and their unique requirements, hamper state planning processes, and affect the smooth implementation of these schemes. Public policy innovations and their diffusion have been important aspects of fiscal federalism and uniform mega policies by the centre, subsuming interesting state-level initiatives, clearly affect these possibilities. In recent times, the absorption capacity of states, desperate and unproductive spending in the last quarter of the financial year to keep the account statement neat, and leakage of resources are questions that surface time and again in various schemes mooted by the centre. In this context, a comprehensive evaluation of various schemes should have preceded the exercise of the Chaturvedi Committee. This would have lent the process a more scientific basis for restructuring instead of a simple approach relying on outlay-based cut-offs. Such an evaluation programme would also have thrown light on the physical and financial flexibility norms to be followed in some detail.

Reforms Inevitable: The current system of administration of the schemes needs reforms. One of the most important gaps is the way distinction is being made between CSS and ACA-based schemes. While generally, ACA-based schemes are 100 per cent Central assistance schemes, particularly Flagship Schemes, in several of these schemes State contribution is required in varying degrees like AIBP and JNNURM to avail of the central funds. The CSS also prescribe different share of the States. These shares vary, as mentioned earlier, from Nil to 65 per cent. Conceptually, both these schemes pass on funds from the Central Government to the State Governments with some conditionality or counterpart fund request and effectively these are CSS. The difference has arisen because of the historical evolution and the way these are being budgeted, financed and controlled and also difference in release of funds. In case of AIBP, for example, evaluation is being done by Planning Commission and based on its recommendations and that of the Ministry funds are released by the Ministry of Finance.

In case of JNNURM, such an evaluation and Draft Restructuring of CSS 25 assessment is being done by Ministry of Urban Development and based on their recommendations, ACA is released by Ministry of Finance. In case of CSS, the budgets are allocated to concerned Ministries and the entire process of releases is also done by them. There does not appear to be any major distinction between ACA based schemes and CSS except that ACA forms part of State Plan size while CSS do not. The number of States, particularly the North-East States, Bihar and Jharkhand have often represented that they have limitation of resources and are not able to provide State's share to enable them to access the required funds under CSS. This is particularly important for schemes like SSA. where the counterpart funds are tothe extent of 35 per cent and the sector is extremely critical for every State. Simultaneously, it is also important to ensure that the States have adequate financial participation to ensure a sense of ownership of the scheme by them. It has been argued that if 100 per cent grants come from the Central Government, the ownership gets diluted. An important area impacting on efficient implementation of CSS has been the need for flexibility in many of the schemes. India with its different geographical regions, varied requirements of States, different levels of infrastructure development, demographics and economic growth, growing urbanization and density of population requires flexibility for States to plan their development.

The flexibility should be in terms of ability of the State to spend part ofthe funds for meeting certain special needs which may be complementary to or meeting the objective of the CSS. This flexible provisions must enable the State to meet any special Draft Restructuring of CSS 26 requirements because of above variations. Such flexibility is also required to enable overall optimum use of the financial resources of States and the Centre. Many of the areas in which CSS are being framed often fall in the domain of the State Governments functions or are part of the Concurrent List. Education and electricity are areas of Concurrent List. But apart from this, in agriculture, rural development, nutrition, land development, employment and rural housing CSS havebeen made to meet needs of our Federation. It is necessary that these schemes take into account the on-going schemes of the States in these areas. The expenditure on these schemes in these sectors by different States varies depending on its own resources and priorities.

In similar activities money may be provided under CSS as well as from State Government. There is, hence, a need to take into account the nature of schemes being run in the States and implement CSS with such flexibility so that convergence leads to better results. These results could be in the form of improvement in the quality of service. For example, if money is provided under IAY for construction of houses and the State Government is also putting its own resources, it may be possible to construct a house with a cement roof, along with a toilet and rooms which have better interior. Under, Rajiv Gandhi Gramin Vikas Yojana (RGGVY), State Governments have been provided funds for electrification of villages. Villages have been uneven size and size of population and may often have several habitations.

Flexibility is necessary with the State Government to enable an effective convergence. This may include increasing the size of the transformers to take up load or providing financial support for far-off villages which do not have a good sub-transmission system. Often in the absence of such flexibility, the full objective of the schemes cannot be met. In several schemes flexibility is required in terms of norms. In a number of schemes, like IAY and PMGSY, the norms for hilly regions, densely populated States, like Kerala, which may have shortage of land or North-East and J&K, where the rural roads may pass through high quality land which may need to beacquired, need to be different in both physical and financial terms. The cost of project is different in different areas. These need to be fully taken care of. For example, the costof buildings in the North-East and in the far-eastcorners of North-East has great variations.

It will be useful to consider the extent to which we can provide flexibility to meet these needs. Yet another example is the cost of cooking in the MDM scheme. Given the rise in Wholesale Price Index, it will be useful to revise norms every two years, so that the purpose of the scheme is met. If this is not done, either the food is likely to be of poor quality or it may not be cooked at all. The schemes which we design provide for individual components which are needed for the development of the sector. We need to develop sectoral or sub-sectoral schemes which address varying aspects of the development needs. While part of the resources of such schemes could be used to address issues concerned to all States, a second component should be flexible part which States may use as required by them in accordance with gaps and to get convergence. Rashtriya Krishi Vikas Yojana (RKVY) is a good example of this.

This provides for a large number of sectors in the field of agriculture. A number of schemes accordingly need to be merged at the Central level, so, that major areas of the concerned department get covered and technology and Central resources can flow for the benefit of the States. In a number of departments, there are large number schemes. In agriculture, for example there are a total of 13 schemes. Similarly, in Animal Husbandry and Dairying there are 15 schemes. It is possible to merge many of them into a comprehensive scheme for development of sub-sectors. Schemes with small outlays are a major disadvantage. These envisage expenditure of small amounts spread over the country. These need to be weeded out. In fact, an earlier Committee on CSS has considered this question and argued that any CSS which had an outlay of less than Rs. 300 crore should not be taken up at all. It is important that the funds we provide should be able to make a dent in the State's economy. All such schemes need to be weeded out. An important issue in the CSS isthe transfer and release of funds and norms which are prescribed for it. There is a need to provide transparent guidelines which provide for allocation of funds under CSS, so that States are able to plan their resources better.

A recent effort to bring complete transparency in this regard has been made in RKVY. The allocation of funds under this schemeis formula-driven. There have been two criticisms on this approach. Firstly, it has led to an uncertain fund position in the State under this scheme. No programmes can, therefore, be run on a long-term basis on such a scheme since the State which if not able to provide adequate budget provision in the agriculture sector does not get funds under RKVY. This approach cannot be adopted for every sector, as it is constrained by the State's resources and overall budget allocations. Therefore, while adopting the RKVY structure its strengths and weaknesses are required to be kept in mind. The current system also suffers from a major drawback on manner of transfer of funds to States under CSS. Funds are being released under CSS to State Governments or independent societies, of which senior officials of State Government are in-charge or at District level to DRDA. It is not possible in the current system to monitor the actual flow of funds under these schemes and release to the States or various societies to whom it is transferred directly.

There is need to use technology and financial accounting methods for effective monitoring of funds under these schemes. An effort in this regard in the Planning Commission has already been started. Following assessment has been made in Planning Commission that "The present system of budget and account classification suffers from several weaknesses. The lack of uniform coding for plan schemes across the States makes it difficult to trace releases under a particular scheme from the Centre to the ultimate user as it flows through state budget system. A significant proportion of central plan resources are also transferred to implementing agencies of State governments by way of direct transfer outside the State Consolidated Funds. These transfers cannot be traced on line in terms of their final use. These problems are planned to be addressed through a new multidimensional budget and accounting classification being prepared by a Committee set up by the Ministry of Finance. Further, the Central Plan Scheme Monitoring System (CPSMS) has been initiated by the Controller General of Accounts in collaborationwith the Planning Commission to serve as a comprehensive management information and decision support system for monitoring of the Plan schemes of the Government.

CPSMS seeks to have interface with state treasuries and State AGs to obtain real time expenditure information for schemes for which funds are transferred from the Central Ministries to the consolidated fund of the States. It also has the challenging task of integrating thousands of implementing agencies through Core Banking Solution (CBS) of the individual banks so that fund movement is tracked at each successive stage starting with the initial release from the Centre till the money actually reaches the ultimate beneficiaries. On full implementation, CPSMS is expected to provide customized information of fund deployment and utilization vertically under each scheme to programme managers and horizontally across schemes in one geographic area. Inputs provided by the system would be vital for programme management and policy planning. The information on fund utilization should also be placed in the public domain for greater public awareness, public participation inthe policy making and execution and toward enhanced transparency in Government operations." This will ensure that no new CSS is introducedwithout uniform budget code from the CGA. As mentioned earlier, the transfer of funds is currently being done through several ways. In a number of schemes, funds are being directly transferred at district-level, in some others, these are given to the State Government which in turn transfer the funds to district-level and Panchayati Raj Institutions (PRIs).

The system of transfers needs a review as it dilutes State Government's responsibility on use of funds transferred directly outside the State budget. Two considerations have to be kept in mind while examining this issue. Firstly, the accountability of the State Government under the present system has to be strengthened. The transfer of funds directly at the district-level or to Panchayats or urban local bodies makes these organizations accountable but the State Government under whom these organizations work has often argued that, since, they have not transferred the funds through States budgets, they are not responsible for its proper utilization. It is important in our federal system that State Governments are fully involved in such transfers and these take place through their budgets. This involves delays which will have to be addressed. Secondly, transfers should be such that funds to the lowest utilizing organizational level reach quickly. This merits to some extent, the transfer of funds directly to the Panchayats where many of these funds are to be utilized. These concerns will need to be addressed for an effective fund transfer mechanism. One of the major problems in the CSS is poor implementation of schemes in several States. This points to a design gap in the schemes.

These schemes either do not provide for a concurrent evaluation and assessment or where they do, this is not done in an independent manner so as to get an effective feedback. Example of an excellent third party evaluation is the Guidelines prescribed for PMGSY and system of evaluation evolved for this. Guidelines for this have been issued by Ministry of Rural Development. Under this evaluation is done at the level of both State and Central Governments. These monitors are appointed in an independent manner and have a responsibility to visit the districts for seeing the progress of work. This has given very good results and the rural roads programme of PMGSY is generally accepted to be an effective programme. It is important that all CSS have such a mechanism installed. This evaluation could be across the country through series of sample surveys or independent monitors giving their assessment after visiting the States and seeing the programmes in certain districts. It could also be through evaluation by a certain institutes. Not enough time has been devoted to this part of the CSS design. The gaps in the schemes have, therefore, quite often been noticed after almost Plan period is over. This restricts the ability for mid-course correction and doing modifications which can improve the design of the programme and improve the effectiveness of the programme.

Suggestions

The centrally sponsored schemes carry substantial amounts of grants transferred from the Government of India (GoI) to states to influence expenditure in areas that are Constitutional responsibilities of states and addressing national objective of critical importance. We have seen that the percentage allocation from Central Plan Assistance towards CSS has been increasing at a rapid pace over the years. The Centre for Budge and Policy Studies (CBPS) has made a detailed study on the CSS. Their findings can be summed up as under:

In general, most departments opine that CSS have served an important purpose and, therefore, must continue. This is despite having problems with some or the other aspect of the specific scheme in many cases. However, a large number of issues and learning emerged through an analysis of the implementation experience of various schemes. Although the nature, design, purpose, structure, funding patters and mechanisms vary quite largely from one scheme to the other, certain common learning emerged which could act as ready check list for future planning or restructuring of the scheme/s.

Provision of adequate human resources to plan, implement and monitor the scheme is considered critical. A number of existing schemes are well-placed in this regard whereas many suffer due to lack of adequate provisions. CSS has good record on investing in professional development of human resources, which needs to continue. But the departments also felt that the training and capacity building component is more sustained if the focus is on the respective departmental staff rather than those hired for short term.

The consultations with almost all the departments in the state revealed that despite the presence of monitoring structures, formats and pre-determined frequencies, monitoring is generally weak for a variety of reasons. There is a need to move from filing up and collecting monitoring formats to utilization of the same in decision-making. The use of IT is highly recommended. Keeping the sensitive relationship between the centre and the state, third party monitoring may seem to be an appropriate method.

There is constant debate on the primary responsibility of providing quality services across departments, and burden sharing between the State and Centre. One of the largest problems with inter-governmental transfer schemes is the overlapping jurisdiction of multiple agencies. While in general the Additional Central Assistance Schemes are 100 per cent centrally assisted and CSS have some state contribution ranging from 10 per cent to 50 per cent, the definition of CSS remains unclear. Chaturvedi committee points out that the distinction between CSS and ACA based schemes is artificial as both are conceptually the same. Greater clarity in such definitions is indeed desirable.

Flexi funds can be introduced at the central, state and district level within the scheme, between schemes and between sectors. Flexi funds could help in filling the gaps in regional variations, encourage innovations and reduce procedural delays. The risks associated with the introduction of flexi funds, as identified by the departments, include the possibilities of vested interests influencing the investments at the cost of real priorities, and diversion of funds in paying salaries and financing state sectors schemes. Well-designed and detailed guidelines and monitoring system need to be in place to minimize such risks. We have suggested that 80 per cent of the funds can come through CSS while 20 per cent of the funds should be allotted to flexi fund kitty. Chaturvedi Committee also suggests allotting 20 per cent of funds as flexi funds.

We have suggested eleven criteria for the selection of proposals to be funded through flexi funds. This includes assessing the proposals on beneficiary targeted, assessing the need of the scheme, assuring that it is not duplicating any ongoing efforts, if the project/scheme proposed will help in filling the gaps in the sector, is it important, innovation, feasibility, sustainability, scalability, cost effectiveness and clarity.

Flexi funds can also be used an incentive for states that have made greater investments in particular sectors, that are considered priority. For instance, Karnataka and other states who had introduced free textbooks before SSA initiation could be given the equivalent amounts as flexi funds to be used for some other purpose within the sector.

References

Anitha Rath, Growing Centralization of Social Sector Policies in India, *EPW*, 26-01-2013, Volume XLVIII, No. 4.

Bagchi, Amaresh (2007): "Role of Planning and the Planning Commission in the New Indian Economy: Case for a Review?", *Economic and Political Weekly*, 42 (44), pp. 92-100.

_______ (2008): "Globalisation and Federalsim: Uneasy Partners ? *Economic and Political Weekly*, 43 (38), pp. 41-48.

Chaturvedi Committee (2011): "Report of the Committee on Restructuring of Centrally Sponsored Schemes (CSS)", Planning Commission, New Delhi.

Dev, S. Mahendra and Jos Mooij (2002): "Social Sector Expenditures in the 1990s: Analysis of Central and State Budgets", *Economic and Political Weekly*, 37 (9), pp. 853-66.

Government of India (2008): "Manual for integrated District Planning", Planning Commission, New Delhi.

Government of India (2008): Eleventh Five-Year Plan, 2007-2012, Volume I-Inclusive Growth (New Delhi: 8. Planning Commission and Oxford University Press).

Punchhi Commission (2010): "Report of the Commission on Centre-State Relations: Centre-State Financial Relations and Planning", Volume III, Government of India, New Delhi.

Rangarajan Committee (2011): "Report of the High Level Expert Committee of Efficient Management of Public Expenditure", Planning Commission, New Delhi.

Rao, M. Govinda and Nirvikar Singh (2005): *Political Economy of Federalism in India*, New Delhi: Oxford University Press.

www.narendramodi.in/text_of_pms_speech_at_red_fort

4

Decentralized Governance and Issues of Accountability and Transparency

The Case of PRIs in Karnataka

S. Harsha

Panchayats in Karnataka have a historical background since the ancient time. However, it was the Mysore Local Boards Act 1902, which gave a formal shape to the Panchayat system. There after a series of changes have taken place with many amendments for providing a gradual enlargement of scope and functions of these bodies. For instance the Mysore Village Panchayats and Local Boards Act 1959, put a milestone with the recommendations of Venkatappa Committee (1950) and D.H. Chandrashekariah Committee (1954). Later the Zilla Parishads, Taluk Panchayat Samitis, Mandal Panchayats and Nyaya Panchayats Act of 1983 regarded as a landmark in the history of local government in India, since it demonstrated for the first time the willingness of a State government to divest itself of substantial powers and functions in favour of sub-state institutions (Satish Chandran, 1994). Karnataka was the first state to pass the legislation on 7th April, 1993, which included the provisions of 73rd Constitutional Amendment Act and it came into force from 30th April, 1993. The three-tier structure of Panchayat Raj with Zilla Panchayat at the district level, Taluk Panchayat at the taluk level and Grama Panchayat at the village level are given impetus to promote development projects in terms of infrastructure, poverty alleviation, education, health and improvement of living conditions in rural areas. The available literature (Aziz, 1993; Sivanna, 1990; Meenakshisundaram, 1994; Manor, 2000; Aziz *et al.*, 2002) on the functioning of Panchayats in Karnataka reveals that it has achieved success to some extent in implementing plans and programmes of decentralization.

It has been observed that micro level accountability mechanisms support decentralization, participation and competition and allow the public to influence the quality and quantity of the public services (Camille, 1997). The proponents of good governance like Soren Villidsen (1999) and Manor (1999); Heller (2001), argue that decentralization ensures more accountability, transparency and participation and thereby it reduces the extent of corruption. Heller observes that strengthening and empowering local government has been justified not only on the grounds of making government more efficient but also on the grounds of increasing accountability and participation. The advantages of decentralization center around increased popular involvement and their control over decision-making and access to services. The local people can also put pressure on local authorities to influence public servicing and thereby reducing financial mismanagement. The common opinion of good governance view is that transparency improves the incentives and pressure for public sector performance while lowering the scope for corruption, reducing transaction costs and improving the efficiency.

Accountability, transparency and increased people's participation in governance reduce the scope for corruption (David Brown, 1999). Thus it is believed that decentralization ensures accountability between the elected representatives and the officials and between the elected representatives and the people (Crook and Manor, 1998). Further, more decentralization tends to produce greater transparency and facilitates more people participation. It also leads to closer contact between the government officials and the local people, which will allow better information, more realistic and effective plans for government and programmes.

Decentralization allows greater representation for various political, religious, ethnic and tribal groups in development decision-making and it could lead to the development of administrative capacity among local governments. More importantly, it institutionalizes the participation of citizens in development planning (Rondinelli and Cheema, 1983).

Regarding the issue of transparency in PRIs, Saxena mentions that information regarding flow of funds and expenditure are still not generally available at the GP level, even though this may have been disseminated through billboards at the block level. The operation of funds involves the lowest Panchayat functionary along with the Pradhan, while the block staff performs supervisory functions. Thus, while other Panchayat members and villagers are not involved in the monitoring of funds and the implementation of schemes, supervision functions from above are carried out by agencies, which also routinely intervene in the implementation and decision-making.

The independent audit functions of the State are also quite weak and open to corruption. Further, he argues that the present system is such that even honest Sarpanches/Pradhans find it difficult to carry out their functions without greasing the palms of officials and meeting the expenditure on their official duties from the public funds.

More or less Inbanathan (2002) also favours this view. He points out that both accountability and transparency are weak in the Panchayats. Most of the people do not have access to even Panchayat information, which is in the public domain. Powerful or influential persons could get information from the official sources. Newly entered members and relatively poor could not access information. More significantly, the Gram Sabhas are poorly functioning. Large numbers of Grama Panchayat members were not even regular to Village Panchayat meetings. These imply that the lack of accountability and transparency as well as poor participation and thereby corruption, seen in various forms in Panchayats, negatively affecting the quality of governance. It is also argued that when administrative and political powers are decentralized, the opportunities for bribe collecting multiply. Even World Bank vice-president for Asia Jean Michel Severino recently admitted that, "Decentralization will lead to less governance and more corruption spread around country, disruption of public service and fiscal burden" (Raymond, 2000). Based on the theoretical background of accountability and transparency, an attempt has been made below to outline the issues of accountability and transparency in the PRIs of Karnataka.

Ward Sabha

Based on the recommendations of Karnataka Working Group Report (2002), Karnataka government has provided for Ward Sabhas by effecting Amendments to Karnataka Panchayat Raj Act. Ward Sabha should meet at least once in six months. The quorum for the meeting of a Ward Sabha should be not less than one tenth of the total number of members of the Ward Sabha or twenty members whichever is less. Another requirement is that thirty per cent of the voters attending the Ward Sabha should be women and there should be proportionate representation to Scheduled Castes and Scheduled Tribes in the Ward Sabha.

Some of the important powers and functions of Ward Sabha's are:

(i) To generate proposals and determine the priority of schemes and development programmes to be implemented in the area of the Ward Sabha and forward the same to place it before the Gram Sabha for inclusion in Gram Panchayat development plan; and

(ii) To identify the most eligible persons from the area of Ward Sabha for beneficiary oriented schemes on the basis of criteria fixed and prepared list of eligible beneficiaries in the order of priority and forward the same to the Gram Panchayat for inclusion in its development plan.

Gram Sabha

The 1993 Act provides for a three-tier structure of Local Government and Gram Sabha. Abdul Nazir Sab (1986), an architect of the 1983 Act, stated that the Gram Sabhas would be the main institution through which the elected representatives would be accountable to the people. Based on the recommendations of "Karnataka Working Group Report on Decentralization (2002)", Government has streamlined the powers and functions of Gram Sabha by passing an Amendment Act. The Gram Sabha consists of all voters in a village and has to meet at least once in six months, provided that a special meeting of Gram Sabha shall be convened if a request is made by not less than ten per cent of the members of the Gram Sabha with items of agenda specified in such request and there shall be a minimum three months period between two special meetings of the Gram Sabha.

The quorum for the meeting of a Gram Sabha shall be not less than one tenth of the total number of members of the Gram Sabha, or hundred members whichever is less. As far as may be, at least ten members from each Ward Sabha within the Panchayat area shall attend the meeting and not less than thirty per cent of the members attending the Gram Sabha shall be women. As far as may be, the persons belonging to the Scheduled Caste and Scheduled Tribe shall be represented in proportion to their population in the Gram Sabha. The Gram Sabha, exercises and discharges following powers and functions:

(a) To consider and approve the annual plan prepared by the Gram Panchayat.
(b) To generate proposals and determine the priority of all schemes and development programmes to be implemented in the Panchayat area.
(c) To identify and select the most eligible persons from the

Panchayat area for beneficiary oriented schemes on the basis of criteria fixed by the Gram Panchayat, Taluka Panchayat (Block), Zilla Panchayat or the government and to prepare a list of beneficiaries in the order of priority after considering the priority lists of individual beneficiaries sent by the Ward Sabhas. Such list shall be binding on the concerned Gram Panchayat, Taluk Panchayat, Zilla Panchayat or the Government, as the case may be.

All resolutions in respect of any issue in the meetings of the Gram Sabha should be passed by the majority of the members present and voting. There was no provision for Ward Sabha and there was no quorum requirement for holding Gram Sabha meetings when the study was undertaken. In Thandaga and Kainadu GPs, Gram Sabha's were conducted in all selected venues, however, in Sirigere and Bharamasagara, they were confined to GP headquarters. In the selected GPs publicity was not given to Gram Sabha through tom tom outside GP headquarters and in Sirigere and Bharamasagara, the publicity was not given in the GP headquarters.

Realizing that Gram Sabha and Ward Sabha's are not convened regularly, Karnataka government in June, 2013 brought about amendment to Karnataka Panchayati Raj Bill 2013 and added a punitive clause. The new bill specifies that heads and members will face termination if they "fail to convene two consecutive meetings". The bill also holds Panchayat Development Officer (PDO) and Executive Officer (EO) responsible and allows government to take disciplinary action if they fail perform duty in regard to Gram and Ward Sabha meetings. Regional commissioners have been empowered to initiate action against both presidents/members and PDOs for failing to perform duties.

Panchayat Jamabandhi (Social Audit by Public)

As a transparency mechanism 'Jamabandhi' which is being implemented by the Gram Panchayats deserves special mention. Under this new mechanism, the citizens are given an opportunity to take a close look at the working of their Gram Panchayats. Through this mechanism citizens can have access to Gram Panchayat's records, registers, budget documents, accounts, JGSY Muster Rolls, Measurement Book, Supply Bill and even they can question the processes followed by the Gram Panchayats in the selection of beneficiaries, development projects etc.

Panchayat Jamabandhi is an annual public inspection of the accounts and registers of the GPs preferably between August 15 and September 15. The Jamabandhi team is to be headed by a Taluk level officer and is to be assisted by two other officials/assistants. The GP Secretary has to make necessary arrangements for holding the Jamabandhi meeting. The Junior Engineer of the TP should be present in the meeting. On the day of the meeting the Jamabandhi Officer inspects the account registers in the presence of the public, who should be given ready access to the information or details sought by them. The Jamabandhi Officer and his team inspect the work spots in the presence of the public or the persons who had given complaint about the selected/completed works. The team should prepare a detailed report with its findings and submit it to the executive officer, Taluka Panchayat (TP). The report should contain details of procedural irregularities, financial misappropriation and substandard works, if any. The Secretary of the GP has to present the report in the ensuing Gram Sabha meeting and the executive officer should present the same in the monthly review meeting of the secretaries and also to publish in the local newspapers.

Further, the process had made the secretaries of the Grama Panchayats to be more responsible and accountable to their scheduled tasks and responsibilities. This, indeed, is a clear evidence to the fact that Jamabandhi has to some extent ensured accountability of the functionaries of panchayats to the citizens.

Primacy of Elected Representatives over Officials

In stark contrast to Kerala and Tamil Nadu Acts, Karnataka Panchayati Raj Act 1993 describes ZP, TP and GP Adhyakshas as the 'Executive Heads' and thereby making the officials accountable to them.

The Karnataka Panchayati Raj Act provides that an elected body or its office bearers hold a superior position over the officials. Section 197 relating to functions, powers and duties of Chief Executive Officer of the Zilla Panchayat States that subject to the general powers of the Adhyaksha the CEO shall perform his functions. Section 193 States that Adhyaksha shall be the Executive head of the ZP. Section 152 States that Adhyaksha shall be the executive head of the Taluka Panchayat. The Section 156(1) relating to functions, powers and duties of EOs, States that subject to the powers of Adhyaksha of TP under Section 152, the EO shall perform his functions. Thus, the GP Secretary, TP Executive Officer and CEO of the ZP are supposed to carry out all the functions allotted to them subject to the orders and supervision of the Adhyakshas of the respective local bodies.

Though the superiority of the elected functionaries is recognized in the Act, it should, however, be pointed out that if an elected body makes a decision which is clearly not in accordance with the general policy laid down by the State Government or the higher level Panchayat bodies, the concerned officer not only has the duty but also the right to offer his dissenting views. In case, the elected body is intransigent about its decision, the officer is obliged to inform the officials at the higher or State level for necessary advice and action on points in dispute.

The 1993 Act, drawing on the provisions of the 74th Amendment, provides for the District Planning Committee (DPC). The DPC consolidates the plans formulated by Zilla, Taluk, Gram and Nagar Panchayats and Muncipalities in the district. Based upon this integration, the DPC is expected to prepare a draft development plan for the district as a whole. The Section 310 of the Karnataka Panchayati Raj Act makes it mandatory for the State to constitute a District Planning Committee in each district. In sharp contrast to other states where district MLA is the chairperson, in Karnataka ZP President is the chairperson of DPC.

Another forum at the State level which could facilitate interaction between State leadership and the Panchayat members is the State Panchayat Council. Section 310 of Karnataka Panchayati Raj Act 1993, provides for the Constitution of the State Panchayat Council with the Chief Minister as Chairman, Minister for Rural Development and Panchayati Raj as Vice-Chairman, five other ministers nominated by the Government and the Secretary of Rural Development and Panchayat Raj Department as Member Secretary. Thus, the Institution of State Panchayat Council also gives primacy to elected representatives of Panchayats and it provides them opportunity to ventilate their grievances with the state leadership.

Sakala (Timely and Improved Service Delivery)

The Karnataka Guarantee of Service to Citizens Act 2011, is a land mark in the recent developments in local governance and devolution. The Karnataka Guarantee of Services to Citizens Act 2011 is known as '*Sakala*' which has been implemented by the Department of Personnel and Administrative Reform (DPAR) with the support of National Informatics Centre (NIC). The Karnataka Sakala Services Act, a leading light to other States in the country, is now effectively being implemented in 30 departments/organizations providing 265 services to the citizens of Karnataka.

'Right to Public Services' is widely recognized as a mechanism to reduce corruption among the government officials and to increase transparency and public accountability. Legislation on right to public services comprises statutory laws which guarantee time and quality bound delivery of various public services rendered by the government to citizens and provides mechanism for punishing the aberrant public servant who is deficient in providing the service stipulated under the statute.

There are total 151 services in 11 Departments including Rural Development and Panchayati Raj, Government of Karnataka which had been selected under the Guarantee of Service to Citizens (GSC). Among the Sakala Schemes, the poor people have to avail more from the Department of Rural Development and Panchayati Raj. Under the Department of Rural Development and Panchayati Raj, 13 essential services which have a direct impact in shaping the quality of public goods and in turn on the well-being and entitlement of rural citizens' are listed under the Act.

Concluding Observations

Notwithstanding the novel and laudable features of the Karnataka Panchayati Raj Act, there are some aberrations which hinder the effective utilization of transparency and accountability mechanisms.

The pre-requisite of decentralized planning is the identification of beneficiaries in the Gram Sabha by involving people and their representatives. There are studies which have documented that there instance of Panchayats not holding the ward and Gram Sabha's regularly. In some Panchayats Gram Sabhas are convened to identify the beneficiaries, there were many cases of misidentification of beneficiaries reported in the selected Panchayats.

The new punitive clause of termination of the membership for not convening Ward and Gram Sabha has been considered as a draconian legislation by the opposition parties.

The state level co-ordination body State Panchayat Council has not been made functional.

Jamabandhi is also plagued by several shortcomings. The lack of awareness among the people, officials deputed on Jamabandhi duty most often did not undertake field visits along with the affected persons and usually action was initiated only against officials. A field study by Sivanna and Babu revealed that the programme ensured both vertical and horizontal accountability particularly among the officials.

References

Government of Karnataka. RDPR. (2002). "Report of the Working Group on Decentralization".

Harry, Blair. (2000). *Participation and Accountability at the Periphery: Democratic Local Governance in Six Countries*, World Development, Vol. 28 (1), 21-39.

Inbanathan Anand. (2002). *Power, Patronage and Accountability in the Pancayats of Karnataka*. ISEC, Bangalore.

Manor, James. (1999). *The Political Economy of Decentralization*, The World Bank, Washington, DC.

Saxena, N.C. (1999), *Improving Effectiveness of Government Programmes—an Agenda of Reform for the 10th Plan*. Planning Commission Government of India, New Delhi.

Sivanna, N. and M. Devendra Babu. (2002). *Panchayat Jamabandhi in Karnataka: An Evaluation Study*. Institute for Social and Economic Change, Bangalore, *Mimeo*.

Sorenvilladsen (ed.) (1999) *Good Governance and Decentralization: Public Sector Reforms in Developing Countries*. Nordic Consulting Group, Gylling.

SECTION-II
Excluded Section, NGOs, Public Opinion and Gender Mainstreaming

5

Local Self-Government in India and Excluded Sections

Welfare and Political Dimensions

V. Ramakrishna

Introduction

Social inequalities existed in the villages and these have continued for centuries. Under these circumstances, soon after Independence the concept of social justice figured in the Constitution of India. Thus, the Constitution of India made an attempt to provide equal social opportunities for the development of personality of all the people in the society, without any discrimination on the basis of caste, sex or race. However, social inequalities continued for a long time in the Indian society. The reasons may be several. The people from higher social strata had received education, and they controlled and managed land. They took up income-earning activities. On the contrary, the lower strata people were denied education, and they were deprived of their right to manage and control land. Thus, they were forced to take up low-income earning activities. Particularly, in the villages the lower strata people took up supportive works for the people who had taken up agricultural activities, such as Carpentry, Blacksmith, Leather work, and labour.

Due to the above-mentioned reasons the marginalized became the weaker sections of the society. Therefore, after Independence, India was one among the countries which went in for social and economic transformation of the rural population. As a preferred condition, rural development became a definite strategy for the improvement of the living conditions of the rural poor. In this direction the Government of India made efforts to solve problems such as poverty, ill health, illiteracy, and backwardness of varied nature prevailing in rural areas, by giving greater attention to the uplift of the rural poor (Shivanna, N. 1990).

Further, the marginalized sections, i.e., SC, ST, and OBC have become an important component in defining of the development policies because of their socio-economic deprivation in the traditional society like India. The political involvement of the upper castes is still more in institutions like Assembly and Parliament. The reservation of seats was 15 per cent in State Assemblies and Parliament. On the contrary there was no representation from the larger sections of the marginalized castes i.e., from the backwards (Singh, S.N. 1996). As a result of this, at present, political participation in India is limited to only a few upper castes. As they manage and control the political system, land pattern. The upper caste people did not mind in formulating and execution of welfare and developmental policies intended for the weaker sections. It can be seen in the failure of several programmes. Among these are Community Development Programmes (CDP) and National Extension Programme (NEP). These programmes were implemented in tune with the upper caste people in the rural areas.

Review of Literature

Sukla Deb Kanoongo (1996), in his research on women's leadership in the Panchayati Raj with special reference to the State of West Bengal, found that many of them, in spite of being educated, in spite of having a tradition of political activity in the family and of having great support from their respective parties, are unable to participate in the whole process in a meaningful way. Many are finding the responsibilities very demanding, some are thoroughly engaged in their domestic responsibilities and some do not maintain good health. He also felt that the socio-cultural factors acted as a deterrent in many cases.

Ujwala Hiremath (1997) conducted a survey of 40 women members of ten village Gram Panchayats in Karnataka. Her studies show the same trend that is seen at the national level politics-members of influential families always seem to have an edge over the rest. Majority of the members were illiterate-thumb impression ones. However, it was interesting to note that all these women had a manifesto of development items for the village-shelter for the poor, electricity, toilets, roads, schools, water facility, doctors for primary health centres, sewing machines for young girls and many other things, including old-age and widow pensions, employment for youth, girls education, transport facilities, etc.

Sudha Pai (1998) cautioned, after brief study of three villages from Meerut district in Uttar Pradesh, that female literacy, independent voting rights and change in the status in the family and society are required for women to play active role in the village politics. The Pradhanis played an almost insignificant role in the functioning of the Gram and Block Panchayat level bodies. They have never attended any meeting or made any decision about allocation of funds to individuals or schemes.

Nagendra Ambedkar (2000) in his book on "Panchayati Raj at Work" explained the origins and growth of Panchayati Raj Institutions in India and structural patterns of Panchayat Raj in Rajasthan. The author also has given importance to electoral system of the local bodies. Further, he analysed the socio-economic and political background of the Panchayat Raj elite, their perceptions and orientations of various issues, pertaining to the Panchayati Raj Institution, finally he analyzed the leadership in panchayats and the qualities, attitude of the leaders towards weaker section of the society.

In other study Aziz (1994) found more or less the same phenomena. While dealing Buch, Jain and Chaudhary (1999) conducted Study on Women in Panchayati Raj in Madhya Pradesh. The study was conducted in three district socio-cultural zones where the ST, SC was others are numerically dominant. So far as their socio-profile is concerned, the study documented that maximum number of PRI leaders (307 out of 343) are from the marginalized groups. 283 women and 80 men participated in the study. Majority of the leaders are above the age of 25 years "they are engaged in agricultural work. In fact, either they are the wage earners or cultivators. Although, there is slight district wise variation but majority of the respondents are from below the Poverty line. More than 50 per cent are illiterate. Even in the case of chairpersons out of 72, 23 are illiterate. Most of them had no affiliation with any of the political parties in the formal sense. 53 respondents are landless but a good number of them (126) Possess either or more than 5 acres of land. It is interesting to note that a good number of respondents have discontinued labour work after becoming PRI leaders but even today 92 are engaged in this work. The study concluded that PRI is numerically imitated by the leaders of lower Socio-economic status in M.P."

Similar observation was made by Lele (2001) In course of the Comparative Study between Traditional Village Panchayat and the modern Gram Sabha in Maharashtra from the point of view of empowerment of the weaker sections, the author opined that of course platform of statutory Gram Sabha is theoretically opened for the marginalized but in the real sense it is not. In fact, alienation from the political processes seems to prevail and that is why even reservation has not helped to make the marginalized more vocal. This then creates the right conditions for the domination of traditional power of the upper castes and classes. The other factor is economic dependence of the marginalized on the dominants. For those who work on the fields or run small shops or are service providers, opposing the gender is unthinkable. They would be digging their own graves by opposing the upper castes and rich farmers on whose fields they work and earn their daily wages. Beside personal loans are also made available by the same people, those who constitute the gender. Thus opposing the gender could mean starvation as a result of boycott by the rich peasants and others.

Committees Appointed from Time to Time

After the Community Development Programme was launched in 1952, it was realized that without an agency at the village level, which could represent the entire community, assume responsibility and provide the necessary leadership for implementing development programmes, real progress in rural development could not take place. It was against this background that a Committee headed by Balwant Rai G. Mehta was appointed in 1957 to make recommendations for revitalization for the Panchayati Raj system define its role in the development process. The report of the Committee recommended that public participation in community works should be organized through statutory representative bodies. Community Development can be real only when the community exercises necessary powers through its chosen representatives. Therefore, it recommended the establishments of statutory elected local bodies.

The Report of the Committee was influential in creating a three-tier Panchayati Raj structure with District Panchayat at the top and Grama Panchayat at the bottom. The intermediate tier was co-terminus with Community Development Blocks. Most of the States amended their laws to conform to the recommendations of the committee. However, the Panchayati Raj Institutions (PRIs) could not function well as elections were either not held or were frequently postponed or they were denied funds or in most of the cases superceded. The Ashok Mehta Committee Report in 1978 was influential in bringing about a shift in emphasis between the first and second degeneration of panchayats from development per se to local Government in its full meaning. Originally, panchayats found a place only in the Directive Principles of State Policy. The 73rd and 74th Constitutional Amendments revitalized the Panchayats and Urban Bodies by giving them Constitutional status, providing for regular elections and reserving 1/3 seats for women and introducing representation for marginalized groups.

73rd Constitutional Amendment Act

To provide the constitutional support to the Panchayati Raj Institutions (PRIs), a Constitutional Amendment Bill was introduced in 1989 by Sri Rajiv Gandhi the then Prime Minister with an intention of transferring power to the people; it relates to Part IX of the Constitution. This bill was passed by the Lok Sabha on the 10th August, 1989. However, it failed in Rajya Sabha and could not become the part of the Constitution. After the defeat of both the bills, another bill that is 73rd Constitution Amendment Bill was introduced in the Lok Sabha. The attempt extending the Constitutional benefits to the Panchayati Raj Institutions, thoroughly the 64th Constitutional Amendment Act of 1988 and 74th Amendment Bill of 1990 did not succeed. Another attempt was made by introducing the Constitutional Amendment Bill on 16th September, 1991. After the series of discussions in the parliament, the matter was referred to joint select committee of parliament for detailed examination. Accordingly joint committee presented its report to parliament in July, 1992. The Lok Sabha finally passed the bill on December 22nd, 1992 and the Rajya Sabha on December 23rd, 1992. The President of India accorded this asset on April 20th, 1993. Finally, the 73rd Constitutional Amendment Act of 1992 came into effect on April 24th, 1993 (Panchayati Raj at a Glance: 1964). There shall be three-tiers of Panchayats at the village, intermediate and district levels. So, only those states having population not exceeding 20 lakhs have the discretion not to constitute the panchayats at the intermediate level. Under Article 243 the president can make special dispensation for Union Territories.

Direct Elections: All seats in a Panchayat at every level are to be filled by direct elections from territorial constituencies demarcated for this purpose, with the ratio between the population of such constituency and the number of such constituency and the number of seats allotted to it being the same throughout the Panchayat area. Reservation of seats: There shall be reservation of seats at every level for SC/STs in proportion to their population in a given Panchayat area and for women to the extent of not less than one-third of the total number of seats. Likewise, the office of the Chairpersons in the Panchayats at each level shall be reserved for women, to the extent of not less than one-third of the total numbers in the office of Chairpersons of Panchayats. In addition, the legislature of any state can make provision for reservation of seats in any panchayats at any level in favour of the backward classes.

Five Year Term: The term of office of panchayat at every level shall be for five years and if dissolved earlier or on expiry of the term, elections must be completed within six months from the date of dissolution or expiry.

Finance Commission: By 24th April, 1993, that is, the coming into the effect the Constitutional (73rd Amendment) Act 1992 and thereafter at the expiration of every fifth year, a Finance Commission shall be constituted in every fifth year. A Finance Commission shall be constituted in every state to go into the governing principles of the distribution and revolution of financial resources between the state and the panchayats at every level and the measures to improve the financial position of the panchayats.

State Election Commission: The direction and control of the preparation of electoral rolls and the conduct of all elections in the panchayats shall be vested in a state election commission, to be constituted by the state concerned.

Eleventh Schedule: Finally, the XI Schedule comprising 29 items has been added to the Constitution which ought to provide an effective role to the PRIs in the planning and implementation of works of local significance. Activities ranging like drinking water, agriculture, land and water conservation to communications, poverty alleviation programmes, family welfare, education, libraries and cultural activities, maintenance of community as sets etc.

Karnataka Panchayati Raj Act 1993—Salient Features

The 1993 Act establishes a three-tier Panchayati raj system in the state with elected bodies at Grama, Taluka, and District level for greater participation of the people and for more effective implementation of Rural Development Programmes. The three-tiers of the Panchayati Raj System are:

(1) Gram Panchayat/Village Panchayat,
(2) Taluka Panchayat, and
(3) Zilla Panchayat.

Outstanding Features of 1993 Act

As a part from the creation of three-tier Panchayat system in the state based on population as per published data of census, the features of 1993 Act are as follows (The Karnataka Panchayati Raj Act 1993).

1. The act facilities the Constitution of Grama Sabha in each village.
2. It provides for reservation of seats in favour of SCs and STs in proportion of their population and subjected to minimum of 15 and 3 per cent respectively at all levels.
3. The Act provides for reservation of 1/3 of seats to women at all levels.
4. It also provides for reservation of 1/3 of seats to persons belonging to Backward Classes.
5. The Act also provides for reservation of 1/3 of seats in each category (SCs, STs, and Backward Classes and General) at all levels for women. The seats reserved shall be allotted by rotation to different constituencies in panchayat area.
6. The office of the Chairperson and Deputy Chairpersons are also reserved at all levels for the persons belonging to SCs, STs and Backwards Classes and Women.
7. The Act envisages the Constitution of State Election Commission, the finance commission and district planning committee. The finance committee is to recommend periodically the policy on finance to Panchayati Raj Institutions.
8. The new law stipulates that the elections to Gram Panchayat are to be conducted on non-party basis. This is intended to minimize the local conflicts during election time. However, participation of political parties has been allowed for upper level Panchayats.
9. The new Act substantially increases the power of State governments to supervise and control Panchayati Raj Institutions (PRIs). The Secretary of Panchayat Raj Department and the Divisional Commissioner are empowered accordingly for this purpose. They are entitled to issue instructions, conduct enquiry, and call for proceedings of Zilla Panchayat and performance of Panchayati Raj Institutions. The government is also authorized to add or delete any programme or scheme in the functions of Panchayati Raj Institutions.
10. All the Adhyakshas of Taluka Panchayats can be members of Zilla Panchayats. All the MLAs, MLCs, and MPs can be Members of Zilla Panchayats and Taluka Panchayats.

11. As regards to finance, every Gram Panchayat will receive annual grant of rupees one lakh towards development activities.
12. The proceeds of heavy cash levy, on land revenue and surcharge on stamp duty will be passed on to Gram Panchayats and Taluka Panchayats. The Panchayati Raj Institutions will receive resources from State Government also.

Objectives and Methodology

The present chapter intends to analyze the involvement of weaker sections representatives in the institutions of Panchayati Raj in Gulbarga and Afjalpur Taluk of Gulbarga District. It also intends to assess the awareness, commitment, ability and problems of weaker sections representatives in the process of implementing the welfare policies for SC, ST and OBC, historical descriptive and analytical methods have been employed in the present study.

To examine the status of weaker sections in village Panchayats of Gulbarga and Afjalpur Taluks in Gulbarga District and to compare the status of weaker section's representatives with the representatives of other castes in Panchayati Raj Institutions of Gulbarga District. To identify the education level of weaker sections representatives in Panchayati Raj Institutions of Gulbarga District. Awareness towards the working of Panchayati Raj Institutions, suggest policy implementations for the effective involvement of weaker section and to implement welfare policies for weaker sections through Panchayati Raj Institutions.

Political Participation of Weaker Sections

It is widely believed that the analysis of age, education, caste, family structure, occupation, income, land holding, party affiliation, etc., are important in determining the nature of leadership. The data relating to socio-economic background of elected respondents of Panchayati Raj institutions were collected in the per cent study to get an insight into the emerging pattern of rural leadership in the Afjalpur Taluk of Gulbarga District. The socio-economic conditions play an important role in characterizing the social life and behaviour of an individual. The socio-economic status of an individual affects the patterns of interaction in the society. It is, therefore, essential to analyse the socio-economic background of the relationship between the leader and the environment. In a developing society like ours where forces of caste and kinship influence the social life and acute disparity in the standard of living and sub culture among various groups and regions are existing, a study of the socio-economic conditions of SC, ST and OBCs respondents would help reveal sociologically significant dimensions (Singhi, N.K. 1974).

The socio-economic, educational and political background of the leaders would also enable us to anticipate as to what they are capable of doing, what we should expect from them and how well they are equipped to discharge the responsibilities developed upon them by the electorate (Sashilata Puri, 1978). Knowledge of socio-economic background of a community is an indispensable prerequisite, for the understanding of the thought or behaviours of its members. This holds good for all human communities, and more so in the case of SC/ST and OBC communities, which are intrinsically more traditional in their structure.

Table 5.1: Distribution of Respondents by Nature of Members

Sl. No.	*Institution*	*Frequency*	*%*
1.	VP	44	58.67
2.	TP	23	30.67
3.	ZP	8	10.67
4.	Total	75	100.00

Source: Compiled from the Data Collected from Field Work.

Table 5.1 is to discuss the nature of members in the study area. It is evident from the table that there are three types of members, i.e. (1). Village Panchayat members are 44 constituting 58.67 per cent, Taluk Panchayat members are 23 constituting 30.67 per cent and Zilla Panchayat members are 8 constituting 10.67 per cent.

Table 5.2. Distribution of Respondents by Position in PRI's

Sl. No.	*Position*	*Frequency*	*%*
1.	Presidents	10	13.33
2.	Vice-Presidents	17	22.67
3.	Members	48	64.00
4.	Total	75	100.00

Source: Compiled from the Data Collected from Field Work.

Table 5.2 is intended to discuss the position of respondents in the Institutions of PRIs Afjalpur Taluk. The response and the study area have been grouped into three categories that is 1. Respondents 10 constitute

13.33 per cent, vice-presidents 17 constituting 22.67 per cent and members 48 constituting 64.09 per cent.

Table 5.3: Distribution of Respondents by Sex-wise

Sl. No.	Sex	Frequency	%
1.	Male	49	65.33
2.	Female	26	34.67
3.	Total	75	100.00

Source: Compiled from the Data Collected from Field Work.

Table 5.3 discusses the sex-wise distribution of respondents in the study area. It is evident from the table that out of the total 75 respondents, the highest number 49 constituting 65.33 per cent are male and 10 respondents constituting 13.33 per cent are female.

Table 5.4: Caste-wise Distribution of Respondents

Sl. No.	Caste	Frequency	%
1.	SC	25	33.33
2.	ST	10	13.33
3.	OBC	40	53.33
4.	Total	75	100.00

Source: Compiled from the Data Collected from Field Work.

Table 5.4 is intended to discuss the caste-wise distribution of the respondents in the study area. The Table 5.4 shows that out of the total sample 75, respondents belonging to SC are 25 constituting 33.33 per cent, STs are 10 constituting 13.33 per cent and OBCs are 40 constituting 53.33 per cent.

Table 5.5: Distribution of Respondents by Age-group.

Sl. No	Age	Frequency	%
1.	18-25	22	29.33
2.	26-35	34	45.33
3.	36-45	8	10.67
4.	46 & Above	11	14.67
5.	Total	75	100

Source: Compiled from the Data Collected from Field Work.

Table 5.5 is intended to analyse the distribution of respondents by age. It is observed from this table that the age-group of the respondents has been grouped into 4 categories. Among these the highest number of respondents 34 constituting 45.33 per cent are from the age-group of 26-35, followed by 22 respondents constituting 29.33 per cent belonging to the age-group of 18-25. Further, the table shows that the lowest number 8 respondents constituting 10.67 per cent are from the age group of 36-45.

Table 5.6: Distribution of Respondents by Religion

Sl. No	*Religion*	*Frequency*	*%*
1.	Hindu	53	70.67
2.	Buddhism	15	20.00
3.	Muslims	4	5.33
4.	Others	3	4.00
5.	Total	75	100.00

Source: Compiled from the Data Collected from Field Work.

Table 5.6 is to analyse the Distribution of Respondents by Religion. This table also shows that out of the sample 75 respondents, the highest number 53 respondents constituting 70.67 per cent are Hindus, followed by 15 respondents constituting 20 per cent are Buddhists; these Buddhists are converted from a particular caste among the SC. In the study area there are 4 respondents constituting 5. 33 per cent belonging to Muslim OBCs, and 3 respondents constituting 4.00 per cent belonging to other religions.

Table 5.7: Distribution of Opinion by Caste about the Objectives of Panchayati Raj Institutions

Sl. No.	*Opinion*	*SC*	*%*	*ST*	*%*	*OBC*	*%*	*Total*	*%*
1.	Yes	19	76	5	38.46	10	27.03	34	45.33
2.	No	6	24	8	61.54	27	72.97	41	54.67
3.	Total	25	100	13	100.00	37	100.00	75	100.00

Source: Compiled from the data collected from the field data.

Table 5.7. Reveals that the caste wise distribution of respondent's opinion about the objectives of Panchayati Raj Institutions (PRIs). The table reveals that out of the total 75 respondents, the highest number of respondents across the castes does not know about the objectives of

Panchayati Raj Institutions. The caste-wise distribution of opinion reveals that there are 25 respondents from SC. Among these the highest number 76 per cent of respondents are aware of the objectives of Panchayati Raj Institutions. Whereas, only 24 per cent of respondents do not know the objectives of Panchayati Raj Institutions.

The respondents belonging to STs opined the different opinion than SC respondents. The highest number 61.54 per cent respondents out of 10 do not know the objectives of Panchayati Raj Institutions and whereas 38.46 per cent of respondents are aware of the objectives of Panchayati Raj Institutions.

So for as concern of the OBC respondents, out of the total 40, the highest number 30 respondents do not know the objectives of Panchayati Raj Institutions. The over all observation of the table is that majority of SC respondents are aware of the objectives of Panchayati Raj Institutions. And on the other hand majority of respondents from STs and OBC are not aware of the objectives of Panchayati Raj Institutions.

Table 5.8: Distribution of Respondent's Opinion by Education about the Objectives of Panchayati Raj Institutions

Opinion	*Illiter-ates*	*%*	*Up to 10th*	*%*	*PUC*	*%*	*Degree*	*%*	*Total*	*%*
Yes	9	37.5	5	17.24	3	20	7	100	24	32
No	15	62.5	24	82.76	12	80			51	68
Total	24	100	29	100.00	15	100	7	100	75	100

Source: Compiled from the data collected from the field data.

Table 5.8 shows that the education wise distribution of representative's opinion about the objectives of Panchayati Raj Institutions. The table reveals that out of the total respondents belonging to illiterates, the highest number 62.5 per cent of respondents do not known the objectives of Panchayati Raj Institutions, and 37.5 per cent respondents are awarded of the objectives of Panchayati Raj Institutions. Among the total, 29 respondents who are studied up to SSLC, the highest number 82.76 per cent are not known about the objectives of Panchayati Raj Institutions, only 17.24 per cent are known. The respondents who have studied up to PUC are 15 in total, among these the highest number 80 per cent respondents does known the objectives of Panchayati Raj Institutions. It is evident from the table that the respondents who are studies up to degree are 7 in total and these respondents have understood the objectives of Panchayati Raj Institutions.

The overall observation of the table is that most of the respondents with lower educational level such as illiterates, studied up to 10th and pre-University education (PUC) are not understood the objectives of Panchayati Raj Institutions in the study area. On the other hand the graduation as the level of education of the respondents are fully understood the objectives of Panchayati Raj Institutions.

Table 5.9: Distribution of Opinion by Caste Towards the awareness of 73rd Constitutional Amendment Act

Sl. No.	*Opinion*	*SC*	*%*	*ST*	*%*	*OBC*	*%*	*Total*	*%*
1.	Yes	18	72	6	60	10	25	34	45.33
2.	No	7	28	4	40	30	75	41	54.67
3.	Total	25	100	10	100	40	100	75	100.00

Source: Compiled from the data collected from the field data.

Table 5.9 discusses the caste-wise distribution of respondents towards the awareness of 73rd Constitutional Amendment Act. The respondents in Panchayati Raj Institutions are supposed to be understood the provisions of 73rd Constitutional Amendment Act. Because, the radical changes have taken place in the institutions of Panchayati Raj in India by 73rd Constitutional Amendment Act. The Table 5.9 reveals that the respondents the highest number 72 per cent of respondents belonging to SC are aware of 73rd Constitutional Amendment Act. The respondents belonging to STs have opinioned that the highest number 60 per cent of respondents are not aware of 73rd Constitutional Amendment Act and only 40 per cent of respondents are aware. So for as concern of the respondents belonging to OBC's, the highest number 75 per cent of respondents are not aware of 73rd Constitutional Amendment Act and only 25 per cent of respondents are aware.

The findings of the table are that the most of respondents belonging to SCs and STs are aware of 73rd Constitutional Amendment Act. And the majority of respondents from ST, and OBC, are not aware of 73rd Constitutional Amendment Act. Therefore, it is viewed that SC and ST respondents has consciousness towards the working of Panchayati Raj Institutions in the study area.

Table 5.10 reveals the educationwise distribution of respondents towards the awareness of 73rd Constitutional Amendment Act. It is evident

Table 5.10: Distribution of Opinion by Education Towards the Awareness of 73rd Constitutional Amendment Act

Sl. No.	*Education*	*Yes*	*%*	*No*	*%*	*Total*	*%*
1.	Illiterates	7	15.22	15	51.72	22	29.33
2.	Up to 10th	23	50.00	9	31.03	32	42.67
3.	PUC	9	19.57	4	13.79	13	17.33
4.	Degree	7	15.22	1	3.45	8	10.67
5.	Total	46	100.00	29	100.00	75	100.00

Source: Compiled from the data collected from the field data.

from the table that the highest number 51.72 per cent of respondents from illiterates are not aware of 73rd Constitutional Amendment Act. And the highest number 50.00 per cent, 19.57 per cent and 15.22 per cent of respondents from 10th, PUC, and Degree as education level respectively are aware of 73rd Constitutional Amendment Act.

The findings of the table are that the most of illiterate respondents are working in Panchayati Raj Institutions without understanding the provisions of 73rd Constitutional Amendment Act. The most important finding of the table is that the respondents with minimum level of education and above are working in Panchayati Raj Institutions with the awareness of 73rd Constitutional Amendment provisions.

Table 5.11: Education-wise Distribution of Respondent's Opinion Towards the Accuracy of the Existing Reservation Provisions in Panchayati Raj Institutions

Sl. No.	*Education*	*Yes*	*%*	*No*	*%*	*Total*	*%*
1.	Illiterates	17	58.62	7	26.92	24	32
2.	Upto 10th	10	34.48	22	84.62	32	42.67
3.	PUC	2	6.90	12	46.15	14	18.67
4.	Degree		0.00	5	19.23	5	6.67
5.	Total	29	100.00	26	100.00	75	100

Source: Compiled from the data collected from the field data.

Table 5.11. Discusses education-wise distribution of respondent's opinion towards the adequacy of the existing reservation provisions in Panchayati Raj Institutions. The table shows that the highest number 58.62 per cent of respondents from illiterate opined that the existing reservation provisions are adequate. The majority of respondents, i.e. 84.62 per cent, who have studied up to 10th opined that the existing reservation provision in Panchayati Raj Institutions are not adequate and only 34.48 per cent have satisfied with the existing provisions. The majority of respondents who studied upto PUC and degree respectively 46.15 per cent and 19.23 per cent are opined that the existing reservation provision are not sufficient in the Panchayati Raj Institutions.

The overall observation of the table is that the illiterate respondents in Panchayati Raj Institutions have not understood the reservation provisions and the respondents educational level as 10th, PUC and Degree have understood the reservation provisions and they want to increase number of seats for SC, ST and OBC in Panchayati Raj Institutions.

Table 5.12: Caste-wise Distribution of Respondent's Opinion Towards Specific Earmark of Allocations and Expenditure for the Welfare of SC, ST, and OBC in Panchayati Raj Institutions

Sl. No.	*Opinion*	*SC*	*%*	*ST*	*%*	*OBC*	*%*	*Total*	*%*
1.	Yes	19	76	7	70	30	75	56	74.67
2.	No	6	24	3	30	10	25	19	25.33
3.	Total	25	100	10	100	40	100	75	100.00

Source: Compiled from the data collected from the field data.

Table 5.12. Reveals that the caste-wise distribution of respondent's opinion towards specific earmark of allocations and expenditure for the welfare of SC, ST, and OBC in Panchayati Raj Institutions. It is evident from the table that the majority 76 per cent of respondents belonging to SCs wanted a specific earmark of allocations and expenditure for the welfare of SC and STs in the institutions of Panchayati Raj, and 24 per cent of respondents opined that their should not be a special earmark for SC and STs in Panchayati Raj Institutions. Respondents belonging to STs opined that the highest number 70 per cent wanted a special earmark and 30 per cent does not want a special earmark of allocations and expenditure for the welfare of SC and STs. The highest number 75 per cent respondents belonging to OBC wanted a special allocations and expenditure where as 25 per cent are not in favour of special earmark for the welfare of SC and STs in Panchayati Raj Institutions. The overall observation of the table is that the majority of respondents belonging to weaker sections wanted a special allocations and expenditure for the welfare of SC ST and OBC's in Panchayati Raj Institutions.

Table 5.13. Reveals that caste-wise distribution of representative's opinion towards their reaction if the funds intended for weaker sections

Table 5.13: Distribution of Opinion by Caste Towards their Reaction if the Funds Intended for Weaker Sections are not Implemented by Panchayati Raj Institutions

Sl. No.	*Opinion*	*SC*	*%*	*ST*	*%*	*OBC*	*%*	*Total*	*%*
1.	Yes	18	72	8	80	25	62.5	56	74.67
2.	No	7	28	2	20	15	37.5	19	25.33
3.	Total	25	100	10	100	40	100	75	100.00

Source: Compiled from the data collected from the field data.

are not implemented by Panchayati Raj Institutions. The table shows that 72 per cent of respondents belonging to SC expressed that they will keep quite and 28 per cent opined that they protest in different forms in case the funds from Central and State Governments intended for the welfare of these sections are not utilized by Panchayati Raj Institutions. The respondents belonging to STs, the highest number 80 per cent of respondents opined that they will keep quite and only 20 per cent of respondents will protest in various forms. The respondents belonging to OBC's, the highest number 62.5 per cent of respondents will keep quite and 137.5 per cent of respondents opined that they will protest in different forms in case funds intended for the welfare of weaker sections by Centre or State governments are not implemented. The overall observation of the table is that the majority of respondents across the castes in Panchayati Raj Institutions are not committed for the utilization of funds given by Central and State Governments for the welfare of weaker sections.

Conclusion

Social inequalities existed in the villages and these have continued for centuries. Under these circumstances, soon after Independence the concept of social justice figured in the Indian constitution. Thus, the constitution of India made an attempt to provide equal social opportunities for the development of personality of all the people in the society, without any discrimination on the basis of caste, sex or race. Therefore, after Independence, India was one among the countries which went in for social and economic transformation of the rural population. As a preferred condition, rural development became a definite strategy for the improvement of the living conditions of the rural poor. In this direction the Government of India made efforts to solve problems such as poverty, ill health, illiteracy, and backwardness of varied nature prevailing in rural areas, by giving greater attention to the uplift of the rural poor. By this case study we came to know that the representatives belonging to weaker sections are able to implement welfare policies for the development of SC, ST and OBC in the study area. Due to the illiteracy and ignorance of weaker section's representatives, several welfare policies intended for the welfare of SC's, ST's and OBC's are not implementing properly in the institutions of Panchayati Raj and suggest for effective implementation of these policies for the welfare of weaker sections and bring them to the main stream as well as equal opportunity as stipulated in the Constitution of India.

References

Aziz, A. (2000), "Democratic, Decentralization—Experience of Karnataka".

Buch, N., Jain, U. and Chaudhary, S.N. (1999), *Women in Panchayati Raj in Madhya Pradesh*, (Mimeo) Bhopal: Mahila Chetna Manch.

Hiremath, Ujwala, (May, 1997), *Women in Grassroot Politics*, Vol. 44, No. 2, *Social Welfare*, p. 13.

Lele, M.K. (2001), "Local Government: Conflict of Interests and Issues of Legitimization", *Economic and Political Weekly*, Vol. XXXVI, No. 51, Dec. 22-28.

Maheshwari, S.R. (1988), *Local Government in India Vs. Lakshmi Narain Aggrawal*, Agra, p. 61.

Nagendra Ambedkar, (2000), *New Panchayat Raj at Work*, ABD Publishers, Jaipur, India.

Pai, Sudha, May 2, 1998, "Pradhanis in New Panchayats" Field Notes From Meerut District, *Economic and Political Weekly*.

Panchayati Raj at a Glance (as on 31st March, 1964), New Delhi, 1965.

Ram Reddy, G. (1982), "Panchayati Raj and Rural Development in Andhra Pradesh, India" in Norman T. Uphoff, *Rural Development and Local Organization in Asia*, Macmillan India Pvt. Ltd., Delhi, p. 78.

Sashilata Puri (1978), "*Legislative Elite in an Indian State: A Case Study of Rajasthan*", New Delhi: Abhinav Publications, p. 31.

Shivanna N. (1990), "*Panchayati Raj Reforms and Rural Development*", Usha Prakashan Mandir, Allahabad, p. 2.

Singh, S.N. (1996), "*Reservation Policy for Backward Classes*", Rawat Publications, Jaipur, New Delhi.

Singhi, N.K. (1974), "*Bureaucracy, Positions and Participation*", New Delhi: Abhinav Publications, p. 55.

Sukla Deb, Kanoongo, (January-March, 1996), Panchayati Raj and Emerging Women Leadership, Vol. 46, *Social Welfare*, p. 86.

Sweeta Mishra. (1994), *Democratic Decentralization in India*, Mittal Publications, New Delhi, 1994, p. 67.

6
NGOs Role in Rural Development
An Empirical Study in Telangana State

Ch. C. Prasad and P. Shreenivas

Civil society is playing an increasingly important social and economic role around the world. One of the more positive e moves of the 1980s has been recognition of the essential development role of civil society. People are creating new institutions at both the local levels and national levels to provide for needs that are not being met by either the market place or the public sector. Non-Governmental Organizations (NGOs) are important actors from civil society.

In the literature on Non-Governmental Organizations variety of terms gained currency. (A long list of acronyms has developed around the term "NGO". These include Civil Society Organization (CSO), Donor Organized NGO (DONGO), Environmental NGO (ENGO), Government Operated NGOs (GONGO), International NGO (INGO), Technical Assistance NGO (TANGO), Grassroots Support Organization (GSO), Market Advocacy NGO (MANGO) Third Sector, etc.). The World Bank's working definition on NGO is inclusive, specifying only the such organizations be: (a) largely or entirely independent of governments; (b) working for humanitarian or cooperative rather than commercial ends, and to relieve suffering, promote the interests of the poor, protect the environment, provide basic social services, or undertake community development.

Governments and international agencies themselves came to acknowledge the ability of NGOs to do what many governments have proven unable to do, i.e., to get a range of essential goods and services to the poor. NGOs now have greater diversity, credibility and creativity than ever before. In the developing countries they have often managed to engage with local populations and to command their trust in ways which governments find impossible. In view of growing importance of NGOs in development process, an attempt is made in this chapter to examine the NGOs role in rural development of Telangana State. The chapter is based on empirical study conducted with the following three objectives:

(a) To examine the initiatives and interventions of NGOs in rural development;
(b) To identify the constraints and limitations of NGOs in the implementation of development progarammes in rural areas; and
(c) To assess the NGOs impact and suggest measures to achieve integrated rural development.

Methodology

The present study is undertaken in Nalgonda district of newly carved Telangana State. The study selected all the four Revenue Divisions of the district viz., Bhongiri, Nalgonda, Miryalaguda and Suryapet. The study selected one active NGO from each Revenue Divisions on random basis to examine the activities and programmes that are undertaken in their adopted villages since inception. The factors like year of establishment, nature of activities, composition of members, area of operation are taken into consideration while selecting NGOs for the study.

The research sample includes 400 respondents consists of 240 beneficiaries and 40 each from the categories of local political leaders, village elite, functionaries and members of NGOs, and grassroots officials. Interviews, informal discussion and non-participative observation techniques are extensively used to ascertain the perceptions of the respondents on the role of NGOs in rural development. The chapter is divided into two sections. Section I explains the profiles of the district under study and selected NGOs; and Section II discusses the major findings of the study and suggests measures, for strengthening NGOs mechanism to achieve integrated rural development.

SECTION-I: OBJECTIVE OF RURAL DEVELOPMENT IN INDIA

Rural development is a process aimed at improving the well-being and self-realization of people living outside the urbanised area through collective effort. The World Bank defines rural development as a strategy to improve the socio-economic life of specific group of people called rural poor. The group includes small farmers, tenants and the landless. The objectives of rural development, therefore, extend beyond any particular sector. They encompass improved productivity, increased employment and thus higher income for target groups as well as minimum acceptable levels of food, shelter, education and health. The World Bank holds the following vision of rural development:

- Rural growth is must be widely shared with private and competitive agriculture and agri-business as the main engines of growth.
- Family farms and non-farms enterprises provide ample remunerative employment opportunities to men and women.
- Rural people will manage the soils, water, forest, grass lands and fisheries in sustainable manner.
- Rural people are linked to well-functioning markets for products, inputs and finance.
- Rural people should have access to medical care, clean water and sanitation, family planning services, educational opportunities and sufficient nutrition foods.
- Essential legal frameworks, public investment, and productive and social service are provided and financed in a decentralised and participatory manner.

After sixty-seven years of independence, India still lives in villages. Rural development is an integral part of India's development. In the context of modern India rural development is defined as integrated development of area and the people through optimum development and utilization of local resources physical, biological and human, and by bringing about necessary institutional, structural and attitudinal changes by delivery of a package of services to encompass not only the economic field, i.e., agricultural, allied activates, rural industries, but also establishment of required social infrastructure and service in the areas of health, nutrition, sanitation, housing, drinking water and literacy, with ultimate objectives of improving quality of life of the rural poor. Rural development in Indian context covers the following aspects:

- Changing the attitude of rural people towards development of transformation of village community;
- Promotion of democratic leadership at the grassroots level by

setting local self-governments;

- Provision of basic needs such as drinking water, health care, better sanitation, housing and employment;
- Development of both farming and non-farming activities so as to generate gain full employment without adversely affecting the environment;
- Improving infrastructural facilities in villages, particularly transport and communication facilities; and
- Ensuring a smooth life for the rural population by promoting communal harmony and unity, literacy, education and cultural activities.

In recent years many NGOs come forward in the State to work in various fields in rural areas like education, health, social reforms, organizing old age homes, women empowerment and other social and economic development. In India NGOs can be registered in four ways, viz. (1) Trust, (2) Society, (3) Section-25 company, (4) Special Licensing Registration can be done with the Registrar of Companies (ROC). The following laws of constitutional articles of the republic of India are relevant to the NGOs:

- Article 19(1)(c) and 30 of the Constitution of India.
- Income Tax Act 1961.
- Societies Registration Act 1860.
- Section 25 of the Indian Companies Act 1956.
- Foreign contribution (Regulation) Act 1976.

In Telangana NGOs are registered under the societies Registration Act of 1860 or the Cooperative Societies Act of 1926 or Trust Act of 1882.

Profiles of Select District and NGOs

Nalgonda district is one of the backward district of Telangana State. The districts is connected with Medak and Warangal district in the north, Khammam and Krishna district in the east, Guntur and Mahabubnagar district in the South and Ranga Reddy district in the west. The District is divided in to four revenue divisions viz., Nalgonda, Suryapeta, Miryalaguda and Bhongiri covering 59 Mandals and 1135 villages. The district covers a total geographical area of 35.51 lakhs of acres.

As per the census of India 2011 provisional population figures, the district has 34, 83,648 total population, it includes 28,21,905 rural population and 6,61,743 urban population. The district has 65.05 per cent literacy rate it includes 61.00 per cent in rural area and 82.19 per cent in urban areas of the district as per provisional population figures of 2011 census. The total area of cultivation in the district measures to 10.47 lakh acres, out of which 65 per cent of the area cultivates dry crops, while 35 per cent of the area wet crops mostly paddy.

NGOs in the Nalgonda Districts have been established and working prior to formation of the district, for example, the Arya Samaj was established in Nalgonda town in the year of 1924. After a few years same organization was started in 1935 in Miryalaguda town and in 1945 in Suryapet. The organization took social issues like widow marriages and education development, Further, the organization established a school named as "Vidikandhra Balika Vidyalayam and a library Bharathi Nilayam Libraries in the District."

The Indian Red Cross Society is another important voluntary organization which was started on 17th November, 1958 by Mr. Sravan Kumar, IAS Officer of the district. In 1906 the organization "Vignana Chandrika Mandali" was started by famous personality Sri Komaraju Laxman Rao. This organization concentrated on the issue of literacy development. Subsequently, the movement was turned into a library movement. NGOs are supplementing the efforts of government by implementing government sponsored schemes and extending financial assistance to the beneficiaries with the supporting of funding agencies, in rural areas.

In the district presently 96 NGOs working in different fields. These organizations were registered under Societies Registration Act 1860 of 1350 Fasali of Telangana. The organizations are undertaking programmes with collaboration of different government agencies like District Rural Development Agency (DRDA), S.C. and S.T. Corporations and Women and Children Welfare, etc. The NGOs have been working in the district in various fields with different objectives. The NGOs in the district are promoting different activities such as agriculture development, irrigation development, community development, health, education and also bringing awareness on public issue like AIDS and family planning, watershed management and other key areas of rural development. The NGOs facilitating beneficiaries in providing finance through financial institutions to undertake productive activities for their livelihood. As per the Planning Commission, Government of India, the number of NGOs in Nalgonda district under different ministries is given in the Table 6.1.

Table 6.1: NGOs Registered in Planning Commission under different Ministries in Nalgonda district

Sl. No.	*Name of the Ministry*	*Total Registered No.*
1.	Ministry of Rural Development	34
2.	Ministry of Human Resource Development (HRD)	22
3.	Ministry of Social Justice and Empowerment	21
4.	Ministry of Environment and Forest Department	13
5.	Ministry of Tribal Affairs	06

The present study has identified the following four NGOs selected each form one Revenue Division of the district viz.:

(A) Society for Action with Rural Poor (SARP)
(B) Society for Women Education and Environment Training (SWEET)
(C) Association for Needy and Kindle the Illiterate Through Action (ANKITA)
(D) Mano Prakash Human Services (MPHS).

The above selected NGOs are actively working in different facets of rural development such as irrigation, agriculture, poverty alleviation and health education in Nalgonda district. The following paras briefly explain the profile of select NGOs:

(A) Society for Action with Rural Poor (SARP)

Society for Action with Rural Poor (SARP) is a registered non-profit, non-religious, non-governmental and social development organization. It was established in the year 1985 under Societies Act 1350 Falsie, with registration number 886/1985. The basic objectives of the SARP is to serve poverty stricken and drought prone areas of Telangana region of the State. It works with rural communities with special focus on children, women, adolescent girls, disabled, aged, farmers and other vulnerable sections of the society. The organization aims at empowerment of poor and marginalized communities. Besides, concentrating on vulnerable, marginalized, deprived and oppressed sections of the society, SARP also concentrate on the infrastructure development, environmental and agriculture issues.

SARP has adopted Dattaipalli village in Turkapalli Mandal in Bhongiri revenue division. The NGO has been implementing watershed programme in the village with the support of National Bank for Agriculture and Rural Development (NABARD), Government of India, Drought Prone Area Programme (DPAP), District Water Management Agency (DWMA) and Telangana State Rural Livelihood Programme (TSRLP). The NGO is implementing watershed management activities through the participation of village communities.

(B) Society for Women Education and Environment Training (SWEET)

Society for Women Education and Environment Training (SWEET) is a registered NGO Societies Registration Act, 1350 Falsie. It was established in the year 1990. The focus of SWEET is to empower rural poor, women and persons with disability through participatory development with an emphasis on local need and resources. The main activities undertaken are formation of women self-help groups, leadership development trainings for women, awareness meetings on women's issues, health education, HIV and AIDS and Child rights, promoting girl child education, steps to remove child labour, awareness on child right, natural resources development through activities under TSRLP and WDF with the support of NABARD etc.

SWEET NGO has adopted three villages namely Aettipamula, Gollapalli and Kolimera in Kattangur mandal of Nalgonda revenue division. These villages are located adjacent to NH-9 highway. In Aettipamula and Gollapalli villages NGO has been undertaking awareness programme for farmers on "SRI" is an abbreviation of "System of Rice Intensification" (SRI). The significance of this cultivation method is farmers utilize non-pesticide management techniques and proactive organic farming to achieve maximum yield with less capital investment. This programme facilitates farmers to secure agriculture machinery and seeds with subsidy from agriculture department. SWEET NGO organizes skill development programmes to farmers to create skills for utilization of machinery like Weder, marker etc.

(C) Association for Needy and Kindle the Illiterate Through Action (ANKITA)

Association for Needy and Kindle the Illiterate Through Action (ANKITA) is registered NGO establish in 1994 under the Registration Act XXI of 1860. The NGO is non-profit, non-political and secular voluntary organization striving for rural poverty alienation. ANKIT has been working in 62 Gram Panchayats in six mandals viz., Damerchala, Pedavoora, Vemulapally, Neredcherla, Munagala and Mothey of Nalgonda District.

One of the prestiages programmes undertaken by ANKIT in the district is establishment and running of worksite schools. ANKIT has been organizing eighteen worksite schools in eight mandals of the district. The schools are established to impart basic education to migrate families children with the support of Rajeev Vidhya Mission.

(D) Mano Prakash Human Services (MPHS)

Mano Prakash Human Services (MPHS) NGO was established in the year 2000. It is registered NGO. The NGO Registered under the Andhra Pradesh (Telangana Area), Public Societies Registration Act 1350 Fasali (Act 1 of 1350 F) with registration number 9060/2000. It was formed by a group of social workers and educated locals. It works for the development of various marginalized sections of society like handicapped children, tribal, scheduled caste; street and working children, small farmers and victims of various communicable diseases like leprosy, TB and AIDS. The NGO adopts reaching out approaches which are suitable to the target group.

MPHS mainly concentrating to organize HIV and AIDS awareness programmes for sex workers who reside in adjacent villages of National Highway (NH-9) on either side of Kodada and Suryapet road. The programme is called HIV/AIDS Avahan Project and received financial assistance from Alliance (Bilgate Foundation). The organization is running clinics with qualified doctors for female sex workers and male sex workers. The NGO assisting them to form community based organization to solve their problems.

The above selected NGOs are both operational and advocacy types. The primary purpose of an operational NGO is the design and implementation of development related projects, whereas, the purpose of an advocacy NGO is to promote a specific cause. The NGOs have traditional hierarchical organization structure with family board governance system. They have adopted some villages to implement government sponsored development and awareness programmes. The major beneficiaries of the NGOs are marginalized sections of village community. The forthcoming section highlights the major findings of the study and suggest measures for strengthening NGOs management to achieve integrated rural development.

SECTION-II: MAJOR FINDINGS AND SUGGESTIONS

Contextual understanding of rural development has been changing over the years. There is a shift in the emphasis on the discourse on rural development form 'intellectual idealism' to 'techno-bureaucracy', and eventually to the present 'participatory development'. All these changes in the perspectives on rural development have been associated with changing approaches and strategies. There is growing emphasis on such criterion as sustainability, participation and decentralization, while formulating strategies for rural development. These criteria have assumed greater significance in the era of globalization as rural development and requirements of globalization raise a debate.

Over the last decade there has been a dramatic growth in the number of NGOs involved in development aid, in both developed and developing countries. Today India has a vibrant NGOs sector. India is estimated to have 3.3 million registered NGOs. With rapid deterioration on performance side of the government agencies, the NGOs role and importance has increased manifold. The reason behind this is that government structures are not geared for integrated development like agriculture, energy, environment, water resources, equity and social justice.

NGO is one of the interventions in a society to achieve development. It acts as catalyst to enhance development process. Therefore, there is a need to assesses the impact of NGO practices that how they contribute to different facts of development. Measurement of NGO performance is a very complicated and complex phenomenon due to qualitative nature of its contribution. It is argued that performance of NGO need not be evaluated on the same yardsticks as those for judging the performance of a commercial organization. The major findings of the study are presented below:

- Rural people have more positive attitude towards significance and role of NGOs in rural development. More than fifty per cent of respondents have acknowledged NGO as a development agency in their locality and created awareness among them on various development activities and programmes of the government.

- NGOs are playing key role in social mobilization to execute quality development activities in rural areas. They are contributing for a grassroots democracy by involving people in the development process.
- NGOs are influencing local administration. They created livelihood opportunities for people and brought awareness on appropriate technologies and scientific practices in rural community.
- NGOs enlarged the scope of rural development programmes by independently formulating its own activates based on their own perception of rural needs.
- NGOs not only helping local people, but also acting as facilitators to institutions that are involved in rural development process like Banks. NGOs are offering help and suggestions to these institutions in implementing their rural development programmes at grassroots level.
- NGOs are acting as watchdog by mobilizing social, political and legal action at appropriate level to prevent arbitrary exercise of state power by exposing government lawlessness. This role is more fundamental for proper social development and legitimate social action.
- NGOs activities have arrested social evils in rural areas such as bonded labour, child marriages, untouchability and contributed to bring awareness on social and health issues especially on HIV and AIDS.
- NGOs skill development activities have contributed to enhance agriculture production and generated innovative agriculture cultivation to produce market based crops. These developments have controlled migration of people from rural to urban areas.
- NGOs activities and programmes have brought participative culture and attitude among villagers particularly to resolve their common problems without external intervention.
- One problem encountering by all the NGOs in the villages is hostile attitude of higher castes and landlords. Due to sincere efforts of NGOs these sections fail to get wage labourers for various works and the available labour demanding higher wages.

The NGOs activities have brought a social change in the villages and almost brought down the hegemony of higher castes in various facets of rural life. Unlike in the past, their domination in social and political areas has declined and space created for marginalized sections due to continuous efforts of NGOs.

Inspite of success stories of NGOs in rural development, there is also criticism over the working of NGOs in rural development. Some of the respondents in the study have expressed dissatisfaction over the functioning of NGOs. The following reasons are expressed by them:

(a) NGOs dance with the tunes of local affluent sections and could not go against their will;
(b) NGOs have nexus with local political leaders and elite;
(c) NGOs have close relations with local officials; and
(d) NGOs only perform activities for publicity.

A negligible percentage of respondents also have expressed multiple reasons for ineffective functioning of NGOs viz.:

(i) The salaries of NGOs staff are very low and it resulted low commitment towards organization;
(ii) NGOs financial management is not transparent;
(iii) NGOs are always in search of projects for sustenance than the completion of the projects on hand; and
(iv) NGOs are functioning as family establishments and not democratic.

Though a negligible respondents have expressed criticism over the working of NGOs in rural development but their opinion cannot be denied. The criticism expressed by them are applicable not only to NGOs under study but NGOs in general. The experts and academicians in the field also have acknowledged the above criticism over the functioning of NGOs in rural development. The study clearly brings out that NGOs would yield fruitful results if the following suggestions are brought in the management of NGOs:

(i) All Rural Development Programmes whether sponsored by the Central or State Government should be executed with the collaboration of NGOs at the grassroots level.

(ii) Local political leaders, local officials, and local elite should become co-opted members in all the NGOs who undertake activities or programmes in their locality.
(iii) A separate directorate should be created to extend needed support to NGOs and monitor their activities.
(iv) Networking of NGOs who are working in similar area is needed.
(v) Capacity building and effective financial management are needed to strengthen the working of NGOs.
(vi) Government should provide space for NGOs in selection of needy persons as beneficiaries for different rural development schemes.
(vii) NGOs need to appoint permanent staff with scale of pay to improve their morale, motivation and commitment among personnel.
(viii) The financial management of NGOs must be transparent.

Conclusion

The new critical approach to development has shifted focus from structure (state) to actors (civil society). The top-down approach has been displayed by bottom-up community approach. NGOs are now an important part of the civil society and legitimate negotiations on behalf of the people. In most of the third world countries, and also in India, NGOs are now playing an important role in the rural development processes.

The new economic policies heralded in the early 1990s in India acknowledge the role of NGOs in implementing developmental programmes. A plethora of NGOs operate in Telangana in various fields in general, rural development in particular. The study highlights that rural people have more positive attitude towards significance role of NGOs in rural development. NGOs are not only influencing local administration and institutions involving in rural development but also inculcating participative culture and attitude to achieve grassroots democracy. They are enlarging the scope of rural development and acting as watchdog to prevent arbitrary exercise of state power. Further, measures like establishment of separate directorate, networking of NGOs in similar field, democratising NGOs management and transparent financial management will go a long way to improve the role of NGOs in rural development. The Telangana State by acknowledging the role of NGOs in rural development, formed an NGO with World Bank assistance i.e., The Society for Elimination of Rural Poverty. Despite the increasing assertiveness of NGOs role in rural development, they cannot be a substitute to states and governments.

References

Behar (ed.) (2005), *Globalization and Rural Development*, Common Wealth Publishers, New Delhi.

Clark, John, (1991), *Democratizing Development: The Role of Voluntary Organization*, East Scan, London, Kumarian Press.

Koter, David C., *Getting to the 21st Century: Voluntary Action and the Global Agenda*, Kumarian Press, 1990.

Nanda, B.R., (2010), "*NGO Management*", Surendra Publication, New Delhi.

Patar A.R., (1985), "Rural Development—A Challenging Task for Voluntary Agencies", *Kurukshetra*, Vol. 34(1), New Delhi, October.

Prasad, B.K., (ed) (2004), *NGOs and Development*, Anmol Publications, New Delhi.

Rajesh Mishra, (2008), *Voluntary Sector and Rural Development: Concept, Practice and a New Approach to Remove Rural Poverty*, Rawat Publications, New Delhi.

Rural Development: Sector Policy Paper, World Bank, Washington DC, 1975.

Satyam Sundaram I., (1997), *Rural Development*, Himalaya Publishing House, New Delhi.

Soorya Moorthy, R., and Gangadar, K.D., (2006), *NGOs in India: A Cross Sectional Study*, Rawat Publication, New Delhi.

World Bank Operational Directives, 14.70, the World Bank, Washington DC, 1989.

7

People's Opinion on Nainital Local Government's Performance in Tourism

S.K. Sathyaprabha

Introduction

Local governance has significant role in tourism sector as both local government and tourism are interdependent for their development. Local governments are practically acting agents for the conservation of the local area which needs the support of the local people. It is undeniable that the relationships between the environmental conservation, local governments and local people inseparable and inevitable. To have sustainable development of the local area as well as the tourism industry, it is essential to involve the local people in all its developmental activities. Studies have examined the involvement and participation of Indigenous people in the tourism development process (Tosun, C., 2000). A similar idea was put forth by Simmons (1994) the relationship between tourism development and indigenes participation indicates that community involvement is, indeed, crucial in order to avoid more likely uncertainties and misunderstandings about tourism development in the area.

Definition

Local Governance

UNDP defines, "Local governance comprises a set of institutions, mechanisms and processes, through which citizens and their groups can articulate their interests and needs, mediate their differences and exercise their rights and obligations at the local level. The building blocks of good local governance are many: citizen participation, partnerships among key actors at the local level, capacity of local actors across all sectors, multiple flows of information, institutions of accountability, and a pro-poor orientation."

Urban Tourism

Urban tourism can be defined as an intensive development of tourism in urban areas with specific plans from government at all levels and an economy that is fully generated by tourism activities.

Urban tourism basically deals with urban infrastructure nature based tourism, and is aimed "to conserve the urbanization and improves the well-being of local people".

Background of the Study

The local governance role in the tourism is very essential for the development of area infrastructure because the local urban government knows the quality of that area. Local government is a key player in Nainital Urban tourism sector. Local government manages the natural and cultural resources that tourism relies on, provides core infrastructure, attractions and facilities, and often funds regional marketing and visitor information.

The local government is responsible for the planning and management of Nainital natural and cultural resources. The local administrative department is very helpful for the local citizen and visitors. The local government is providing attractive facilities for the public and tourism aspect also.

It also provides the core utilities and infrastructure on which the tourism industry is based. This includes district and city roads, lighting, water and sewerage, public transport systems. Local government operates attractions such as museums, art galleries, sports stadium, convention centres, parks, events, tours, and other amenities.

Local government enables regional marketing and provides visitor information by being the primary source of funding for Regional Tourism Organizations (RTOs) and the Visitor Information Network (VIN). There is very good IT facility for getting information about the Nainital place and other tourist spots, all offices and hotels are attach with the internet facilities for people welfare. Thus, the research on linkage between the local governance and nainital urban tourism in the people's point of view would be greatly helpful for both the tourism department and the local government institution to aware about the shortcomings as well as to improve their quality of service.

Objectives of the Study

- To understand the role of local governance in Nainital Urban Tourism in the perspective of local people.
- To analyze the issues involved in the improvement and maintenance of Nainital Urban Tourism.

Scope and Limitations of the Study

The researcher has chosen Nainital for this research study as it is a popular tourist place in India more infrastructural developmental programmes has been initiated by the Government of India. Since, the study was conducted at Nainital district where custom, tradition and culture are different from other parts of India, the results could not be generalized to any other states of India. At the same time special efforts could be taken on basis of suggestions of this research report as this study is a very specific and it is applicable only to Nainital. The scope for this research is high since researches on urban tourism relating to local governance are very rare in India.

Research Methodology

The researcher is interested to know whether the local communities are benefited by the economic gains of Nainital urban tourism department. For the process of this research data was collected from the public which includes the local people who are involved in tourism activities, vendors, guides and the tourists, etc. Totally data was collected from 50 respondents. Simple random sampling method was used to collect the data. Questionnaire and informal interview were the tools used to collect the primary data for the study. The secondary data was collected from were collected form the Nainital Nagar Palika Parishads, JNNURM Division, Uttarkhand Jal Sansthan (UJS), Nainital Lake Region Special Area Development Authority (NLRSADA), Lake development authority, Jalagum department, Mission butterfly, Nainital forest department, Nainital zoo, PWDDRDA office, manuals of the JNNURM, manuals of the URBAN development programmes, official research reports of JNNURM, the official records maintained by the Nainital Nagar Palika

Parishad. Books, Newspaper articles, Journals relating to Urban Tourism and Urban Studies, articles published in web sites form the secondary source of the study. All these sources primary and secondary sources were utilized by the researcher for the study. The responses collected through the questionnaire were entered in Microsoft Excel worksheet. Tables and figures were drawn by converting the data into percentages for analysis and interpretation.

Analysis and Interpretation

This section consists of assessment of local people on Nainital local government. Among the total number local people utilised for this part of analysis 23 per cent of the respondents are living in Nainital for less than 10 years. But 27 per cent of the respondents are living for more than 10 years and 50 per cent of them are natives of as they are living since they born. Table 7.1 gives the people's opinion about Nainital Tourism. Regarding the Tourism encouragement for variety of cultural activities by the local population cultural activities, more than half (53%) of the respondents agreed to it. At the same time nearly 23 per cent of the respondents disagreed and another 23 per cent of respondents are undecided.

Table 7.1: People's Opinion about Nainital Tourism

Responses	*Percentage*			
	Cultural activities	*Employment opportunities*	*Income generation*	*Cross-cultural exchange*
Strongly Disagree	10	7	0	0
Disagree	13	17	0	0
Undecided	23	0	0	10
Agree	40	43	60	50
Strongly Agree	13	33	40	40
Total	100	100	100	100

Source: Primary Data.

The response for Tourism providing employment opportunities, totally a very high per cent (76%) of the respondents agreed and the remaining 24 per cent of the respondents disagreed.

Tourism generates income is accepted by 100 per cent of the respondents. Totally 90 per cent of the respondents agreed that meeting the tourists is promoting their cross-cultural exchange and 10 per cent of the respondents are undecided about the statement. Thus the local people are having a good opinion about the Nainital Tourism.

Table 7.2 shows the Development in Nainital tourism in the past five years. Generally, the quality of life of local people has no change as per 20 per cent of the respondents. But 33 per cent of the respondents said the quality of life has improved and 47 per cent of the respondents said significantly improved.

In the past five years the employment opportunities for the people has improved because of tourism as 57 per cent of the respondents said as improved and 43 per cent of the respondents said significantly improved.

Table 7.2: Development in Nainital Tourism for the past five years

Responses	*Percentage*						
	Quality of life	*Employment opportunities*	*Household income*	*Quality of goods and services*	*Income-generating projects*	*Entrepreneurial training*	*Accessibility (transport and communication)*
Significantly Worse	0	0	40	0	0	30	0
Worse	0	0	27	0	13	23	0
No Change	20	0	16	20	17	13	0
Improved	33	57	17	50	40	20	57
Significantly Improved	47	43	0	30	30	13	43
Total	100	100	100	100	100	100	100

Source: Primary Data.

Except 15 per cent of the respondents none of the respondents gave positive answer for improvement in their household income because of tourism in the past five years. Fourty per cent of respondents said it is significantly worse, 27 per cent of the respondents said it is worse and 17 per cent of them said there is no change in their household income. Only 17 per cent of the respondents accepted that there is improvement in their household income.

The Quality of goods and services has significantly improved in the past five years in Nainital as a sum of 80 per cent of the respondents accepted as improved and significantly improved. The remaining 20 per cent of the respondents said there is no change their quality of goods and services in general.

Table 7.3: Suitable Means of Involving Local People in Tourism Development

Responses	*Percentage*					
	People Investment	*Tourism Work*	*Decision-making*	*Tourism benefits*	*Tourism survey*	*Seminar, Conference & Workshops*
Strongly Disagree	0	0	0	0	0	40
Disagree	0	20	13	23	10	23
Undecided	17	17	33	10	27	10
Agree	43	37	40	47	37	27
Strongly Agree	40	27	13	20	27	0
Total	100	100	100	100	100	100

Source: Primary Data.

Table 7.3 shows the responses of the people on suitable means of involving local people in tourism development.

By encouraging the local people to invest in the tourism sector a high majority (83%) of respondents are in favour this as 43 per cent of the respondents agreed and 40 per cent of the respondents strongly agreed. The remaining 17 per cent of the respondents are undecided. Thus, none of them is against this view of investing in tourism sector.

For the development of the tourism local people has to be encouraged to work with the tourism. The statement is agreed by a sum of 64 per cent of the respondents as 37 per cent of the respondents agreed and 27 per cent of them strongly agreed. But 20 per cent of the respondents are disagreed with the statement and 17 per cent of them are undecided.

A sum of 53 per cent of the respondents agreed (40%) and strongly agreed (13%) that Local People should take part actively in tourism decision-making process. 33 per cent of the respondents are undecided and 13 per cent of respondents are disagreed.

Sharing tourism benefits is a means of involving local people in the tourism is accepted by 67 per cent of the respondents and disagreed by 23 per cent of them. Ten per cent of the respondents remain undecided.

By responding to a tourism survey local people could be involved in tourism is agreed by a sum of 64 per cent of the respondents as agreed (37%) and strongly agreed (27%). But 10 per cent of the respondents are disagreed and 27 per cent of the respondents are undecided.

The faith on seminar, conference, workshops for tourism development is very low as none of them strongly agree and just 27 per cent of the respondents are agreed to it. Totally 63 per cent of the respondents disagreed (23%) and strongly disagreed (40%).

Thus, according to the people's view Encouraging local people to invest in the tourism sector, Encouraging local people to work for the tourism sector and Responding to a tourism survey are the suitable means of involving local people for tourism development.

Table 7.4 shows the Appropriate Role of Local People in Tourism Development. Totally 70 per cent of the respondents supported that they should take the leading role as entrepreneurs as 43 per cent of them agreed and 27 per cent of the respondents are strongly agreed.

Majority of the respondents (73%) accepted that local people should take the leading role as workers at all levels for tourism development as 43 per cent of the respondents are agreed and 30 per cent strongly agreed. None of them disagreed upon this point of view.

Table 7.4: Appropriate Role of Local People in Tourism Development

Responses	*Percentage*						
	Entre-preneurs	*Workers*	*Decision-Making*	*Consulted Tourism Policies*	*Final Decision by Tourism Authorities*	*Should Not Participate*	*Financially Supported*
Strongly Disagree	0	0	0	0	0	40	0
Disagree	17	0	0	0	0	33	17
Undecided	13	23	0	0	17	27	10
Agree	43	43	63	77	53	0	47
Strongly Agree	27	30	37	23	30	0	27
Total	100	100	100	100	100	100	100

Source: Primary Data.

Hundred per cent of the respondents said that Local people should have a voice in decision-making process of local tourism development as 63 per cent agreed and 37 per cent strongly agreed. Again a cent per cent of the respondents accepted that Local people should be consulted when tourism policies are being made as 77 per cent of the respondents agreed and 23 per cent of the respondents strongly agreed.

Local people should be consulted, but the final decision has to be taken by tourism is the response of 83 per cent of the respondents as 53 per cent of them agreed and 30 per cent of the respondents strongly agreed.

All the respondents wanted the local people participation in tourism as 40 per cent of them e strongly disagreed and 33 per cent of the respondents disagreed.

A sum of 74 per cent respondents agreed that Local people should be financially supported to invest in tourism development as 47 per cent of the respondents agreed and 27 per cent of them strongly agreed.

Thus, the respondents wants the local people to take the leading role as entrepreneurs, as workers at all levels so that they have a voice in decision-making process of local tourism development, should be consulted when tourism policies are being made and should be financially supported to invest in tourism.

Table 7.5: Assessment of Nainital Tourism Functions

Responses	*Percentage*				
	Bamboo Fencing	*Closed-Circuit Television*	*Disaster Management*	*Naini Lake Pollution*	*National Lake Conservation Project*
Strongly Disagree	23	0	0	0	0
Disagree	43	17	27	30	0
Undecided	20	10	10	7	0
Agree	13	43	43	47	53
Strongly Agree	0	30	20	17	47
Total	100	100	100	100	100

Source: Primary Data.

Table 7.5 shows the respondents Assessment of Nainital Tourism Functions. Bamboo fencing on Nainital's hillside roads has prevented hillside accidents is disagreed by 23 per cent of the respondents and strongly disagreed by 43 per cent of the respondents. Twenty per cent of the respondents are undecided and a small percentage (13%) of the respondents is agreed.

About 43 per cent of the respondents are agreed and 30 per cent of them strongly agreed as Closed-Circuit Television (CCTV) Cameras installed across the hill resort has solved problems like traffic jams and pick-pocketing. But 17 per cent of the respondents are disagreed and 10 per cent of the respondents are undecided.

There is enough disaster management and security measures for the land sliding or any other threat is by 43 per cent of the respondents and 20 per cent of them strongly agreed. Nearly 27 per cent of the respondents are disagreed and 10 per cent of the respondents are undecided.

The Naini Lake in Nainital has spiritual importance is now being polluted by garbage and sewerage water is agreed by 47 per cent of the respondents and strongly agreed by 17 per cent of the respondents.

Now a days, some of the Schools/NGOs/voluntary organisations are involved in cleaning the lake. They are as follows:

- Government Girls Inter College, Nainital
- Sherwood College, Nainital.
- St. Joseph's College Mallital, Nainital.
- Birla Vidya Mandir, Nainital.
- National Service Scheme and National Cadet Corps of Kumaon University Nainital.

Nearly half of the respondents (53%) are agreed that National Lake Conservation Project (NLCP) in Nainital is working well and 47 per cent of the respondents are strongly agreed the same. Thus, 100 per cent of the respondents assessed the National Lake Conservation Project as satisfactory.

So except in bamboo fencing the assessment of Nainital Tourism Functions in Closed-Circuit Television, Disaster Management, Naini Lake Pollution control and National Lake Conservation Project are satisfactory level is more than 50 per cent.

Major Findings of the Study

- All the respondents are the habitants of Nainital among them half of them are natives of as they are living since they born, quarter per cent of them are living for more than 10 years and the remaining are living in Nainital for less than 10 years.
- More than half per cent of the people agreed that the tourism encourages variety of cultural activities by the local population.
- More than three quarters of the people opinioned as Tourism providing employment opportunities.
- A cent per cent of the people have the view that Tourism generates income.
- Majority of ninety per cent agreed that meeting the tourists is promoting their cross-cultural exchange.
- Regarding the improvement in the quality of life of the local people four-fifth of them responded positively as the quality of life has improved and the remaining responded as no change.
- In the past 5 years the employment opportunities for the people has improved because of tourism and it is agreed by more than half of the people (57%) and the rest of them gave a strong

reply as there is significant improvement. Thus, all the respondents admit the above statement.

- Although people acknowledge the employment opportunities more than four fifth of them gave a negative comment about their household income as worse.
- The quality of goods and services has significantly improved in the past five years in Nainital as a sum of 80 per cent of the respondents accepted as improved and significantly improved.
- Most of local people are interested for partnership with the tourism sector as more than four-fifth of them showed concern for it.
- More than four-fifth the local people expect an encouragement to work with the tourism.
- About half of local people are awaiting to take part actively in tourism decision-making process.
- More than three-fifth of the local people felt that sharing tourism benefits is a means of involving local people in the tourism.
- Similarly local people could be involved in tourism survey is well accepted by three-fifth of them.
- The faith on seminar, conference, workshops for tourism development is very low as none of them strongly agree and just more than one quarter of the local people agreed to it.
- Seven-tenth of the local people urges to take the leading role as entrepreneurs.
- Nearly three quarters of them suggested that local people should take the leading role as workers at all levels for tourism development.
- A cent per cent of them wants to take the privilege of being a part in decision-making process of local tourism development and they hope to be consulted when tourism policies are being made.
- Most of local people reflected that Bamboo fencing on Nainital's hillside roads has not prevented hillside accidents.
- Nearly three quarter of the local people accepts that Closed-Circuit Television (CCTV) Cameras installed across the hill resort has solved problems like traffic jams and pick-pocketing.
- About three-fifth of the local people are answered that there are enough disaster management and security measures for the land sliding or any other threat is made available by the local government.
- Majority of the local people accepts the pollution of Naini Lake and now days, some of the Schools/NGOs/voluntary organisations are involved in cleaning the lake.

- National Lake Conservation Project (NLCP) in Nainital is working well as all the local people agree it.
- Except in bamboo fencing the assessment of Nainital Tourism Functions in Closed-Circuit Television, Disaster Management, Naini Lake Pollution control and National Lake Conservation Project are satisfactory level is more than 50 per cent.

Conclusion and Suggestions

According to the research findings the role of local governance in Nainital Urban Tourism in the perspective of the local people are satisfactory. The local people participation in all the tourism activities is excepted as most of the people have the tourism as their livelihood and main business.

Most of the local people families residing in this hilly area are predominantly depend on tourism related business which is leading to expect more from the government sector. Since Local Government Institution has an important responsibility in enhancing tourism in its areas as it will bring in more income, these local people could also be involved in its process which in turn will reflect in the sustainable development of the lives of local people and their area.

According to the people's view encouraging local people to invest in the tourism sector, to work for the tourism sector, involve in tourism survey are the suitable means of involving local people for tourism development and also they want to take the leading role as entrepreneurs, as workers at all levels so that they have a voice in decision-making process of local tourism development.

For the betterment of Nainital tourism healthy environment, good and cheap transportation system, developing new attractive tourist sport, improvement in the local infrastructure and sanitation facilities, Modern and stylist boat in the Nainital Lake and keeping the bank of lake clean, Opening Tourism Information Centre working twenty four hours which gives greater access of information for the tourist are some of the suggestions.

References

Kumar, V. and Arvind Kumar (2009), Assessment of Socio-Economic Impact of Tourism/Eco-Tourism at Barabar and Nagarjuni (B And N) Hills in Bihar (India) *Journal of Environmental Research and Development*, Vol. 4, No.

2, October-December 2009. Available atwww.jerad.org/ppapers/dnload.php?vl=4&is=2&st=601ý

Simpson, M.C., (2007), *Community Benefit Tourism Initiative: A Conceptual Oxymoron*, Oxford: Oxford University Press.

Singh, S.K. and P. Nag (1999), *Tourism and Trekking in Nainital Region*, Concept Publishing Company, New Delhi.

Titus, Amalu and Amin Ajake (2012), An Assessment of the Employment Structure in the Tourism Industry of Obudu Mountain Resort, Cross River State, Nigeria, *Geo-Journal of Tourism and Geosites*, Year V, No. 1, Vol. 9, May, 2012 available at http://gtg.webhost.uoradea.ro/PDF/GTG-1-2012/2_106_Titus.pdf-

Thodupuzha, M. Joseph (2008), *New Governance Paradigm: Issues in Development*, Kalpaz Publications, New Delhi.

Tosun, C., (2000), Limits to Community Participation in the Tourism Development Process in Developing Countries, *Tourism Management*, 21(2), 613-633.

Tosun, C., (2006), Expected Nature of Community Participation in Tourism Development, *Journal of Tourism Management*, 27(3), 493-504.

Tourism Policy of India: An Exploratory Study, Equitable Tourism Options (EQUATIONS) 1994, Bangalore.

Towards Democratising Tourism, Equitable Tourism Options (EQUATIONS) (2004), Bangalore.

8

Do Construction-Related Projects at the Local Level Contribute to Gender Mainstreaming?

Evidence from Kottayam, Kerala

Nisha V. Nair

Introduction

One of the remarkable features of Kerala's People's Plan Campaign (PPC) was its introduction of a Women Component Plan (WCP) as an integral part of the local level planning process. This was a unique development in the country. Launched a year after the Beijing Conference on Women and the Platform for Action (PFA), the 'people's plan campaign' sought to integrate women at every stage of the planning process. For example, women's issues constituted a separate chapter in the development report. Gender was a component in all the training programmes organised during the five stages of the plan campaign. Efforts were made to include as many women as trainers at state, district and local levels. From the second year of the Ninth Plan onwards, it was made mandatory that ten per cent of Plan Funds should go for projects exclusively meant for women. Each individual project was to have a statement in it relating to its gender implications. Similarly, when the panchayat plan was finalised, it was made mandatory to have some reference to gender by devoting a section for that purpose.

In Kerala, the whole project of mainstreaming gender was confined to the 10 per cent plan funds alone and no conscious attempt was made for enhancing women's share in the total expenditure over the years. The process dimension that makes planning a form of debate between men and women and among women themselves was absent. To quote Healey, "Planning as debate has the potential to confront those who 'currently' hold power at the level of ideology and philosophy as well as materially" (quoted in Moser, 1993: 88). Planning should become iterative and process–intensive. At the same time one needs to be aware that participation of poor women can come only if the benefits are in sight in the immediate future. Early emphasis on strategic interests of women such as focusing on the gendered division of labour can scuttle the process. Talking about strategic interests to women whose survival needs are not met can turn out to be a futile exercise.

The study examines the construction-related projects under Women Component Plan (WCP) implemented in Kerala at the local level by selecting five Grama Panchayats randomly from the five taluks in Kottayam District in Kerala. The paper draws on data relating to a ten-year reference period (1997-2007) collected from each of the five panchayats through field visits as well as through interviews of panchayat representatives (50 males and 50 females). The main objective of study is to understand the nature of construction-related projects under WCP, the increasing tendency to go for such projects and whether such projects are of any benefit to women.

Review of the Literature

A few studies related to WCP are available. But most of them are of a cursory nature. The Kerala Development Report 2008 brought out by the National Planning Commission had made a study of four panchayats in Trivandrum to see how gender issues were factored into the planning processes and how much flow of funds came for women. The study found that projects in housing, drinking water, sanitation and roads, which should have been included in the general category since they benefit both men and women, were often included in the WCP even as the panchayats conformed to the ten per cent allocation criteria. (Government of India, 2008: 419). A study done by Eapen (2004) showed no difference in the quality of spending in WCP projects in panchayats headed by women. The study found a decreasing trend in allocation for productive sector projects, which was seen as not in the interest of women. In other words, women may not gain much from increasing allocations to service and infrastructure sectors as they benefit both men and women. It was also found that the projects tended to be in line with the socially defined roles of women-focusing more on their practical (survival-related) gender needs.

Eapen (2007) found that there is a correlation between the tendency to go for higher allocation in the general infrastructural projects of the panchayat and reduction in the flow of resources to women from the general expenditures. She also found the absence of a sustained stream of imaginative projects aimed at income-generation by Self-Help Groups (SHGs).

The ten per cent of the funds earmarked for projects which directly benefit women did not involve, in theory, the neglect of women's interests and needs in the general projects. Further, projects that benefit both men and women such as roads, sanitation units, electrification, smokeless chullahs were not to be included in the WCP. Housing scheme for women-headed households and for those households where there are no adult males could be treated as coming under WCP (Vijayan, 2004; Seema and Mukherjee, 2000). Vegetable cultivation, goat rearing, poultry etc., were to be avoided under the WCP. If productive projects of this kind had to be included in the WCP, control over their organisation and income also had to rest with women. The *Anganwadi* nutritional programme and pre-primary education etc., were not to be included in the WCP. Construction of *Anganwadis* which do not provide separate meeting spaces exclusively for women could not be included in the WCP. Women's projects were to be implemented through groups. Women below poverty line recommended by Kudumbasree, SHGs and neighbourhood groups who were engaged in small savings and credit could be assisted under the WCP. Micro-enterprise development of women, basic infrastructure creation, marketing facilities, entrepreneurial development etc., could be assisted on a priority basis. The small groups of women entrepreneurs formed by the industrial department could be assisted under WCP subject to certain guidelines. Local bodies could also include projects relating to study of the status of women in their jurisdiction. Honorarium of *Anganwadi* workers was allowed to be included under WCP by the State Planning Board to bring the workers close to the Panchayat and make them participate in the organization of Gram Sabha (Isaac and Franke, 2000: 166). A study found that given the highly circumscribed manner in which the WCP was factored into the process of planning, it was only natural that it did not produce conflict either in the panchayat or in other participatory forums like the Gram Sabha. Ideally, it should have produced a sort of 'agonism' as conceived by Chantal Mouffe (Nair, 2011: 210). Another study points out that WCP has been relegated to the status of one of the regular sources of Kudumbasree financing (Nair and Moolakkattu, 2014: 270).

Profile of the Panchayats

Njeezhoor Panchayat located in the midlands was formed in 1953. Politically, the Panchayat is dominated by the Congress-led United Democratic Front (UDF). It is not industrially advanced. Kanjirappally panchayat formed in 1958 is in the highland region. It is also a UDF bastion with the Left Democratic Front (LDF) also occasionally coming to power. Thalappalam Panchayat falling in the midland region of the District was formed in 1953, and UDF, mainly Congress, dominates the panchayat. Thrikkodithanam, formed in 1968, is an LDF-dominated Panchayat in the midland region. It has the highest density of population among the five Panchayats. The Panchayat has more mixed cultivation than the type of monoculture (rubber) that is found in all the three aforesaid Panchayats. Nattakom Panchayat was founded on 27th July, 1953. The Panchayat stands second in the District with respect to income from non-agriculture sector. Politically, the Panchayat is evenly matched between the Marxist-led and Congress-led coalitions. Broadly, the Panchayats with rubber as the main source of income such as Kanjirappally, Thalappalam and Njeezhoor are relatively prosperous compared to Thrikkodithanam and Nattakom. For details see Table 8.1.

Table 8.1: Demographic Indicators

Name of the Panchayat	*Njeezhoor*	*Kanjirappally*	*Thrikkodithanam*	*Thalappalam*	*Nattakom*
Area	28.91 km²	52.47 km²	13.31 km²	22.73 km³	20.04 km²
No: of wards	14	23	20	13	22
Population	17651	37017	28468	12150	41702
Sex Ratio	997	974	1014	951	1035
Female Literacy (in %)	95	93	87	93	95.47
Male Work Participation	55.74	53.27	50.22	55.99	47.92
Female Work Participation	13.49	9.60	9.55	13.45	11.08

Source: Panchayat Level Statistics 2006, Kottayam.

Women Component Plan (WCP) and Construction Related Projects

Of the five Grama Panchayats the WCP expenditure of Thalappalam was the highest. This is not because of the quality of the WCP projects, but because the plan fund devolved to the Panchayat was the smallest compared to the other four. Overall the performance of the five Grama

Panchayats was poor as is evident from the fact that more than half the allocated amount (54.59) was unspent. Further, out of the total amount envisaged and spent under WCP, the major share of the fund available was utilised for construction-related projects as can be seen from Table 8.2. Construction projects are popular with the panchayats members across gender because they are more visible, easier to complete before the plan period ends and had greater scope for rent seeking.

Table 8.2: Amount envisaged and actually spent under WCP in construction-related projects (percentage) during 1997-2007

Panchayat	*Amount envisaged (%)*	*Amount spent (%)*	*Total expenditure under WCP (%)*
Njeezhoor	61.77	53.28	44.20
Kanjirapally	52.57	56.95	51.26
Thrikodithanam	76.4	73.81	40.04
Thalappalam	61.32	61.48	71.70
Nattakom	26.46	18.1	28.82
Total	54.85	55.97	45.59

Source: Plan documents 1997-2007.

In all Panchayats other than Nattakom the amount set apart for projects having a construction component and expenditure registered was above 50 per cent, as can be seen from Table 8.2. Nattakom Panchayat registered poor performance in all the years. Since the Panchayat was

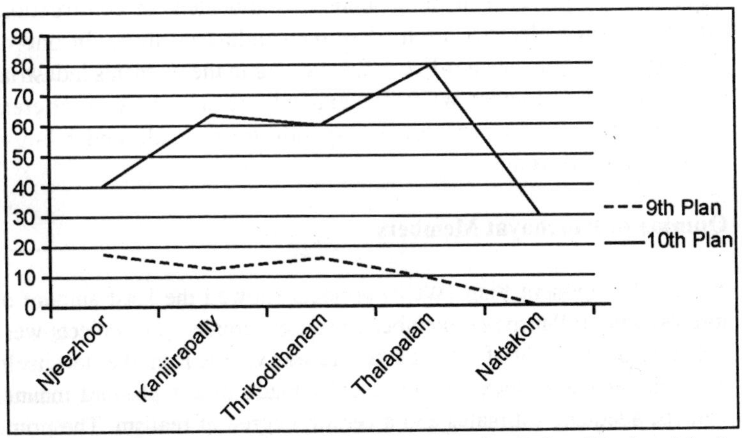

Fig. 8.1: Expenditure per cent of WCP (Construction Related Projects) in the Ninth and Tenth Llan

close to the District headquarters, construction of a working women's hostel was envisaged and for three years in a row funds were set apart for the project. However, it could not be implemented because of a dispute with the revenue department over the ownership of the building site.

Figure 8.1 shows that there was a remarkable increase in the expenditure per cent in the Tenth plan. This shows a shift from productive sector projects in the Ninth Plan to construction-related projects in the Tenth Plan. One reason for the increase in Tenth Plan expenditure is that the nature of projects changed from individual projects to group projects with greater outlay.

Table 8.3: Construction-related projects under different sub-sectors (%)

Projects	*Amount envisaged*	*Amount spent*
Women's Houses	34.59	49.36
Women's Industrial units	50.58	36.76
Women's Conference Halls etc.	14.83	13.88
Total	100	100

Source: Calculated from Plan documents 1997-2007.

The construction-related projects can be categorised into three on the basis of the nature of the projects. House construction projects meet the housing needs of the female-headed households. Table 8.3 reveals that out of the total amount envisaged for construction-related projects, more than 50 per cent of the amount was allocated for construction, maintenance or electrification of women industrial units. In one of panchayat, the Panchayat office is functioning in the women's industrial centre constructed under WCP. The expenditure side shows a different picture where 49.36 per cent of expenditure is made under house construction for women.

Opinion of Panchayat Members

Women Component Plan (WCP) projects showed the least amount of interest among Panchayat members, male or female. The projects were not seriously thought of and their failure was visible from the start itself. The ten per cent allocation was usually made in a haphazard manner without adequate estimates and a certain degree of realism. The prime consideration was to meet the requirement of the District Planning Committee.

Majority of the members (67%) (both male and female) admit that construction-type projects are increasing as years go by. Out of the 67 per cent of the members who agree that construction type project is increasing, 47 per cent of them attribute it to the reason that they are easier to implement. Some female members strongly feel that house construction projects are good as they benefit the whole family. A female member and president of the Panchayat says that house construction will not lead to women empowerment—the real goal of WCP.

In Kanjirappally Panchayat women conference halls have been built in most of the wards under WCP. The halls are used by Kudumbasree members to conduct meetings. Earlier such meetings were held in the houses of Kudumbasree members, which was inconvenient. Gram Sabha meetings are also conducted in these halls. A Panchayat member says that in future it can be used for personal needs of citizens of the ward for nominal charges, which could go to the Kudumbasree funds. He thinks that WCP has come to mean nothing more than setting apart 10 per cent for women which may or may not be useful for them. He is of the opinion that 60 per cent of Plan Fund should be set apart for infrastructure sector because people need roads rather than other things, and he adds that 90 per cent of the members agree with him on this.

There is also a general impression that 10 per cent is enough to take care of women's needs and no further allocation need to be made in other projects in the general sector for women. The ten per cent was originally envisaged as the minimum and in this case 10 per cent is generally seen as the maximum. In other words, although the introduction of this quota was meant to prevent flow of benefits from the plan campaign to women below a certain threshold, this had to be assured through other projects like Asraya and EMS housing scheme.

Do construction-related projects under WCP benefit women? It can be seen that the major share of the expenditure is made for house construction for widows and other female-headed families which partly addresses the housing needs of these hapless women. But if WCP funds are spent exclusively on housing and buildings, this is not going to be an optimal strategy for women's economic empowerment. Women industrial units often need allocation for a number of years for completion and such units are often set up without looking closely at the forward and backward linkages. The net result is that such buildings are used for purposes that do not benefit women. Women conference hall should be used for the benefit of women. It has been found that all construction projects other than housing did not benefit women.

The shift from productive sector to the infrastructure sector in the general projects in all Panchayats has also had an effect on the WCP. More WCP funds need to be allocated to the productive sector even though many such projects often fail and may not contribute to higher expenditure. The WCP did not have much impact on women's income generation, not to speak of addressing their strategic gender needs.

In effect, the ten per cent has amounted to a situation in which there was absolutely no concern with the needs of women in other projects, thereby pegging the direct benefits that women can derive from the projects to the share of WCP. Here too, the benefits did not directly come to women, particularly those from the construction projects.

Over the years, gender has taken a back seat with disability, old age, destitute and EMS housing etc. taking up greater attention. The lack of state government's consistent endorsement of the importance of gender considerations in the planning process was seen to be one of the main hindrances to mainstreaming gender issues into planning at local level. In sum, the mainstreaming that has taken place is more mechanical and superficial than substantial.

Conclusion

The shift to more and more construction-oriented projects is a general trend in most Panchayats in Kerala and this not unique to WCP projects. But this encourages many Panchayats to construct buildings in the name of women which could be used later for general purposes. This shift deprives many poor women of the opportunity to tap the WCP funds to earn an income by engaging in productive activities such as agriculture, animal husbandry and so on. Such projects are seen as challenging and cumbersome for elected representatives to implement. In the absence of sustained commitment to the WCP by women representatives themselves, the WCP can only be carried out only in this lacklustre fashion. While some projects like women's houses can be useful for women, the construction of women's industrial units and conference halls for women will not be of much benefit to them. Given the fact that an elected woman representative sees herself as a representative of the entire electorate in a constituency, it is difficult to inculcate in her a special interest in a programme meant for women alone. It is here that women's organisations have to step in and play a major role to sustain interest in gender issues relating to local level development.

References

Eapen, Mridul (2004). Report on Gender Analysis of Select Gram (Village) Panchayat Plan-Budgets in Trivandrum District, Kerala, paper presented at the Consultation on *Impact of Macroeconomic Policies on Women,* 25 November, 2004, New Delhi, Human Resources Development Centre, UNDP. available from http://wcd.nic.in/gbsummary/Mridul.pdf, viewed on 10 December, 2010.

Eapen, Mridul (2007). Gender Budgeting and Decentralised Governance. In M.A. Oommen (ed.) *A Decade of Decentralisation in Kerala: Experience and Lessons* (pp. 209-244). New Delhi: Har Anand.

Government of India (2008): *Kerala Development Report*, New Delhi: National Planning Commission and Academic Foundation.

Issac, Thomas T.M. and Franke, Richard (2000). *Local Democracy and Development, People's Campaign for Decentralized Planning in Kerala.* New Delhi: Left Word.

Moser, C.O.N. (1993). *Gender Planning and Development: Theory, Practice and Training.* London: Routledge.

Nair, Nisha V. (2011). Participatory planning and gender mainstreaming: Case study of a village panchayat in Kerala. *Gandhi Marg,* 33(2), 187-215.

Nair, Nisha V., and Moolakkattu, John S. (2014). Women Component Plan at the Village Panchayat level in Kerala: Does it live up to its promise? *Indian Journal of Gender Studies*, 21(2), 247-276 (forthcoming)

Seema, T.N., and Mukherjee, V. (2000). Gender governance and citizenship in decentralised planning. Paper presented at the International conference on democratic decentralisation, Thiruvananthapuram, May 23-27.

Vijayan, Aleyamma and Sandhya J. (2004). *Gender and Decentralised Planning in Kerala*, Trivandrum: Caxton Press.

9
Government Accounting
DRDA in Goa and its Accounting Procedure-Guidelines

Anthony Rodrigues

Poverty alleviation through Self-employment and Wage-employment programme is the theme of rural development. It is District Rural Development Agency at the District level which overseas the implementation of different anti-poverty programme. District Rural Development Agency (DRDA) came into existence with effect from 1.4.1980. Previously it was known as Marginal Farmer and Agricultural Land Development Agency (MFALDA). Later on it became Small Farmer Development Agency (SFDA). These agencies were only to cater the development of Marginal Farmers and Agricultural Labourers in rural area. Now, District Rural Development Agency has embraced manifold activities for upliftment of rural poor.

District Rural Development Agency has traditionally been the principal organ at the district level to oversee the implementation of anti-poverty programmes of the Ministry of Rural Development. This agency was created originally to implement the Integrated Rural Development Programme (IRDP). Subsequently, the District Rural Development Agencies were entrusted with number of programmes of both State and Central governments. From 01 April, 1989 a separate District Rural Development Agency Administration has been introduced to take care of the administrative costs.

Objectives of the Study

1. To study and evaluate the various schemes of DRDA-districtwise.

2. To study whether the schemes provided by the government are really benefiting the people.
3. To study the accounting procedure followed by DRDA as a system of government Accounting.

Research and Methodology

The purpose of this study is evaluating the various schemes implemented by DRDA and to see that whether the schemes really benefited the rural people or the backward class people and if the DRDA is functioning according to the guidelines of the Government.

Start of the Problem

Research and Methodology

The purpose of conducting this study is to study and evaluate the various schemes implemented by the government and to see that whether the schemes really benefited the rural people or the backward class people.

Methodological Assumptions and Limitations

(a) Study is concentrated on DRDA and evaluation of schemes.
(b) The study is conducted purposely to see that the people are really benefited from the scheme.
(c) Data collected and analysed is from 2001-02 to 2007-08.

Rural Development Department, Government of Goa

Rural India which encompasses three fourths of the Country's population is characterized by low income levels, inadequate to ensure a quality of life compatible with physical well being. The Ministry of Rural Development, spearheading the frontal attack on rural poverty, through its various programmes endeavoured to reach out to the last and most disadvantaged sections of society, provide them with avenues of employment, be it self-employment or wage-employment, and to improve infrastructure relating to their life support system.

In State of Goa this task is entrusted to two District Rural Development Agencies viz., District Rural Development Agency-North Goa and District Rural Development Agency-South Goa. The Agency came into existence when the Government established the Small Farmers Development Agency (SFDA) which has been amalgamated with the then Rural Development Agency on 4.11.1980. District Rural Development Agencies were established by bifurcating the then Rural Development Agency into District Rural Development Agency, North-Goa and District Rural Development Agency, South-Goa with the objective to take the administration at the nearest steps to the people. The Agency works at Panaji and Margao. North Goa is having jurisdiction over 6 development blocks of North Goa District namely, Tiswadi, Bardez, Pernem, Bicholim, Ponda and Sattari and District Rural Development Agency, South Goa is having jurisdiction over five development blocks namely, Sanguem, Quepem, Canarcona, Salcete and Mormugao. These Agencies are implementing the programmes with the assistance of the Block Development Officers at the block level.

Role and Functions of the District Rural Development Agency

"India lives in its villages"—this axiom is as true today as it was over fifty years ago. The majority of our population lives in the rural areas. The all round socio-economic transformation of Rural India is a must for the nation to realize its potential and secure the position it deserves among the comity of nations. Government of India therefore, accords a high priority to Rural Development and is accordingly implementing a number of Programmes aimed at sustainable holistic development of the rural areas. A strategic pro-poor policy in terms of which the rural poor are treated as a net resource replete with their own ideas and experience, well in tune with the local conditions forms an integral part of the Development Strategy. In the process, the disadvantaged sections of society receive a high priority.

Schemes Implemented by District Rural Development Agency

Integrated Wastelands Development Programme

The broad objectives of the programme are:

(i) Development of wastelands based on village/micro-watershed plans. The stake holders prepare these plans after taking into consideration the capability of land-site conditions and local needs; and

(ii) Promoting the overall economic development and improving the socio economic condition of the resource poor and disadvantaged sections inhabiting the programme areas.

Wastelands/Degraded Lands

As per the Report of the Technical Task Group constituted by the Planning Commission, 1987, the wastelands are the degraded lands which can be brought under vegetative cover with reasonable efforts and which are currently under-utilized and the land which is deteriorating for lack of appropriate water and soil management or on account of natural causes. Broadly, the following are the causes of degradation:

(i) Increasing biotic pressure on the fragile ecosystem;
(ii) Population pressure, unplanned urbanization and rural poverty;
(iii) Break down of traditional institutions for managing Common Propert Resources; and
(iv) Lack of appropriate management practices.

There are various estimates of total wastelands/degraded lands in the country. The Department of Land Resources follows the National Remote Sensor Agency estimates. According to the latest *Wasteland Atlas of India* brought out by the NRSA in May, 2000, out of 329.00 million hectares of total land, 63.85 million hectares (20.17% of the total area) are the wastelands which are categorized as follows:

Table 9.1: Forest and Non-Forest Area

Category	*Area (lakh hectares)*	*%*
Forest	140.65	22
Non-Forest	497.87	78
Total	638.52	100

Source: DRDA Goa.

Watershed Approach

On the recommendations of the Hanumantha Rao Committee, the two Area Development Programmes and the development of wastelands are to be taken up through community participation following a watershed

Table 9.2: The Category-wise Details of Non-Forest Wastelands are as given below:

Categories	*Area (in lakh hectares)*
Upland with or without scrubs	194.01
Water logged	16.56
Saline/Alkaline land	20.48
Shifting cultivation land	35.14
Sands-inland/coastal	50.02
Mining/Industrial Wastelands	1.25
Barren Rocky/Sheet Rock	64.58
Snow Covered/Glacial	55.78
Degraded pastures/grazing land	25.97
Steep Sloping Area	07.65
Gullied/Ravinous land	20.55
Degraded land under plantation	5.83
Total	497.87

Source: DRDA Goa.

approach under common guidelines with effect from 1st April, 1995. A watershed is a geo-hydrological unit, which drains into a common point. It is a project based, ridge to valley approach for *in-situ* soil and water conservation, afforestation etc. and it includes:

(i) Focus on village common lands.
(ii) Equity in sharing the benefits.
(iii) Institutionalized community participation at the village level for implementation and post project maintenance.
(iv) Emphasis on sustainable rural livelihood support systems through Self-Help Groups and User Groups.
(v) Capacity building as a vital component.
(vi) Committee systems at the State and District level for monitoring and implementation.
(vii) Decentralized planning and decision-making by the local people of the watershed area.

Funding Pattern

Integrated Wastelands Development Programme is a 100 per cent Central Sector Scheme. Ongoing Watershed Projects Under Employment Assurance Scheme.

Hariyali Project

The scheme Hariyali came into effect from 1/4/2003 with the following objectives:

(i) Harvesting every drop of rainwater for purpose of Irrigation, Plantations including horticulture and floriculture, pasture development, fisheries etc. to create sustainable sources of income for the village community as well as for drinking water supplies.

(ii) Ensuring overall development of Rural areas through the Gram Panchayats and creating regular sources of income for the Panchayats from rainwater harvesting.

(iii) Employment generation, poverty alleviation, community empowerment and development of human and other economic resources of the rural areas.

(iv) Mitigating the adverse effects of extreme climate conditions such as drought and desertification on crops, human and livestock population for the overall improvement of rural areas.

(v) Restoring ecological balance by harnessing, conserving and developing natural resources i.e. land, water, vegetative cover especially.

(vi) Encouraging village community towards sustained community action for the operation and maintenance of assets created and further development of the potential of the natural resources in the watershed.

(vii) Promoting use of simple, easy and affordable technological solutions intuitional arrangements that make use of, and build upon, local technical knowledge and available materials.

Sampoorna Grameen Rozgar Yojana (SGRY)

The Sampoorna Grameen Rozgar Yojana have the following objectives:

Primary Objective

The primary objective of the Scheme is to provide additional wage employment in all rural areas and thereby provide food security and improve nutritional levels.

Secondary Objective

The secondary objective is the creation of durable community, social and economic assets and infrastructural development in rural areas.

Swarnajayanti Gram Swarozgar Yojana (SGSY)

Anti-poverty Programmes have been a dominant feature of government initiatives in the rural areas. The Programmes have been reviewed and strengthened in the successive years in order to sharpen their focus on reduction of Rural Poverty. The results achieved, in the meanwhile, are worth noting. In percentage terms, rural poverty, has reduced from 56.44 per cent of the country's population in 1973-74 to 37.27 per cent in 1993-94. Some States have been more successful in reducing their poverty (rural) during this period. These States are Andhra Pradesh (48.41% to 15.92%), Goa (46.85% to 5.34%), Gujarat (46.35% to 22.18%), Karnataka (55.14% to 29.88%), Kerala (59.19% to 25.76%), Rajasthan (44.76% to 26.46%), Tamil Nadu (57.43% to 32.48%), and West Bengal (73.16% to 40.80%). However, the cause of concern is that the estimated number of the rural poor is still about 244 million which has led to further review and restructuring of the Anti-poverty Programmes. The Swarnajayanti Gram Swarozgar Yojana is the result of such latest review and restructuring of the Programmes. The Swarnajayanti Gram Swarozgar Yojana has been launched with effect from 1.4.1999 as a new Self-employment Programme. With the coming into effect of the Swarnajayanti Gram Swarozgar Yojana, the earlier Programmes of Integrated Rural Development Programme (IRDP), Training of Rural Youth for Self-Employment (TRYSEM), Development of Women and Children in Rural Areas (DWCRA), the Ganga Kalyan Yojana (GKY) as well as the Million Wells Scheme (MWS) are no longer in operation.

Rural Housing

Housing is one of basic requirements for human survival. For a normal citizen, owning a house provides significant economic security and dignity in society. For a shelter less person, possession of a house brings about a profound social change in his existence, endowing him with an identity, thus integrating him with his immediate social milieu.

According to the 1991 Census, the rural housing shortage was 13.72 million consisting of 3.41 million households without houses and 10.31

million living in unserviceable kutcha houses. It has also been estimated that another 10.75 million houses would be needed to cover the population growth during 1991-2002, at the rate of an annual growth of 0.89 million houselessness. The 1991 Census further indicates that about 40.82 per cent of the total of 112 million rural households remains in one-room tenements, 30.65 per cent in two-room houses and 13.51 per cent in three-room units or more. In terms of roof type, the percentage of houses having grass, straw and thatch is about 33 per cent, mud and unburnt bricks 6.05 per cent and tents 4.22 per cent. Apart from this, in terms of quality of walling, 47.27 per cent of the total households have grass and straw walls and about 4 per cent have tent and cloth walls. Nearly 70 per cent of the rural houses are either unserviceable kutcha (9%) or serviceable kutcha (25%) or of semi-pucca (35%) category as per Census 1991. Over 90 per cent of the rural houses have no provision for toilet as per the Census 1991. This suggests that there is a clear correlation between poverty and housing: a poor person either does not have a house or lives in an unserviceable kutcha house.

Indira Awaas Yojana (IAY)

The objective of Indira Awaas Yojana is primarily to help construction of dwelling units by members of scheduled Castes/Scheduled Tribes, freed bonded labourers and also non-scheduled Castes/Scheduled Tribes rural poor below the poverty line.

Credit-cum-Subsidy Scheme

There were a large number of households in the rural areas which could not be covered under the Indira Awaas Yojana, as either they do not fall into the range of eligibility or due to the limits imposed by the available budget. On the other hand due to limited repayment capacity, these rural households cannot take benefit of fully loan-based schemes offered by some of the housing finance institutions. The need of this majority can be met through a scheme which is part credit and part subsidy based, Funding:

The Centre and the State, in the ratio of 75:25 share the funds respectively.

National Social Assistance Programme (NSAP)

The Government of India has introduced National Social Assistance Programme on 1.8.1995 and it has namely two components.

National Old Age Pension Scheme

Under this programme, Pension of Rs. 200 per month is eligible. The following criterion is applied for availing the benefit under this scheme:

(i) The age of applicant (Male or Female) shall be 65 years and above.
(ii) The applicant must be destitute in the sense of having little or no regular means of substances from his/her own source of income or through financial support from family members of other sources.

National Family Benefit Scheme

Under this scheme, an assistance of Rs. 10,000 is given to the family on the death of its Primary Bread Winner. The following criteria is adopted to obtain assistance under this scheme.

The Funds position during the year 2006-07 under National Family Benefit Scheme (NFBS) is as follows:

(i) The primary bread winner shall be the member of the household, male or female whose earning contributes substantially to the total household income.
(ii) The death of such a primary bread winner should have occurred whilst he or she is in the age-group of 18 to 64 years, i.e. more than 18 years and less than 65 years of age.
(iii) The bereaved household qualifies as on below poverty line to receive the assistance.

Swabhimana

(i) To create and support appropriate initiatives and opportunities, whose include employment generation activities, for the weaker sections of the society and the unemployed and economically backward people of the State of Goa so as to provide them with a regular sustained income.
(ii) To encourage and develop the production of traditional and indigenous items which are characteristic and unique to the State of Goa and to standardize these products thus assuring quality and genuineness of these products.

The programme will be implemented through the following four categories of stakeholders:

(a) State Government (through the Department of Rural Development and the District Rural Development Agencies).
(b) Self-Help Groups.
(c) Financial Institutions/Bankers.
(d) Independent Marketing Agency.

Balika Samrudhi Yojana (BSY)

The Balika Samrudhi Yojana (BSY) covers the girl child in families below poverty line as defined by the Government of India in rural areas, who are born on or after 15th August 1997. The Girl Child in India generally has a low status and enjoys fewer rights, opportunities and benefits of childhood as compared to bcy child. The Balika Samrudhi Yojana is a part of the long-term strategy to change attitude and behavioural pattern towards the girl child while raising her status.

A post birth grant amount of Rs. 500 is given to girl child. In addition to this, an annual scholarship is also given for attending the school and after successfully completing years of schooling as detailed below:

Table 9.3: Annual Scholarship of Girl Child

Sl. No.	*Std.*	*Amount of Scholarship*
1.	I Std. to IIIrd Std.	Rs. 300 per annum for each class
2.	IVth Std.	Rs. 500 per annum
3.	Vth Std.	Rs. 600 per annum
4.	VIth Std. to VIIth Std.	Rs. 700 per annum. for each class
5.	VIIIth Std.	Rs. 800 per annum
6.	IXth Std. to Xth Std.	Rs. 1000 per annum for each class

Source: Ballika Samridhi Yojana.

Goa Grameen Urja Yojana (GGUY)

The objective of the scheme is to all Below Poverty Line families installation of Domestic one Liquified Petroleum Gas (LPG) connection, pollution free (fuel), to minimize the use of firewood, thus decreasing the pressure on forest and at the same time helping maintaining pollution free environment.

The Below Poverty Line families who are notified as per Below Poverty Line Census can avail the benefit under this scheme, as per entitlement. The programme will be implemented as a State Scheme. All the Below Poverty Line eligible families will be covered under the scheme during eleventh Five Year Plan.

Assistance under the Scheme

Every Below Poverty Line family covered under the scheme shall be provided with Domestic Liquified Petroleum Gas connection with 2 cylinders, one gas regulator with its accessories and 2 burners one gas stove of Indian Standard Institution (ISI) mark.

Goa Rural Employment Guarantee Scheme (GREGS)

The State of Goa has made its own scheme namely "Goa Rural Employment Guarantee Scheme" based on the National Rural Employment Guarantee Act which is a Landmark Legislation in the country. Goa Employment Guaranteed Scheme is expected to make significant prudent in the poverty situation in the rural areas. The Scheme is designed as per National Rural Employment Guarantee Act (NREGA-2005) passed by the Parliament.

The objective of the Scheme is to provide for the enhancement of livelihood, security of the household in the rural areas in the State of Goa by providing at least 100 days of the guaranteed wages employment in a financial year to every household whose adult member volunteer to do unskilled manual work.

Reports of District Rural Development Agency Schemes

Swarnajayanti Gram Swarozgar Yojana (SGSY)

The Physical progress of the Scheme during the last seven years under Swarnajayanti Gram Swarozgar Yojana Scheme are shown below:

Table 9.4: Progress of Scheme SGSY

Year	*No. of beneficiaries assisted*
2001-02	573
2002-03	666
2003-04	364
2004-05	683
2005-06	625
2006-07	711
2007-08	415

Source: Questionnaire.

The difficulties faced by the beneficiaries under Swarnajayanti Gram Swarozgar Yojana is that Banks are reluctant to grant loan to the beneficiaries as there are many defaulters.

Details of Achievement of Individual Cases and Self-Help Groups under Swarnajayanti Gram Swarozgar Yojana.

Table 9.5: DRDA-North Beneficiaries

Sl. No.	Name of the Block	Target	Year 2006-07			
			Cases identified	Cases recommended	Cases sanctioned by bank	Cases pending in bank
1.	Bardez	126	213	213	172	41
2.	Bicholim	52	98	98	52	13
3.	Ponda	77	90	90	52	39
4.	Pernem	53	55	55	59	07
5.	Sattari	75	86	86	80	16
6.	Tiswadi	17	37	37	13	16
	Total	400	579	579	428	132

Source: DRDA Annual Reports.

Table 9.6: DRDA-South Beneficiaries

Sl. No.	Name of the Block	Target	Year 2006-07			
			Cases identified	Cases recommended	Cases sanctioned by bank	Cases pending in bank
1.	Sanguem	57	55	55	44	11
2.	Quepem	37	62	62	74	2
3.	Canacona	57	62	62	75	2
4.	Salcete	61	90	85	83	7
5.	Mormugao	06	9	9	7	2
6.	Total:	218	278	273	283	24

Source: Questionnaire.

Marketing and Infrastructure Support to Swarozgaris

To provide marketing support to the Swarozgaris (beneficiaries under Swarnajayanti Gram Swarozgar Yojana) the Agency assists the beneficiaries to participate and to make them confident not only in local exhibitions but also State/National level exhibitions.

Position of Funds

Table 9.7: The Financial Position of the Scheme during the year 2006-07 is as below:

(Rs. in lakhs)

Name of the District	*Year*	*Opening balance as on 1.4.2005*	*Released by*		*Other receipts*	*Total*	*Exp. upto March 2006*
			Centre	*State*			
North-Goa	2006-2007	1.74	35.30	11.76	2.45	51.25	43.99
South-Goa	2006-2007	7.55	7.35	2.45	0.19	17.54	17.51

Source: DRDA Annual Reports.

Table 9.8: Financial Position of the Scheme during the year 2006-07 and 2007-08

	North Goa		*South Goa*	
	2006-07	*2007-08*	*2006-07*	*2007-08*
Total Subsidy released Rs in lakhs	26.87	25.64	15.12	11.03
Revolving Fund released to SHGs Rs in lakhs	5.70	7.86	1.04	1.19
The Expenditure incurred for undertaking skill training	4.57	1.09	0.12	—

Source: DRDA Annual Reports.

Goa Bazaar

The Goa Bazaar is a special project under Swarnajayanti Gram Swarojgar Yojana to provide Marketing support to Swarojgaris. The total cost of the Project is Rs. 9.83 crores, which has been approved by the Government of India. This would create a permanent structure in the form of Marketing Centre "Goa Bazaar" for sale of product of Swarojgaris a training Centre at Goa Bazaar will also be established as part of the project, to upgrade the skill of the rural micro-enterprises, Self-Help Groups and Swarojgaris for higher productivity and capacity building, the process of land acquisition is completed and an area of 40,839 sq. mtrs. has been acquired. The total expenditure incurred upto October, 06 is Rs. 104.65 lakhs. The Chief Architect PWD has prepared the drawings of the different structures that are to be constructed in the land acquired for construction of Goa Bazaar. The drawings are sent for their concurrence before preparing the detailed Project Reports.

However, the following works are to be taken up on Priority basis:

(1) Soil Investigation/Foundation Exploration, the estimated cost of which is Rs. 1,80,210. The said work is tendered and work order will be issued to the successful Agency.
(2) Survey and Plotting for a Grid Pattern, the estimated cost of which is Rs. 51,600.
(3) Improvement of the land by filling moorum, the estimated cost of which is Rs. 71,06,918.

Sampoorna Grameen Rozgar Yojana (SGRY)

Projects Sanctioned to the Village Panchayats

Table 9.9: During the year 2006-07, the Funds received and Expenditure incurred under the Scheme is as under

(Rs. in Lakhs)

Year	Name of District	Opening balance	Funds received		Other receipts	Total availability	Exp. incurred
			Central	State			
2006-07	North Goa	13.94	250.58	130.00	11.78	406.30	393.63
2006-07	South Goa	3.53	91.04	30.35	0.31	125.23	115.00

Source: Questionnaire.

The proposals under this scheme are prepared by the Panchayats and forwarded to the District Rural Development Agency through Block Development Officer for Administrative approval. The proposals from the Panchayats complete in all respects and based on funds available with the Panchayats are approved by the District Rural Development Agency.

During the financial year 2006-07, 32 number of projects were sanctioned to the Village Panchayats of North Goa wherein total amount involved is Rs. 449.75.

During the financial year 2006-07, 111 number of projects were sanctioned to the Village Panchayats of South Goa wherein total amount involved is Rs. 100.12.

The scheme could not make much progress during the year 2007-08 as the Government of India extended National Rural Employment Guarantee Scheme to this State and Sampoorna Gramin Rozgar Yojana will be merged into National Rural Employment Guarantee Scheme.

Rural Housing

Indira Awaas Yojana (IAY)

Table 9.10: Position of funds and expenditure incurred during the year 2006-07 and 2007-08 is as below (New Construction)

(Rs. in Lakhs)

Year	Name of the District	Opening Balance	Funds released		Other Receipts	Total Availability of Funds	Expenditure
			Central	State			
2006-07	North-Goa	2.52	88.90	29.64	1.08	122.14	117.68
2007-08	North-Goa	4.46	61.73	20.58	0.26	87.03	36.09
2006-07	South-Goa	0.08	19.46	9.03	0.10	28.67	28.63
2007-08	South-Goa	2.67	27.71	9.00	—	39.38	11.42

Source: DRDA Goa.

Table 9.11: Upgradation

(Rs. in Lakhs)

Year	Name of the District	Opening Balance	Funds released		Other Receipts	Total Availability of Funds	Expenditure
			Central	State			
2006-07	North-Goa	0.02	16.66	20.56	0.23	37.47	37.21
2007-08	North-Goa	0.22	11.57	3.86	0.02	15.67	14.13
2006-07	South-Goa	—	3.72	1.74	—	5.46	3.23
2007-08	North-Goa	0.54	5.54	1.66	—	7.74	2.40

Source: DRDA Goa.

Government of India instructed to provide land to landless Below Poverty Line beneficiaries to construct their houses. It is submitted that wherever, Government land is available, 100 sq. mts. be allotted to them and cover all the landless families. Land acquisition is required to be processed. Placed before the house for information and decision.

The difficulties faced while implementing the IAY Scheme is that beneficiaries are not in a possession of Form XIV. Land documents are not in the name of the beneficiaries and Land Owners are reluctant to issue N.O.C. for the construction of new house.

If the house is registered in the name of the owner, the proposal is sanctioned for the upgradation of the house.

Table 9.12: Houses completed (Year 2006-07) (South-Goa)

Sl. No.	Block	New Houses		Upgradation		Credit-cum-subsidy	
		Houses completed	Expenditure	Houses completed	Expenditure	Houses sanctioned	Expenditure
1.	Sanguem	18	2.39	8	0.36	—	—
2.	Quepem	31	5.06	45	2.15	9	1.13
3.	Mormugao	—	—	—	—	—	—
4.	Salcete	15	1.80	16	0.65	4	0.48
5.	Canacona	132	19.38	1	0.07	1	0.12
	Total	196	28.63	70	3.23	14	1.73

Source: DRDA Goa.

Credit-cum-Subsidy

Table 9.13: Position of Funds and Expenditure incurred during the year 2006-07 and 2007-08 is as below:

Year	Name of the District	Opening Balance	Funds released		Other receipts	Total availability of Funds	Expenditure
			Central	State			
2006-07	North-Goa	0.20	5.56	6.86	—	12.62	7.58
2007-08	North-Goa	5.05	3.86	1.78	0.01	5.54	3.88
2006-07	South-Goa	—	1.15	0.53	0.10	1.78	1.73
2007-08	South-Goa	0.12	1.39	0.60	—	2.11	1.50

Source: DRDA Goa.

Table 9.14: Physical achievements under Credit-cum-Subsidy

Year	Name of the District	Target	Achievement
2006-07	North-Goa	40	60
2007-08	North-Goa	28	79
2006-07	South-Goa	18	14
2007-08	South-Goa	19	12

Source: DRDA Goa.

National Social Assistance Programme

Table 9.15: The Taluka-wise number of Beneficiaries under the Scheme, during the year 2006-07, are as given below:

Sl. No.	Name of the Block	No. of Beneficiaries
1.	Ponda	679
2.	Pernem	501
3.	Bardez	603
4.	Sattari	444
5.	Bicholim	251
6.	Tiswadi	219
7.	Sanguem	68
8.	Quepem	165
9.	Canacona	123
10.	Salcete	227
11.	Mormugao	129
	Total	3409

Source: DRDA Goa.

Table 9.16: The Funds Position during the year 2006-07 and 2007-08 (Upto October 7) under National Old Age Pension Scheme (NOAPS) is as follows:

(Rs. in lakhs)

Year	Name of the District	O.B.	Central	Other Receipts	Total availability of funds	Expenditure
2006-07	North-Goa	6.04	25.00	0.28	31.32	28.63
2007-08	North-Goa	2.68	25.00	1.16	28.84	17.12
2006-07	South-Goa	25.56	10.50	0.45	36.06	6.48
2007-08	South-Goa	20.07	10.50	—	20.07	15.12

Source: DRDA Goa.

Accounting System/Procedure Followed

Maintenance of Cash Book

1. The DRDAs/ZPs/DLCs in NSAPs are required to maintain separate Cash Book for each Scheme. Against each entry in the cash book, name of the block and implementing agencies should be indicated. The Cash Book shall be maintained by all the District Rural Development Agencies. The transactions relating to schemes of other Ministries should not be included in these Cash Books.

Table 9.17: Physical Achievement under National Family Benefit Scheme during the year 2006-07

Sl. No.	*Name of the Block*	*No. of Beneficiaries*
1.	Ponda	30
2.	Pernem	25
3.	Bardez	58
4.	Sattari	53
5.	Bicholim	33
6.	Tiswadi	3
7.	Sanguem	23
8.	Quepem	30
9.	Canacona	14
10.	Salcete	39
11.	Mormugao	5
	Total	313

Source: DRDA Annual reports.

2. DRDAs each Block is required to maintain separate Cash Book for each scheme. The transactions relating to schemes pertaining to other Ministries should not be included in these Cash Books.
3. The name of the Bank and the Bank Account no. of the Scheme should be written on the first page of the Cash Book as it will be useful to the Inspecting Officers and Audit Officers.
4. Cash Book shall be closed on every transacting day. All receipts and payments should be posted in the Cash Book on regular basis. After balancing the amount it should be signed by the Cashier and DDO.
5. The Cash Book should be certified, summerised, closed and signed on the last working day of the month by the Project Director, DRDA/CEO, Zila Panchayat/DLC on NSAP.
6. All receipts of money should be entered in the Cash Book on the day they are received. Interest Earned on scheme fund should also be reflected in the Cash Book.
7. The monthly closing balance should have details of Balances available in the Bank Pass Book, entries in the Cash Book and Cash in Hand. Balance should also be supported by the copies of Bank Pass Book. A certificate in this regard should be recorded at the close of every month.
8. There may be some debits and credits for Bank charges, commission or interest, which will appear in the Monthly Bank statement. These items should be incorporated in the Cash Book

in the following month, so, that Cash Book balances agree with the Bank Balance.

Maintenance of Scheme Ledger

1. Each DRDAs/ZPs/DLCs on NSAPs should maintain Scheme wise Ledgers. Different pages of Ledgers should be for different Blocks. Thus, there will be numbers of ledgers equivalent to the number of Schemes in the District and each Ledger will have detail of Blocks, date of release of Advance, Amount of Advance released, voucher number, cheque number and date of receipt of UCs/Adjustment Bill.
2. At the end of the month a scheme-wise abstract should be prepared showing Monthly Advances and the monthly adjustment/ expenditure in respect of each scheme and each Block.
3. (a) Each Block should maintain a Scheme-wise Ledger with different pages for different Panchayats, under which name of the Panchayats/Village, date of release of Advances, Amount of advance, Cheque number and date of receipt of UCs/Adjustment Bill should be given.
   (b) At the end of the month a scheme-wise abstract should be prepared showing the release and monthly Expenditure in respect of each scheme in each Panchayat.
4. Trial Balance for the month using General Ledger and Cash Book should be prepared. If Trial Balance is not tallied then error of posting in Cash Book and Ledger should be checked.

Guidelines for Payments

1. BDOs/Implementing Agencies will receive their funds from DRDAs/ZPs as advance and adjustment bills should be submitted to DRDAs/ZPs to settle the advance. There is no limit on reimbursement, however, second advance for the same project can be be given subject to the condition that 60 per cent funds has been utilised/expenditure incurred out of advance already issued. However, third advance cannot be given till the first advance is fully settled.
2. All payments exceeding Rs. 1,000 shall be made in Cheque/ DD, in cases where it is not possible to make payment by Cheque/ DD then such reasons should be recorded in the Cash Book.

The Drawing and Disbursing Officer will satisfy himself about the mode of payment.

3. All payments should be supported by documents such as bills/ receipts and cash memos.
4. When disbursing the payments, the Accountant/Accounts Officer should obtain the signature of the payee acknowledging receipt of the cheque or cash as the case may be. This signature must be affixed in appropriate space.
5. All paid vouchers be retained for the **period of 5 years** from the date of adjustment/settlement of Advance, or till the Statutory Audit for that period is completed, **whichever is later.**
6. Bills and Vouchers which have been paid by cheques shall be divided into the following classes, namely: (i) salary and establishment Bill, and (ii) other bills. Each class of bills should be pasted in a separate guard file and shall be consecutively numbered in order of payment. But sub-vouchers which have been paid in cash out of the permanent advance, shall be separately filed together with the recoupment vouchers covering them.
7. A system of debit voucher for each payment (whether by cheque or in Cash) may be introduced. The debit voucher may indicate sanction number, particular of expenditure, ledger head under which it is classified and mode of Payment (Cheque/DD/Cash). The debit voucher may be approved by the Accounts Officer and shall form the basis for posting the Cash Book.
8. Payment made to Blocks/Panchayats and Other implementing agencies be entered in Payment Register.

Procedure for Bank Reconciliation

1. The DRDAs/ZPs and Banks should reconcile their accounts on monthly basis. Pass Book should be updated twice in a month i.e. on 10th and last working day of every month. The Bank Reconciliation Statement should be pasted in the Cash Book at the end of each month.
2. The Balance appearing in Pass Book/Bank Statement should be reconciled with entries shown in Cash Book. In the event of any cheques issued during a month remaining uncashed at the close of the month,
3. At the end of each Month a summary of the outstanding cheques

issued but not presented to Banks should be prepared indicating date, cheque no., amount and Payees name.

4. Cheques older than 6 months from the date of issue and not presented to the Bank should be investigated by the PD/CEO, ZP and then written back in Cash Book noting the reference number, date of payment voucher and head of Accounts liability for payment in future after following the procedure.
5. All moneys remitted to the Bank to the Credit of the Society and all payments made by the Bank on cheques or otherwise on account of the society shall be entered in a Pass Book. The Pass Book shall remain in the custody of the Accounts Officer and it shall be sent to the Bank at least twice in a month. The Bank should update entries of Receipt and Payment, balance the account and sign the Pass Book. The amount should be entered in words as well as in figures. On receipt of the Pass Book by the Bank, the receipt and payment upto date, shall be entered therein and when the Book is received on the last working day of the month, the account shall be balanced and signed by the Agent of the bank, the amount being entered in words as well as in figures. The Pass Book shall be returned to the Office of the Society (DRDA) as soon as the entries prescribed in this rule have been made in it.
6. The Project Director/CEO, ZP shall examine the Pass Book at least once in a month and shall immediately call the attention of the Bank to any discrepancy that may appear between the credits and debits shown in the Pass Book and these shown in the accounts of the Society.

Guidelines for Annual Financial Statements

The following Annual Financial Statements shall be prepared by the DRDA/Agency for each scheme.

Receipts and Payments Accounts

The summary of the Receipts and Payments should be tallied with the cash book. The Proforma of Receipts and Payment Account may be seen at It has following features:

(1) It starts with an opening balance on the debit side showing cash in hand and balance in bank.

(2) Receipts are recorded on the debit side and payment on the credit side.
(3) Both receipts and payment are classified under suitable headings.
(4) All transactions occucring during the year shall be recorded in this account. In other words, receipts and payments pertaining to the previous year, current year and next year are recorded in it. Moreover, it records receipts and payments of both capital and revenue nature.
(5) This account ends with a closing balance which represents cash in hand or bank balance at the end of the year. If however, it shows a credit balance, it means it is bank overdraft.

Income and Expenditure Account

It is prepared on the principles of Profit and Loss Account of a Non-Profitable organisations. Special features of the account are:

(1) Expenditure is on the debit side of this account and Incomes are recorded on its credit side.
(2) Items of only revenue nature are shown. Items of capital nature are excluded.
(3) Expenses and Incomes are adjusted in the following manner:
    (i) Include all figures relating to the current year only even if the items are not fully settled in cash;
    (ii) Exclude figures relating to future or previous years; and
    (iii) Interest earned on funds of each scheme should also be shown as Income.

Steps for Preparing Income and Expenditure Account out of Receipts and Payments Account

For this purpose the following steps may be necessary:

(1) Exclude the opening and closing balances of the Receipts and Payments Account.
(2) All items of capital nature recorded in the receipts and payments account should be excluded.
(3) Any income and expenditure of the previous year or next year must be excluded.
(4) Any income earned but not received during the year should be

provided for, similarly of expenditure incurred but not paid should be recorded in.

(5) Items like depreciation, bad debits etc., which are not paid in cash, must be taken into account.

(6) All items of capital nature appearing in receipts and payments account but not shown in the income and expenditure account should be shown in the balance sheet.

Balance Sheet

(i) The Balance Sheet must be prepared for every financial year in the prescribed Proforma.

(ii) The Balance Sheet should show all balance of Assets and Liabilities Account at close of the year with the comparative figure for previous period.

(iii) Accounts Officer and Project Director/CEO must sign the Balance Sheet, before forwarding it either for audit or to Executive Committee.

(iv) The necessary annexure to the Balance Sheet should be numbered in sequence and attached thereof.

(v) The annual accounts along with Balance Sheet shall be subjected to Audit.

(vi) The Audited Annual Accounts along with the Balance Sheet and Audit Report should be sent to the Ministry of Rural Development Government of India and the State Government by the 30th September Every Year.

Schedules

The Annual Financial Statements should be accompanied by the following Schedules:

(i) Schedule of Assets created during the year.
(ii) Schedule of Grants/Subsidies received.
(iii) Schedule of Interest Earned on unutilised funds kept in Banks.
(iv) Schedule of Establishment Expenses (For DRDA Admn. only).
(v) Schedule of Other Administrative Expenses.
(vi) Schedule of Expenditure on Grants and Subsidies.

After the preparation of Annual Financial Statements, as mentioned above, the Project Director shall lay them before the Governing Body for their approval.

Utilisation Certificate

The DRDAs/ZPs/DLCs shall submit utilization certificate along with Annual Statement of Accounts. The Blocks and other executing agencies shall render their accounts against advance given to them by the DRDA. The UCs shall be signed by the PD/CEO.

Conclusion

1. DRDAs/ZPs and Blocks are responsible for the correct accounting of money distributed to the implementing agencies. They are supposed to supervise and control the whole accounting functions of Blocks/Panchayats. Project Directors/CEOs are supposed to carry out essential checks
2. The accounts of the each District Rural Development Agency (DRDA)/ZP/DLC and Block shall be maintained on accrual basis/double entry system like other commercial organisation.
3. DRDAs/ZPs/DLCs/Block and Panchayats should maintain a consolidated Receipt and Payment Account register common for all schemes on the basis of Pass Book, Cash Transaction as recorded in the Cash Book and posted in Ledger.
4. Interest earned on funds of each scheme should be added in the scheme fund. Income and Expenditure Account should depict the same separately.
5. Principal of one Bank account for each scheme must be followed by DRDA and line level. Second Bank Account for the same scheme, if at all required could only be opened with the approval of the State Secretary (RD). Multiplicity of Bank Accounts for one scheme is not permissible.
6. Funds received both from Central and State Governments should be kept in the Savings Bank Accounts only. Funds in no case be kept in the Fixed Deposits/Term Deposits. All existing FDs/TDs should be encashed and transferred to the respective scheme account.
7. Scheme Account should be maintained only in Nationalised/ Cooperative/Regional Rural Banks. In no case funds are to be kept or transferred in Treasuries, or in Personal Ledger Account,

Treasury Savings Accounts, Treasury Public Deposit Account etc.

8. State Share received against each scheme should also be transferred in the respective scheme account maintained in the Banks. No funds should be kept in Treasuries.
9. (i) Funds transferred to Block Development Officers/ Implementing Agencies shall be reflected as advance to them and be adjusted against the receipt of adjustment bills. Second advance for the same project can be given subject to the condition that 60 per cent funds have been utilized/ expenditure incurred out of advance already issued. However, third advance cannot be given till the first advance is fully settled.
   (ii) Advances to BDO should be shown as advance in the Cash Book and Balance Sheet and not as final Expenditure on the scheme.
   (iii) Expenditure on the scheme should be on the basis of adjustment bills or on receipt of the utilisation certificates.
10. DRDAs/ZPs should prepare following Scheme-wise Annual Statements as per:
    (i) Receipt and Payment Account
    (ii) Income and Expenditure Account
    (iii) Balance Sheet
    (iv) Utilisation Certificate
    (v) A statement of Annual Opening and Closing Balance of each Scheme.
    (vi) A certificate of Imprest adjustments at the end of Financial Year.
11. Payments to state P.W.D., Forest Department and to other Implementing Agencies for various works may be termed as Deposit works for which separate accounts may be kept and executing agency shall render the account of each deposit and expenditure against such work every month to the DRDAs/BDOs as the case may be.
12. The DRDAs Accounts Officer shall acknowledge the receipt of funds received from the Banker of the Ministry. The acknowledgement receipt, in the prescribed proforma, should reach to the Pay and Accounts Officer.
13. Subsidies from SGSY scheme fund should not be released by the lead Bank/DRDA to branches before the receipt of the

intimation from the branch bank confirming that the loan release cases of the beneficiaries have been processed and sanctioned. Thereafter, subsidy equal to sanctioned amount should be released on monthly basis. Instances of refund of unutilized subsidy by the bank branches may be reduced to the minimum.

14. DRDAs are not authorised to take overdraft from the Banks. No overdraft at any stage be paid to DRDAs on behalf of any scheme of Government of India. Bank should not entertain any such request as Government of India is not liable for such payment.
15. Flow of funds from DRDAs/ZPs/Blocks/Gram Panchayats and Implementing Agencies should be through cheque/Demand Draft only.

Recommendations

Summary of Accounting Records to be maintained by the DRDAs/ZPs

1. Cash Book
2. Ledger
3. Journal
4. Cheque Issue Register
5. Register of Receipt Books
6. Register of Cheque Books
7. Register of Advance Implementing Agencies
8. Register of risk fund/managerial subsidies Bank account register to record the cheques issued against the balances in different banks and to work out the balance from time to time.
9. Register to review the progress of expenditure against the budget allotments for:
   (i) administrative expenses under different ledger heads;
   (ii) expenditure on subsidies for different programmes in different sectors; and
   (iii) risk fund/managerial subsidy.
10. Permanent advance Account (Petty cash book and recoupment vouchers).
11. Provident funds accounts if any for employees of the DRDA/ DRDS, under the rules of the society.
12. Register to record the recovery and remittance of (i) Provident Fund Contributions, (ii) Income tax, (iii) Loans and Advances

(iv) Register to watch the disposal of Audit objections (AGs inspection, CAs audit).

13. Assets register in GFR Form 19.
14. Bank reconciliation register with separate folios for the reconciliation of balances sheet with different branches of the bank by the DRDAs.
15. Any other register considered necessary in connection with the work of maintenance of accounts.
16. Register of Consolidated Receipt and Payment.
17. Deposit Register in a format to be maintained for EMD, Security Deposit and Income Tax Deduction.
18. Scheme-wise Ledger having Block-wise Detail.
19. Petty Cash Book.
20. Recoupment Register (for Imprest).
21. Register of Audit and settlement of Audit Objections.
22. Block wise Scheme wise Register for watching Utilisation from BDOs Implementing Agencies for amount advanced to them. The Register should show the following items also:
    (a) Funds advanced to the Blocks under different Schemes.
    (b) Expenditure intimated by the Blocks against advances.
    (c) Amount Outstanding against each BDO pending adjustment.
23. A monthly account showing the allotment and expenditure under each item, shall be prepared and put up before the PD/CEO.

References

Chan, J.L. (2003). "Government Accounting: An Assessment of Theory Purposed Standards," *Public Money and Management,* 13-20.

Gauthier, Stephen J. (2001). *Governmental Accounting, Authority and Financial Reporting*. Government Finance Officers Association, I.

Governmental Accounting Standards Board. (2002). *Codification of Governmental Accounting and Financial Reporting Standards* (Statement 34 Edition), as of June 30.

Hepworth, N. (2003). "Preconditions for Successful Implementation of Accrual Accounting in Central Government," *Public Money and Management,* 37-44.

Milan, V. *The Harmonization of Government Accounting and the Role of IPSAS,* pp. 3-18, McGraw-Hill.

Sutcliffe, P. (2003). "The Standards Programme of the IFAC Public Sector Committee," *Public Money and Management.*

Wynne, A. (2011). Annual Financial Reporting by Governments–What Is Africa's Best Practice? Harare: African Capacity Building Foundation.

Web Sources

www. DRDAgolaghat.org/programs/sgry/asp
www.DRDAgolaghat.org/programes/sgsy/ruralhousing
www.Rural.nic.in
www.pbplanning.gov.in/pdf
www.swabhiman.org
www.Gramin Bharat.com
www.Bharatnirman.gov.in
www.nrega.nic.in
www.drdagoa.nic.in
www.wcdhry.co.in/ballika samridhi_yojana.htm
www.ruralbazaar.nic.in

SECTION-III
Women Empowerment, Sustainable Development and New Economic Initiatives

10
Women Empowerment through Micro-Enterprises

Y. Gurappa Naidu and C. Krishnamurthy

Introduction

In the recent past, there have been a renewed concern and commitment on the part of the governments for the all round development of women. The enhanced commitment led to the emergence of a novel and landmark strategy in the name of 'empowerment' which is dominated the governments' thinking and approach all over the globe towards women welfare. That is the reason why the socio-economic advancement of a country can best be judged by the status and position which it can bestow upon women. Building up of a nation is practically impossible with one section of its population inactive and ignorant. Just like "A bird cannot fly with its one wing only", "a nation would not march forward if the women are left behind". Women have been subjected to drastic discrimination in all walks of the life and are denied and deprived of the equality of status and opportunities in the social, economic and political spheres despite their significant contribution to the social and economic progress of the country. It is crystal clear that women literacy and participation of educated women in decisions within and outside family strongly influence the relative respect and regard for women's well-being.

The empowerment of women for the last two decades has been widely recognized as a central issue in determining the status of women. It covers aspects such as women's control over material and intellectual resources. Empowerment is a process, but not an event, which challenges traditional power equations and relations. In recent past the two landmark initiatives have become very important for the empowerment of women, one being the reservation of seats in local bodies for women and the other being the Programme for Development of Women and Children in Rural Areas (DWCRA). The DWCRA programme, initiated in 1980s, is based on the concept of Self-Help Group (SHG), and has emerged as the most successful programme in promoting the empowerment of women. The State of Andhra Pradesh (AP) has become a role model for other states. The SHGs in AP have recorded a rip-roaring success in eliminating the poverty among the rural women and in empowering them in different spheres. The impact of SHGs in Andhra Pradesh has been appreciated by the World Bank.

There are multiple goals achieved by the SHGs such as inculcation of saving habits, provision of credit for consumption and productive purpose, entrepreneurship development, developing leadership qualities, gender sensitivity and awareness about the socio-political, economic and cultural issues to the extent of initiating development programmes by women, which in turn ensure the overall development of the women in rural area. In India, it was only in the 1970s that the shift in approach from welfare to development has emerged with reference to the weaker sections of the society including women. Sixth Plan emphasized the potential of women to become agents of development. In 1980s, the Integrated Rural Development Programme (IRDP) that takes the family as a unit of development and stands for an integrated development of those living below the poverty line was improved and refined in order to make it more effective, particularly in the case of rural women. The Eighth Plan, which corresponded the beginning of liberalization and market-friendly economy, marks a major shift in the developmental strategy.

Empowerment is a multi-dimensional process, which should enable the group of individuals to realize their full identity and powers in all spheres of life. It also means equal status to women. Empowering women socio-economically through increased awareness of their rights and duties as well as access to resources is a decisive step towards greater security for them. Empowerment includes higher literacy level and education for women, better health care for women and children, equal ownership of productive resources, increased participation in economic and commercial sectors, awareness of their rights and responsibilities, improved standards of living and acquiring self-reliance, self-esteem and self-confidence.

Majority of the rural population is unskilled and asset less and purely depending on wage paid employment. Large scale unemployment of rural artisans is due to dearth of demand for their products. Most of the small and marginal farmers possess low holdings and their low farm income pushes them into debt trap and poverty. Women in rural areas are underemployed and their potentialities are underutilized due to poor financial background. Rural poor are unable to fulfil the security obligations of banks to get financial assistance and very often exploited by rural money-lenders and usurers. The benefits of the anti-poverty programmes have not reached the poor as expected resulting in poor recovery of loans. Micro-credit programmes facilitate the poor women to take up micro-enterprises, generate gainful employment and income with low capital investment. This approach is quite suitable for the rural poor because it generates savings of the group members and the repayment performance is good due to regular generation of income. Good recovery of bank loans facilitates recycling of funds which leads to economic empowerment of women and further to social and political empowerment.

Against this background, the present study has been undertaken with the following objectives: To evaluate the impact of micro-enterprises undertaken by women through SHGs in the generation of their income, employment, asset status and to assess the impact of micro-enterprises on the empowerment of women.

Methodology

The study covers all the three regions of the State of AP: Telangana, Coastal Andhra and Rayalaseema. From each region, one district was selected based on the incidence of poverty. Among the different districts of each region which have higher percentage of BPL households, one district with the highest number of BPL households has been selected as first stage units of sampling. Accordingly, Mahabubnagar district from Telangana region, Chittoor district from Rayalaseema region and West-Godavari district from Coastal Andhra region have been selected for the study. From each selected district three revenue divisions and from each sleeted revenue division, one revenue mandal were selected using random sampling procedure as the second stage units. Finally, the study covered Farooq Nagar, Kottakota and Devarakadra Mandals from Mahabubnagar district. Kalakada, Yerpedu and Penumuru Mandals in Chittoor district. Chantalapudi, Elamanchili and Nidadavolu Mandals from West Godavari district. From each selected revenue mandal, five gram panchayats were selected as third stage units and from each selected gram panchayat, two self-help groups were chosen as fourth stage units of sampling. Thus, the sample SHGs covered by the study are ninty and from each SHG, the president of the SHG and four other members who have taken up diverse micro-enterprises were selected randomly as the respondents constituting the last stage units of sampling. On the whole, this study covers 3 districts, 9 revenue mandals, 45 gram panchayats, 90 SHGs and 450 SHG members in the state of AP.

The primary data was collected by directly through structured schedule from the group leaders and members of SHGs in three selected districts of AP to obtain their views and opinions on micro-enterprise activities undertaken by the respondents through SHGs. The micro-enterprise activities undertaken by the sample respondents through SHGs are broadly grouped as milk vending, flower vending, sheep/goats, small business, petty business, milk production, handloom/lace, Tailoring/laundry and other activities.

Socio-Economic profile of the Sample SHG Members

The knowledge of socio-economic profile of the sample members facilitates proper understanding of the economic conditions of the sample households and the impact of the micro-enterprises on the improvement of their economic position.

- Out of the 450 sample respondents, scheduled castes constitute 14.89 per cent, scheduled tribes constitute 0.44 per cent and 47.50 per cent belong to backward communities. The members of other castes constitute 31.78 per cent.
- Those who are in the age-group of 18-30 years constitute 28.00 per cent while 37.78 per cent are in the age-group of 30-40 years. This shows that majority members are in the age of active economic participation, i.e. less than 40 years. The members who are in the age group of 40-50 years constitute 22.22 per cent while 12 per cent are above 50 years of age.
- As many as 65.11 per cent of the sample members have pucca houses and 8.67 per cent live in semi-pucca houses. The members owning katcha and thatched houses constitute 26.22 per cent of the total sample. The average value of the katcha and thatched houses is worked out to Rs. 62,500, the average value of semi-pucca houses to Rs. 97,850 and the average value of pucca houses is estimated at Rs. 1,30,277.30.
- Among the sample members, 24.67 per cent are illiterates, 47.11 per cent have primary education and 24.44 per cent have

secondary education. This provides an evidence that the members of the SHGs are mostly illiterates or having primary education.

- Of the sample members, 48.22 per cent have no land of their own and the remaining 233 members (51.78 %) have own land. Out of which 54.08 per cent have land holdings of less than 1 acre and 22.75 per cent have land holdings in the range of 1-2 acres. The above trend shows that most of the SHG members are landless or marginal farmers.
- Of the 450 households, 56.89 per cent have some own livestock. The total value of all the livestock owned by the 256 sample households is estimated at Rs. 1,26,71,600 and the average value of livestock per household possessing livestock is worked out to Rs. 49498.44.
- The average value of farm and household assets of the sample farm assets is worth of Rs. 10,67,100. Only 41.11 per cent have own farm assets. The average value of farm assets per household is estimated at Rs. 5,768.11 and the average value of household assets per household is accounted for Rs. 6752.
- The average value of all assets per household is worked out to Rs. 2,44,344.00. The average value of assets per household is the highest for households running milk vending business (Rs. 3,57,471.93) followed by households engaged in milk production (Rs. 2,74,663.11) and households who maintain sheep/goat farming (Rs. 2,58,365.91). The lowest value of assets per household is recorded by the sample households who run tailoring/laundry shops (Rs. 1,48,852.38) followed by households who are engaged in other activities (Rs. 1,56,733.33).

Impact of Micro-Enterprises

Micro-enterprises are assumed to be suitable instruments for economic betterment of rural poor particularly rural women. Majority of rural women remain unemployed and underemployed for most of the days in a year. Micro-credit programmes through SHGs, help the rural poor to run micro-enterprises which generate income and employment and make them to cross the barriers of the poverty levels. An attempt is made to present and analyze the different costs incurred and income generated of different micro-enterprise activities undertaken by the women members of SHGs covered by the study. Through the above analysis, the cost and profitability of different activities have been evaluated so as to assess the impact of micro-finance on economic empowerment of women. The distribution of sample SHG members by micro-enterprise activity indicate that 57 out of 450 representing 12.67 per cent have taken up milk vending as their micro-enterprise activity, 34 sample members representing 7.55 per cent have taken up flower vending, 44 representing 9.78 per cent are engaged in sheep/goat rearing as their micro-enterprise activity. Of the sample members 59 have undertaken small business as their micro-enterprise activity accounted for 13.11 per cent while petty business was taken up by 53 members. The largest sample i.e.,103 out of 450 representing 22.89 per cent of the total SHG members are engaged in milk production while 63 representing 14.00 per cent have taken up tailoring/laundry as their micro-enterprises. The lowest number constituting 19 representing 4.22 per cent have undertaken handloom and lace-weaving and other activities are taken up by 18 out of 450 constituting 4.00 per cent of the sample members covered by the study.

Table 10.1 presents the economics of different types of micro-enterprises engaging by the sample SHG members. The conclusions that can be drawn from the table are:

(1) The total cost of maintaining/organizing milk vending business by 57 sample members has been estimated at Rs.54,38,853 per annum and the average cost per member is worked out to Rs. 95,418.47. The gross income earned from milk vending business by all the 57 members has been estimated at Rs. 79,84,943 per year and the average per member is worked out to Rs. 1,40,086.72. The total net income realized by all the 57 members is estimated at Rs. 25,46,090 and the average net income earned per member is worked out to Rs. 44,668.24. From the above, it can be concluded that an investment of Rs.100 on milk vending activity fetches a net return of Rs.46.81 per annum.

(2) Flower vending is the micro-enterprise activity taken up by the 34 sample members of SHGs. The total cost of maintenance is worked out to Rs. 28,02,637 and the gross income earned by all the members is accounted for Rs. 38,52,117. The total net income has been estimated at Rs. 10,49,480 and the average net income per member is worked out to Rs. 30,867.06. On an average, an investment of Rs.100 on flower vending business fetches a net income of Rs. 37.45 per year. The total cost of rearing and maintenance of sheep/goats of 44 sample households as micro-enterprise is estimated at Rs. 53,59,622 and the gross income

Table 10.1: Economics of Micro-Enterprises Organized by the sample SHG Members in three sample districts of Andhra Pradesh

Sl. No.	Particulars of Cost/Income	Name of the Micro-Enterprise									
		Milk Vending	*Flower Vending*	*Sheep/ Goats*	*Small Business*	*Petty Business*	*Milk Production*	*Handloom/ Lace*	*Tailouring/ Laundry*	*Other Activities*	*Total*
A.	Cost of Production/Maintenance										
1.	Inputs	2759132	1701440	3319389	6774106	5119596	1642772	377700	1264290	1918920	24877345
2.	Labour	2562250	1063900	1981960	3260950	2089256	2894000	672656	21,97250	1195060	17917282
3.	Interest on working capital	27591	17014	33193	67741	51195	16427	3777	12642	19189	248769
4.	Interest on fixed assets	89880	20283	25080	43212	44844	164060	17020	79656	25646	509681
	Total	5438853	2802637	5359622	10146009	7304891	4717259	1071153	3553838	3158815	43553077
B.	Income										
1.	Micro-Enterprise	7984943	3852117	7776243	14340957	10329191	7217035	5181398	5791229	4133911	66607024
2.	Net Income	2546090	1049480	2416621	4194948	3024300	2499776	4110245	2237391	975096	23053947
3.	Average Income	44668.24	30867.06	54923.20	71100.81	57062.26	24269.67	216328.68	35514.14	54172.00	51230.99

realized by all the members has been worked out to Rs. 77,76,243. The total net income earned by the sample members is worked out to Rs. 24,16,621 and the average net income realized per member is accounted for Rs. 54,923.20. On the whole, an investment of Rs. 100 in sheep/goat farming provides a net benefit of Rs. 45.09 per year.

(3) The total cost of maintaining small business has been worked out to Rs. 1,01,46,009 and the total gross income realized by the 59 members involved in small business has been estimated at Rs. 1,43,40,957. The total net income earned by all the members is worked out to Rs. 41,94,948 and the average per member to Rs. 71,100.81 per year. On the whole, an investment of Rs. 100 in small business fetches a net return of Rs. 41.35 per year on an average. Petty business run by 53 SHG members has accounted for a cost of maintenance of Rs. 73,04,891 and it has fetched a total gross income of Rs. 1,03,29,191. The total net income earned by all the 53 members out of petty business has been accounted for Rs. 30,24,300 and the average per unit is worked out to Rs. 57062.26. The net return earned per an investment of Rs. 100 in petty business has been worked out to Rs. 41.4 per year.

(4) The average cost of maintaining and feeding milch animals is worked out to Rs. 47,17,259 and the gross income earned by 103 sample members engaged in milk production has been estimated at Rs. 72,17,035. The total net income earned out of milk production is accounted for Rs. 24,99,776 and the net income per annum per member is Rs. 24,269.67 on an average. An investment of Rs. 100 on milch animals could generate a net income of Rs. 52.99 on an average.

(5) Among all the micro-enterprise activities taken up by the sample members, hand loom or lace weaving is the most profitable activity which is undertaken by 19 sample members. The total cost of maintenance of handloom/lace weaving units is Rs. 10,71,153 and the total gross income to Rs. 51,81,398. The total net income realized by the members is Rs. 41,10,245 and the average net income per member is Rs. 2,16,328.68. An investment of Rs. 100 on handloom/lace weaving units provides a net income of Rs. 383.72. As many as 63 sample members maintains tailoring/laundry units. Maintaining the tailoring/laundry units accounts for a total cost of Rs. 35,53,838 per

annum. The total gross income reported by the 63 sample households is Rs. 57,91,229 and the total net income is Rs. 22,37,391. On an average, a net income of Rs. 35,514.14 has been realized by each member. The net benefit realized by the member per investment of Rs. 100 on tailoring and laundry units is worked out to Rs. 62.96 per year.

(6) Among the sample members, 18 members have reported other activities. The total cost of production/maintenance is Rs. 31,58,815 and the total gross income earned is Rs. 41,33,911. The total net income is accounted for Rs. 9,75,096 and the average per unit for Rs. 54,172.00. The net income earned out of an investment of Rs. 100 in other activities is estimated at Rs. 30.87 per year.

The average income per household undertaking different micro-enterprise activities is presented in Table 10.2. The Table 10.2 analyses the impact of different micro-enterprises on income generation of sample households and the results are given below the Table 10.2.

Table 10.2: The average income per household of sample households undertaking different micro-enterprise activities through SHGs

Sl. No.	*Name of the Micro-enterprises*	*No. of SHG Members*	*Income excluding MEA*	*Income from MEA*	*Income per household*	*% of income from MEA*	*% of Income increased due to MEA*
1.	Milk Vending	57	37255.89	44668.24	81924.13	54.52	119.89
2.	Flower Vending	34	28029.40	30867.06	58896.14	52.41	110.13
3.	Sheep/Goat Rearing	44	18000.00	54923.20	72923.20	75.31	305.13
4.	Small Business	59	15538.98	71100.81	86639.79	82.06	457.54
5.	Petty Business	53	16891.31	57062.26	73953.57	77.16	337.83
6.	Milk Production	103	32732.73	24269.67	57002.40	42.58	74.14
7.	Handloom/lace Weaving	19	16894.74	216328.68	233223.42	92.76	1280.45
8.	Tailoring/laundry	63	30730.15	35514.14	66244.20	53.61	115.57
9.	Other activities	18	5499.99	54172.00	59671.99	90.78	984.96
	All Activities	450	25351.32	5123100	76582.32	66.90	202.08

Note: MEA–Micro-enterprise Activities.

(1) As many as 57 SHG members have taken up milk vending as micro-enterprise. The average income of the househoids excluding micro-enterprise income is accounted for

Rs. 37,255.89 and the income from micro-enterprise is worked out to Rs. 44,668.24 registering an increase of income by 119.89 per cent. The percentage of income from micro-enterprise works out to 54.52.

(2) The average income of 34 sample households who have undertaken flower vending as micro-enterprise excluding micro-enterprise income is worked out for Rs. 28,029.40 and the income from micro-enterprise is worked out to Rs. 30,867.06 registering an increase of income by 110.13 per cent. The percentage of income from micro-enterprise in the average total income works out to 52.41.

(3) A total of 44 sample members engaged in sheep/goat rearing as micro-enterprise indicate that the average income excluding micro-enterprise income is accounted for Rs. 18000 and the income from micro-enterprise is worked out to Rs. 54,923.20 registering an increase of income by 305.13 per cent. The percentage of income from micro-enterprise works out to 75.31.

(4) As many as 59 SHG have taken up small business as micro-enterprise. The average income per household excluding micro-enterprise income is worked out to Rs. 15,538.98 and the income from micro-enterprise is accounted for Rs. 71,100.81 registering an increase of income by 457.54 per cent. The percentage of income from micro-enterprise in average total income is worked out to 82.06.

(5) About 53 sample members who maintained petty shops as micro-enterprise from assistance provided by SHGs shows that the average income of the household excluding micro-enterprise income is accounted for Rs. 16,891.31. The income from micro-enterprise is estimated to Rs. 57,062.26 registering an increase of income by 337.83 per cent and the income from micro-enterprise in the average income is worked out to 77.16 per cent.

(6) The average income excluding of micro-enterprise income of 103 sample households who have undertaken milk production as micro-enterprise has been estimated at Rs. 32,732.73. The income from micro-enterprise is accounted for Rs. 24,269.67 indicating an increase of income by 74.14 per cent. The percentage of income from micro-enterprise in the average total income is worked out to 42.58.

(7) As many as 19 SHG members have taken up handloom/lace

weaving as micro-enterprise. The average income per household excluding micro-enterprise income is accounted for Rs. 16894.74 and the income from micro-enterprise is worked out to Rs. 2,16,328.68 showing an increase of income by 1,280.45 per cent. The percentage of income from micro-enterprise in the total income per household works out to 92.76.

(8) The average income of 63 sample households who maintain tailoring/laundry units as the micro-enterprise excluding micro-enterprise income is worked out for Rs. 30,730.15. The income from micro-enterprise is accounted for Rs. 35,514.14 recording an increase of income by 115.57 per cent. The percentage of income from micro-enterprise in the average total income is estimated at 53.61.

(9) The 18 sample households who have taken up other micro-enterprise activities have reported an average income of the households excluding micro-enterprise income is Rs. 5,499.99. The income from micro-enterprise is accounted for Rs. 54172.00 showing an increase of income by 984.96 per cent.

Among all the micro-enterprise activities undertaken by the SHG members, milk production was taken up by a large number of members. The average income from all sources of 103 sample households undertaking milk production from SHG assistance is estimated at Rs. 57,002.40. Out of the income from all sources, income from milk production is Rs. 24,269.67 per household accounting for 42.57 per cent of the average income of all sources.

Handloom/lace weaving activity appears to be high income yielding than other micro-enterprise activities which was undertaken by 19 sample households and their average income from all sources per household is worked out to Rs. 2,33,223.42. Out of the average income as much as 92.76 per cent is from micro-enterprise alone which has fetched an average income of Rs. 2,16,328.68 per household.

On the whole, out of the average income per household of Rs. 76,582.32, micro-enterprise is the major source of income fetching a net income of Rs. 51,230.99 accounting for 66.90 per cent of the income from all sources. This shows the positive impact of micro-enterprises on the income generation of poor households. Of the various types of micro-enterprises handloom/lace weaving has accounted for maximum average income per household of Rs. 2,16,328.68 followed by small business with a net income of Rs. 71,100.81, petty business fetching an income of Rs. 57,062.26 and sheep/goat rearing yielding an income of Rs. 54,923.20.

The sample respondents were interviewed on the problem they face in the organization of the micro-enterprise undertaken through SHGs. A majority (56.67%) of the sample members reported that they have not faced any problems in the organization of micro-enterprise. About 43.33 per cent of them expressed that they had to face some problems in the organization of micro-enterprises.

Among the sample members who have reported problems, 89.74 per cent have reported maintaining as a problem, 85 per cent expressed the problem of less production, 64.10 per cent reported the problem of non-availability of inputs and 52.32 per cent expressed less net income as the problem.

A majority (93.11%) of the total sample consider that the micro-enterprises undertaken by them are more relevant to women and have positive attitude as far as the relevance of micro-enterprises to women is concern, hundred per cent reported that it helped the poor in raising their family income, 94.99 per cent expressed it increases the earning capacities of women, 93.08 per cent reported that it enhances the additional employment opportunities by utilizing ideal women labour. Those who come under the category of any other reason constitute about 57 per cent of the total sample. The reasons under any other category are: helpful to increases the economic and social status, developing skills, giving motivation, capacity building, improving literacy rate etc.

Conclusions

Micro-financial activities of SHGs are able to provide women a means to overcome the problem of poverty. Micro-finance could be a solution to help them to extend their horizon and offer them social recognition and empowerment. Steps should be taken to increase literacy level of women and making them aware about women rights and entitlements. Literacy and numeric training is needed for the poor women to benefit from the micro-credit schemes. The members should be given necessary training and guidance for the successful operation of the micro-enterprise. There is a need for establishing a computerized Management Information System for SHGs to monitor their performance on a regular basis.

Proper marketing support is required to the old SHGs and infrastructure facilities to the newly formed SHGs. Steps should be taken for imparting more training to SHGs on book keeping, leadership, decision-making and organization micro-enterprises. State level federations should be formed by the government for promoting marketing tie up. Marketing facilities for the sale of products of SHG may be created. Periodical exhibitions may be organized where the products of SHG can be displayed. These steps help to improve institutional capacity to handle marketing activities independently.

The micro-enterprise activities undertaken by the women members through SHGs have improved the socio-economic conditions as well as participation of women in decision-making and contributed for the empowerment of women in the state. It made a silent revolution in the rural womenfolk by enabling them to become self-dependant and self-reliant, providing a forum for members for discussing their socio-economic problems and equipping women with basic skills required for money transaction. On the whole, the micro-enterprise activities undertaken by the members ensure for women empowerment in dimensions which include economic, social and political empowerment and of course in psychological empowerment of women.

However, the following conclusions emerge out of the results of the study. The results provide ample evidence to confirm that the micro-credit programmes through self-help groups have positive impact on generation of income and on providing gainful employment especially to rural women who remain idle or unemployed. The additional income generated by the micro-enterprises enable them to come out of the poverty level. Added to this, the micro-credit programmes through self-help groups promotes savings among rural women. In fine, the micro-credit programmes through self-help groups are the very suitable instruments for empowerment of women.

References

Aruna Goel, (2009), *Women Empowerment: Myth and Reality*, Deep and Deep Publications, New Delhi, p. vii.

Leelamma Devasia and James Antony, (2004), "Social Development Issues in SHGs", *Social Welfare*, January, p. 4.

Sreelakshamma, K., (2008), *Empowerment of Women in India*, Serials Publications, New Delhi, p. viii.

Sreelakshmamma, K., *Empowerment of Women in India*, *op. cit.*, pp. 27-29.

11
The Status and Specific Impacts of MGNREGP on Rural Masses

B. Ananda Naidu

Introduction

The grim unemployment situation in India led to the introduction of several wage employment programmes since India's Independence in 1947. The Central and various State Governments introduced several wage employment and self-employment programmes from time to time to mitigate the unemployment situation in India. The erstwhile wage employment programmes suffered with several defects and at the same time the Central and State governments allocations for the implementations of these programmes are inadequate. Moreover, no wage employment programme guaranteed certain number of days of employment to rural households. So, the MGNREGS is unique in its content as well as statutory status. It is the Scheme which legally guaranteed hundred days of employment to all households irrespective of their social and economic status.

Soon after the formation of the Government by United Progressive Alliance (UPA) in 2004, an agenda for governance was set through the National Common Minimum Programme (NCMP) with regard to poverty alleviation and rural prosperity/development. It is envisaged in the NCMP that the UPA's economic reforms will be oriented primarily to spreading and deepening rural prosperity, to significantly improving the quality of public systems and delivery of public services to bring about a visible and tangible difference in the quality of life of ordinary citizens of the country. To achieve the objectives of spreading and developing of rural prosperity, generation of employment, augmenting and modernization of rural infrastructure, including roads, housing for the weaker sections in the rural areas and providing drinking water to all sections and strengthening of livelihood in rural areas were highlighted. With this agenda, a conference of Chief Ministers was convened by the Ministry of Rural Development on 29-30th June, 2004, so that a collective effort is made to achieve the objectives for which a road map was outlined in the NCMP. The theme of the conference was "Poverty alleviation and rural prosperity through Panchayati Raj Institutions".

In accordance with the priorities set in the NCMP the programmes of Ministry of Rural Development were reviewed. A new ambitious programme like National Rural Employment Guarantee Scheme was initiated and other programmes of Ministry of Rural Development were consolidated, modified and restructured. The National Rural Employment Guarantee Act, 2005 was notified in September 2005. The programme was launched on February 2nd, 2006 in 200 districts in the first phase all over India.

The launch of MGNREGS by the Central Government is guided by the successful implementation of the Maharashtra Employment Guarantee Scheme (MEGS), which has been implemented for three decades in Maharashtra, where the demand for unskilled wage work is not declined. The MGNREGS is not a new wage employment programme. There are several such programmes before this Scheme. But the previous employment programmes were not adequate in fulfilling the demands of rural poor. The experiences gained in implementation of different wage employment programmes like National Rural Employment Programme (NREP, 1980), Rural Landless Employment Guarantee Programme (RLEGP, 1983), Jawahar Rozgar Yojana (JRY, 1989), Employment Assurance Schemes (EAS, 1993), Jawahar Gram Samridhi Yojana (1999), Sampooran Grameen Rozgar Yojana (2001) and National Food For Work Programme (NFFWP, 2004) during the past three decades, were also taken into account while formulating the Act. With the launch of the Mahatma Gandhi National Rural Employment Guarantee Act (MGNREGA) on 2nd February, 2006, entire NFWP programme was subsumed into it. SGRY programme in 200 districts was also subsumed into MGNREGA in the first phase in 2006-07. SGRY programme in additional 130 districts was subsumed into MGNREGA in the second phase in 2007-08. The entire SGRY programme was subsumed into MGNREGA with effect from 1st April, 2008.

Objectives of the Study

The specific objectives of the study are as follows:

1. To discuss the need, importance and features of MGNREG Programme.
2. To examine the performance angle of the MGNREG Programme in Ananthapuram district.
3. To assess the impact of MGNREG Programme on selected beneficiaries in Ananthapuram district, and
4. To evaluate the achievements and failures of the MGNREG Programme and to offer some suggestions for the proper implementation of the programme.

Sampling

The MGNREG programme has been extended to all sections of the society irrespective economic social and political status of rural families. All the revenue villages, hamlets in the district are covered by the programme. For effective study of the impact of the programme on beneficiaries, a purposive random sampling method was followed. For the collection of respondents views and ideas on the impact of the MGNREG Programme, one Gram Panchayat from each of the three revenue divisions were selected by taking into account the financial, caste, demographic factors of the beneficiaries. From each selected Gram Panchayat 40 beneficiaries were by purposive random sampling technique. So the universe of the sample constitutes 120.

Coverage of Districts under MGNREGP

The MGNREG Act is applicable to areas notified by the Central Government. In its first phase, it was notified in 200 districts across the country. In the second phase the Act has been notified in the financial year 2007-08 in an additional 130 districts, bringing the total of number of districts covered by MGNREGA to 330. In these districts, pre-existing wage employment programmes, the National Food For Work Programme (NFFWP) and the Sampoorna Grameen Rozgar Yojana (SGRY) were merged with NREGA. The remaining rural areas of the country have been notified on 28th September, 2007 where NREGA will come into force w.e.f. 1st April, 2008. The Table 11.1 gives a clear picture of state wise coverage of districts under three phases of MGNREGP implementation.

Table 11.1: Phase-wise Districts notified under Mahatma Gandhi National Employment Guarantee Act

S. No.	*Name of the State/UT*	*Phase I*	*Phase II*	*Phase III*	*Total*
1.	Madhya Pradesh	18	13	19	50
2.	Odisha	19	5	6	30
3.	Bihar	23	15		38
4.	Andhra Pradesh	13	6	3	22
5.	West Bengal	10	7	2	19
6.	Jharkhand	20	2	2	24
7.	Chattisgarh	11	4	3	18
8.	Maharashtra	12	6	15	33
9.	Gujarat	6	3	17	26
10.	Rajasthan	6	6	21	33
11.	Dadra and Nagar Haveli	0	0	1	1
12.	Goa	0	0	2	2
13.	Meghalaya	2	3	2	7
14.	Arunachal Pradesh	1	2	13	16
15.	Nagaland	1	4	6	11
16.	Manipur	1	2	6	9
17.	Mizoram	2	2	4	8
18.	Tripura	1	2	1	4
19.	Sikkim	1	2	1	4
20.	Assam	7	6	14	27
21.	Himachal Pradesh	2	2	8	12
22.	Uttar Pradesh	22	17	32	71
23.	Uttaranchal	3	2	8	13
24.	Jammu & Kashmir	3	2	17	22
25.	Karnataka	5	6	19	30
26.	Kerala	2	2	10	14
27.	Tamil Nadu	6	4	21	31
28.	Andaman and Nicobar Islands	0	0	3	3
29.	Lakshadweep	0	0	1	1
30.	Puducherry	0	0	2	2
31.	Punjab	1	3	16	20
32.	Haryana	2	2	17	21
33.	Daman and Diu	0	0	2	2
34.	Chandigarh	0	0	1	2
	Total	200	130	295	625

Source: Ministry of Rural Development, Government of India.

Salient Features of the MGNREG Act

The responsibility of implementation of the scheme lies with the states as the states have been given the responsibility to prepare, finalize and approve the schemes of 'shelf of projects' (annual action plans) which ensure 100 days of guaranteed manual unskilled employment to every rural household who is willing to work. The plan prepared will be given wide publicity through local newspapers for the generation of awareness among the people. Following are the salient features of the MGNREGP.

1. **Registration of Employment Seekers:** The registration of employment seekers will be made at the Gram Panchayat level along with their full particulars. After a proper enquiry for a period of at least five years. A job card will be issued with photograph. The employment seekers will submit their applications to the Sarpanch of the Gram Panchayat or the Programme Officer at the Block level.
2. **Availability of Employment Opportunities:** At least 100 days of employment in financial year will be provided to all adult members of a registered family taken together in a financial year, who are willing to do unskilled manual work in such a manner that one-third opportunities are available to women. However, there is no upper ceiling on the number of days of employment. The programme officer at the block level will be responsible for making available the manual work within 15 days of the application. The job seeker will have to work together for not less than a fortnight thereby that he/she will continuously work for at least 15 days at a given point of time. An advance application can also be made for the employment. The intimation for offering employment shall be given in writing and through public notice.
3. **Minimum Requirement for Starting a New Work:** If the job seekers cannot be absorbed on the ongoing work, minimum 50 applicants are required for starting a new work. There has to be perfect liaison between Gram Panchayat and Programme Officer for success of the scheme.
4. **Provision of Wage:** At the National level average minimum wage rate will be Rs. 60 per man-day though it has been left to the State Governments to fix wage rates in the state, which shall be equal to seven hours of working. The disbursement of wage shall be made weekly, but not later than a fortnight. In case the work site is beyond 5 km of radius, then the applicant will be entitled to 10 per cent extra wages for travelling allowance.

5. **Wage-Material Ratio:** The cost of material component of works including wage to skilled and semi-skilled workers will be restricted to 40 per cent of the total project cost.
6. **Institutional Mechanism:** The MGNREG Act envisages separate mechanism for the proper implementation of the scheme. For this purpose a separate mechanism from Central level to village level is arranged.

Objectives of the Programme

The following are the important objectives of the MGNREGP:

- The primary objective of the Scheme is to provide livelihood security to the households in rural areas, in notified districts by providing not less than 100 (one hundred) days of guaranteed wage employment in every financial year to every household, whose adult members volunteer to do unskilled and manual work.
- Creation of durable assets and strengthening the livelihood resource base of the rural poor.
- If an applicant is not provided with such employment within 15 days of receipt of his/her application seeking employment or from the date on which the employment has been sought in the case of an advance application whichever is later, he/she shall be entitled to daily unemployment allowance subject to the entitlement of the household at the rate which shall not be less than one fourth of the wage rate for the first 30 (thirty) days of the financial year and not less than one half of the wage rate for the remaining period of the financial year.
- As far as possible the applicant shall be provided work within the village. If an applicant is provided employment outside a radius of five kilometers of the village where he/she resides at the time of applying he/she should be paid an extra 10 per cent of the prevailing wage rate to meet additional transportation and living expenses.
- Priority shall be given to women in such a way that at least one-third of the wage seekers shall be women who have registered themselves and requested for work.
- In case the payment of wages is not made within a fortnight, the workers shall be entitled to receive payment of compensation as per the provisions of the Payment of Wages Act 1936 (Act 4 of 1936).

- There shall be no discrimination solely on the ground of gender and the provisions of the Equal Remuneration Act of 1976 (Act 25 of 1976) shall be complied with.
- Workers are entitled for work site amenities like safe drinking water, shade for children and periods of rest, first-aid box with adequate material for emergency treatment of minor injuries and other health and occupational hazards.
- If the number of children below the age of six years accompanying the women, working at any site is five or more, one woman worker shall be engaged to look after such children and she shall be paid wage rate.
- Any injury caused to a person employed under the Scheme by accident arising out of and in the course of his/her employment, such person is entitled to medical treatment free of charge.
- Where hospitalization of the injured worker at the worksite is necessary, such arrangements shall be made including accommodation, treatment and medicines. The injured worker shall be paid daily allowance not less than half of the wage rate required to be paid had the injured been engaged in the work.
- If the person employed dies or becomes permanently disabled by accident arising out of and in the course of employment, he/she shall be paid an ex-gratia at the rate of Rs. 25,000 or such amount as may be notified by the Central Government, and the amount shall be paid to the disabled or legal heirs of the deceased, as the case may be; and
- Any personal injury caused by accident to a child accompanying any person employed under the Scheme, such person is entitled to free of charge medical treatment for the child and in case of death or disablement, an ex-gratia as determined by the government.

Expansion and Growth of MGNREGP in India

The Act is applicable to areas/districts notified by the Central Government from time to time. In these districts, pre-existing wage employment programmes, the National Food For Work Programme (NFFWP) and the Sampoorna Grameen Rozgar Yojana (SGRY) were merged with NREGA. MGNREGA has provided basic income security to a large number of beneficiaries. It provided employment to around 5 crore households, on an average, every year. This is almost one-fourth of the total rural households in the country. Since, its inception Mahatma Gandhi NREGA has generated 1575 crore man days of employment up to December, 2013. From financial year 2006-07 up to financial year 2013-14 (up to December 2013) over Rs. 1,55,000 crore has been spent on wages. This is almost 70 per cent of the total expenditure. The Scheme's notified wages have increased across all States since 2006. The average wage earned per beneficiary has risen from Rs. 65 per man day in 2006 to Rs. 124 by 2013. Table 11.2 gives the progress of the scheme in India during the last eight years.

It is evident from the Table 11.2 that during eight years of MGNREGP implementation the number of households benefited by the scheme is more than double. To be more precise in 2006-07 2.10 crore households were benefited and by 2012-13 it increased to 4.98 crore households. The man days are also doubled. The participation rate of Scheduled Castes ranges between 22 to 31 per cent. On the other hand, the participation rate of Scheduled Tribes ranges from 16 to 36 per cent. Comparing to above two social categories the participation rate of women is high, which ranges from 40 to 54 per cent. The average person days per households gradually increased during first four years of study. But it decreased during 2010-2011. The total work under taken under the scheme is increased more than 13 times during eight years of study. On the other hand, work completion rate increased less than three times. The cause for poor work completion rate can be attributed to disputes with regard to some specific works, lack of coordination etc. Among the completed works high percentage of works are undertaken for water conservation. Around 10 to 20 per cent of completed works, irrigation works for SCs and STs were taken up. Rural connectivity works and land development works ranges from 10 to 21 per cent and 11 to 16 per cent respectively. Various provisions under the Act and its Guidelines aim to ensure that women have equitable and easy access to work, decent working conditions, equal payment of wages and representation on decision-making bodies. From financial year 2006-07 up to financial year 2013-14 (up to December 2013) the women participation rate has ranged between 40-51 per cent of the total person days generated, much above the statutory minimum requirement of 33 per cent. In the current financial year, 2013-14, (up to December, 2013) 3.8 crore households were provided employment and 135 crore Man days of employment were generated. In the current financial year, 2013-14, Rs. 17,832 crore (76% of the total expenditure) has been on wages. As in each of the previous years, the programme had high work participation for marginalized groups like SC/ST (39%), in 2013-14 (up to December, 2013).

Table 11.2: Growth of MGNREGP in India during the years 2006-07–2013-14

Year	*2006-07*	*2008-09*	*2008-09*	*2009-10*	*20 10-11*	*20 11-12*	*20 12-13*	*2013-1-4) (till Dec., 13)*
Total Job Card Issued (in crores)	3.78	6.48	10.01	11.25	11.98	12.5	12.79	12.72
Employment ovided to households (in crores)	2.1	3.39	4.51	5.26	5.49	5.06	4.98	3.81
Man days (in crores)								
Total:	90.5	143.59	216.32	283.59	257.15	218.76	229.86	134.8
SCs	22.95 (25%)	39.36 (27%)	63.36 (29%)	86.45 (30%)	78.76 (31%)	48.47 22%)	50.96 (22%)	31.53 (23%)
STs	32.98 (36%)	42.07 (29%)	55.02 (25%)	58.74 (21%)	53.62 (21%)	40.92 (19%)	40.75 (18%)	21.09 (16%)
Women	36.4 (40%)	61.15 (43%)	103.57 (48%)	136.4 (48%)	122.74 (48%)	105.27 (48%)	117.93 (51%)	73.33 (54%)
Others	34.56 (38%)	62.16 (43%)	97.95 (45%)	138.4 (49%)	124.78 (48%)	129.38 (59%)	138.14 (60%)	82.18 (61%)
Man days per HH (Days)	43	42	48	54	47	43	46	35
Budget Outlay (in Rs crores)	11300	12000	30000	39100	40100	40000	33000	33000
Central Release (in Rs crores)	8640.85	12610.39	29939.6	33506.61	35768.95	29189.77	30009.96	29885.92
Total available fund (including OB) in Rs. crores.	12073.55	19305.81	37397.06	49579.19	54172.14	48805.68	45051.43	37084.76
Expenditure (in Rs. crores.) (% against Available funds)	8823.35 (73%)	15856.89 (82%)	27250.1 (73%)	37905.23 (76%)	39377.27 (73%)	37072.82 (76%)	39657.04 (88%)	24848.75 (67%)
Expenditure on Wages (in Rs. crores)	5842.37 (66%)	10738.47 (68%)	18200.03 (67%)	25579.32 (70%)	25686.53 (68%)	24306.22 (70%)	27128.36 (72%)	17832.19 (76%)
Total works taken up (in lakhs)	8.35	17.88	27.75	46.17	50.99	80.77	106.51	111.64
Works completed (in lakhs)	3.87	8.22	12.14	22.59	25.9	27.56	25.6	11.17
Works break up (in lakhs)								
Water conservation	4.51 (54%)	8.73 (49 %)	12.79 (46%)	23.43 (51%)	24.26 (48%)	48.81 (60%)	49.26 (46%)	45.41 (41%)
Works on individuals land	0.81 (10%)	2.63 (15 %)	5.67 (20%)	7.73 (17%)	9.15 (18%)	9.16 (11%)	11.81 (11%)	12.62 (11%)
Rural Connectivity	1.8 (21%)	3.08 (17 %)	5.03 (18%)	7.64 (17%)	9.31 (18%)	13.86 (17%)	13.04 (12%)	12.62 (11%)
Land Development	0.89 (11%)	2.88 (16%)	3.98 (5%)	6.38 (4%)	7.04 (4%)	6.32 (8%)	6.58 (6%)	5.78 (5%)
Any other activity	0.34 (4%)	0.56 (3%)	0.28 (1%)	0.98 (2%)	1.06 (2%)	2.31 (3%)	9.87 (9%)	9.65 (9%)
Rajiv Gandhi Seva Kendra	—	—	—	—	0.17 (0.33%)	0.29 (0.36%)	0.3 (0.28%)	0.29 (0.26%)
Coastal Areas	—	—	—	—	—	—	0.00061 (0.001%)	0.00407 (0.004%)
Rural Drinking Water	—	—	—	—	—	—	0.03062 (0.03%)	0.08757 (0.08%)
Fisheries	—	—	—	—	—	—	0.02791 (0.03%)	0.03508 (0.03%)
Rural Sanitation	—	—	—	—	—	—	15.59 (15%)	25.12 (23%)
Aanganwadi	—	—	—	—	—	—	—	0.00664 (0.01%)
Play Ground	—	—	—	—	—	—	—	0.00876 (0.01%)

Source: http://nrega.nic.in

Around 111.64 lakh works were undertaken (including new works as well as spill-over works from the previous FY), of which 41 per cent relate to water conservation, 23 per cent for the provision of rural sanitation, 11 per cent relate to works on land owned by SC/ST/BPL, IAY beneficiaries, small farmers or marginal farmers as defined in the Agriculture Debt Waiver and debt relief schemes or beneficiaries under the Scheduled Tribes and other traditional forest dwellers (Recognition of Forest Rights Act, 2006), 11 per cent rural connectivity and 5 per cent for land development.

MGNREGP in Andhra Pradesh

The implementation of NREGA calls for the formulation of Rural Employment Guarantee Scheme by the State Governments. The Scheme so formulated would have to provide for the minimum features specified in Schedule-I of the Act and may prescribe conditions, which are without prejudice to the conditions specified in Schedule-II of the Act. Accordingly, the Government of Andhra Pradesh has formulated the rules and regulations for the implementation of the Scheme on 28th January, 2006 to provide not less than one hundred days of guaranteed wage employment in a financial year to every household in rural areas covered under the scheme and whose adult members volunteer to do unskilled manual work subject to the conditions stipulated in the Act.

Expansion of MGNREGP in Andhra Pradesh

The MGNREGP was extended to all 22 rural districts of Andhra Pradesh in a phased manner. Table 11.3 gives the phase-wise expansion of the programme in the state.

Table 11.3: Phase-wise Coverage of Districts under MGNREGP in Andhra Pradesh

Sl. No.	*Phases*	*Month and Year*	*Districts Covered*
1.	Phase-I	February 2006	Adilabad, Anantapuram, Chittoor, Kadapa, Karimnagar, Khamam, Mahabubnagar, Medak, Nalgonda, Nizamabad, Vijayanagaram, Warangal
2.	Phase-II	May 2007	East Godavari, Kurnool, Guntur, Nellore, Prakasam and Srikakuklam.
3.	Phase-III	April 2008	Krishna, Visakhapatnam, West Godavari.

Source: Ministry of Rural Development, Government of Andhra Pradesh.

The Table 11.3 shows that during the first phase the MGNREGP was launched in 13 districts of Andhra Pradesh, out of which all nine districts are from Telangana region of the state. In Rayalaseema region 3 districts and in coastal Andhra only one district was covered. The fundamental reason for the inclusion of large number of districts in Telangana and Rayalaseema region is that these districts are not well developed, when compared to other coastal districts of the state. During the second phase the scheme extended to 6 districts of the state, in which 5 districts are from coastal Andhra and one from Rayalaseema region. In the last phase 3 districts of coastal Andhra were covered under the scheme. In all 22 out of 23 districts were covered by the scheme. As this scheme is intended to provide employment for the rural poor, the district of Hyderabad is not covered under this scheme.

Caste-wise Beneficiaries

The MGNREGP aims at bringing economic equality by giving large share of access and opportunity to the disadvantaged and economically weaker sections of the society, such as Scheduled Castes, Scheduled Tribes and Below Poverty Line (BPL) households. The Table 11.4 gives the caste wise employment details of beneficiaries in Andhra Pradesh.

As shown in Table 11.4 the number of households working under MGNREGP in the state has gradually increased during first four years of study in case of all social categories except minorities. During the eight years of its implementation the percentage of registered households remained same in case of all social categories. With regard to total wages as well as number of person days more or less same trends could be noticed in case of different social categories.

Number of Days of Household Employment

By providing hundred days of work to a rural household, the Act provides an income supplement for poor households. The NREGA wage is critical in this MGNREGA offered nearly hundred days of work and the Scheme's impact on the labour market was substitutive; it drew a sizeable, mostly female, workforce away from agriculture and to make up, farm wages had to go up 50-70 per cent. Table 11.5 gives a clear picture of man days provided for each household.

It is evident from Table 11.5 that the number of households availing statutory hundred days of employment never exceeded 21.74 per cent in

Table **11.4**: Caste-wise Household Employment Analysis in Andhra Pradesh

Particulars	*2006-07*	*2007-08*	*2008-09*	*2009-10*	*2010-11*	*2011-12*	*2012-13*
BC-No of Regd., HHs	6380635	6380635	6380635	6380635	6380635	6380635	6380635
BC-No of working HHs	1038619	2298593	2810805	3054440	3015645	2385884	2890569
BC-Total wage (Rs. in lakhs)	24441.87	78453.47	92145.41	176465.35	144856.6	123129.9	168787.3
BC-Days worked	30086700	95207310	112197101.5	197049722	152166217	129708361	163420816
SC-No of Regd., HHs	3243014	3243014	3243014	3243014	3243014	3243014	3243014
SC-No of working HHs	625053	1252036	1478032	1539380	1505964	1300971	1449235
SC-Total wage (Rs. in lakhs)	15443.91	45153.25	48117.76	84292.82	67104.03	74081.88	79496.36
SC-Days worked	19136195	54790252	58326943	94323554	70533004	76801872	75982786
ST-No of Regd., HHs	1515348	1515348	1515348	1515348	1515348	1515348	1515348
ST-No of working HHs	288212	560055	695532	773687	764693	647061	739056
ST-Total wage (Rs. in lakhs)	6814.15	21190.55	24290.87	52922.01	47061.54	50490.95	53144.47
ST-Days worked	8269458	25472836	28969036	56726486	46435269	50435095	48754014
Minorities-No of Regd., HHs	180687	180687	180687	180687	180687	180687	180687
Minorities-No of working HHs	18152	43080	59922	63429	67726	56914	68441
Minorities-Total wage (Rs. in lakhs)	504.78	1795.44	2355.08	3785.62	3343.89	2965.42	3606.05
Minorities-Days worked	602540.5	2128958	2779743	4191903	3511992	3071399	3428714
Others-No of Regd., HHs	2186452	2186452	2186452	2186452	2186452	2186452	2186452
Others-No of working HHs	222914	574330	719657	708664	701733	542014	667829
Others-Total wage (Rs. in lakhs)	6440.23	19159.07	21382.45	35327.02	29841.63	26385.46	35429.39
Others-Days worked	8037733	23563690	26033194	39909158	31702269	27421016	34003066

Source: Ministry of Rural Development, Government of Andhra Pradesh.

Table 11.5: Distribution of Households by person days of Employment provided under MGNREGP in Andhra Pradesh

Year	*No. of HHs working*	*No. of HHs completed 100 days*	*No. of HHs completed 75-100 days*	*No. of HHs completed 50-75 days*	*No. of HHs completed < 50 days*	*Total Wage (Rs. in Lakhs)*	*Avg. Wage per Day*	*Avg. Days of Employ-Provided per HH*
2006-07	2174798	67242	69175	174793	1863588	53140.12	81.09	30.13
2007-08	4685014	410526	288818	551974	3433696	163956.4	82.38	42.48
2008-09	5704026	481097	357115	694790	4171024	185936.5	82.45	39.54
2009-10	6078836	1321236	577645	844240	3335715	349233.2	89.95	63.8
2010-11	6225241	963695	626087	1016971	3618488	324997.1	96.98	53.83
2011-12	5006979	973647	481590	734456	2817286	289356.6	97.19	59.46
2012-13	5811230	1046490	672928	1008303	3083509	346916.3	105.14	56.78

Source: Ministry of Rural Development, Government of Andhra Pradesh.

the State. In 2008-09 only 8.43 per cent of households got 100 days of employment in Andhra Pradesh. On the other hand more than half of the households got less than 50 days of employment during all the 7 years of study. The households which got 75 to 100 days of employment ranges between 3.18 per cent to 11.58 per cent. The number households which got 50 to 75 days of employment in 2006-07 is 8.04 per cent and they increased to 17.35 per cent by 2012-2013. The total wage amount gradually increased during first four years of study. It is welcome move to note that the average wage per day is showing upward trend in the State. The average days of employment provided to households is also encouraging.

Progress Made under MGNREGP in Ananthapuram District

Ananthapuram District, which is located in the Rayalaseema region, is the biggest and driest of all the drought prone districts of A.P. In this district it is clearly estimated that the droughts occur at least thrice in a decade. The Irrigation Commission and other Central Commissions have been identified the whole district as drought prone. This district is included as one of the districts as pilot districts for undertaking welfare activities. A single dry crop i.e. ground nut is raised under rain fed conditions in most parts of the district. Agriculture is the main source of economy of the district. The work force engaged in agriculture is more than three fourth's of the total work force. The demand for labour in agriculture sector is highly uncertain and seasonal. This is leading to migration of labour in a large scale to the nearest cities. The drought conditions are creating an ecological imbalance and converting the district into a desert. Drought prone areas are more vulnerable to denude the forests and exhaust the natural resources like water, soil, minerals, etc. By result the rivers and other streams dry up. Consequently, the underground water levels vanish and the area under irrigation is declined. The instant result is the decrease in agriculture production. This is leading to food problem. All these uneven conditions are making the lives of agricultural labourers and farmers rigorous and not bearing. As a result numbers of farmers' suicides are reported in the district.

Keeping all the above facts in view the Government of India has decided to implement the ambitious MGNREGP in Ananthapuram district in the first phase itself. The programme was formally launched at Bandlapalli village of Ananthapuram district on 2nd February, 2006 by the former Prime Minister of India Mr. Manmohan Singh. In spite of

Table 11.6: Year-wise Household Wage Earners in Ananthapuram District

Year	*Household registered*		*Household working*	*Household total days*	*Household total wage (in lakhs)*	*Household avg. wage*
2006-07	7,65,815	29.63	2,26,919	90,50,874	8182.52	90.41
2007-08	7,65,815	45.79	3,50,645	1,74,55,903	14567	83.45
2008-09	7,65,815	41.17	3,15,255	1,35,98,280	11846.65	87.12
2009-10	7,65,815	44.80	3,43,079	2,35,46,692	22972.34	97.56
2010-11	7,65,815	38.49	2,94,758	1,49,00,126	15091.05	101.28
2011-12	7,65,815	30.27	2,31,842	1,89,01,004	20181.73	106.78
2012-13	7,65,815	34.66	2,65,421	1,78,72,559	21305.05	119.21
2013-14	7,65,815	34.84	2,66,794	1,63,59,322	20495.37	125.28

Source: District Water Management Agency, Ananthapuram.

many other schemes under taken for the betterment of rural poor, it is the only programme that has mobilized the rural folk involvement.

Household Wage Earning Analysis

Table 11.6 gives the details of year-wise household wage and wage seekers in Ananthapuram District.

Table 11.6 indicates that the numbers of registered households in the district are constant throughout eight years of study. Among the registered households, the per cent of working households ranges between 29.63 per cent to 45.79 per cent. It means that the working households never crossed at least 50 per cent mark in the district. The total number of household days reached from 90,50,874 to 2,35,46,692 days by 2009-10. But they declined to 1,49,00,126 in 2010-11, and again increased to 1,89,01,004 days in 2011-12. The gradual decrease can be observed in next two years also. The average wage per household in 2006-07 is Rs. 90.41 and it gradually increased and reached the highest point of Rs. 125.28 by 2013-14.

Household Employment

The NREGA guarantees 100 days of employment in a financial year for all rural households. Table 11.7 gives a clear picture of person days provided for each household.

It is crystal clear from Table 11.7 that the households who worked for statutory minimum 100 days are not evenly distributed in the district. The per cent of households which got less than 50 days of employment is

Table 11.7: Distribution of Households by person days of Employment provided under MGNREGP in Ananthapuram District

Year	*No. of HHs working*	*No. of HHs completed 100 days*	*No. of HHs completed 75-100 days*	*No. of HHs completed 50-75 days*	*No. of HHs completed < 50 days*	*Total Wage (Rs in Lakhs)*	*Avg. Wage per Day*	*Avg. Days of Employ-Provided per HH*
2006-07	2,26,919	13,773	12,446	26,457	1,74,243	8,113.57	90.4	39.55
2007-08	3,50,645	34,183	29,102	53,308	2,34,052	14,419.82	83.45	49.28
2008-09	3,15,255	26,064	24,225	45,878	2,19,088	11,715.76	87.11	42.66
2009-10	3,43,130	80,766	36,386	52,264	1,73,714	22,706.34	97.55	67.83
2010-11	3,46,736	61,592	39,558	58,336	1,87,250	20,672.03	102.4	58.22
2011-12	2,42,386	77,355	27,048	35,087	1,02,896	20,536.87	106.83	79.31
2012-13	2,71,579	69,415	38,446	47,294	1,16,424	21,496.32	119.32	66.34
2013-14	2,69,118	56,212	48,548	49,590	1,14,768	20,431.28	125.36	60.56

Source: District Water Management Agency, Ananthapuram.

gradually decreasing. On the other hand the per cent of households which got 100 days of employment, 75 to 100 days of employment and 50 to 75 days of employment are gradually increasing in the district. In 2006-07, around 6.07 households got minimum 100 days of employment. The average wage per day is also showing definite improvement in the district. It can be concluded that year by year there is improvement in number of man days of employment for each households under the MGNREGP.

Impact of MGNREGP on Wages

Since India's Independence Minimum Wages Act were passed by the Union as well as several State Governments. But in practice, these Acts were confined to papers, especially in rural India. After the launching of MGNREGP the Minimum Wages Act came in to lime light. After the implementation of MGNREGP, the daily wages for agricultural labour was automatically increased. But this increase is not universal. In some areas the old rates are still continuing. So, during the study the respondent's views with regard to increase or decrease of wages is ascertained and presented in the Table 11.8.

Table 11.8: Impact of MGNREGP on Daily Wages of Agricultural and Allied Activities Labourers

Sl. No.	*Amount of change*	*No. of Beneficiaries*	*Percentage of total*
1.	No Change	14	11.67
2.	Little Change	39	32.50
3.	Moderate Change	44	36.67
4.	Significant Change	12	10.00
5.	Change for Worse	3	2.50
6.	Don't Know	8	6.66
	Total	120	100.00

Source: Field Data.

The Table 11.8 indicates that nearly 79 per cent of respondents reported some amount of change in their daily wages after the initiation of MGNREGP. Among them 32.50 per cent reported little or insignificant change and 36.67 per cent reported significant change. Only 10 per cent reported significant change. Around 11.67 per cent reported neither positive nor negative improvement in wages. Only 2.50 per cent reported negative impact of MGNREGP on their daily wages. About 6.66 per cent denied to response.

Impact on Migration

Nearly three-fourths of the Indian agricultural/cultivable land is un irrigated. That is why agriculture in India is rightly considered as a gamble of monsoons. The yielding depends largely on rains. Besides, this large area under cropping in India is confined to only kharif season. So for nearly half of the year, the agricultural labour left without employment and which forces them to migrate to urban areas for work during un season. The fundamental motive behind launching various wage employment programmes is to limit the migration of labour in rural areas. The MGNREGP is also started with that motive. So, during the study the impact of MGNREGP on rural migration was ascertained and presented in the Table 11.9.

Table 11.9: Impact of MGNREGP on Migration of Rural Labour

Sl. No.	*Mode of Change*	*No. of Beneficiaries*	*Percentage of total*
1	Decreased	81	67.50
2	Increased	21	17.50
3	Don't Know	18	15.00
	Total	120	100.00

Source: Field Data.

A glance at the Table 11.9 makes it clear that 67.50 per cent of respondents reported that there is a gradual decline in the migration of labour after launching of MGNREGP. It is quite astonishing to note that nearly 17.50 per cent reported negative impact of MGNREGP on rural migration. They reported that the wages which they are getting under the MGNREGP is not sufficient to meet their minimum needs, as the programme provides employment for only one person. Besides this, the programme providing employment for only-fourth of a year. All these resulted in migration of labour. About 15 reported neither positive nor negative impact of the programme.

Impact of MGNREGS on Asset Creation

The creation of assets is another important aim of the MGNREGP. The maintainance of assets created under the scheme will be considered as permissible work under MGNREGP. The same applies to the maintenance of assets created under other programmes but belonging to the sectors of works approved in Schedule-I of the Act. On the basis of MGNREGP legislation the Andhra Pradesh State Government in its guidelines says that, "to ensure sustainable assets and a holistic approach to planning", a project approach should be adopted towards defining a work. The views of the sample respondents on the creation of assets are presented in the Table 11.10.

Table 11.10: Impact of MGNREGP on Asset Creation

Sl. No.	Type of Change	No. of Beneficiaries	Percentage of total
1.	No Change	77	64.17
2.	Increased	12	10.00
3.	Don't Know	31	25.83
	Total	120	100.00

Source: Field Data.

The Table 11.10 makes it clear that nearly 64.17 per cent of respondents reported *status* with regard to creation of assets. Only 10 per cent reported positive change. It is important to note that more than one-fourth of respondents reported neither positive nor negative impact. One of the reason observed is that they have no proper idea on assets.

Impact of MGNREGP on Income

As per the MGNREGA legislation each beneficiary should be paid minimum wages as prescribed by the Act. At present the Standard Schedule Rate (SSR) is fixed as Rs. 80 per day which is minimum for each labour. There was ceiling of Rs. 125 per day for each labour. These wage rates are expected to enhance the income level of a family. The beneficiary perception on income generation is presented in the Table 11.11.

Table 11.11: Impact of MGNREGP on Income Generation

Sl. No.	Type of Change	No. of Beneficiaries	Percentage of total
1.	Increased	94	78.33
2.	Decreased	—	—
3.	Don't Know	26	21.67
	Total	120	100.00

Source: Field Data.

The Table 11.11 indicates that 78.33 per cent of respondents confirmed that there is a real increase in their income levels after starting work in MGNREGP programme. About 21.67 per cent expressed neither negative nor positive impact of the scheme on their income levels. It is interesting to note that none of the respondents given negative impact of the scheme on their income levels.

Suggestions

- There is a low awareness among some workers of MGNREGP. To come out of this anomaly more awareness campaigns have to be conducted to educate the people about the provisions of the programme.
- There is delay in making the payment of wages in the case of some workers. To avoid this appropriate steps are to be taken by the government to maintain the uniformity in wage payment.
- Some of the worksite facilities are very poor. So the steps should be taken to provide adequate worksite facilities. For this purpose separate mechanism should be evolved.
- For comprehensive participation of rural masses should be allowed to involve in planning for MGNREGP.
- Designing special Statement of Rates (SoR) for women, preferably through conducting a systematic time and motion study, to ensure that they earn the set minimum wages.
- Improving the quantity of employment of MGNREGP by implementing all entitlements of workers including payment of the legal minimum wages, work site facilities and dependable first aid facilities. In addition, it is important to add some minimum social security such as health insurance. In other words, MGNREGP work needs to move towards quality employment.

Conclusion

While concluding this study, one can observe that the positive and negative impacts of MGNREGP on rural masses empowerment cannot be ignored on the grounds that these are unintended or not covered under the main objectives of MGNREGP. By addressing these impacts will not only help women's empowerment but it will also help in achieving medium and long term goals of MGNREGP and help in moving towards optimum use of labour in the economy. It will also help in moving towards some desirable national level social policies.

References

Akhtar, Jawed, S.M., Abdul Azeez, N.P. and Maisroof Md., (2011), "Towards Millennium Development Goals and the Role of MGNREGA", *Kurukshetra*, Vol. 60, No. 2, December, pp. 40-44.

Charan, Chanchal, (2012), "Working of MGNREGA in Bihar and Millennium Development Goals", *Southern Economist*, October 15, pp. 49-55.

Dutta, Puja, Murgai Rinku, (2012), Ravallion Martin and Dominique Van De Walle, "Does India's Employment Guarantee Scheme Guarantee Employment?" *Economic and Political Weekly*, Vol. XLVII, No. 16, April 21, pp. 55-64.

Gundegowda and Nagaraju, G.H. (2012), "Impact of MGNREGA Programme and Poverty: A Case Study", *Southern Economist*, Vol. 1, No. 10, September, 15, pp. 37-39.

MGNREGA Sameeksha, An Anthology of Research Studies on the Mahatma Gandhi National Rural Employment Guarantee Act, 2005, 2006-2012, Ministry of Rural Development Government of India, New Delhi.

Rao Gandhara, G. and Rao Mohana, L.K. (2011), "Women Participation in MGNREGA in India", *Southern Economist*, Vol. 50, No. 9, September 1, pp. 34-38.

Report to the People (2nd February, 2014), Mahatma Gandhi National Rural Employment Guarantee Act, 2005, Ministry of Rural Development Department of Rural Development Government of India, New Delhi.

Roy, Aruna and Nikhil Dey "Much More than a Survival Scheme", *The Hindu*, 31-8-2012.

Singh, Sajjan, (2011), "Role of the Panchayats in Implementing NREGA in Sirsa district: An Analysis", *The Indian Journal of Political Science*, Vol. LXXII, No. 3, July-September, 2011, pp. 819-832.

Tiwari, Rakesh Et. Al, Sekhar Soma, H.I.; Ramakrishna Parama, V.R; Indu, K. Murthy, Kumar Mohan M.S. Kumar Mohan, B.K; Harshad Parate, Varma Murari, Sumedha Malaviya, Ananya S. Rao, Sengupta Asmita, Kattumuru Ruth, Ravindranath, N.H. (2011); "MGNREGA for Environmental Service Enhancement and Vulnerability Reduction: Rapid Appraisal in Chitradurga district, Karnataka", *Economic and Political Weekly*, Vol. XLVI, No. 20, May 14, pp. 39-47.

12
Gandhian Approach to Simple Living and Development

Ashok S. Anikivi

PART I: CONCEPT OF SIMPLE LIVING

Introduction

Mahatma Gandhi was the eminent and distinguished Indian in the human history of all times. He was the political emancipator of India. Even after six decades of his assassination, his enormous corpus of his concepts and the "Story of his experiment with Truth" and "Non-violence is a part of his legacy." His ideas and actions are still a guiding force to save the entire humanity. An eminent writer John Haynes Holmes notes "when all the kings and princes and great captains of our times, who make so much noise and accupy so central place upon the stage, when these have long since been forgotton, everyone of them, the Mahatma will still be known and referred as the greatest Indian since Gautama Buddha, and as the greatest man since the Jesus Christ"[1] (Janardhan Pande, 1998).

Mahatma Gandhi sought to apply those moral values which are considered as most precious in personal life, truth and love-in the difficult domain of political and social action. Gandhism is a living thought for resolving the social, political problems of the day of course, Gandhism is becoming more and more principles in each and every field. Infact the future generation will recall Gandhis idea's. Accordingly, "Gandhi in his life and writings, reasserted the value, efficacy and significance of the moral and spiritual norms and precepts. He believed in the categorical imperatives of truth, non-violence, purity non-possessiveness, simplicity and Godliness[2].

Gandhi assumed a unique place among modem Indian thinkers. He was not merely a thinker but also led popular movements to eliminate evils of social life and to recognize society on the basis of equality and social justice. Gandhi visualized for India an ideal society in which advantages and privileges will not be monopolized by anyone section of society but will be shared by all. He wanted to establish an egalitarian society based on principles of equality and justice.

Sustainability means making provisions for future while living now. Whatever, we have we should use those resources and handover to the next generation. It also implies give more importance to quality of life rather than higher material standards of living. Simple living covers a number of different voluntary practices to simplify one's life style. For instance, these may include limiting one's possessions or increasing self-sufficiency. As simple living may be delineated by individuals being satisfied with what they need rather than want[3] (Linda Breen Pierce, 2000). But asceticism commonly encourages living simply and refraining from luxury and indulgence, not all proponests of simple living are ascetics[4] (Griffiths, Michel B. Flemming Christiansen and Malcolm Chapman, 2010). So, simple living is different from those living in forced poverty, as it is a voluntary life style choice.

Simplicity of Life

The purpose of this chapter is to examine Gandhian concept of simple living and how it will help sustainable living and development. No doubt, Gandhi believed in a life of simplicity and self-sufficiency. However, Gandhi's life offers us many key lessons—he practiced simplicity and minimalism in all aspects of his life. And he left a huge legacy to show how one can live in a life of simplicity and thereby lead to sustainable living.

Adherents may choose simple living for a variety of personal reasons, such as spirituality, health, increase in "quality time" for family and friends, reducing personal ecological footprint stress, personal taste frugality. Others mention socio-politcial goals aligned with the anti-consumerist movement, including conservation, growth, social justice, ethnic diversity and sustainable development.

The modern day economy is spreading consumerism and making man material oriented. It has led to profiteering, the exploitation of the common people, exploitation of society excessive consumption of resources deterioration of moral standards and hence the need for understanding Gandhian way of simple living.

Simple living can also be a reaction to materialism and conspicuous consumption. "Gandhi emphasised simplicity and an ascetic life as the basis of his personal life and he transformed these values into the wider sphere of the society. It does not require much justification to argue that he overgeneralised a personal experience on which his theory of trusteeship rested, and certainly this was a weak and shaky foundation"[5] (Patil, V.T. ed.1983).

Further, Gandhi consistently emphasised simplicity and satisfaction of the basic needs of human life as the corner stone of his whole economic philosophy. He was of the opinion that the earth was endowed with enough resources to meet every mans basic needs[6] (G. Parthsarthy, 1981). However, on the otherhand, the greed of men for competitive acquisiveness leading to concentration of wealth in the hands of a small privileged and influential section of the society positively deprived the basic needs of the majority in the society. Through trusteeship, Gandhi wanted to establish an economic order through a proper scheme of distribution of wealth to all members of the society. But more important than this consideration was his concern to remove selfishness from human beings by appealing to the moral consciousness of the individuals. Gandhi was of the opinion that since the state was a soulless machine and represented violence in a concentrated and organized from[7] (*The Modern Review*, 1935). The state was unable to appeal to the superior moral ethos of man with a view to transform their minds and heart from selfishness and acquisitiveness to one of common good.

Moreover, Gandhi wish for an ethical solution to an economic problem. He depreciated the powerful play of psychological factors like human greed and acquisitiveness in the material world. Gandhi seems to apply an ethical framework towards the building up of an equitable economic order based on trusteeship. He took a very simplistic view of group dynamics and group conflicts in a feudal or traditional world order. Gandhi's stress on satisfying fundamental requirements of human beings and the simplicity of life were contrary to the existing social environment which build very heavy importance on a material civilization. So, it must be remembered that "simplicity is also a relative term; it depends upon the circumstance and on surroundings, and in the modem world, where science has made great striking progress and industrialization has taken grip over the whole human society, now to say that we will run away from it would be not only unreal, but it would be giving up good things in order to escape from bad things"[8] (Morarji Desai,1981). However, beneath such situations acquiescence of trusteeship principle would turn out to be a reversion to industrial primitivism in an age depicted by the scientific and technological revolution.

Throughout his life Gandhi convinced the capitalist class to work as trustees of the people. It has been affirmed that "Gandhiji was rather disillusioned in the end and held that his capitalist friends could never become the trustees of the people. The capitalists went to him for their own purpose mostly... but Gandhi could not tum the heart of even one capitalist. They remain what they were..."[9] (Acharya Kripalani, 1953). Gandhiji was indeed the ultimate minimalist a man who passed away a pauper but who impressed the lives of many and continue to inspire us within his massage even today. When Gandhi died he has less than ten possessions comprising a spectacles, sandals watch and eating bowl. Undoubtedly, he was a man of non-possession and did not even possess a abode. Gandhi firmly believed that each one endeavoured to have what he actually needed and did not attempt to accumulate for tomorrow. Therefore, he emphasized on the virtues of non-possession that means we should not strive to accumulate more than we actually needed as would leave enough for others. Therefore, Gandhi argues: "Nature produces enough for our wants from day today, and if only everybody look enough for himself and nothing more, there would be no pauperism in this world, there would be no man dying of starvation in this world"[10] (Bhardwaj, K.K. 2004).

The Concept of simplicity, i.e., "the deliberate and voluntary restrictions of wants"[11] (J.L. Nehru, 1962) differs with forced poverty and in its ideal form means complete renunciation or non-possession. "The doctrine of simplicity or deliberate and voluntary restriction of wants or non-possession probably come to Gandhi from stealing. Thus in common parley stealing means to take any thing belonging to another without his permission"[12] (Gandhi, M.K., 1945). Even taking away something in the belief that it is nobody's property[13] (*Ibid.*) might be included in theft. Further, Gandhi wanted to expand the meaning of theft. So, he affirmed, "It is theft to take something from another even with his permission, if we have no real need of it"[14] (*Ibid.*). In addition "If we devote some thought to the subject, we shall find that we can get rid of quite a number of our wants. One who follows the observance of non-stealing will bring about a progressive reduction of his own wants"[15] (*Ibid.*).

However, non-stealing involves not merely reduction of present wants, but also not worrying for the future wants. Meanwhile Gandhiji notes: "One, who observes the principle of non-stealing, will refuse to bother himself about things to be acquired in the future"[16] (*Ibid.*). Again, "possession implies provision for the future. A seeker after truth a follower of Law of love cannot hold anything against tomorrow"[17]. The ideal of non-possession (*aparigraha*) as mentioned in the *Ishopanishad.* It also strengthen to the ideal of the *Bhagavadgita* which maintains that we have a claim merely to so much as would satisfy our hunger, otherwise desiring more than that is like theft be worthy of punishment. While endorsing his debt to the *Bhagavadgita*, Gandhi candidly affirmed: "I understand the *Gita* teaching of non-possession to mean that those who desired salvation should act like a trustee who, though having control over great possessions regards not an iota of them as his own"[18] (Gandhi, M.K., 1927).

The doctrine of Trusteeship has several cardinal implications. Firstly, it applies with regard to accumulated wealth and earning beyond one's needs. It aims that any superfluous wealth should be held in trust. It also mean an ideal of economic equlity in the ideal state. Secondly, it implies case of equality of rights not of rewards. Gandhiji does not like to cramp the intellectual attainments of the people and allows them to make full use of their talent in the interest of the community. Thirdly, it discards the case of nationalization or abolition of private property. Instead it desires a change of heart or mentality. Fourthy, Gandhiji is not in favour of the modern capitalist system, because he rejects the law of inheritance.

Thus, Gandhi observes "Life is not a bundle of enjoyments but a bundle of duties. That which separates man from beast is essentially man's recognition of the necessity of putting a series of restraint on worldly enjoyment"[19] (Ramesh Bhardwaj, 2007). "An individual wedded to non-stealing, will reduce his present wants but what should he do of his already acquired possessions? Gandhi derived his theory of trusteeship and wanted a man to retain this property in trust for the benefit of the society"[20] (Dhawan, 1990). Accordingly, simplicity or non-possession or non-stealing of Gandhi's idea means decreasing present wants to minimum, not accumulating things for the future use and to hold the already acquired surplus things as a trustee for the society. As far as non-possession is concerned Gandhi said: "From the stand point of pure truth, the body too is a possession. Love and exclusive possession can never go together. Theoretically, when there is perfect love, there must be perfect non-possession. The body is our last possession. So, a man can only exercise perfect love and be completely disposed, if he is prepared to embrace death and renounce his body for the sake of human service"[21] (Ramesh

Bhardwaj, 2007). This obviously indicates that a person should sacrifice for the sake of service of the humanity.

Apparently, the concept of absolute non-possession or simplicity cannot be achieved completely "only the fewest possible, if any at all", Gandhi noticed, "can reach this ideal. We ordinary seekers may not be repelled by seeming impossibility. But we must keep the ideal constantly in view, and in the light thereof, critically examine our possessions and try to reduce them"[22] (Gandhi, M.K.). Gandiji did not bother about the final goal or future. For him one step was enough[23] (Gandhi, M.K. 1934). Gandhi was also aware of the difficulties involved in it. "I cannot tell you the truth that, when this belief come to me, I discarded everything immediately. I must confess to you that progress at first was slow. And now, as I recall those days of struggle, I remember that was also painful in the beginning. A time came when it become a matter of positive joy to give up those things... Exploring the cause of that joy, I found that, if I kept anything as my own, I had to defend it against the whole world.... And, then I said to myself: "possession seems to me to be a crime"[24] (*Speeches and Writings of Mahatma Gandhi*, 1931). Gandhiji's stress on manual productive labour, small self-sufficient units, and simple way of life follows from the principles hitherto discussed. To him don't produce anything even beyond necessary. Otherwise exploitation takes place.

Modern life has become so complicated and interwoven. An individual who is always trying to multiply his wants, even beyond a minimum limit, not only make himself unhappy but also brings unhappiness and misery on others, the great economist Robbins tells us, 'means are limited'. So Gandhi notes, "our ignorance or negligence of the Divine Law which gives to man from day today his daily bread and no more, has given rise to inequalities with all the miseries attendant upon them. The rich have superfluous store of things which they do not need, and which are, therefore, neglected and wasted, while millions are starved to death for want of sustenance"[25] (Gandhi, M.K., 1945).

In this way "simplicity of life and of economic and political order provides a more suitable environment for the establishment of a non-violent society than an order based on excessive centralization, mechanization and production on gigantic scales"[26] (Mashruwala, 2007). Further, Gandhiji's thought is creativity in simplicity, the good relationship between human being and nature, has to meet the need of human being and not his greed.

Some instances can be stated from the life of Gandhi to prove his trust in simplicity. "The government had fixed upon the monthly sum of

Rs. 150 for Bapus expenses, because, he was a state prisoner. Major Martin the Jail Superintendent, brought a whole lot of furniture, crockery and all sorts of utensils the very first day. "For whom have you brought all this?" Asked Bapu, "Take it away please" Major Martin was Puzzled. He said, propitatingly, I have written and told the Government that at least 300 rupees a month should be spent on an honoured guest, like you. I have every hope that government will agree. Bapu said, "That is all very well. But after all, all the money would come from the Indian Treasury, would it not? I do not want to increase the burden on my country. I hope that, my boarding expenses will not come to more than 35 rupees a month. Had my health permitted, I would have eaten 'C' class food. But to my shame fruit is for me a sheer necessity, so is 'goat milk'. So, all the paraphernalia comfort was sent away"[27] (Kaka Kalelkar, 1950).

Gandhi was a man of "Simple living and High thinking". When he returned to India as a Barrister, he always walked to the court from his house. Thus, "When Bapu sat down to write, he would up the letters he had received carefully cut out the parts of the letter paper that had not been written on, and write his answers on them"[28] (*Ibid.*). The above illustrations clearly indicates that Gandhiji followed the life of simplicity throughout his life. Gandhiji, has firm conviction that the Western philosophy which is a materialistic one. So he inquires, "Is mans happiness increasing in the same proportion in which his belongings are increasing"[29] (*Speeches and Writings of Mahatma Gandhi*). The answer is obvious. "As it is, the rich are discontented not less than the poor. The poor man would fain become a millionaire and the millionaire a multi-millionaire"[30] (Gandhi, M.K.). In addition, "The human mind is like a restless bird, the more it gets, the more it wants and still remains unsatisfied"[31] (*Ibid.*).

Gandhiji said simple living is the foundation for economic equality. His economy aims at is to furnish all people with their full requirement of food, clothing shelter, education, medical care sanitation, etc., A well known historian, Arnold Toyanbee, speaks of corporate benefits of simple way of life: "No doubt we have a far greater capacity to reconstruct as well as to destroy than Chinese and Romans had. On the otherhand, a simpler social structure has far greater spontaneous recuperative power than a more complicated one has..."[32] (Arnold Toynbee, 1947).

Basic Tenets of Simple Living

Gandhi was actually born into a prosperous family and had a very privileged upbringing, which included a prestigious education in England.

Though born into wealth, he finally gave it all away and through the course of his life managed to let go of material trappings. The view of Gandhi on simple living are:

Accumulate Little

Gandhiji believed in possessing little except the clothes he wore and some utensils for cooking and eating. He used to give away or auction any gift that was never given to him. "Just as once must not receive, so one must not possess, anything which one does not really need. It would be breach of this principle to possess unnecessary food stuffs, clothing or furniture. For instance, one must not keep a chair if one can do without it. In observing this principle one is led to progressive simplification of one's own life"[33] (Gandhi, M.K., 1959). Again he wrote: "God never stores for the tomorrow. He never creates more than what is strictly needed for the moment"[34] (Gandhi, M.K., 1957). Further, "If each retained possession on only of what he needed, not one would be in want and all would live in contentment"[35] (*Ibid.*). It may not be possible these days for us to get down to less than ten possessions like Gandhi did, but start cutting down to bare basics. Recycle, give things away, or auction your unwanted possessions. Always, we tend to spend a lot of time and energy looking after our possessions. By having fewer things to possess and look after, your life automatically becomes simpler Gandhiji knew well that the full realization of principle of non-possession was no easy task.

Eat Simple Food

Gandhi never had a problem with being over weight. He followed a strict vegetarian diet and frequently cooked his own simple food, which was locally produced. "The greatest problem he faced on his arrival in London was food. He could not like insipid vegetarian food available there and he could not take non-vegetarian food. In fact in his long journey by ship and for first few days in London he solely depend on the provisions which he had brought with him from Bombay"[36] (Our Bapu, 1990).

Further Gandhi wrote in *Harijan*: "If we did so, our wants would be minimized. Our food would be simple. We should then eat to live, not live to eat. Let anyone who doubts the accuracy of this proposition try to sweat for his bread, he will derive the greatest relish from the production of his labour, improve his health, discover that many things he took were superfluities"[37] (Gandhi, 1935). Gandhi ate this simple food from a small bowl, a reminder to eat moderately, and at the same time he ate mindfully, often accompanied by prayers. He divided food into three categories: (a) Vegetarian, (b) Flesh, and (c) Mixed.

"Vegetarian diet, besides grains, pulses edible roots, tubers and leaves, includes fruits, both fresh and dry. Dry fruits includes nuts like almonds, pistachio, walnut etc."[38] (Gandhi, M.K., 2009). Gandhi advised fresh vegetables, a fair amount of leafy vegetables must be taken every day. He never suggested potatoes; sweat potatoes, suran etc., which supply starch mainly among vegetables. According to Gandhi, "food should be taken as a matter of duty even as a medicine to sustain the body, never for the satisfaction of the palate. Thus, Pleasurable feelings comes from the satisfaction of real hunger…"[39] (*Ibid.*). Further he argues: "There is a great deal of truth in the saying that man becomes what he eats. The grosser the food the grosser the body"[40] (Gandhi, M.K., 1933). So, eat simply and moderately.

Dress Simply

Gandhiji had great love for simplicity. He was so simple in dress. He was called '*Naked Fakir*'. Gandhiji wore simple clothes that conveyed his message. There is anecdotal story of the time when Gandhiji met the King of great Britain in London and he wore his simple wrap around cloth. At that time a journalist enquired Gandhi, "Mr. Gandhi did you feel-under dressed when you met the King?" Gandhi replied, "The king was wearing enough clothes for both of us". Though it may not be practical to weave your own clothes; you can simplify your life by dressing for comfort, not to impress. Thus, Gandhi wrote that "the washerman' s bill was heavy and as he was besides by no means noted for his punctuality, even two to three dozen shirts and collars proved insufficient for me. Collars had to be changed daily and shirts, if not daily, at least every alternate day. This meant a double expense, which appeared to me unnecessary. So, I equipped myself with a washing outfit to save it. I bought a book on washing, studied the art and taught it also to my wife. This no doubt added to my work, its novelty made it a pleasure"[41] (Bharatan Kumarappa, 2011). As far as simplicity of dress, is concerned Gandhi again wrote: "The national dress.... Is the most natural and the most becoming for Indian. I believe that our copying of the European dress is a sign of our degradation, humiliation and our weakness, and that we are committing a national sin in discarding a dress which is best suited to the Indian climate and which, for its simplicity, art and cheapness, is not to be beaten on the face of the earth and which answers hygenic requirements"[42] (Gandhi, M.K., 1947).

Lead a Simple Stress Free Life

Gandhi never got stressed. He meditated daily and spent hours in reflection and prayer. Gandhiji was essentially a man of religion. Be began the day with prayer and also end his day with it. He spent his time at *Ashram* for worship were 4-15 to 4-45 a.m. and in the evening 7-00 to 7-30 p.m. When he was in tour he never missed his prayers. He belived that the meaning of prayer is to invoke Divinity in your person and attempt to achieve complete identification with God. Further, 'Prayer' according to Gandhiji "is complete meditation and melting into the Highest self through one occasionally does lapse into imploration like that child to his father"[43] (Bhardwaj, K.K., 2004). Though he was a world leader and idolised by millions, he continued to lead a simple life with few distractions and commitments. He would even interrupt his political meetings to go off and play with children. And despite all his needs being taken care off, Gandhi still insisted doing his own simple things. He advocated self-sufficiency and simple work.

Let your Life be Your Message

Gandhiji preached what he practiced. He preferred to let his life do the talking for him. By living a simple life, Gandhi was able to devote his life to his chosen higher purpose. He was totally focused in his commitment to his people and the world. "The message of simple life is the need of India today. False desires are at the root of artificial life which dangerous. Gandhiji thought the essence of the *Gita*—the truth of self-restraint and self control. We must not become the victims to desires"[44] (H. Sreenivasaiah, 2011). Start living a simple life from today and you will release a lot of time and energy. This will give you the space to create the life you really want to live, a life that is inspired and inspiring.

PART II: GANDHIAN CONCEPT OF SUSTAINABLE DEVELOPMENT

The concept sustainable development has been defined by the World Commission on Environment Development (Brundtland Report, 1987), as "meeting the needs of the present without compromising the ability of future generations to meet their own needs." Further, the Group of Seven approved the Brundtland Report's definition of sustainable development at the Toronto Summit in 1988, and it was incorporated in Principle 4 of the "Rio Declaration," which states: "In order to achieve sustainable development, environmental protection shall constitute an integral part of the development process and can not be considered in isolation from it." Thus, the phrase 'sustainable development' links the meta-narratives of 'environmentalism' and 'economic development' in ongoing dynamic tension. However, this dynamic tension reveals multiple and ambiguous meanings of sustainable development.

At very surface level, the concept of sustainable development seems a notion of natural resources management, which has acquired a high conservationist status today. It is not surprising that sustainable development has become the ideal paradigm for addressing the unsustainable use of natural resources such as land, water, soil, sea and minerals. Often, Politicians and other academicians of society meet to deliberate over the devastating effects of unsustainable development. Interestingly, such meetings are concerned about the symptoms and not the causes of problems such as poverty, unfair trade relations, deepening global economic disparities, disease, pollution and the damage to the environment. The outcomes of these meetings may be seen in the form of pledges and signed agreements, as can be seen in Johannesburg World Summit for Sustainable Development. The major shortcomings of these texts are that they do not consider the context within which sustainable or unsustainable development takes place. Politicians get caught up in the application of the most commonly used notions and principles of sustainable development. For them, sustainable development refers to utility and management of resources, and to speak of sustainable development is to speak of an attempt to overcome crisis by to maintaining, sustaining and supporting economic development through modification of destructive characteristics of human technological activity.

At practical level, sustainability is understood mainly as: holding companies liable for environmental damages, implementing charges on unsustainable practices, putting the burden of proof on potential polluters to prove that their activity will do not harm, enforcing laws requiring regular company reports on their pollution releases, asking for independently verified reports from all companies involved in production processes regarding their progress towards environmental friendly goals, providing mechanisms for public input and participation in company decisions that may have negative environmental or social impacts. At people level, it has become a kind of slogan. Universities, local communities, non-profit organizations, states, even some industrial companies have adopted it. Further, groups who say they are working toward sustainable development aim to mix values of social equity, environmental responsibility and economic viability. As sustainable development moves into the mainstream, the largely amorphous concept gets bent into many different shapes. However, today, typical words used to characterized sustainability seem quite very positive and charismatic sustainable programmes should be democratic, equitable, environmentally benign and holistic-while allowing for a healthy economy. Many advocates say true sustainability will require a systemic shift in how society addresses issues ranging from resource allocation to urban planning. Other more radical fighters for sustainable development appeal for immediate changes in thinking, in societal values and beliefs, even in human nature. At theoretical level, academics consider sustainable development as an interdisciplinary science, the subject of which is composed of contribution from ecology, economics, anthropology, sociology and psychology, and computer science. Its range is bolstered by other cross-disciplinary work such as system science and non-linear dynamics; chaos, catastrophe, and complexity theory and showing up regularly in the literature. In short, sustainable development characterizes many things. If this concept is to become meaningful to the world at large, then it is better to deconstruct the underpinned discourse.

Sustainable Life-Gandhian Way

Gandhi's intervention in this debate of sustainable development can be reformulated on the basis of his ethical assumption about nature of human being, their needs and its relation to nature. Although, he had a plan to execute these assumptions into reality and to develop, an economic structure, what he said non-violent economic nature, however, this chapter restricts itself only to the evaluation of his ethical perspective as an intervention in the discourse of sustainable development.

Regarding Gandhi's intervention in the debate of sustainable development, one might consider the very idea of 'economic man' which is root of all contemporary development discourse that discuss about sustainability. Gandhi in his ethics rejects this very idea of 'economic man' as it was his conviction that one's behaviour as an economics agent cannot be isolated from one's behaviour as an autonomous moral agent. It is at this point Gandhi talks about 'limitation of wants' and self-restraint of individual that has personal as well as social and environmental dimension.

At personal level, Gandhi considers limitation of wants essential for spiritual or moral development. Extending this to social level, at the same time one can see, demand will be controlled and it would free certain resources that could be used to produce those requirements of those who do not have enough resource to live in. Further, it can check the resources some of which may be overexploited. By this Gandhi's ethics work on to solve the problem of consumerism and unsustainable resource use.

In fact, Gandhi's ethics call for a paradigm shift. His idea of wants has psychological basis. His view is human wants, given the freedom of choice, are insatiable. The societal approach to accept this and then use the science and technology for want satisfaction was not a sustainable approach; one might derive this from his ethical perspective. In Gandhian paradigm, value of an economic activity is evaluated less by the dividends it pays to shareholders than by its effect on the bodies, soul and spirits of the people employed in it. The first basic principle of Gandhi's economic thought is a special emphasis on 'plain living' which helps in cutting down wants and being self-reliant. This leads to make a distinction between 'Standard of Living' and 'Standard of Life', where the former merely states the material and physical standard of food, cloth and housing.

Deeply influenced by the Indian cultural tradition and also as he had taken quite advanced education in England, he, therefore, could claim to have comparative views of the living lifestyle and progress of both India and the West. As early as in 1909, in his small but perceptive publication, *Hind Swaraj*, Gandhi stated, that the civilization of the West that is influencing India in the name of modernity is a destructive monster. It is a civilization which equates consumerist lifestyle and abundance with development. It can not be civilization in real sense of the term (*Hind Swaraj*, 2007: 35). Further, he said that it seeks to increase physical comforts of the people. We should keep patience to see that such a civilization will invite its own destruction. Gandhi had not only the vision about environment; he not only exhorted his country men to be critically aware of uncritical acceptance of technology and eating up with the west in terms of its living standard. Thus, Gandhi seems presenting a critique of meta-narrative of development at very ethical level as well as policy level cautioning against what was later on to be known as the 'consumerist culture' and a 'waste-centric society'. Gandhi seems also concerned about the resource utilization as he suggested that by imitating the West, India (with its vast population) tried to reach the living standard of England, the resources of the earth will not be enough. This seems futuristic and also a warning to present generation about the limit of resource availability.

Gandhi's celebrated and often quoted statement, "the Earth has enough to satisfy the need of all the people, but not for satisfying the greed of some," can be analyzed to understand his intervention in discourse of sustainability. However, analysis presented here is made in the broader framework of his view on human being, its need and its relation to nature. For Gandhi man is neither an economic man nor is he a mere a collection of atoms. The pursuit of material self interest should not be the only objective of his life. Man is made in the image of God and to attain emancipation is his ultimate destiny. Services, sacrifice, suffering are the major motivation which sustain societies. Man in nature and society is really the necessary principle for saving earths. Thus, he makes a distinction between 'need' and 'want' of the human being and warns people to be aware from this distinction (Bhole, 2000:36).

Regarding nature his view is; nature not exists merely for man's conquest, exploitation and use. Everything in nature has its own purpose or objective of existence which is independent from the objective of man. Nature like man is creation of God. There is unity of all life, nature and universe. Man's activity must centre on all human beings, and all generation of human beings all living and non living beings in nature. These ought to be inter-generational, inter-special balance in all activities of man. This earth is given in man's trust to preserve, conserve, renew and not to defile, degrade despoil and destroy.

In Gandhian paradigm, the objective of humanity is to achieve harmonic (materiel, mental and spiritual) growth, happiness for all, and inner as well as outer peace (Mehta, 1985:49). The maximization of production and consumption of material good and bridging the gap between the poor and rich in respect of material prosperity and scientific, technological progress cannot be the primary pursuit of man. The best principle or consumption ethics for sustainability is minimization of wants. There is no scarcity of resources if austerity is practiced by all. The individual and social lifestyle should not be resource-intensive and technology-intensive. Satisfaction of basic needs of all is necessary and sufficient condition for and development. Further, development should take into account the cultural characteristics or specificities of various places. Similarly, it should give people a strong sense of belonging, identity and firm roots.

In Gandhian paradigm, the prime institution or structure or organization of society is not the market or state but it is self-sufficient, self-reliant, self-governing small and local villages. The organization principle of mechanization, centralization, specialization and large scale should be replace by those of decentralization and maxim of small is beautiful. The mode of production and social relation should be simple, labour intensive, and participative (Anantu, 1990). Consumption and production should be at local level. Sustainable development is a paradox. It is a self-contained deconstruction in which one term endlessly undoes the other at many levels. Sustainable development qualifies the privileged conception. The term exposes the hidden environmental costs of the development of the industrialized North. Sustainable development has multiple shades and it seems politics of North to sustain the global resources especially of South when they have already depleted their resources (Prem Anand Mishra, 2012).

PART III: GANDHI ON RURAL DEVELOPMENT

Mahatma Gandhi as a visionary of India, had a very clear perception of its villages and made an emphatic assertion that "India lives in her seven and half lakhs of villages". He further believed that India will have to live in villages, not in towns, in huts not in palaces. He held this conviction by saying that "If village perishes, India will perish too. He found that the progress of a country like India lies in the empowerment of the majority who lives in the villages. They should be encourged to attain self-sufficiency at all levels. Gandhiji found the only way of bringing hope of good living to the rural peoples by making the village the central place in the economic programme Rural development as outlined by Gandhiji contained self-sufficiency, inter-dependence for other wants and development of Village Industries. He wanted to bring about rural reconstruction with sound scientific and spiritual values. Through his 18-Point Constructive Programme, Gandhiji successfully implemented his rural reconstruction activities in Sevagram Centre near Wardha in 1935.

Gandhiji's ideal village belongs to the pre-British period, when Indian villages were the small republics undisturbed by the periodical visitations of barbarious hordes This republican character of the villages was destroyed by the British rule. Therefore, in Gandhian plan of rural reconstruction, the ancient republican village without any kind of exploitation served as a model unit. Gandhiji aimed at the attainment of Village *Swaraj* and said in 1942, My idea of Village *Swaraj* is that it is a complete republic, independent of its neighbours for its own vital wants and get inter-dependent for many others in which dependence is a necessity. Thus, every villages' first concern will be to grow its own food crop and cotton for its cloth. It could have a reserve for its cattle, recreation and playground for adults and children. Then if there is more land available, it will grow useful money crops, thus excluding ganga, tobacco, opium and the llke. The village will maintain a village theatre, school and public hall. It will have its own water works ensuring clean water supply.

Gandhiji fully understood the consequence of Western type of industrialization in India. He was conscious of the fact that far industrialization would destroy the Indian society by eliminating our decentralized rural industries and further leads to improvement. The once self-sufficient and self-contained rural villages have been drained progressively. He wanted to reverse this trend and bring about a rural reconstruction based on sound scientific and spiritual values. He said, my deal village will contain intelligent human beings. They will not live in dirt and darkness as animals. Men and women will be free and able to hold their own against anyone in the world. There will be neither plague nor cholera nor small pox, none will be idle, no one will wallow in luxury. Everyone will have to contribute his quota of manual labour.... It is possible to envisage railways, post and telegraphs and the like. Gandhian strategy of rural reconstruction was based on Village *Swaraj* and *Swadeshi* Movement. The basic principle of Village *Swaraj* as outlined by Gandhiji are trusteeship, *Swadeshi*, full employment, bread labour, self-sufficiency, decentralisation, equality, *Nai Talim*, etc. Thus, the idea of ideal village of Gandhian dream was a comprehensive one, encompassing the economic, social, political and educational dimensions.

Eighteen Points Constructive Programme

In 1935, Ghandhiji started his rural reconstruction activities Sevagram to implement his idea of Constructive Programme which are included Items such as the use of *Khadi*, Promotion of Village Industries, Basic and Adult Education, Rural Sanitation, upliftmen of the Backward Classes, the Welfare of Women, Education in Health and Hygiene, Prohibition and Propagation of the Mother Tongue. He incorporated all these activities under his 18-Point Constructive Programme and consider it as the truthful and non-violent way of winning *'Poorna Swaraj'*. Constructive Programme is not a fragmented approach. It is an attempt to develop society at the grassroots level with the resources that are available locally.

He said, thirty-four years of continuous experience and experiment in truth and non-violence have convinced me that non-violence cannot be sustained unless it is linked to conscious body labour and finds expression in our daily contact with our neighbours. This is the Constructive Programme. It is not an end, it is an indispensable means and, therefore, is almost convertible with the end. The power of non-violent resistance can only come from honest working of the Constructive Programme.

The Constructive Programme may otherwise and more fittingly be called construction of *Poorna Swaraj* or complete independence by truthful and non-violent means. The 18-Point Constructive Programmes included the following items:

1. Communal unity
2. Removal of untouchability
3. Prohibition
4. *Khadi*
5. Other Village industries
6. Village sanitation
7. New or basic education (*Nai Talim*)
8. Adult education
9. Women
10. Education in health and hygiene
11. Provincial language
12. National language
13. Economic quality
14. Kisans
15. Labour
16. *Adivasies*
17. Lepers
18. Students

Communul Unity

Everybody should be agreed about the significance of communal unity, which means an unbreakable heart unity. Thus, it has a wider significance than political unity. For the attainment of communal unity, every social worker should aim at developing and encouraging the bond of love and regard among the Hindu, Muslim, Christian, Zoroastrian and Jew members and cultivate a unity based on such mutual love and regard.

"In such a happy state, there would be no disgraceful cry such as

'Hindu-water' or 'Muslim-water' or 'Hindu-tea' or 'Muslim-tea'. There would be no separate rooms or pots for Hindus and non-Hindus in schools and colleges, no communal schools, colleges and hospitals." Gandhiji found that social stability of the country cannot be achieved without the social unity between these communities. He pleaded and laboured for the Hindu-Muslim unity to consolidate corporate strength for better purposes in India. For this Gandhiji recommended the following measures:

Removal of Untouchability

Untouchability is a social evil and should not be looked upon as a mere political necessity The socio-economic evils associated with this system must be abolished. According to Gandhiji, there should be perfect social equality among the people in the society No social superiority should be entertained by any individual or by a section of the society on the ground of birth or knowledge or religion or any other consideration. Gandhiji fought against social superiority in any form and carried on his crusade against the doctrine of racial superiority in South Africa and evil practices of untouchabilty in India.

He has the opinion that no one is born as untouchable and unequal. The practice of untouchability is a sin against God as the *Harijans* and non-*Harijans* are the children of the same God. He found untouchabiltity as the worst evil effect of Hinduism and worked for their temple entry for religious equality. In 1932, Gandhiji introduced *Harijan Sevak Sangh*, a non-political association for their self-improvement. He suggested their economic self-reliance through the adoption of spinning and weaving. He advocated non-violent methods to be adopted by them for their self-employment and for proper realisation of their rights.

Prohibition

Gandhiji considered drinks, intoxicating drugs and gambling as the social evils which eat into the very vitals of the social system and its values. He suggested the various measures to be undertaken to implement prohibition by the Government, Social Organizations and Social Workers. He realised the fact that the drinks and drugs harden the heart of man and endanger it with cruelty and is the root cause of many a social evil. The moral loss is greater than the financial loss; the physical disease may harm body but the drinks and drugs sap both the body and the soul.

Khadi

Khadi mentality means decentralization of production and distribution of the necessaries of life. *Khadi* has to play an important role in the village economy of India. It can give the poor at least three things: cloth, work and self-confidence to articulate themselves. Gandhiji considered *Khadi* as an inevitable means for the all-round development of the Nation. In 1934 Gandhiji wrote in *Harijan*, "*Khadi* is the sun of the village solar system. The planets are the various industries which can support *Khadi* in return for the heat and substance they derive from it. Without it, the other industries cannot grow... and also without the revival of the other industries, *Khadi* could not make further progress. For, villagers to be able to occupy their spare time profitably, the village life must be touched at all points."

Other Village Industries

According to Gandhiji village economy cannot be completed without the essential village industries such as hand-grinding, hand pounding, soap-making, paper-making, match-making, tanning, oil-pressing, etc. The village industries give employment to millions of people and provide an outlet for the creative skill and resourcefulness of the people. Large scale industries will eliminate the spinning wheel and the handloom, and through the large-scale industries, the wealth will be concentrated in the hands of a few. On the contrary, the village industries will lead to distribution of national income among the millions of people in thousands of villages.

Village Sanitation

The ideal vlllage envisaged by Gandhiji could be constructed on the basis of the principles of public hygiene and sanitation. The houses which are to be built with locally available material will have sufficient light and ventilation. Each house or a cottage shall have a courtyard to grow vegetables for domestic consumption and to house cattle. The village streets and lanes will be kept clean. Each village shall have its own water works to ensure clean water supply.

The constructive workers shall make the villages models of cleanliness by teaching the villagers to maintain cleanliness in and around the village, including public wells, tanks and rivers.

New or Basic Education (Nai Talim)

Gandhiji developed the idea of *Nai Talim*, for the "all round drawing of the best in child and man, body, mind and spirit". According to him literacy in itself no education, it is not the end of education. "His philosophy of education was based on his experiments with physical, literary and moral training at the Tolstoy Farm in South Africa. The vocational training was given through carpentry, shoe-making, gardening, etc. Literacy classes as well as spiritual training were conducted by him and others. He realized that the spirit of the children could not be trained through books alone. He was convinced that it is the life and character of the teacher which moulds the moral life of the students. He drew hls conclusions and inferences from the experiences which he gained at the Tolstoy Farm and followed it in India".

Adult Education

According to Gandhiji, adult education should not end with bare acquaintance with the alphabet. The literary education of illiterate adults should go hand in hand with the spread of the knowledge which is useful to the villagers in their daily life. During the transitory stage towards complete literacy, the social workers shall engage themselves in adult education of the illiterate people. This will lead to the eradication of illiteracy from the country.

Women

Gandhiji believed that the same soul resides in both man and woman and both of them have equal opportunities to develop their personality. They are inseparable pair; and one cannot live without the other.

According to Gandhiji: In a plan of life based on non-violence, woman has as much right to shape her own destiny as man has to shape his. But as every right in a non-violent society proceeds from the previous performance of a duty, it follows that rules of social conduct must be framed by mutual co-operation and consultation. They can never be imposed from outside. Men have not realized this truth in its fullness in their behaviour towards women. They have considered themselves to be lords and masters of women instead of considering them as their friends and co-workers. Though both man and woman posses equal mental abilities, they differ in certain respects. Woman posses greater degree of non-violence than man. As a mother, she exhibits greater degree of suffering, sacrifice and love. She is the mistress of the house, keeper and distributor of the bread in the house and takes greater interest in the management of the house. After completing her house work, she can take up some constructive activities.

Education in Health and Hygiene

According to Gandhiji it is the duty of the social workers to explain the simple rules of health and hygiene to the villagers.. The way of life of the social workers should be a living message to others in health and hygiene. They should maintain good health by following the rules of health and nature cure. They have to make attempts to get purified water for the villagers.

Gandhiji considered the fundamental laws of health and hygiene are as follows:

> Think the purest thoughts and banish all idle and impure thoughts. Breathe the freshest air day and night. Establish a balance between bodily and mental work. Stand erect, sit erect and be neat and clean in every one of your acts, and let these be an expression of your inner condition. Eat to live for service of fellow men. Do not live for indulging yourselves. Hence, your food must be just enough to keep your mind and body in good order. Man becomes what he eats. Your water, food and air must be clean and you will not be satisfied with mere personal cleanliness, but you will infect your surroundings with the same three-fold cleanliness that you will desire for yourselves.

Provincial Languages

"Gandhiji was in favour of regional languages as media of instruction at all stages of education. The social workers have to carry on the fight for establishing the supremacy of the regional languages at all levels of education and administration. Gandhiji recognized English as the language of international commerce and diplomacy and appreciated the English literature which has rich literary treasure and which gives an insight into the Western culture and thought." But, he recommended it would be taught as one of the subject and gave importance to the regional languages as it is the language of the rural masses.

National Language

According to Gandhiji, the national language of in a should be Hindi and he put forward the following arguments in favour of Hindi as national language.

(i) It is spoken by the single largest group of people who are spread over a number of states in North India and understood by many in the South.
(ii) It is easy enough to learn Hindi to the people of Gujarat, Maharashtra and W. Bengal. Within a few months, they can have sufficient command over this language.
(iii) Though the Dravidian languages are different from Sanskrit, they have profusely borrowed words from Sanskrit vocabulary which has also enriched Hindi language.
(iv) Hindustani is spoken by the Hindus and the Muslims in the Northern India. While the learned Hindus have Sanskritized Hindi which cannot be easily understood by the Muslims. The Muslims of Lucknow have persionized it, which has become unintelligible to the Hindus. Thus, the Sanskritized and Persionized Hindi represents two expressions of the same language Simple Hindi (Hindustani) is to be favoured.
(v) The religious, commercial political and social activities can be carried out throughout India through Hindi medium.
(vi) It is easy for the officials to learn this language.

Economic Equality

Economic equality means that everyone shall have sufficient and nutritious food to eat, proper shelter to live in, adequate khadi to wear, timely medical relief and necessary facilities for education. It also implies abolition of the eternal conflict between the capital and the labour by the levelling down of the rich in whom bulk of the Nation's wealth is concentrated and the levelling up of the poor. For this, the constructive workers shall strive to level down the few rich and level up the semi-starved millions through trusteeship system. It does not mean that everyone would literally have the same amount but it means that everyone should have enough for one's needs.

Kisans

Kisans form the bulk of India's population and are the backbone of this rural country. Majority of the India's population depend on agriculture and associated occupations such as cattle farming, dairying, poultry, piggery, etc. Hence, Gandhiji insisted on the social workers to render effective service in the village. In order to do this, they must acquire sufficient theoretical as well as practical knowledge about agriculture. According to him, the agriculture of a village should be planned in such a manner that each village shall be self-sufficient in its food requirements. If geographical conditions permit, the farmers should cultivate cotton required for the village. Gandhiji was in favour of farmer's organisations, but which are to be directed to redress the grievances of the peasants. But, it should not be used for low-level competitions for political gains of certain individuals.

Labour

According to Gandhiji, he who tills the land should own the land. The land owners should not think that the possession of land gives them any superiority over the tenants and the landless labourers. They should recognize that the tenants and the landless labourers possess the same soul which they possess. The land owners whose agricultural income is surplus should act as trustees for the benefit of the agricultural labourers and others. The land owners should not take more than the needs and should lead a sample life. They should engage themselves in the upliftment of the poorer sections of the village and should become partners in the peaceful evolution of soclo-economic change.

Adivasis

Under his 18-Point Constructive Programme, Gandhiji included the welfare of *Adivasis* also. He said, "Though they are the sixteenth number in this programme, they are not the least in point of importance. Our country is so vast and the races so varied that, the best of us cannot know all there is to know of men and their condition. As one discovers thls for oneself, one realises how difficult it is to make good our claim to be one nation, unless every unit has a living consciousness of being one with every other."

Lepers

According to Gandhi, service to the lepers is service to the suffering humanity. He sad, "India is perhaps a home of lepers next only to Central Africa. Yet they are as much a part of society as the tallest among us. But the tall absorb our attention though they are least in need of it. The lot of the lepers who are much in need of attention is studied neglect. I am tempted to call it heartless which it certainly is, in terms of non-violence."

Students

Gandhiji wished that the students should possess the following qualities:

(i) The students must have initiative, they must not be imitators
(ii) They must possess freedom. However, they must exercise freedom with restraint and humility.
(iii) They should have purity of heart which ensures the purity in personal life.
(iv) They are *brahma* chams, They must maintam self-control in thought, word and action and should preserve the vital energy.
(v) They should cultivate the sense of service to the community.

Gandhiji wished that the students should wear *Khadi* clothes and engage themselves in constructive programme. They will study the literature about spinning with all its economic, social, moral and political implications. During their vacation, they must conduct day and night schools for the illiterates. They could clean the *Harijan* Quarters, their children and give simple lessons in hygiene both to the young and the grown up. According to Gandhiji students must not take part in party politics. The students are to study, they are researchers, but not politicians. It is not possible for the student to be active politicians and to be real students simultaneously. They can study the programmes and ideologies of the various political parties and listen to their point of view. They should have freedom of opinion and can openly sympathize with any party which they like. But they should not support political strikes and demonstrations.

Conclusion

Gandhiji blended his simplicity with his humility. He observes: "You may have occasion to possess or use material things, but the secret of life lies in never missing them". Gandhi's life was his message or in other words the great truths that he profounded, he concretely tried to realize in his own life and in the lives of the people. Gandhi like a religious preachers, philosopher and noble men of different times.[45] (K.M. Munshi and Aiyer (ed.) and countries was a believer in the philosophy of 'simple living and high thinking' and wanted to build his socio-politico-economic structure on it. Gandhiji's stress on simplicity is of epochal significance. Simplicity is regarded as a quest for primitivism. But with mounting population figures, simplicity is a logical demand of the times, because the earth, simply, does not have the resources to cater to the material needs of such a mounting population touching the four or more 500 crores (500 million) figure. An economy based on "Simple Living" or Limited wants Gandhiji further claims, would neither invite aggression nor itself be tempted to commit aggression. To those who accept "Simple Living" or subsistence living as the highest value, what Gandhiji says is certainly relevant. In the political sphere simplicity will mean reducing power i.e., establish village republics or *Ram Rajya*. Therefore, Gandhi, wished to decentralize power by converting every village into a self-sufficient republic having its own legislature executive and judiciary all combined into one. The message of his life is India's urgent need is the worlds need today, as the human race is facing crisis, perhaps the greatest crisis in human history. Finally, his greatest contribution to the entire mankind "his principle of truth, non-violence and his philosophical way of simple living like poorest of the poor". He lived in a hut and dressed in two pieces of cloth like the poorest man in India.

References

1. Quoted in Pande, Janaradhan (ed.), *Gandhi and 21st Century* (New Delhi, Concept Publishing Company, 1998), p. 77.
2. *Ibid.*, p. 18.
3. Linda Breen Pierce, (2000), *Choosing Simplicity.*
4. Griffiths, Michael, B. (2010), *Flemming Christiansen and Malcolm Chapman.*
5. Patil, V.T., (1983), *Studies on Gandhi*, (ed.), Sterling Publishers Pvt. Ltd., New Delhi, p. 105.
6. G. Parthsarthy, (1981), "Integrated Rural Development: Concept Theoretical Base, and Contradictions", ed. T. Mathew, *Rural Development in India*, (New Delhi, Agricole Publishing Academy), p. 31.
7. *The Modern Review*, October, 1935, p. 413.

8. Morarji Desai, (1981), Gandhi Contemporary World, in K.P. Mishra, S.C. Gangal, (ed.) *Gandhi and the Contemporary World* (Delhi, Chanakya Publications), pp. 14-15.
9. Acharya Kripalani, (1953), *Gandhian Outlook and Techniques* (New Delhi, Ministry of Education, Government of India) pp. 16-17.
10. Quoted in Bharadwaj K.K., (2004), *Gandhian Thought* (New Delhi, Sudha Publications Pvt. Ltd.), p. 68.
11. *Jawaharlal Nehru: An Autobiography* (Bombay, Allied Publishers Pvt. Ltd., 1962).
12. *Gandhi, M.K.*, (1945), *From Yaravada Mandir* (Ahmedabad, Navajivan Publishing House).
13. *Ibid.*
14. *Ibid.*
15. *Ibid.*
16. *Ibid.*
17. *Ibid.*, chapter-VI.
18. Gandhi, M.K. (1927), *The Story of My Experiments with Truth* (Ahmedabad, Navajeevan Publishing House), pp. 221-22.
19. Ramesh Bhardwaj, *Thus Spoke Gandhi*, (Quotes of Mahatma Gandhi), (New Delhi, Gandhi Sahitya Bhandar, 2007), p. 32.
20. G.N. Dhawan, *The Political Philosophy of Mahatma Gandhi*, p. 94.
21. Ramesh Bhardwaj, *op. cit.*, p. 86.
22. *Yaravada Mandir, op.cit.*, chapter VI.
23. *Harijan*, 20-04-1934.
24. Address delivered at the Guild House, Landon, September 23, 1931, *Gandhi*, p. 1066.
25. From *Yaravada Mandir, op. cit.*
26. K.G. Mashruwala, (2007), *Gandhi and Marx*, (Ahmedabad, Navajivan Publishing House), p. 84.
27. Kaka Kalelkar, *Stray Glimpses of Bapu*, pp. 86-87.
28. *Ibid.*, p. 88.
29. "Speches and wirtings of Mahatma Gandhi", (Madras, G.A. Natesan and Co., 1922), p. 350.
30. *Yaravada Mandir*, chapter VI.
31. *Ibid.*
32. Arnold Toynbee (1947), *International Affairs*, p. 468.
33. Gandhi, M.K., (1959), from *Yaravda Mandir*, p. 23.
34. *Ibid.*, pp. 23-24.
35. *Ibid.*
36. *Our Bapu*, (1990), (New Delhi, Diamond Pocket Book Pvt. Ltd.), p. 16.
37. *Harijan*, 29-06-1935.
38. Gandhi, M.K., (2009), *The Moral basis of Vegetarianism* (Ahmedabad, Navajivan Publishing House), p. 5.
39. *Ibid.*, p. 13.

40. *Harijan,* 05-08-1933.
41. Bharatan Kumarappa (2011), *Gandhiji's Autobiography,* Abridged (Ahmedabad, Navajivan Publishing House), p. 97.
42. Gandhi, M.K. (1947), *India of My Dreams*, (Ahmedabad, Navajivan Publishing House), p. 305.
43. Bhardwaj, K.K. *Gandhian Thought*, *op. cit.*, p. 78.
44. H. Sreenivasaiah, (2011), *Relevance of Gandhiji* (Bangalore, Karnataka Gandhi Smaraka Nidhi Gandhi Bhavan), p. 30.
45. K.M. Munsi and N.C. Aiyer, (ed), *Gandhis View of Life*, p. 143.

13

A Sustainable Environmental Project

Nagaland Environmental Protection and Economic Development (NEPED) and its Impact on Jhum Cultivation in Nagaland

Merensangla Longkumer and A.K. Makar

Introduction

Nagaland, located in the north-eastern region of India, with an estimated population of over 1.5 million, covers an area of 16,579 km. Agriculture is the main land use and occupation in Nagaland. Traditional agriculture has rich and diverse history. For the past years, jhuming has met the household needs of most of the Nagas and is a way of life for the Nagas. However, with increasing population pressure and changing lifestyle, the Nagas faced challenges of meeting livelihood needs and sustaining their environmental resources. The jhum cycle has been falling from 15-20 years to an average of 9 years. Over time the soil started to deteriorate and there had been decreased in the yield and the forest biodiversity gradually started deteriorating. So, it was necessary to develop alternative land use systems in Nagaland. However, traditional shifting cultivation methods need not be eliminated, but modified by adopting agro forestry and enriched fallow management systems.

With a view to help farmers improve the land use system, and to protect the remaining forests, the Nagaland Environmental Protection and Economic Development (NEPED) project was established partnering with the Government of Nagaland, International Development Research centre and India-Canada Environment facility. Beginning in 1995, NEPED has worked at the community level to encourage adoption of agro-forestry by planting trees in jhum fields. As majority of the population in the state are forest based subsistence farmers, NEPED focused on issues like shifting cultivation, environment protection, economic development and empowerment of people.

The principle, goal and operation of NEPED are as follows:

(i) Sustainable livelihood, environment protection and development, putting rural people first.
(ii) The project goal is sustainable management of the natural resource base, which would benefit the people of Nagaland. This project is specifically designed to improve lands under jhum.
(iii) The project operation follows a participatory approach by involving the jhum farmers themselves in the selection, development and testing of agro-forestry technologies.

Building Upon Traditional Agriculture: The Premise of NEPED

Interventions to improve livelihoods and strengthen natural resource management practices for food security and environmental sustainability must be done in a culturally appropriate way that involves communities up front and centre. The need to find ways to add value to the shifting cultivation system and improving it was of paramount importance. The foremost problem was the cultural reliance on jhum cultivation and the large scale depletion of the natural forest caused by timber extraction. Various schemes have been implemented to decrease the incidence of jhum cultivation, but these met with limited success. The increase in jhum cultivation both in intensity and extent far outstrips the results of implementation of past schemes to contain the practice. Also, the efforts made to replenish the forest cover have been lagging behind the rate of degradation.

In Nagaland, out of a total area of 7,000 sq.km. of jhum land, around 500 sq.km. is cleared of vegetation and burned annually for jhum cultivation. About 70 per cent of the rural families subsist on jhum cultivation. As the land belonged to the people and is not owned by the state, there is hardly any way of regulating the land utilization.

Although the practice has adverse effects, the following aspects cannot be ignored:

(i) Jhum assures a measure of food security for most of the people.
(ii) In ecologically sensitive and hilly terrains like Nagaland,

application of modern technologies has limitations. Jhum on the other hand is the base for development and application of low input technologies like low external agricultural input technology.

(iii) The sustenance of agro-biodiversity of Nagaland may be attributed to the jhum practice.

The Concept

(i) Trees as a jhum crop. Jhum is a mixed crop system and adding one more tree crop will do no harm.

(ii) Sowing of non-traditional winter crops like wheat, barley, pea and other cover crops after the harvest of traditional crops like rice, maize, millets etc. in jhum fields.

(iii) Selected shade loving cash crops can be planted among the trees. These trees can yield income during the fallow period, which is also the gestation period of the trees.

(iv) By adopting proper crop rotation and combination of trees and other crops, jhum cultivation can be turned into the main tool for economic development in Nagaland.

Research Methodology

There are eleven districts in Nagaland, viz.,

1. Kohima, 2. Dimapur, 3. Wokha, 4. Mokokchung, 5. Zunheboto, 6. Phek, 7. Mon, 8. Tuensang, 9. Peren, 10. Longleng, and 11. Kiphire.

Within Nagaland, the Human Development Index (State Human Development Report, 2004) is highest in Dimapur (0.73), followed by Mokokchung (0.71) and Phek district (0.450). Thus, for the present study, based on these index, Dimapur, Mokokchung and Phek were selected.

Dimapur, being the gateway of the State has easy access to communication, transportation and infrastructures needed for any developmental activities. The State's only railway station and airport are located in the district. So, based on its convenience and easy availability of resources for the research work, Dimapur was selected as one of the study area.

Mokokchung, one of the fast developing district of Nagaland and the cultural centre of the AOs. The AOs are considered the forward tribe of all the tribes among the Nagas. NEPED has been quiet successful in implementing its activities in Mokokchung.

Phek, one of the eleven district of Nagaland, lacking behind from other districts in many areas mainly because of poor transportation and communication, but yet the people are known for being hardworking, needs special focus and policy intervention to tap its vast unexplored resources. For the present study, Phek was selected as one of the study area to determine how much NEPED has succeeded in improving the economic status of the people in this backward area.

The basic criterion for the selection of the respondents is that one should be a beneficiary of NEPED. The respondents were selected randomly from the sample villages. From each selected villages, a total of 10 respondents were selected randomly. A total of 280 respondents were selected altogether for the present study.

The primary datas were collected directly from the selected respondents with the help of the structured schedule, by employing personal interview method.

The secondary datas were collected from the records of NEPED office and their various publications.

Findings and Discussions

The aim of this project was to make jhuming a more sustainable activity by adding value in the form of trees. NEPED concentrated on tree plantations in the farmer's jhum field and spreading the message of the advantages of planting trees in the jhum fields. One remarkable feature of NEPED was to go only for locally and easily available and fast growing tree species like Alder, Albizzia sp, Cetrella, hollock, and gomari.

The NEPED project established tree planting in jhum fields in a high proportion of villages across the State. The NEPED project has inspired most farmers across Nagaland to plant trees on their own land. The evidence of extensive tree planting is everywhere and can be observed casually as one drives to different areas across the State.

In the present study, an assessment on effectiveness of the project on spreading awareness on environmental protection without eliminating the jhum practices was carried out in the three selected districts.

Table 13.1 and Fig. 13.1 revealed that there had been 100 per cent awareness in tree planting in all the three districts. One of the remarkable outcomes of the project was the way tree planting was widely adopted by

Table 13.1: Assessment on Effectiveness of the Project on Spreading Awareness on Environmental Protection

Sl. No.	*Features*	*Districts*			*Overall*
		Phek	*Dimapur*	*MKG*	
1.	Increased Awareness in Tree Planting	60 (100)	180 (100)	40 (100)	280 (100)
2.	Do You Support NEPED's Policy of Planting Trees in Jhum Land	60 (100)	180 (100)	40 (100)	280 (100)
3.	Increased Awareness on Extenting Jhum Cycle (With Fallow Management)	60 (100)	180 (100)	40 (100)	280 (100)
4.	Increased awareness on forests in village	60 (100)	180 (100)	40 (100)	280 (100)
5..	Awareness on Importance of Forests in Village	50 (63.3)	120 (66.7)	30 (75)	200 (71.4)
6.	Creation of community forest after NEPED inter intervention in the village	10 (16.7)	20 (11.1)	20 (50)	50 (17.9)
7.	Restriction on afforestation increased after NEPED intervention	20 (33.3)	90 (50)	30 (75)	140 (50)
8.	Awareness on forests conservation for better environment, Fresh Air and to prevent the extinction of SP, After NEPED intervention	40 (66.7)	120 (66.7)	20 (50)	180 (64.3)
9.	Increased Knowledge and Practise on Soil Conservation	60 (100)	130 (72.2)	40 (100)	230 (82.1)
10.	Increased Knowledge on Weed Management	50 (33.3)	140 (77.8)	30 (75)	220 (78.6)
11.	NEPED was the pioneer in planting trees for improving environment	60 (100)	180 (100)	40 (100)	280 (100)
12.	Do you support NEPED's policy of planting trees of local SP.	40 (66.7)	180 (100)	30 (75)	250 (89.3)

Note: *Figures in parentheses indicate percentage.

both farmers and entrepreneurs all over the state. The project had tremendously spread awareness on tree planting and its importance.

The respondents were 100 per cent supportive of NEPED'S policy of planting trees in jhum fields in all the three districts. The project established tree planting in jhum fields in a high proportion of villages across the state. The respondents were of the view that planting trees has helped them meet the increasing demands for timber and environmental sustainability.

According to the respondents, there had been 100 per cent increased awareness on extending jhum cycle with fallow management. They were of the view that the villagers had realised the need for extending the jhum cycle and its benefits and had been practising suitable fallow management techniques such as going for crops that could generate cash early and restore

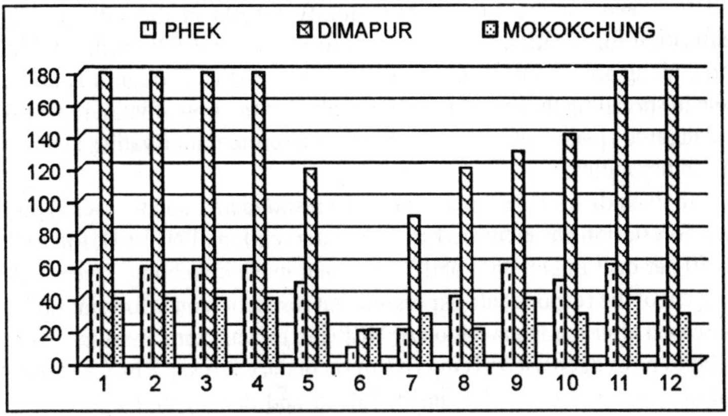

Fig. 13.1: Assessment on the effectiveness of the project on spreading awareness environmental awareness and protection

the soil fertility while ensuring food needs as well. Integration of such crops into jhum cultivation is one pathway to an improved jhum system.

The respondents expressed that the project had increased (100%) awareness on improving the jhum system practices in Nagaland. They said that before NEPED intervention they never felt the need for the modification or improvement of the jhum cultivation they had been practising. But with the advent of the project, the villagers had realized the need for improving the jhum cultivation instead of eliminating it as it is a part of Naga culture and application of modern technologies is not possible in hilly terrains like Nagaland. So, the project had made them realised that planting trees along with the crops can go a long way in enhancing the traditional shifting cultivation.

There had been 63.3 per cent increased awareness on importance of forest in Phek, followed by 66.7 per cent in Dimapur and 75 per cent in Mokokchung. Overall, there had been 71.4 per cent increased awareness on importance of forests among the respondents in the village and it is quite an achievement. According to the respondents, the project has shown them the importance of conserving forests and the interdependence of forest and agriculture and if the forests are harnessed well, it can create opportunities for economic activities and employment opportunities and as well as environmental sustainability.

In Phek district, 16.7 per cent of the respondents felt the need for creation of community forests, followed by 11.1 per cent and 50 per cent in Dimapur and Mokokchung. Overall, 17.9 per cent of the respondents felt the need for creation of community forests in the village. The realisation for creation of community forest was not felt untill NEPED came along and changed the mindset of the people. Though it is taking time in spreading the awareness, the gradual extinction of vulnerable and endangered species of plants has been an important motivating factor to the communities.

In Phek district, 33.3 per cent of the respondents said that restriction on afforestation has increased after the intervention of NEPED, followed by 50 per cent in Dimapur and 75 per cent in Mokokchung. Overall, 50 per cent of the respondents expressed that restriction on afforestation has increased after the intervention of NEPED. Infact, jhum areas in several villages have decreased giving rise to secondary forests. The Chakesang Public Organisation (CPO) has resolved and demarcated a portion of their community forests as a biodiversity conservation zone. After the CPO resolved to ban rampant burning of jungle, the dynamics of plant succession in the direction of climax forest had been observed in many locations in the district of Phek.

There has been remarkable spread of awareness on forests conservation for better environment, fresh air and preservation of extinct sp. after NEPED intervention in Phek (66.7%), Dimapur (66.7%) and 50 per cent in Dimapur. Overall, 64.3 per cent spread of awareness on forests conservation for better environment, fresh air and preservation of extinct sp. after NEPED intervention. According to the respondents, they have understood and became more aware about the crucial role forests play in the life-support system. They were of the view that forests maintain the delicate ecological balance, conserve soil and recharge underground water resources. This fact has been realized by the village community.

The increased knowledge and practise on soil conservation is 100 per cent in Phek, 72.2 per cent in Dimapur and 100 per cent in Mokokchung. Overall, there is 82.1 per cent increased knowledge and practise on soil conservation. The farmers understand the need for soil conservation practices because of the existence of traditional practices to control soil erosion using physical and biological barriers, but these are not always effective because they are not used in irregular manner. NEPED has attempted to build upon these traditions and bring improvements to these methods.

There had been 33.3 per cent increased knowledge on weed management in Phek, 77.8 per cent in Dimapur and 75 per cent in Mokokchung. Overall, 78.6 per cent increased knowledge on weed management. The NEPED team has shared the importance of integrated weed management at farmer's level through various ways of leaflets, trainings, radio programmes, etc and as a result many farmers have adopted the improved system of weed management in their jhum fields.

According to the respondents (100%), there had been no project or department or any agencies that were involved in planting trees before NEPED. So, NEPED has emerged as the only project in Nagaland that has focused on tree planting for environmental concerns. Though there are some projects and programmes coming up with plantation of trees but NEPED was the pioneer in it.

In Phek district, 66.7 per cent of the respondents supported NEPED's policy of planting trees of local sp, 100 per cent in Dimapur and 75 per cent in Mokokchung. Overall, 89.3 per cent of the respondents supported NEPED'S policy of planting trees of local sp. because they are easily available, suitable to the climate and soil. The respondents were also of the view that many of the local sp. available in Nagaland are not available and are of high value and demand outside Nagaland. So, they were of the view of preserving the local sp. instead of bringing other sp. in high prices.

Table 13.2: Level of Effectiveness of the Project on Spreading Awareness on Environmental Protection

Sl. No.	*Level*	*Score range*	*Districts*			*Overall*
			Phek	*Dmp*	*Mkg*	
1.	Low	Upto 7.53	10 (16.66)	100 (55.55)	—	81 (28.92)
2.	Medium	7.53–10.43	20 (33.33)	80 (44.44)	40 (100)	169 (60.35)
3.	High	Above 294.43	30 (50)	—	0	30 (10.71)
		M = 8.5	8.44	8.00	8.98	
		S.D = 1.00	.1512	0	1.45	

Note: Figures in parentheses indicate percentage.

Table 13.2 and Fig. 13.2 revealed that in Phek, there had been high level (50%) of effectiveness of the programme on environmental awareness and protection, followed by medium level (33.33%) and 16.66 per cent level of effectiveness of the programme on environmental awareness and protection. In Dimapur, there is low level (55.55%) of effectiveness of the programme on environmental awareness and protection followed by medium level (44.44%). Mokokchung had experienced medium level of effectiveness of the programme on environmental awareness and protection.

It is evident from Table 13.2 and Fig. 13.2 that there had been medium (60.35%) level of effectiveness of the project on spreading awareness on

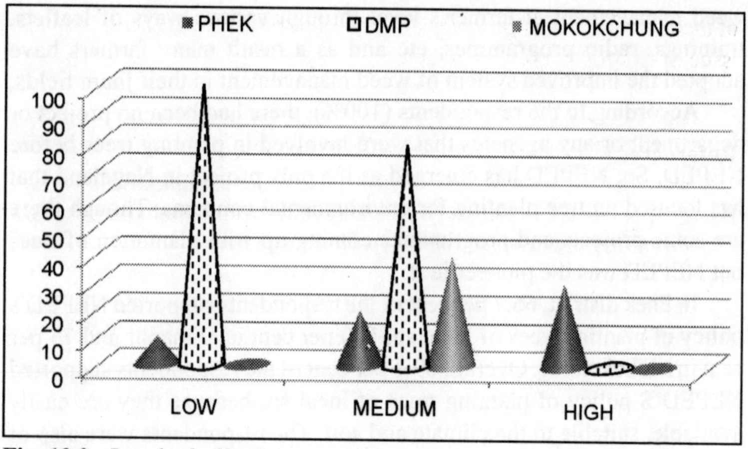

Fig. 13.2: Level of effectiveness of the project on spreading awareness on environmental protection

environmental protection. This is a big achievement for NEPED because Nagaland is such a place where jhuming is an integral part of Nagas and is deeply rooted in their culture which has a direct adverse impact on environment. And no other project or programme has ever tried in creating awareness on jhum and improvement on its practices. So, with zero level of awareness, NEPED has created a revolution in environmental protection and has been successful in achieving medium level of awareness on environmental protection.

Conclusion

The project sought to break the vicious circle of poverty and environmental degradation. It is the poverty of the jhum farmers which forces them into causing environmental degradation and this continued environmental degradation re-enforces their poverty. The mainstay of this project was tree planting. The economic benefits from the trees go hand in hand with environmental benefits. The tree planting has created a long term asset as the elders said "they did for their children". Villagers had become much more conscious of the need to save and renew forests, conserve soils and wildlife, and conserve biodiversity. Villagers in Nagaland are now convinced that planting trees will generate income. They had enthusiastically responded to NEPED and the Government of Nagaland programmes with tree plantation on a massive scale. The project has successfully created a source of income for the poor farmers, while simultaneously addressing the larger issue of environmental degradation.

References

Baerg, R., Vettivel, S.K., Bagai, D.S. (2000) "*Nagaland Environmental Protection and Economic Development Project Performance Assessment*".

NEPED (2006), "*Adding Value to Shifting Cultivation in Nagaland India*", N.V. Press, Kohima, Nagaland.

NEPED and IIRR (1999), "*Building Upon Traditional Agriculture in Nagaland, India*", N.V. Press, Kohima, Nagaland.

14
Empowering People Through Gram Sabha for Inclusive and Sustainable Rural Development

Ch. C. Prasad and P. Shreenivas

Introduction

Panchayati Raj System constitute the foundation on which stands the entire edifice of rural development in India. Pandit Jawaharlal Nehru the first Prime Minister of India laid the foundations of Panchayati Raj at Naguar in Rajasthan on 2nd October, 1959. The basic philosophy of Panchayati Raj System is that the villagers should think, decide and act for their own collective socio-economic interests. According to Article 40 of the Constitution of India, the respective State governments shall take steps to organize Village Panchayats and endow them with such powers and authority as the units of self-governance. The Panchayats have been the back bone of Indian villages to achieve economic development and social justice in rural areas.

The 73rd Amendment to the Constitution of India (1992) is a milestone in the evolution of decentralized governance in India. The Act has given constitutional recognition to rural local Self-Government Institutions. The Eleventh Schedule of the Act lists 29 subjects to Panchayati Raj Institutions (PRIs) which include almost all the aspects of rural development. One of the most important recommendations made by the 73rd Constitutional Amendment is that the Gram Panchayat should invariable conduct Gram Sabha meetings regularly and elicit the opinion of the voters about the priority of development works and in turn implement them to achieve sustainable development. The goal of inclusive growth as envisaged by the government cannot be achieved without effective participation of local people. In view of this, an analysis has been made in the present chapter to examine the role of Gram Sabha in achieving inclusive and sustainable rural development.

Gram Sabha: An Epitome of Participatory Democracy

The idea of Gram Sabha (Village Assembly) is not new although it got more currency after the 73rd Amendment to the Constitution. In pre-independence days under British regime the idea of associating villagers with the Panchayat administration was accepted and incorporated in some of the Provincial Panchayat legislations like Bombay Village Act of 1933, which had the provision of assembling all the adults at a common place where the panchayat would read out the report on the village administration for the preceding year and activities to be taken up in the ensuing year. But the Gram Sabha was not empowered to make changes in the proposals made by the Panchayats. This was obvious because not much was expected from the alien government.

The Gram Sabha corner stone of the participatory democracy, was not functional prior to the 73rd Constitutional Amendment Act *(Article 243(B) of the Constitution refers to Gram Sabha as "a body consisting of persons registered in in the electoral rolls relating to a village comprised with the area of panchayat of the village level")*. Realising the importance of this institution at the local level, the Government declared the year 1999-2000 as the "Year of Gram Sabha". The Gram Sabha is an institution which provides an opportunity to participate meaningfully in governance, to all the people willing and capable of participating in the development process. The Gram Sabha is a concept intending to represent ordinary people's needs and wishes which appeals to the general mass of population irrespective of class, caste, gender distinction and political partisanship. It refers to supremacy of the people.

The Gram Sabha enables each and every voter of the village to participate in decision-making at the local level. It is a constitutional body consisting all persons registered in the electoral rolls of a Village Panchayat. It provides a political forum to people in the village to meet and discuss their common problems and consequently understand the needs and aspirations of the community. It also provides a forum to meet, discuss, debate and analyse the development and administrative actions of elected representatives and thereby ensure transparency and accountability in the functioning of the Village Panchayat. It Act as a watchdog on the working of Gram Panchayats besides facilitating the rural people's participation in the decision-making processes. The Gram Sabha is supposed to play a central role in promoting participatory democracy not only by working as an institutionalised platform to represent each and every section of the community and their needs, but also by functioning as mechanism to monitor and evaluate the development activities carried on by panchayat.

Most of the rural people are not able to distinguish between Panchayat and Gram Sabha. In Panchayati Raj System, Gram Sabha is the corporate body and panchayat is the executive body. In country like India with so much of diversity and unevenness, any mandate is not so easy to put into practice. The realisation of Gram Sabha concept is totally depends on the awareness of local people who are the members of it. Most of the village issues will be resolved in village itself, if people actively participate in the proceedings of Gram Sabha. To achieve inclusive and sustainable development in rural areas and ensure grassroot democracy, Gram Sabha need to function with true spirit.

The Government's concept of rural development hither to remained limited only to the anti-poverty programmes which are implemented by the Ministry of Rural Development. Since, independence various schemes and programmes have been taken up both by the Centre and State governments as anti-poverty measures. Yet the results were not on expected lines. The basic reason was that all these anti-poverty programmes were planned and implemented through the agencies created like District Rural Development Agency (DRDA), etc. There was no involvement of Panchayati Raj Institutions (PRIs). As a result, these programmes failed to become people's programmes. Thus, the Governments felt that implementation of development programmes would be most effective if local people were involved, especially for identification of beneficiaries for development programmes. Taking lessons, now the government has been involving the Panchayati Raj Institutions in a big way in the planning and implementation of development plans. The Gram Panchayats and Gram Sabhas would plan and decide the types of work to be undertaken in the rural areas. The Gram Sabhas would also discuss and approve the plans. They would also supervise and monitor the rural development programmes being executed in the villages. Mahatma Gandhi National Rural Employment Guarantee Act (MGNREGA), 2005 also recognised the important role of Gram Sabha in rural development. The responsibility of development in the rural sector is now on the villagers themselves.

Gram Sabha: Present Scenario

The above discussion clearly highlights that the basic objective of introducing Gram Sabha is to have decentralised planning and evaluation with peoples participation at the grassroot level. The concept of eradication of discrimination and facilitation of peoples participation from all walks of social life in the management of affairs of their locality were the foundation for the emergence of comprehensive society called Gram Sabha. Peoples participation alone can bring sustainable development through good governance at the base level.

The 73rd Constitutional Amendment Act makes the establishment of Gram Sabha mandatory. It however, leaves it to the State Government to spell out its jurisdiction and powers. Most state legislations assign to Gram Sabha a ceremonial and tokenistic role. Most State legislations endorsing proposals, making recommendations, considering annual accounts, reviewing development plans, scrutinising completed works. Other functions entrusted to Gram Sabha include those like promoting harmony and unity in the village, mobilizing voluntary labour and contributions in cash or kind, rendering assistance in implantation of development schemes and promoting programmes for adult education and family welfare. Sixth Round Table organised at Guwahati by the Ministry of Panchayati Raj put together a series of recommendations to make Gram Sabha transparent and accountable, viz.

(a) Activation of the Gram Sabha preferably by statutorily endowing Gram Sabha with the duty of—
   (i) Approving all projects and programmes and plans of the Panchayat;
   (ii) Authorizing the issue of utilization certificates by the Panchayat bureaucracy; and
   (iii) Formation of the sub-committees of the Gram Sabhas to liaise with the counterpart Standing Committees of the Panchayat.

(b) The Constitution of Ward Sabhas to facilitate participative social audit.

(c) The convening of Mahila Sabhas immediately prior to meetings of Ward Sabhas, Gram Sabhas; and

(d) Involving the Right to Information Act and associating public spirited NGOs to make Gram Sabhas truly a people's parliament to furnish the checks and balances, advice and consent on which depends the success of the democratic functioning of an elected executive authority.

The Gram Sabha performs the following functions:

(i) To examine annual statements of accounts, audit report, audit note and to seek clarification from the Panchayat.
(ii) To discuss report on the administration of the preceding years.
(iii) To review programme for the year, any new programme and review all kinds of works under taken by the Gram Panchayat.
(iv) To consider proposals for fresh taxation or for enhancement of existing taxation.
(v) To approve the selection of schemes, beneficiaries, location, identification and implementation of various development programmes.
(vi) To mobilise voluntary labour and contributionin kind and cash.
(vii) To undertake programmes for adult education and family welfare with in the village.
(viii) To promote unity and harmony among all the sections of the rural community.
(ix) To seek clarifications from the members of the Gram Panchayat about schemes, income and expenditure.
(x) To consider the budget prepared by the Gram Panchayat and future development programmes and plans.
(xi) To maintain a complete register for all development works undertaken by Gram Panchayat or any other department.
(xii) To approve Village Plan of Action.

But the real picture of Gram Sabhas functioning at the grassroots level is different and mixed. In a study of 185 Gram Panchayats in Gujarat, Haryana, Himachal Pradesh, Kerala, Madhya Pradesh and Uttar Pradesh, the following were observed in relation to Gram Sabha:

- In many instances Gram Sabha meetings were convened as a matter of formality;
- In most of the meetings the minimum required quorum was rarely fulfilled;
- In nearly 1/3rd cases of study, the records of Gram Sabha meetings were completed even when meetings were not held or there was no quorum;

- The important reason for ineffective functioning of Gram Sabha is due to absence of understanding about its role in the minds of both its members and Gram Panchayat leaders;
- Absence of prior information about the Gram Sabha meeting is the most important reason for poor attendance;
- Whenever Sarpanch and Panchayat members have consulted members of Gram Sabha in advance, participation of members has been substantial and active;
- Confusion about the role of Gram Sabha is mainly due to members perception that it is a programme of a political party or an occasion to identify beneficiaries;
- Except in Kerala and Madhya Pradesh, the advice and suggestions of Gram Sabha are not binding on Gram Panchayat; and
- Most Sarpanches lack skills in conducting meetings.

Above findings indicate that special interventions and awareness—building measures for their proper functioning is required. Unless the Institution of Gram Sabha put to use fully, the Panchayati Raj Institutions in general, and grassroots democracy in particular will not be able to flourish to the desired extent.

Empowering Gram Sabha

The present scenario of functioning of Gram Sabha is a bit critical. In actual practice the Gram Sabha has not raised to the expectations of the law makers and even the spirit of the Constitution of India. The socio-economic and political realities of India with illiteracy, caste and gender biases, the rigid caste hierarchy and the powerful patriarchal norms are also not conducive to bring desired changes through Gram Sabha institution. It cannot be denied that it is not easy for a mandated body to perform its functions, especially when it concerns people, contesting with the social realities of stark power imbalances. Though there are provisions for representation of the weaker section of the society in terms of caste, tribe and gender, implying the same on the ground is a different story all together. Effective functioning of Gram Sabha will only be possible when the common people will start recognising its importance and their role in it. Lack of awareness among the Gram Sabha members often contributes to limited presence and participation. This is more so for the marginalised section of any community who are in a worse position than others. Thus, there is a need to provide support to both community members and also to the elected representatives to understand the importance of Gram Sabha, its roles and their significance, in the whole process of sustainable development.

Non-Participation of the rural thé people as hobbled the development of the Gram Sabha, denying the true benefits of this institution to the people. The participatory approach helps us to reduce development cost, increase perceived and actual benefits and increase awareness among the people and help in the mobilisation of local resources, facilitates smooth and easy project implementation. It further enables people to have access and control over the resources and ensures that the benefits reach to the legitimate claimants. It also creates sustainability aspect and gradually empowers the socially and economically disadvantaged people. The concept of Gram Sabha has also not been grasped clearly, right from the policy-makers to the villagers. The difficulty lies in motivating the villagers to attend the Gram Sabha meetings. In most of the backward villages, in the absence of a common public, the vested interests are likely to influence the proceedings which may not be in the felt need or real interest of the community. Therefore, the office bearers of various village level organizations such as schools, colleges, cooperative societies, banks, *mahila mandals*, youth groups, farmers' associations and voluntary agencies should take part in the meetings, as these institutions are expected to safeguard the interests of the community. Some of these institutions can also assume the role of facilitators of the Gram Sabha and form a link between the Gram Panchayat and Gram Sabha. The community will be able to monitor the services provided by the Government through Gram Sabha with the active participation of all sections of the local community.

Empowering Gram Sabha to achieve inclusive and sustainable development in rural areas several suggestion are made by the experts and voluntary organizations viz.:

- Gram Panchayat should be made responsible to conduct Gram Sabha meetings twice in a year under the direct supervision of Mandal Development officials and the Revenue Officials.
- The exact date of conducting Gram Sabha can be left to the discretion of the village panchayat and its members.
- Beneficiaries of various schemes should be identified and approved only in the Gram Sabha meetings. All the benefits of various schemes should be distributed in the Gram Sabha so that benefits would go only to needy.

- Information regarding all government activities in connection with the Village Panchayat should take place through Gram Sabha. This would create interest among the people to participate in the meetings.
- A film show explaining the public policies and programmes under taken by the government in the field of Agricultural, Rural, Health, Education, Minimum Needs Programmes, Right to Information, Drinking Water to all the local public, Public Distribution System would attract the people towards Gram Sabha meetings.
- A collective participation of the villagers along with Gram Panchayat ward members would go along way in solving the developmental issues in the village in turn this would help in achieving integrated development in the Village Panchayat.
- Print and electronic media should play an important role in providing adequate information about the growing importance of Gram Sabha and create social awareness among the people.
- The salient features of Gram Sabha and the various activities to be constituted during Gram Sabha meetings and agenda has to be informed to the villagers well in advance.
- Ward members/public representatives must disseminate the information about the Gram Panchayat function to the local people in their respective wards and they should motivate them to participate in the Gram Sabha.
- Ward-wise Gram Sabha would enable every voter to participate in the deliberations. The Village Sarpanch and ward members should apprise the ward people about the government programmes sanctioned to the village.

In addition, the Sub-Group of the Taskforce on Panchayati Raj constituted by the Union Ministry of Rural Development has suggested the following recommendations in relation to empower Gram Sabha:

1. Appointment of specified officers of intermediate level or district level Panchayati Raj Institutions as observes of Gram Sabha.
2. Gram Sabha Abhiyan meetings to be conducted throughout the state for two weeks to bring awareness among people.
3. The agenda of the Gram Sabha should be of interest to majority of members and must-cover a range of subjects that vitally affect their day-today-life.

4. They should not act merely as a recommendatory body or debating forum.
5. If the decisions are not capable of being implemented, the Gram Panchayats should report the reasons for non-compliances to Gram Sabhas.

Gram Sabha committees need to be constituted to supervise the operational aspects of Gram Panchayat as one of the vital concept of decentralised administration. The observation reveals that most of the state governments are not serious towards formation of Gram Sabha committees. Few states like Bihar, Goa, Himachal Pradesh, Manipur, Rajasthan and Tripura have formulated vigilance committees to ensure at the grassroot democracy. Though Gram Sabha is empowered to participate in decision-making process of the Panchayat meetings, none of the State government formulated Gram Sabha with development committees at the village level. Further, Social Audit is one strong measure through which empowered Gram Sabha can be achieved. Social Audit a process in which details of the resources, both financial and non-financial, is used by public agencies for development initiatives and is shared with the people through public platforms. The benefits of Social Audit:

- It will bring transparency and accountability in the functioning of Panchayati System.
- It will improve the quality of work and service delivery at all levels.
- It will help to improve peoples participation at Gram Sabha level.
- It will create awareness and knowledge among the Gram Sabha members about the development works being carried out at village level.
- It will force the Panchayat to keep proper records and accounts of the spending made against the grants received from the government and other sources.
- Through Social Audit all the stake holders will be able to gain control over the implementation of development works undertaken by Gram Panchayat.

Social Audits will contribute to the process of empowerment of the beneficiaries and generate demand of the effective delivery of programmes. Special Gram Sabha may be arranged to conduct Social Audits of all the previous works in addition to ongoing development works as an item of discussion in agenda of Gram Sabha. Gram Sabha are to be made effective, active and creative so that the expected result could be accessible to the rural society. It is foremost responsibility of the Panchayati Raj representatives to convey to the people the real nature, function and the real spirit of Gram Sabha. Gram Sabha meeting is a good platform to resolve local issues and found solution to various day to day problems encountering the village. This platform can also be used for initiation of community work.

Most of the basic rural problems, which have hardly any cost effect, can be solved by motivating villagers to participate in Gram Sabha proceedings. The Gram Sabha is the right forum to discuss all issues related to village development. The vibrancy and efficacy of Gram Sabha will remain dismal, if it does not possess the capacity to perform assigned roles and responsibility. This question becomes more pertinent in a socio-cultural milieu where society is deeply fragmented and hierarchical. Therefore, it is urgently needed that marginalised sections of society which has been out from the process of decision-making at grassroots level have to be taken in mainstream through sensitization and capacity building. Gram Sabha can reduce the gap between the desired impact and actual impact of several programmes of the government involving crores of rupees. It also contributes to bring the gains of our democracy and economic prosperity to spread evenly across all sections of the rural society.

Conclusion

Gram Sabha has been described as the institution for direct democracy through participation of local community in decision-making, fixing priorities about the development works, analysing and approving the forth coming programmes, Perusing annual reports and conducting social audits of all the works being carried out at village level. It is a corner stone of the entire scheme of democratic decentralisation was non-functional prior to the 73rd Constitutional Amendment Act. The 73rd Constitutional Amendment Act made the establishment of Gram Sabha mandatory. It acts as a watchdog on the working of Gram Panchayats besides facilitating the rural people's participation in the decision-making processes.

But the real picture of Gram Sabha functioning at grassroot level is different and mixed. There is no unanimity among the states in implementing the functions devolved. Most of the village panchayats have failed to execute the decisions taken of the Gram Sabha. It is unfortunate that a majority of state governments could not show seriousness and have failed to conduct Gram Sabha meetings which is mandatory. However, the recent experience reveals that there is growing awareness among rural people particularly marginalised sections about the significances of Gram Sabha functions and meetings. The goals of inclusive growth and sustainable development as envisaged by the Central and State governments cannot be achieved without empowering Gram Sabha. Measures like creating awareness among marginalised sections of villagers to use their constitutional rights, increasing active participation of people in Gram Sabha meetings, capacity buildings of villagers, women empowerment, active role of media etc., will go a long way to empower Gram Sabha and achieve inclusive and sustainable rural development.

References

Aslam, M., (2004) "Towards Empowering Gram Sabha" in *The Grassroots Governance,* Volume II, No. 2, December.

"Decentralisation and Local Governance", *MA Public Administration Course Material* (MPA-016), School of Social Sciences, Indira Gandhi National Open University, New Delhi, 2006.

Empowering Gram Sabha (A special issue), *Kurukshetra, A Journal of Rural Development Ministry of Rural Development*, Vol. 61, No. 7, May, 2013.

Joshil, R.P. and G.S. Narwani, (2002), *Panchayati Raj in India: Empowering Trends Across the States*, Rawat Publications, New Delhi.

Mathew, George, (2005), Ten-year Journey of New Panchayats in S.S Chahar (ed.); *Governance of Grassroots Level in India*, Kanishka, New Delhi.

Panchayati Raj in India—Status Report 1999, Task Force on Panchayat Raj, Rajiv Gandhi Foundation, New Delhi, March, 2000.

The Constitution (Seventy Third Amendment) Act, 1992. Government of India, New Delhi.

15

Contract Farming System in India

Challenges and Solutions

V. Saravanan

Introduction

In India, 85 per cent of the farmers are marginal or small, operating less than two acres. In fact, 66 per cent operate less than one acre each. How many will have such land to give for contract crops. It is possible that contract farming can work if there is a collectivisation of small farmers. For instance, 10 to 15 farmers get together, form a group and sign a group contract. It brings down the transaction costs, the farmers are better protected and it is essentially, a win-win situation for both the former and the corporate.

Contract Farming has been in existence for many years as a means of organizing the commercial agricultural production of both large-scale and small-scale farmers. In an age of market liberalization, globalization and expanding agri-business, there is a danger that small-scale farmers will find difficulty in fully participating in the market economy. The era of globalization, the concept of 'Contract Farming' is an effective way to co-ordinate and promote production and marketing in agriculture. "Contract Farming can be defined as an agreement between farmers and processing or marketing firms for the production and supply of agricultural products under forward agreements, frequently at predetermined prices."

Eventhough the contract farming will have its own set of pros and cons. One is simple procurement, in the second, the buyer provides some inputs and takes the crop according to the terms and conditions of the contract; and in the third, the buyers provides inputs and planing schedules and is more involved in the agricultural process.

The pros and the high yields and fixed prices. The cons, however are where as born production risk and market risk. Production costs in contract farming are higher as the standard expected is higher. No company offers protection for crop failure. No crop insurance is given and thus production risk is not covered most of the time. Thus, market risk is also not covered fully, especially when the contract prices are based on market prices, as we know that the market prices vary substantially during the season or even during the day. If contract doucment is not fair, how can the farm practice be fair?

Meaning of Contract Farming

A system in which agricultural production is carried out through an agreement between farmers and buyers, that specifies a combination of features such as price, quality, volumes to be supplied and date of delivery, which farmers as suppliers are expected to adhere to, and in response to which buyers are expected to redeem their pledge to acquire supplies at the pre-specified price.

Unequal Relationship

On the surface the system seems to lock both farmers and buyers into what is an equal relationship. But, besides not being arms-length as a result, the relationship is most often unequal, with buyers being large corporations looking for guaranteed supplies at pre-specified prices, and suppliers being competing farmers who are economically weaker partners in the arrangement. In fact, large buyers often subordinate farmers within the relationship by providing them with inputs and or credit, giving the former substantial leverage *vis-à-vis* the latter. Thus, instances of contract farming in India have involved companies such as Pepsi (in potato and groundnut, among other crops), Unilever (tomato and tea), ITC (tobacco and oilseeds) and Cargill (seeds). It is true that large foreign and domestic conglomerates such as these enter into contracts with relatively larger farmers who are better suited to meeting quality and volume requirements. Yet there are huge differences in relative economic weight between producers and buyers that are bound to influence the nature of the relationship.

Yet advocates of contract farming tend to present the relationship as a win-win solution for both sides. While buyers are assured of supplies and can intervene in production to ensure quality, it is argued, empirical studies show that farmers who operate under the contract farming system obtain better and more predictable prices than their counterparts outside the system.

There is, however, the potential for and some evidence of the dangers inherent in the unequal system. While farmers are assured of price, volumes sold depend on the portion of the harvest identified by the buyer as of appropriate quality. This quality angle could be used by powerful buyers to renege on volumes promised to be acquired in the contract in times when demand is low or when harvest fluctuations result in buyers being able to acquire much cheaper supplies from outside the system. Moreover, in years of lean demand, buyers can delay payments—a common experience in the relationship between ancillary suppliers and large buyer firms in the industrial sector.

Even when contract conditions are not implicitly violated, the risk associated with contract farming could be greater if meeting the quality and volume demands of the buyer requires substantial investment on the part of farmers, who undertake that investment on the basis of credit provided or organised by buyers. Shortfalls in production resulting from weather fluctuations, pest attacks and the like would result in much higher losses than would have otherwise been the case.

If farmers are still willing to enter into such arrangements, it is because of the instability and uncertainty inherent in peasant-based, fragmented and largely rain-dependent agriculture. This periodically challenges the viability of crop production and the agricultural sector fails to deliver to the non-agricultural sector its requirement of a marketable surplus of agricultural supplies, especially food. That possibility forces the state to intervene to stabilise agriculture.

Overtime, a government unwilling to mobilise the resources required to finance this comprehensive package, has let the extension services system collapse and reneged on its promise to procure and distribute enough to ensure universal food access at affordable prices. Liberalisation and deregulation are in part a consequence of this failure. Not surprisingly, the 'promotion' of contract farming through deregulation has been partly justified on the grounds that it is a way of introducing better and more modern farming practices into a slowly growing agricultural sector, which is affected by dwindling productivity in many regions. Large commercial buyers, it is argued, would provide the credit, the technical services and the remunerative prices that the state had committed to provide, but has not been adequately successful in ensuring.

The possibility that direct marketing and contractual relationships between vulnerable farmers and large buyers could be damaging for the farmer was what resulted in the regulation of markets through the Agricultural Produce Marketing Committees (APMCs).

APMCs was not only that of providing better marketing facilities, but of establishing regulated markets in which orderly and transparent trading conditions permit price discovery by farmers who might otherwise lose as a result of unequal buyer-seller relationships.

The positive feature here is that contract-farming agreements have to be registered, allowing in principle for monitoring and systems of dispute settlement. But, in as much as the relationship between the contracting parties is unequal, the terms of the contract are bound to benefit buyers and complaints are unlikely to be registered whenever they arise. In the event, after the first flush in which contract terms and contracting behaviour would be adjusted to attract farmers into relationships with large buyers, economic instability and even deterioration could be the fate of those entering the practice.

Farmer has Risk, Capital has Control

It would be best if risks can reside with farmers but control over production and marketing can be acquired by capital. This is what the system of contract farming seeks to do. It does so by enticing farmers into using equipment and inputs that deliver revenues and profits to external producers and produce and deliver outputs that external agents can distribute or process for profit. Since, this penetration of external capital into agricultural production is driven by profit, it is to be expected that the agri-business value chain is modified in ways that leave a smaller share of revenues and value added with farmers. At the end of the twentieth century in the US, it was estimated that around 10 per cent of every dollar consumers paid for food went to the farmer, with 25 per cent accruing to input suppliers and the remaining 65 per cent to those engaged in the transportation, processing and marketing of food output. If that is the intent of contract farming, expecting it to benefit farmers in the long run would be to miss the motivation for the transition to this form of organising agricultural production.

Moreover, the experience in countries other than India suggests that the spread of contract farming has implications not just for those entering into contracting arrangements but the agricultural sector in general. As noted earlier, given the volumes, farming practices and standards demanded by contracting buyers, agreements are normally entered into with larger farmers who have the where withal to meet those demands. Where successful, this excludes smaller producers from markets and encourages acquisition of more land by those who have established successful relationships, leading to intensified peasant differentiation and the reduction of large numbers of poor and marginal peasants to the status of agricultural workers. This too then helps bring the whole of agriculture under the sway of big capital.

Marginal Farmers Worst Affected

Marginal farmers, who constitute 83 per cent of farm households in India, will be the worst affected by contract farming as they lack the surplus to invest and do not have risk-bearing capacity. The expansion of contract farming will also force marginal farmers to lease out their lands to corporate or big farmers at payments below the market price. In a district of Karnataka where rose is cultivated under corporate farming, Scheduled Caste and Scheduled Tribe farmers were forced to lease out their land at one-third of the market price.

Other implications of corporate farming include a shift towards mechanisation and high-value crops such as fruits, vegetables and flowers. There are studies that clearly indicate that such a shift adversely affects the need of the locally available or produced labour-intensive goods and services, a major source of the Rural Non-Farm Economy (RNFE). Another feature of the contract system is cartelisation, where farmers are forced to use seeds, fertilizers, insecticides and credit of a particular company. This decreases the autonomy of farmers.

The proposition that farmers will get extra price in contract/corporate farming lacks conclusive evidence. International experience of corporate farming shows that in the initial phases some margin is transferred to the farmer so as to establish a monopsony. Once it is established, the corporates exert downward pressure on the producer and on labour. A study conducted in 1999 by the Competition Commission, United Kingdom, for the Director General of Fair Trading concluded that practices adopted by organised retailers exerted downward pressure on the incomes of farmers and workers involved in the supply of goods to the retail chain.

Studies in India

Extensive studies were made on almost all agriculture marketing systems prevalent in different parts of India by the working group of the Eleventh Five Year Plan (2007). The findings on the farmers' share in the final consumer price found in different marketing systems may be summarised as follows:

(a) The share of farmers in the final consumer price varies between 24 and 58 per cent.
(b) The share of farmers is highest in the markets controlled by farmers' organisations such as HOPCOM (Horticultural Producers Cooperative Marketing and Processing Society Limited) and Gadat Agricultural Marketing Cooperative Society. Here, the share of vegetable and fruit growers is as high as 75 per cent of the stall price.
(c) The most efficient market system for farmers and consumers is farmers' markets such as Apni Mandi, Rythu Bazaar, Uzhavar Sandhai and Krushak Bazaar.

The farmers' share in the final produce in the government-controlled sugar sector in Uttar Pradesh is almost 80 per cent, while in Amul in the cooperative sector, it is more than 80 per cent.

The provision of Rs.380 crore for the development of the agriculture market reflected the government's seriousness in the matter. Against a target of 1,152, only 51 *Apni Mandis* were set up. Only one wholesale *mandi* was set up against a target of 75. No terminal market became functional against the target of 35 during the Eleventh Plan. So, it is a myth that the farmer may get a higher price only in corporate market formats.

Cold storages set up in various States in the private and public sectors have been abandoned because of high running costs on account of high electricity bills and low profitability. The 50 per cent investment in back-end infrastructure is attached as conditionality in FDI in multi-brand retail, but how it will benefit farmers is not clear. These are post-aggregation logistics and add value to the produce after purchase from the farmer.

Multinational corporations are exerting pressure on the government to ease the conditions attached to FDI in multi-brand retail, especially to make an entry into cities that have a population of less than one million, because it suits their economies of scale, and for the inclusion of agri-produce in Small and Medium Enterprises (SME). There are signals that the government will concede their demands. The pro-corporate attitude of the government is reflected in the draft of the Twelfth Five Year Plan.

Corporate entrants have not fared well in the competition with incumbent traders since existing trading margins, although high, are in fact much less than, for example, in the United States.

The inherent danger of corporatisation of the farm sector is price volatility and the alignment of domestic food prices with international food and oil prices. The prices will be decided in futures markets rather than in physical markets after corporate takeover of the purchase and storage of foodgrain. There was a 13 per cent price rise in wheat after a one per cent reduction in its production in 2007. During this season (2013), the Uttar Pradesh government could purchase only 10 per cent of the targeted wheat.

The need of our economy is to take steps to protect, enhance and defend the livelihood of small and marginal farmers and not adopt policies that "take care and promote the profits of super-rich corporates". If the government feels so concerned about the exploitation of retail by the intermediaries, it should form cooperatives up to the retail level.

History of Food Retailing

The transformation of agriculture into agribusiness in a liberal economic regime attracted major domestic and foreign corporates to the agricultural trade. The Indian retail market (worth Rs. 17, 497 billion in 2008-09) occupied top position in A.T. Kearney's annual Global Retail Development Index (GRDI) for three consecutive years (2005-08). The importance of farm produce in retail is evident from the National Sample Survey Organisation (NSSO) data, which say that the Private Final Consumption Expenditure (PFCE) of 40 per cent of the urban population and 52 per cent of the rural population is on food items. The size of food retail in 2008-09 was estimated at Rs. 10,700 billion, 61 per cent of the total retail value. Besides value, food retailing means regular customer footfalls.

Before economic liberalisation, state intervention in the agriculture market was considered an important instrument of development policy. The state generally controls the agriculture markets through—(1) fixing of minimum price, (2) maintenance of the minimum price through purchase operations by state and cooperative agencies, and (3) formulation of market regulating Acts generally known as the APMC Act and the establishment of necessary infrastructure.

The thrust of the different Five Year Plans was to establish regulated markets and to create storage capacity in the form of warehouses and cold storages, grading facilities, processing units and market intelligence, mainly in the cooperative sector. The private sector was accorded equal status in agriculture marketing in the Tenth Plan (2002-07) as private and cooperative sector participation in the marketing of agriculture produce would break the monopolistic or oligopolistic supply structure. Also, it favoured forward trading in agriculture commodities.

The APMC Act was amended into the Model APMC Act in 2003 to provide a bigger role for the private sector. It includes provisions for setting up private *mandis* and for contract farming. So far, 16 States have adopted different provisions of this Act, but none of them has adopted them fully because of local compulsions.

Major Indian corporates entered agribusiness in different formats during 2000-10. The Bharti group, along with Walmart, opened the first cash-and-carry store in 2006 as a joint venture. The rationale of the government in allowing them was to remove the "intermediaries" to create a "farm-to-fork" model and create infrastructure in the interest of farmers and consumers. But no impact studies were made. The only study made, by the Indian Council for Research on International Economic Relations (sponsored by the Government of India) in 2008, concluded that farmers realised 25 per cent higher price of their produce in the organised retail format. But this study suffered from several weaknesses, starting with its small sample size. It was based merely on interactions with 197 farmers of a single locality of Hoskote, Bangalore, and growers of a single commodity, cauliflower. Clearly, there is no attention to detail, either by design or by default, while the larger agenda of "corporatocracy" is being pushed forward through different political and administrative manoeuvres.

Issues related to Contract Farming

As with any form of contractual relationship, there are potential disadvantages and risks associated with contract farming. If the terms of the contract are not respected by one of the contracting parties, then the affected party stands to lose. Common contractual problems include farmer sales to a buyer other than the one to whom the farmer is contracted (side selling or extra-contractual marketing), a company's refusal to buy products at the agreed prices, or the downgrading of produce quality by the buyer. Side selling by farmers to competing buyers is perhaps the greatest problem constraining the growth of contract farming. Contractors also may default by failing to pay agreed prices or by buying less than the pre-agreed quantities.

The existence of an adequate legal framework is thus crucial for the successful implementation and long-term sustainability of contract farming operations. A system of law is essential to assist farmers and their buyers in the negotiation and drafting of contracts. It is also important to protect them from risks that may occur during contractual execution, such as abuse of power by the stronger bargaining party or breach of the contract. Different countries have enacted policies and legislation to ensure fair contractual practices and offer remedies for dispute resolution.

Another concern about contract farming arrangements is the potential for buyers to take advantage of farmers. Buying firms, which are invariably more powerful than farmers, may use their bargaining clout to their financial advantage. Indeed, if farmers are not well organised or where there are few alternative buyers for the crop or it is not easy to change the crop, there is a danger that farmers may have an unfair deal. Tactics sometimes used are changing pre-agreed standards, downgrading crops on delivery so offering lower prices, or over-pricing for inputs and transport provided. Strengthening farmer organisations to better access appropriate services such as credit, extension services and market information and improving their contract negotiating skills can redress the potential for exploitation of farmers and poorly formulated contracts and their enforcement. There are also proposals for some form of welfare system for contracted farmers akin to the benefits provided in most contractual employment.

Farmer Discontent

A number of situations can lead to farmer dissatisfaction. Discriminatory buying, late payments, inefficient extension services, poor agronomic advice, unreliable transportation for crops, a mid-season change in pricing or management's rudeness to farmers will all normally generate dissent. If not readily addressed, such circumstances will cause hostility towards the sponsors that may result in farmers withdrawing from projects.

Extra-contractual Marketing

The sale of produce by farmers to a third party, outside the conditions of a contract, can be a major problem. Extra-contractual sales are always possible and are not easily controlled when an alternative market exists. For example, a farmer cooperative in Croatia bought cucumbers, red peppers and aborigines on contract. The cooperative's advances to the farmers included all necessary production inputs. Unfortunately members often sold their vegetables to traders at higher prices than the cooperative had contracted. The outside buyers offered cash to farmers as opposed to the prolonged and difficult collection of payments negotiated through the cooperative. Sponsors themselves can sometimes be a cause of extra-contractual practices. There are several companies working with the same crop (e.g. cotton in some southern African countries), they could collaborate by establishing a register of contracted farmers. Managers must be aware of produce being sold outside the project and also be aware of produce from outside being channeled into the buying system. This occurs when non-contracted farmers take advantage of higher prices paid by an established sponsor. Non-contracted crops are filtered into the buying system by outside farmers through friends and family who have crop contracts. Such practices make it difficult for the sponsor to regulate production targets, chemical residues and other quality aspects.

Input Diversion

A frequent problem is that farmers are tempted to use inputs supplied under contract for purposes other than those for which they were intended. They may choose to use the inputs on their other cash and subsistence crops or even to sell them. Clearly this is not acceptable to the sponsor, as the contracted crop's yields will be reduced and the quality affected. Steps to overcome such problems include improved monitoring by extension staff, farmer training and the issuing of realistic quantities of inputs. However, the knowledge that a contract has the advantages of technical inputs, cash advances and a guaranteed market usually makes the majority of farmers conform to the agreement. Unless a project is very poorly managed, input diversion is usually an annoyance rather a serious problem.

Remedies for the Problems of Contract Farming System

A typical contract farming agreement is an agreement between two unequal parties involving large number of illiterate farmers on one side and a mighty sponsoring company on the other. These farmers do not have sufficient means to approach the court of law for resolution of disputes, if any, with the company. It is equally difficult for the company to redress the breach of agreement by the farmers through the present mechanism of civil court. Hence, it is necessary to create a dispute resolution mechanism near to the farmers, which can quickly settle the disputes in quasi-judicial manner. The dispute redressal authority should be a body at the sub-divisional level comprising a representative of the sponsoring company, a farmers' representative and the Sub-Divisional Magistrate of the area under whose jurisdiction the contract farming land falls. The party aggrieved by the decision of the prescribed authority as above may prefer an appeal to an Appellant Authority within thirty days from the date of decision.

The farmers may be required to invest substantial amount of resources to raise the contracted crops and run the risk of incurring huge debt in the event of crop failure, which may result in their displacement from the land, affecting their livelihood. In order to protect the farmers from such displacement, it is considered necessary to prevent, by law, displacement of farmers from their land as consequence of the contract farming agreement.

Participatory Process for Drawing up Contracts

The contracts should be managed in a more transparent and participatory manner, so, that there is greater social consensus in handling contract violation from either side without getting involved in costly as well as lengthy process of litigation. The best contract between parties is the contract of trust and loyalty. The sponsoring companies should discharge some social responsibilities for the farmers in respect of health, hygiene, education, and long-term training in Good Agricultural Practices, Good Hygiene Practices, Good Marketing Practices, etc. This would help in the sustenance of long-term relationship between the farmers and the sponsoring companies. Some governmental incentives should be given to the sponsoring companies for this purpose through a well-designed incentive programme of contract farming through some state agency in the line of Punjab Agro Corporation. The remaining states should amend their respective APMR Acts in the line of the Model Act of the Government of India so as to permit contract farming, direct marketing, and facilitate the appointment of authority for dispute redressal mechanism. The APMC Act should also be amended for the rationalization of market fees, formation of Bureaus of Standards at the state level, and marketing extension, etc.

Lease Market to Develop

In many parts of the country, agricultural tenancy is legally banned, although concealed tenancy exists. Tenants, who do not enjoy security of tenure, cannot participate in contract farming. Hence, legalization of tenancy would be a precondition for enabling the tenant farmers to benefit from contract farming. Although different forms of land tenants including share-croppers can be adopted to maintain the contract farming, security of tenure would be necessary. Leasing of land should be permitted for a relatively long period, making it co-terminus with the life of asset created by mean of investment by the sponsoring company in the farmer's land. A long lease period will ensure security of tenure for the sponsoring companies encouraging them to go in for long term investment in the contracted land.

Incentives to Sponsoring Companies

Some contract farming incentives should be given to the sponsoring companies for disseminating technical knowledge or introduction of new technology amongst the farmers in the line of Punjab Model of partial reimbursement of extension expenditure of the sponsoring companies. At the time of registration itself, a company should given a declaration regarding the technology to be introduced in its contract farming model. This should simply be filed by the registering authority. While transferring a technology through the extension staff, the intellectual capacity of the workers, the technical feasibility, economic viability and cultural acceptability need to be taken into consideration.

Preservation of Bio-Diversity

It has to be ensured through an appropriate state agency that contract farming, which is generally commodity specific and tends to promote monoculture, does not grow beyond proportion to destroy bio-diversity and agricultural ecology. It may be necessary to provide necessary guidelines for land use planning in each region in order to prevent such eventualities. There is a need for widespread awareness for contract farming through campaigns, media, etc.

Stable Models

The Economic Reforms Commission recognises the importance of farm producers' organisations, that is, companies, cooperatives or associations in the corporatisation of agriculture. Through, the recently (April, 2013) amended policy of Small Farmers Agribusiness Consortium (SFAC), benefits of the cooperative sector have been extended to farm producers' companies through the consortium. A provision has been made in the Producers' Company Act for optional conversion of producers' cooperatives to producers' companies.

Compared with the JSC model, producers' organisations are better placed with least social destabilisation. From the point of farm producers, producers' companies are poor substitutes to producers' cooperatives as the farmers' involvement, and the benefits from it, are relatively better than those obtained in the company model. Farmers should be allowed to choose between the producers company and cooperative models. The consortium should extend its support to whatever the farmers prefer without discrimination.

The SFAC encouraged the formation of producers' vegetable cooperatives around big cities. About 70 have been formed in Andhra Pradesh itself. The cooperatives are helping growers to reduce their cost of cultivation and market expenses and improve the net profit. Produce from these societies is being procured by city-based big retailers who make huge profits. If the SFAC can help organise the wholesale markets, it will improve the net profits of the growers without casting a burden on the consumers. Similarly, it can help fruit growers, as it has in Himachal Pradesh.

Finally, it can be said that better experiences are available from the cooperative sector to bring small farms into the corporate model, modernise them and extend the benefits of large-scale farming to farmers. The JSC model is inferior to the cooperative models in this regard, provided the growers are involved more democratically in the functioning of the cooperative set-up. It also requires political will on the part of the ruling class. Will the policy-makers, committed as they are to globalising the Indian economy, allow this? The answer is not difficult to predict.

Concluding Remarks

The various studies done in India and abroad indicate that the corporate system strongly prefers contract farming system. But the experience of the contract farming system is not very encouraging in different parts of the country, mainly because of corporate tactics such as *post-facto* lowering of prices; delays in payments; defaults on contracts in a slut situation, as done by Pepsi in Punjab and mineries in Maharashtra; and improper legislation. The contract system has certain structural characteristics; for instance, the farmer bears the risk even when the decision regarding the choice of crop, input, quality and quantity of crop and schedule of payment rests with the corporate. Moreever, contract farming has a strong bias towards large land owners as they have the surplus to invest and can supply the required quantity, a prerequisite for economics of scale.

The need of our economy is to take steps to protect, enhance and defined the livelihood of small and marginal farmers and not adopt policies that "take came and promote the profits of super-rich corporates". If the government feels so concerned about the exploitation of retail by the intermediaries, it should from co-operatives up to the retail level.

References

Chandrasekhar, C.P. (2013), "Locked into Business" *Frontline*, Vol. 30, No. 14, July 13-26, pp. 8-9.

Prasad Rao (2013), "Exploitative Models" *Frontline*, Vol. 30, No. 14, July 13-26, pp. 10-12.

Pultrone, C. (2012), "An Overview of Contract Farming: Legal Issues and Challenges", UNIDROIT, *Uniform Law Review*, p. 56.

Rangi, P.S. and Sidhu, M.S. (2003), "Contract Farming System, Punjab State Policy Issues", *Productivity*, October-December 2003, Vol. 44, No. 3, pp. 484-491.

Sahat, B.S. *Supply Chain Management in the 21st Century*, MacMillan India Ltd., Delhi, pp. 10-12.

Singh, Gurdev, S.R. Asokan and V.N. Asopa "*Seed Industry in India, A Management Perspective*", Oxford and IBH, New Delhi, pp. 36-38.

Singh, Sukpal "Contract Farming and Agricultural Diversification in the Indian Punjab: A Study of Performance and Problems, *Indian Journal of Agricultural Economics*, 55 (3) July-September, pp. 283-294.

Sudhir Panwar (2013), "Towards Corporatecracy", *Fronteline*, Vol. 30, No. 14, July 13-26, pp. 13-15.

16
Textile Industry and Rural Upliftment under New Economic Initiatives

D. Indrakumar

Background

Manufacturing Industry in India has gone through various phases of development over the period of time. Since independence, the Indian manufacturing sector has travelled from the initial phase of building. The industrial foundation was made during in 1950's and early 1960's. It was controlled through the License-Permit Raj in the period of 1965-1980. Finally, the manufacturing industry went to a phase of liberalization in 1990's, emerging into the current phase of global competitiveness. It has grown at a robust rate over the past ten years and has been one of the best performing manufacturing economy. Manufacturing sector contributes about 16 per cent of India's Gross Domestic Product (GDP) and 50 per cent to the country's exports. The sector employed 44 million people in 1999-2000 to 51 million in 2009-10.

In the recent years manufacturing has been playing a dominant role on account of an increase in volume of global trade as a result of globalization and dismantling of trade barriers under the World Trade Organization (WTO). The improvement in the growth scenario of the manufacturing sector has been significant due to the improvement in the performance with regard to exports. However, India's strategy for industrial development witnessed a paradigm shift after the introduction of new economic reforms in 1991. Industrial development until then was largely based on product market regulations, with capacity licensing.

Though this strategy had successfully created an industrial base, it had encouraged rent seeking to a considerable extent. Economic reforms initiated in 1991 gradually removed licenses. Industrial Policy since 1991 has been more for facilitating the industrial development rather than anchoring it through permits and controls.

With aim to focus industrial development in the country for better employment and income generation, Government of India carry forwarded the liberalized economic process. By simplifying and relaxing the entry barriers for business activities and providing investor friendly laws and tax system especially for foreign investors. However, there is a need to modernize the manufacturing sector simultaneously also have to save the domestic industry. It requires a law should be such that it protects domestic investors and also promote trade through Foreign Direct Investment (FDI). (Devajit, 2012).

The data on manufacturing sector's contribution to total GDP since 1991 shows a fluctuating trend. It is visible from the data that, manufacturing GDP is registered an upward trend over the total GDP of the country. Similarly, it also registered a very low growth rate than the overall GDP growth rate since 1991. The manufacturing GDP has achieved a double digit growth rate (10.82 and 11.3% respectively) in 1994-95 and 2009-10. During the same period the overall GDP growth rate is 6.39 per cent and 8.59 per cent respectively. After 2010 the manufacturing sectors growth rate is very unimpressive among the sectors. It started declined to below 10 per cent (9.73%) in 2010-11 and just around 3 per

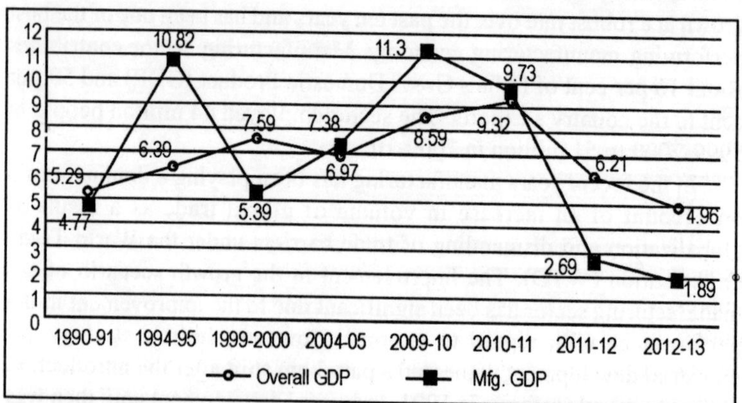

Fig. 16.1. GDP's Growth Rate
Source: Planning Commission, 2013.

cent for 2011-12 and 1.89 per cent for 2012-13 which is lowest growth of the sector since the new economic reforms was introduced in 1991. Global slowdown and it post impacts are largely caused this lowest growth in the manufacturing sector. However, the overall GDP of the country has registered fluctuating trend of growth during the post reform period (Fig. 16.1). The manufacturing growth rate reduced to 2.5 per cent in 2011-12 from 10.3 per cent in 2007-08. The global slowdown in 2008-09 has caused for this decline (Singh, 2013).

It is clear from the Fig. 16.2 the contribution from manufacturing industries shows a fluctuating trend over the years. The share from agriculture is continuously declining since in 1980s. However, the sector still employs more than 50 per cent of the workforce of the country. Even after the twenty years of new economic reforms the contribution from Industrial sector are still nominal. It was 13.95 per cent in 1980-81 to just around 19.17 per cent in 2009-10. It took three decade to get additional three per cent increases to the country's GDP.

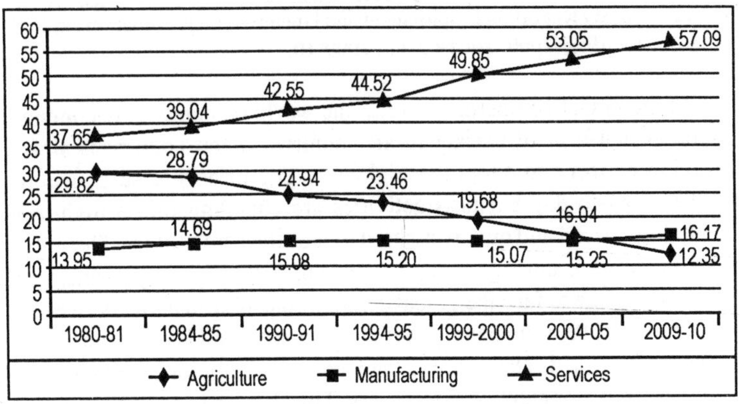

Fig. 16.2: Sectoral Share of GDP over the Years
Source: Reserve Bank of India, 2013.

The Table 16.1 shows the employment trend of major sectors of the economy for the previous decade (1999-2000 to 2009-10). It is really impressive to see the growth of the sectoral contribution in employment during the period. During the first half (1999-2000 to 2004-05) of the decade, all the sectors of the economy has registered an absolute increase in the number of employment generated by them. There was about 1.2 million additional employments were generated by the manufacturing sector alone during this period of five years. The textile sector contributed

0.74 million new employment between 1999-2000 to 2004-05. Whereas, in the second half (between 2004-05 to 2009-10), almost all sectors have lost their employment except the services sector. The manufacturing sector had lost 5.03 million opportunities during this period. Similarly, the textile sector lost 3.17 million jobs between 2004-05 to 2009-10 (Table 16.1).

Table 16.1: Number of Employment in Textile and Manufacturing

(Employment in Millions)

Sectors	Year		
	1999-2000	*2004-05*	*2009-10*
Agriculture	237.67	258.93	242.11
Manufacturing	44.05	55.77	50.74
Textile	11.51	18.92	15.75
Services	94.2	112.81	116.34
Total Employment	396.76	457.46	460.22

Source: NSSO Report on Employment and Unemployment Situations in India for 1999-2000, 2004-05 and 2009-10.

In the era of competitive world, the world economy is becoming a common platform of market to all countries. Each country is slowly adopting or force to adopt these globalisation effects to sustain in the market. Day-to-day business activities are changing into a high-tech, technology based and quality assured to face the competitors. The Indian manufacturing is among the top which is undergoing many phenomenal phase of change to face the global competition. Textile industry in one of predominant player in manufacturing component and is one of the oldest in the entire world. The sector is the leading contributor to the country's economic development over the years. The chapter is makes an attempt to analyse the impact of the globalisation on this sector especially the organised segment of the textile sector is anaysed and presented in the following sections.

Textile Industry in India: An Overview

An Overview

The Indian Textiles Industry has an overwhelming presence in the economic life of the country. Apart from providing one of the basic necessities of life, the textiles industry also plays a vital role through its contribution to industrial output, employment generation, and the export earnings of the country. Textile industry is one of the largest and oldest among the most industrially development nations. India's presence in the international market is significant in the areas of fabrics and yarn. The country is the largest exporter of cotton yarn in the international market and has a share of 25 per cent in the world's cotton yarn exports. India accounts for 12 percentage of the world's production of textile fibres and yarn. Similarly, the country has the highest loom capacity, including the handlooms with a share of 61 per cent in world's handloom capacity. Textile sector contributes about 14 per cent to industrial production, 4 per cent to the Gross Domestic Product (GDP), and 11 per cent to the country's export earnings. Textile is second single largest provider of employment after agriculture in the country. Thus, the growth and all round development of this industry has a direct bearing on the improvement of the economy of the nation. India's textiles and clothing industry is one of the mainstays of the national economy (Ministry of Textiles, 2013).

In value terms, India's Textile & Clothing (T&C) industry is estimated to be worth US$ 78.0 billion in 2010, comprising exports of US$ 22.0 billion and domestic market of US$ 56.0 billion. The industry had grown from US$ 58 billion in 2006 at a Compound Annual Growth Rate (CAGR) of 7.69 per cent. Segment-wise, garments constituted an estimated 64 per cent of the domestic market, followed by household fabrics (nearly 17%), technical textiles (14.3%), and home textiles (4.7%). In terms of textile units, the Indian T&C industry is one of the largest in the world. India has the second-largest installed capacity of spindles in the world after China. With an installed capacity of 43.0 million spindles, India represents 20 per cent of global spindle capacity. India also has one of the highest weaving capacities in the world (61.6% of global weaving capacity), with a presence of 2.2 million power looms, 3.5 million handlooms, and an estimated 92,000 million looms in the organised mill sector.

There are round 2,300 processing units in India. Most of these are independent units, with only 22 units being integrated with spinning, weaving or knitting units. Additionally, there are roughly 27,000 manufacturers, 48,000 contractors and over 1,000 manufacturer-exports of garments in India. India is the second highest producer of cotton after China contributing about 21.5 per cent of world production. In case of jute, India is the largest producer contributing about 64 per cent of world jute production. In case of silk, India is a distant second to China, contributing 15.5 per cent of world production. During the last ten years capacity addition has increased at a Compound Annual Growth Rate (CAGR) of 7.5 per cent for man-made filament yarn, 5.5 per cent for man-made fibres, 4.4 per cent for rotors, and 3.45 per cent for power looms (Ministry of Textiles, 2011).

The Indian textile industry is set for strong growth, buoyed by both strong domestic consumption as well as export demand. Abundant availability of raw materials such as cotton, wool, silk and jute and skilled workforce has made India a sourcing hub. The analysis of sector-wise FDI inflows shows that, the textile sector is one of the most attractive sectors which floated more FDI after the liberalization of the Indian economy (Mathiyazhagan *et al.,* 2005). The potential size of the Indian textile and apparel industry is expected to reach US$ 221 billion by 2021, according to Technopak's Textile and Apparel Compendium 2012. The textiles sector has witnessed a spurt in investment during the last five years. The industry (including dyed and printed) attracted foreign direct investments (FDI) worth Rs 5,831.02 crore (US$ 854.78 million) during April 2000 to May 2013. The report of the Working Group constituted by the Planning Commission on boosting India's manufacturing exports during Twelfth Five Year Plan (2012-17), envisages India's exports of Textiles and Clothing at USD 64.41 billion by the end of March, 2017.

Characteristics of Indian Textile Sector

The textiles sector in India comprises both organised and unorganised segments. More than 70 textile and clothing clusters account for about 80 per cent of total production in the country. There are 39 power loom clusters in the country. Major states with a number of clusters are Maharashtra, Tamil Nadu, Andhra Pradesh, Karnataka, Kerala and Uttar Pradesh. The textiles industry is extremely diversified with hand-spun and hand-woven sectors at one end and the capital-intensive, sophisticated mill sector at the other. The de-centralised power loom/hosiery and knitting sectors form the largest section of the textiles industry. Major sub-sectors of the textiles sector are organised cotton/man-made fibre textiles mills, man-made fibre/filament yarn, wool and woolen textiles, sericulture and silk textiles, handlooms, handicrafts, jute and jute textiles and textiles exports.

The structure of the textile industry is extremely complex with the modern, sophisticated and highly mechanised mill sector on the one hand and the handspinning and handweaving (handloom) sector on the other.

Between the two falls the small-scale powerloom sector. The latter two are together known as the decentralised sector. Over the years, the government has granted a whole range of concessions to the non-mill sector as a result of which the share of the decentralised sector has increased considerably in the total production. Of the two sub-sectors of the decentralised sector, the powerloom sector has shown the faster rate of growth. In the production of fabrics the decentralised sector accounts for roughly 94 per cent while the mill sector has a share of only 6 per cent.

The textile industry in the country is vertically-integrated across the value chain and extends from fibre to fabric to garments. At the same time, it is a highly-fragmented sector, and comprises small-scale, non-integrated spinning, weaving, processing and cloth manufacturing enterprises. The sector has always been an important part of people's lives in India. Much before industrialisation, hand weavers and handloom workers contributed to the growth of the industry. The government framed policies during 1950-1970 for the development of Small Scale Industries (SSIs) in the sector; as a result, the power loom and handloom sectors, mainly small and medium scale enterprises, were decentralised. India's textile industry since its beginning continues to be predominantly cotton based with about 65 per cent of fabric consumption in the country being accounted for by cotton. The industry is highly localised in Ahmedabad and Mumbai in the western part of the country though other centres exist including Kanpur, Calcutta, Indore, Coimbatore, and Sholapur (D&B, 2010).

The textile and clothing trade is governed by the Multi-Fibre Agreement (MFA) which came into force on January 1, 1974 replacing short-term and long-term arrangements of the 1960's which protected US textile producers from booming Japanese textiles exports. Later, it was extended to other developing countries like India, Korea, Hong Kong, etc. which had acquired a comparative advantage in textiles. Currently, India has bilateral arrangements under MFA with USA, Canada, Australia, countries of the European Commission, etc. Under MFA, foreign trade is subject to relatively high tariffs and export quotas restricting India's penetration into these markets. India was interested in the early phasing out of these quotas in the Uruguay Round of Negotiations but this did not happen due to the reluctance of the developed countries like the US and EC to open up their textile markets to Third World imports because of high labour costs. With the removal of quotas, exports of textiles have now to cope with new challenges in the form of growing non-tariff/

non-trade barriers such as growing regionalisation of trade between blocks of nations, child labour, anti-dumping duties, etc. (Naumann, 2006).

Indian textile industry is highly unorganised and fragmented in nature. Highly organised segment of mills for spinning and weaving at one and largely fragmented, unorganised and traditional weaving sectors at another end the Indian textile sector is largely on both the extremes. However, after entering into the World Trade Agreements and Multi-Fibre Agreements the Indian Textile Industry is forced to adopt the global situation. Studies have estimated that every job created in manufacturing has a multiplier effect, creating 2-3 jobs in the services sector. In a country like India, where employment generation is one of the key policy issues, this makes this sector a critical sector to achieve inclusiveness in growth (CII, 2012). Currently, India's manufacturing sector contributes only 1.8 per cent share in world manufacturing. This is in stark contrast to China; where manufacturing contributes 34 per cent to the GDP and is 13.7 per cent of world manufacturing. India's growth has been on the back of a booming services sector which contributes 62.5 per cent of the GDP (Planning Commission, 2012).

Employment of the Sector

The textile industry is the largest industry of modern India. It accounts for over 20 per cent of industrial production and is closely linked with the agricultural and rural economy. It is the single largest employer in the industrial sector after agriculture. If employments in allied sectors like ginning, agriculture, pressing, cotton trade, jute, etc. are added then the total employment is estimated at 93 million (Chavan, 2001). The net foreign exchange earnings in this sector are one of the highest and, together with carpet and handicrafts, account for over 37 per cent of total export earnings at over US$ 10 billion. Textiles, alone, account for about 25 per cent of India's total foreign exchange earnings.

The Fig. 16.3 gives the employment share of the textile sector. During the first half of the previous decade (between 1999-2000 to 2004-05), there was a sharp increase in the employment share. The share in manufacturing employment has increased to 34 per cent from 26 per cent. During the same period, textile sector's employment share in total workforce of the country has also registered a positive growth which increased to 4.16 per cent from 2.9 per cent. However, the in second half (between 2004-05 to 2009-10), the sector has registered a decline in the share of employment.

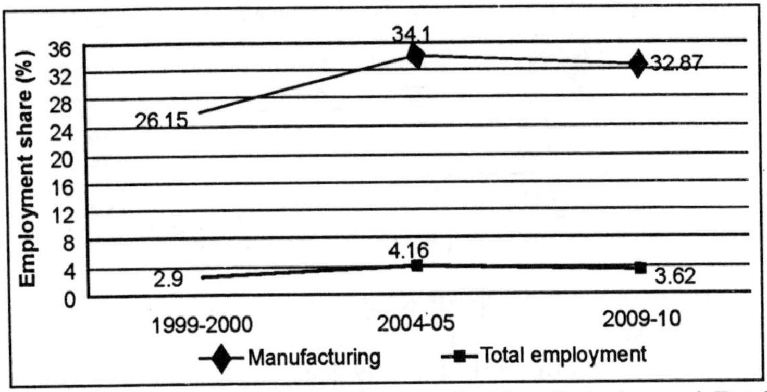

Fig. 16.3: Share of Textile Employment in Manufacturing and Total Employment

Source: NSSO's 1999-2000, 2004-05 and 2009-10 Reports on Employment and Unemployment Situation in India.

Gross Value Addition (GVA) of the Textile Sector

The Gross Valued Addition (GVA) of the textile sector indicates a fluctuating trend between 1994-95 to 2009-10 the period of post-reform in the country. The GVA for both Organised (registered) and unorganised (Unregistered) were assessed separately. During the previous decade (1999-2000 to 2009-10) the growth rate of organised segment has registered 5.80 per cent per annum. On the other hand, unorganised segment (a major component of the sector) had only 1.75 per cent growth per annum. Which means that major component of the sector has not achieved better growth during the previous decade that is a decade of after the new economic reforms. The liberalized economic process allowing the foreign direct investment removing the quotas under small scale industries are some facts which caused the slow growth of the sector. This may also happened that, the sector is slowly moving towards organised part for their sustainability.

Between 1994-95 to 1999-2000, the period immediately after the reforms, the registered segment of the Indian textile sector had posted a negative growth (–0.37%) as compared with 4.93 per cent growth in unorganised segment. Almost after a period of ten years both the segments had registered almost similar rate of growth. In between 2004-05 to 2009-10, the organised segment has registered a drastic growth of 9.3 per cent growth per annum which is 0.73 per cent for the unorganised segment (Table 16.2).

Table 16.2: Growth Rate (CACR) of Gross Value Added of the sector

Category	*1994-95 to 1999-2000*	*1999-2000 to 2004-05*	*2004-05 to 2009-10*	*Decadal Growth Rate 1999-2000 to 2009-10*
Registered	(–) 0.37	2.32	9.39	5.80
Unregistered	4.93	2.79	0.73	1.75
Total	2.69	2.61	4.37	3.48

Source: National Accounts Statistics (NAS) for different periods.

The textile sector's growth trend for the organised component was computed and presented in Fig. 16.3. In the first half of the reference period that is, between 1994-95 to 1999-2000, textile sector has registered a higher growth rate than the overall manufacturing components. The textile sector achieved 5.73 per cent per annum and manufacturing sector altogether achieved only 1.65 per cent for the same period. However, there was a negative growth of textile sector for the period 1999-2000 to 2004-05 whereas, the all manufacturing sector has also reached a very slow growth at the rate of 0.68 per cent per annum. During the entire period two decade after the reforms, this five year (1999-2000 to 2004-05) period was a very stagnant and slow period of growth for both the sectors. Despite, both the sector has recovered from recession and registered drastic growth during the next five years. Between 2004-05 to 2009-10 the textile sector has registered an impressive growth of 5.58 per cent per annum and the manufacturing sector together achieved 6.88 per cent growth per annum. There was no much difference between both the textile and all manufacturing sector for their decadal growth rate of growth (Fig. 16.3).

Investments

India is the world's second largest producer of textiles and garments. Indian textile industry accounts for about 24 per cent of the world's spindle capacity and eight per cent of global rotor capacity. Abundant availability of raw materials such as cotton, wool, silk and jute and skilled workforce have made India a sourcing hub. The size of Indian textile and apparel market stood at US$ 89 billion in 2011 and is expected to touch US$ 223 billion by 2021. Textile plays major role in the Indian economy. It accounts for 27 per cent of foreign exchange inflows and contributes 14 per cent to industrial production and 4 per cent to the Gross Domestic Product (GDP). With over 45 million people, the industry is one of the largest

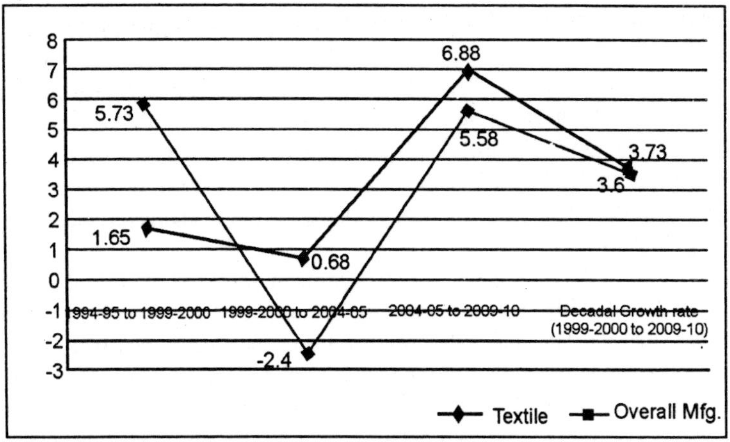

Chart 16.4. Growth Rate (CAGR) of Organised Employment in Textile and Overall Manufacturing.

Source: Computed from annexure table A.3.

sources of employment generation in the country, and also accounts for nearly 11 per cent of total exports. Exports grew to US$ 33.3 billion in Financial Year 2011-12 from US$ 17.6 billion in the year 2005-06, registering a Compound Annual Growth Rate (CAGR) of 11.2 per cent.

The textiles sector has witnessed a spurt in investment during the last five years. The industry (including dyed and printed) attracted Foreign Direct Investments (FDI) worth Rs. 5,831.02 crore (US$ 854.78 million) during April 2000 to May 2013. The net foreign exchange earnings in this sector are one of the highest and, together with carpet and handicrafts, account for over 37 per cent of total export earnings at over US$ 10 billion. Textiles, alone, account for about 25 per cent of India's total foreign exchange earnings (IBEF, 2014).

The Indian textiles industry is set for strong growth, buoyed by strong domestic consumption as well as export demand. The most significant change in the Indian textiles industry has been the advent of Man-Made Fibres (MMF). India has successfully placed its innovative range of MMF textiles in almost all the countries across the globe. MMF production recorded an increase of 10 per cent and filament yarn production grew by 6 per cent in the up to month of February, 2014. Cloth production by mill sector registered a growth of 9 per cent in the month of February 2014 and of 6 per cent during April, 2013 to February 2014. Power loom and hosiery industry of production of clothes increased by 2 per cent and 9 per cent respectively (GoI, 2014).

Organised Textile in India: Growth trend of Economic Indicators

The growth indicators which have been considered to analyze the growth of the industry in India, are: (i) Number of Factories, (ii) Fixed Capital Formation (Fixed Capital), (iii) Employment (number of persons engaged), and (iv) Gross Value Added (output) in various product groups of the textile industry. An analysis of change in major characteristics based on data provided in the Table 16.3.

Growth rate analysis of the organised segment of textile sector presented in Table 16.3 shows that the sector has been growing constantly since 1994-95. The data highlights that during the period 1994-95 to 2009-10, organised component of the textile sector on an average exhibited a positive growth trend. However, during 1999-2000 to 2004-05, there was either a marginal growth or a declining trend. Though, average growth in total manufacturing sector was also positive for all characteristics, this growth was less than the textile sector. Declining trend in many of the indicators was observed during the first two sub-periods, i.e., 1994-95 to 1999-2000 and 1999-2000 to 2004-05. Another salient feature of the data is that growth in output, GVA and wages/salaries was substantially higher as compared to the growth in number of factories and number of workers/ employees.

The number of workers and number of employees engaged in textile sector reported a declining trend during 1994-95 to 2009-10. However, the recent sub-period reported to substantial growth. In general, the rate of growth for different parameters was higher during the period 1994-95 to 1999-2000 as compared to the period 2004-05 to 2009-10. The highest rate of growth (9.96% per annum) was reported by fixed capital during 1994-95 to 2009-10 (Table 16.3).

Number of Factories

The number of factories in textile sector have increased from 12633 in 1994-05 to 19459 in 2009-10 i.e., increased at the compounded annual rate of 2.92 per cent. This rate of growth is much higher than that for the total manufacturing sector (1.72% per year). However, further analysis reveals that the rates of growth in number of factories vary in different sub-periods. In the period 1994-95 to 1999-00 the growth was much higher (6.15% per annum) as compared to other sub-periods (–0.13% and 2.84% per annum respectively during 1999-00 to 2004-05 and 2004-05 to 2009-10). It is interesting to note that except during the period 194-95 to

1999-2000, the rate of increase in total manufacturing industries was higher than the rate of increase in textile sector (Table 16.3).

Number of Factories

The number of factories in textile sector have increased from 12633 in 1994-05 to 19459 in 2009-10 i.e., increased at the compounded annual rate of 2.92 per cent. This rate of growth is much higher than that for the total manufacturing sector (1.72% per year). However, further analysis reveals that the rates of growth in number of factories vary in different sub-periods. In the period 1994-95 to 1999-00 the growth was much higher (6.15% per annum) as compared to other sub-periods (- 0.13 per cent and 2.84 per cent per annum respectively during 1999-00 to 2004-05 and 2004-05 to 2009-10). Except during the period 2004-05 to 2009-10, the rate of increase in total manufacturing industries was less than the rate of increase in the textile sector (Table 16.3 and Annexure Table A.3).

Employment

(a) Workers

As against about 1.01 million workers in 1994-95, the number of workers in textile sector increased to about 1.92 million in 2009-10. The number of workers increased at the compounded annual growth rate of 4.37 per cent during 1994-95 to 2009-10. This is higher than the rate of increase (1.84%) witnessed by number of workers in total manufacturing sector over the same period. However, the increase in number of workers witnessed a fluctuating trend: during 1994-95 to 1999-00, the rate of increase was 5.72 per cent which dropped to just 1.85 per cent during 1999-00 to 2004-05 and increased to 5.59 per cent during 2004-05 to 2009-10. On the other hand, number of workers in total manufacture sector, which declined by 2 per cent during 1994-95 to 1999-00 and increased by just 1 per cent during 1999-00 to 2004-05, increased significantly by 6.77 per cent during 2004-05 to 2009-10 (Table 16.3).

(b) Employees

In addition to workers, there are a number of other persons employed in the industry. These include managers, engineers, technicians, supervisors, etc. They are the high level manpower in the officer grade. While highly

Table 16.3: Growth rate of various Economic Indicators

Economic Indicators	*Compound Annual Growth Rate (CAGR - %)*							
	Textile				*All Manufacturing*			
	1994-95 to 1999-00	*1999-00 to 2004-05*	*2004-05 to 2009-10*	*1994-95 to 2009-10*	*1994-95 to 1999-00*	*1999-00 to 2004-05*	*2004-05 to 2009-10*	*1994-95 to 2009-10*
1. Number of factories	6.15	–0.13	2.84	2.92	1.35	0.72	3.10	1.72
2. Employment								
(a) Workers	5.72	1.85	5.59	4.37	–2.06	0.99	6.77	1.84
(b) Total persons engaged	5.73	1.65	5.58	4.31	–2.40	0.68	6.88	1.65
3. Fixed Capital	24.13	–3.68	11.20	9.96	2.32	–0.19	15.24	5.58
4. Invested Capital	19.66	–3.55	10.54	8.46	2.53	0.78	14.44	5.75
5. Inputs	27.17	–9.48	8.28	7.62	7.06	8.31	11.43	8.92
6. Output	24.77	–8.60	8.37	7.31	6.08	7.64	11.47	8.37
7. Gross Value Added	14.29	–3.86	8.77	6.12	2.82	4.96	11.67	6.41
8. Wages to Workers	0.63	5.68	6.77	4.33	–1.53	–0.16	9.59	2.51
9. Total Emoluments	7.24	2.55	8.23	5.98	0.96	0.87	11.97	4.47

Source: Computed from ASI data for respective years.

technological industry may require more number of employees, traditional labour intensive industry may require lesser number of employees. The unpaid family workers are also included in this category. The difference in the number of total persons engaged and the workers provide the number of such employees/persons. In the textile sector, the growth in the number of persons engaged is almost similar to that of number of workers during 1994-95 to 2009-10. A similar pattern has been observed in the case of total manufacturing sector which indicate that both textile as well as total manufacturing sector are becoming more technological oriented (Table 16.3).

Gross Value Added (GVA)

Value addition by the textile sector as well as by total manufacturing in the country has grown at a very significant rate during the reference period. During the 20 years of post-reform period, the rate of growth in GVA by textile sector and the manufacturing as a whole was almost similar (6% per annum). However, analysis of different quarters indicates a different picture as they exhibited a fluctuating trend. During 1994-95 to 1999-00, GVA by textile sector increased by 14.29 per cent as against just 2.8 per cent by total manufacturing. During 1999-00 to 2004-05, textile sectors' GVA declined by 3.86 per cent per annum while GVA in total manufacturing grew by about 5 per cent per cent during the same period. In the third quarter i.e., 2004-05 to 2009-10, GVA in both textile and total manufacturing accelerated a positive growth of 8.77 per cent and 11.67 respectively (Table 16.3).

Invested Capital

The total capital invested in organised segment of textile sector has increased at a compound annual growth rate of 8.46 per cent during 1994-95 to 2009-10 whereas, it was 5.75 per cent for the total manufacturing. The growth in capital investment has shown fluctuating trends during this period. In the case of textile sector, the rate of growth was 19.66 per cent per annum during 1994-95 to 1999-2000 but registered a drastic decline to negative growth (–3.55% per annum) during 1999-2000 to 2004-05. The sector recovered from the setback during the previous five years and again grew by 10.54 per cent per annum during 2004-05 to 2009-10 (Table 16.3).

Fixed Capital

The fixed capital invested in textile sector was slightly higher than the invested capital of the sector. The sector registered compound growth rate of 9.96 per cent between 1994-95 to 2009-10. Textile sector's growth pattern was similar to that followed by invested capital. The sector has achieved 24.13 per cent of annual growth between 1994-95 to 1999-2000 which more than 10 time of the overall manufacturing sector's growth during the same period. However, the sector has posted a negative growth (–3.68%) between the period 1999-2000 to 2004-05 (Table 16.3).

Input

The trend of the textile sector's input in has increased on an average by 7.62 per cent per annum between 1994-95 to 2009-10. The sector has registered a highest rate of growth (27.17%) during 1994-95 to 1999-2000 and was least (–9.48%) during 1999-2000 to 2004-05. The corresponding rate of growth in total manufacturing industries during 1994-95 to 2009-10 was 8.92 per cent per annum. Overall manufacturing sector' rate of growth is lower than the textile sector. However, the rate of growth in total manufacturing in different sub-periods is higher than the corresponding rates in textile sector (Table 16.3).

Output

During the period 1994-95 to 2009-10, the output of the textile sector has increased by 7.31 per cent per annum. However, the growth was much higher during 1994-1995 to 1999-2000 with 24.77 per cent per annum. A drastic decline was observed during 1999-2000 to 2004-05. Total manufacturing sector followed the same pattern and grew by 8.37 per cent per cent during the entire period and there was consistent increase: 6.1 per cent, 7.6 per cent and 11.4 per cent per annum during 1994-95 1999-2000, 1999-2000 to 2004-05 and 2004-05 to 2009-10 respectively.

The Share of Textile Sector in Overall Manufacturing

As a result of different rates of growth of the textile sector and total manufacturing, the share of various economic characteristics of textile in total manufacturing has changed over time. The share of various economic indicators textile sector in total manufacturing sector is presented in Table

16.4. In general, there was fluctuating trend was observed for major economic indicators of textile in overall manufacturing component. Up to 2004-05 majority of the indicators shows an increasing trend. An increasing trend was observed in the number of factories in the textile sector to total manufacturing sector. This is may be due to various incentives announced by the Ministry of Textiles, Government of India. However, due to the variable rate of growth in number of factories between different periods in both textile and total manufacturing sector, the share of textile sector in the total manufacturing has been changing over the periods. This share increased from 10.27 per cent in 1994-95 to 12.94 per cent in 1999-2000, then to a decline in 2004-05 with 12.41 per cent and again declined to 12.25 per cent in 2009-10.

Similarly, the employment has grown in textile sector's organised component, the share of workers in textile to the total manufacturing witnessed a fluctuating trend. The share of workers engaged in organised textile sector to the total workers in manufacturing sector increased from 14.51 per cent in 1994-95 to 21.27 per cent in 1999-2000 but declined to 22.19 per cent in 2004-05 and 20.99 per cent 2009-10. Thus, above analysis points out that textile sector is losing its labour intensive character (Table 16.4).

The share of total employees in textile sector to that in the total manufacturing is less than the share of ratio of workers. Further analysis indicates that there is a marginal increase in the number of workers per employee and this is true for textile and total manufacturing sector. The textile sector's contributions in total manufacturing in terms of gross value added increased from 7.26 per cent in 1994-95 to 12.33 per cent in 1999-2000 but declined to 7.95 per cent in 2004-05 and again decrease to 6.97 per cent in 2009-10. Capital investment share of organised segment of textile sector to the total manufacturing sector increased to 12.33 per cent in 1999-2000 from 5.75 per cent in 1994-95. There was slowdown in the share of the textile component in the total manufacturing after 1999-2000 (Table 16.4).

The share of fixed capital of the textile sector to total manufacturing sector has increased from 4.52 per cent in 1994-95 to 11.88 per cent in 1999-2000. This investment pattern indicates that, the labour intensive textile sector is becoming more capital intensive. The sector's capital move is towards the modernization of plant and machinery. However, the share of textile in total manufacturing in terms of input has declined from 19.84 per cent in 1999-2000 to 7.01 per cent in 2009-10. Again the share of output of textile sector in the total output of manufacturing sector

Table 16.4: Textile Share in Total Manufacturing

Economic Indicators	Reference Period			
	1994-95	1999-2000	2004-05	2009-10
1. Number of factories	10.27	12.94	12.41	12.25
2. Employment				
(a) Workers	14.51	21.27	22.19	20.99
(b) Total persons engaged	12.96	19.33	20.28	19.08
3. Fixed Capital	4.52	11.88	9.94	8.32
4. Invested Capital	5.75	12.45	9.99	8.40
5. Inputs	8.39	19.84	8.09	7.01
6. Output	8.11	18.26	8.06	7.00
7. Gross Value Added	7.26	12.33	7.95	6.97
8. Wages to Workers	12.43	13.86	18.42	16.17
9. Total Emoluments	9.91	13.40	14.56	12.29

Source: Computed from Annexure Table A.3.

remained to about 7.8 per cent except in 1999-2000 when it grew to 18.26 per cent (Table 16.4).

Analysis of Technical Ratios

Workers per Factory

Though textile sector is considered to be labour intensive, the workers per factory in the sector were higher compared to overall manufacturing sector. In textile sector there were 80 workers per factory in 1994-95 as compared to 57 in total manufacturing. The growth in number of factories in textile was identical to the growth of workers in the sector; as a result, the workers per factory remained almost constant during the period 1994-95 to 2004-05. Worker per factory has shown an increase in 2009-10. However, a normal trend has been observed in the case of total manufacturing sector without much increase or decrease in workers per factory. The decline in workers per factory over the time indicates that industries are moving towards modernization for better use of advanced technology to sustain.

Fixed Capital per Factory

In the textile sector, the fixed capital per factory has drastically increased from Rs. 88.23 lakh in 1994-95 to Rs. 237.89 lakh in 2009-10. In total manufacturing sector, this ratio increased from Rs. 200.45 lakh to Rs. 350.16 lakh over the same period. While fixed capital per factory in textile sector more than tripled during 1994-95 to 2009-10, the ratio in the case of total manufacturing increased by 1.5 times. As like as the number of factories in textile increased at a faster pace than the number of factories in the total manufacturing sector, the rate of growth in fixed capital in textile was higher than that in total manufacturing industries. This scenario proves that textile industry becoming more capital intensive as compared to the total manufacturing sector, and losing its labour intensive character as observed earlier.

Gross Value Added per Factory

The GVA per factory in all manufacturing sector was higher than textile in 1994-95 to 2009-10. The GVA per factory in the case of textile sector increased from 64.93 lakh in 1994-95 to 102.79 lakh in 2009-10. The textile sector has witnessed a compounded annual growth of 3.11 per cent as against 4.61 per cent in the case of total manufacturing sector over the same period. It is worth mentioning that the rate of growth in gross value added was same in both textile and the total manufacturing during the period under reference. Moreover, the share of GVA by textile sector in the GVA by manufacturing sector remained almost constant throughout the period except for 1999-2000. Thus, it is the growth in number of factories in textile sector that restricted the GVA per factory in the sector.

Efficiency

The efficiency of an industry or a sector is defined as the ratio measure of the size of output to the size of input and is generally expressed in percentage terms. Both input and output are measured in same units and hence efficiency is unit less. The efficiency of the textile sector decreased from 1.28 in 1994-95 to 1.17 in 1999-2000. A slight upward to 1.22 in 2004-05 and again experienced a marginal increase by 0.01 to 1.23 in 2009-10. It is observed that efficiency in textile sector has always remained less than or similar to the total manufacturing, though it also exhibited a declining trend. However, the efficiency of textile sector is less than the total manufacturing component. Highly labour intensive in nature, highly depend on other sectors like agriculture etc. may be the factors cause for low efficiency in the sector. There was decline in the efficiency of both textile and all manufacturing industries during the reference period.

Table 16.5: Technical coefficients of the textile sector over the years

Indicator	Unit	Period							
		1994-95		1999-00		2004-05*		2009-10	
		Textile	Mfg.	Textile	Mfg.	Textile	Mfg.	Textile	Mfg.
Fixed cap per factory	Rs. Lakh	88.23	200.45	192.93	210.23	160.94	200.90	237.89	350.39
GVA per factory	Rs. Lakh	64.93	91.83	93.97	98.65	77.66	121.23	102.79	180.66
GVA/Invested capital	Rs. Lakh	0.41	0.33	0.33	0.33	0.32	0.41	0.30	0.36
GVA/Fixed capital	Rs. Lakh	0.74	0.46	0.49	0.47	0.48	0.60	0.43	0.52
GVA per worker	Rupees	81110	162062	119780	206638	89738	250492	104076	313421
Worker per factory	Number	80.05	56.66	78.46	47.74	86.54	48.40	98.76	57.64
Employee per factory	Number	94.63	75.01	92.79	62.12	101.35	62.00	115.63	74.22
GVA per employee	Rupees	68619	122421	101280	158797	76626	195546	88896	243405
Wages per worker	Rupees	24044	28056	18786	28824	22590	27212	23884	30992
Emoluments per employee	Rupees	26032	34016	27936	40289	29198	40677	33048	51324
Output/Input	Number	1.28	1.33	1.17	1.27	1.22	1.23	1.23	1.23
Output per factory	Number	295.39	373.97	662.77	469.75	425.50	654.91	552.86	967.33
Output per worker	Number	3.69	6.60	8.45	9.84	4.92	13.53	6.50	16.78

Source: Computed from Annual Survey of Industries' (ASI) data for respective years.

Productivity

The output of an industry or sector is influenced by a number of input factors like employment, capita, technology, etc. The productivity is defined as ratio of output (or GVA) per unit of input (capital or labour). The most common measures of productivity are labour productivity (GVA per worker or employee) and capital productivity (GVA per rupee of capital invested). Since, input and output units are different, productivity is expressed in units.

Labour Productivity

Labour productivity has been estimated as a ratio of GVA to the number of workers. The labour productivity of the sector, it may be noted that though there are period to period fluctuations. The labour productivity in textile sector has increased from Rs. 81,110 in 1994-95 to Rs. 1,04,076 in 2009-10. The labour productivity of the total manufacturing was quite higher as compared to textile sector and it increased from Rs. 162,062 in 1994-95 to Rs. 3,13,421 in 2009-10. The growth pattern in textile sector and total manufacturing is almost similar. However, the labour productivity growth in textile sector has been found to be fluctuating over the years. This may be due the proportionately higher growth in the number of workers as compared to the growth in GVA. This analysis of labour productivity growth reveals that the labour productivity in textile sector has remained less than the total manufacturing sector. This brings out the need for better resources either in terms of raw material or workforce suitable for the sector. The declining trend in the growth rate of labour productivity in the textile sector in recent years is a matter of concern for the overall competitiveness of the sector (Table 16.5).

Capital Productivity

Capital productivity has been estimated as a ratio of GVA to the invested capital i.e., GVA per rupee of Invested Capital. Capital productivity of textile sector has declined marginally from Rs. 0.41 in 1994-95 to Rs.0.30 in 2009-10. The sector has registered a negative growth in the capital productivity during the reference period. A similar trend was also observed for overall manufacturing components. In was Rs. 0.33 Lakhs in 1994-95 to Rs. 0.36 lakhs in 2009-10. There are no big changes in capital productivity despite the tremendous technological changes in both the textile and overall manufacturing components.

Major Challenges

India has become one of the fastest growing economies in the world over the last two decades, undoubtedly aided in this performance by economic reforms. The striking aspect of India's recent growth has been the dynamism of the service sector, while, in contrast, manufacturing has been less robust. The Manufacturing sector's contribution to the GDP has stagnated at 16 per cent, raising questions about India's development model, including its sustainability, especially for generating adequate employment.

With changing global realities, the manufacturing sector will need to be the safeguard of employment creation over the next decade, in contrast to current employment of only 11 per cent of India's working population. India's long touted demographic dividend can only then be sufficiently exploited through the systematic growth of this sector. These statistics clearly indicate that while manufacturing has not been the engine of growth for the Indian economy, it now needs to grow at a much faster rate (Planning Commission, 2012).

Currently, India's manufacturing sector contributes about 16 per cent to the GDP, and India's share in world manufacturing is only 1.8 per cent. This is in stark contrast to China; where manufacturing contributes 34 per cent to the GDP and is 13.7 per cent of world manufacturing up from 2.9 per cent in 1991. India's growth has been on the back of a booming services sector which contributes 62.5 per cent of the GDP. These statistics clearly indicate that while manufacturing has not been the engine of growth for the Indian economy, it now needs to grow at a much faster rate. With changing global realities, the manufacturing sector will need to be the bulwark of employment creation over the next decade, in contrast to current employment of only 9 per cent of India's working population. India's long touted demographic dividend can only then be sufficiently exploited through the systematic growth of this sector (S. Nayak, *et al.,* 2013).

The history of the textile and clothing industry has been replete with the use of various bilateral quotas, protectionist policies, discriminatory tariffs, etc. by the developed world against the developing countries. The result was a highly distorted structure, which imposed hidden costs on the export sectors of the Third World. Despite the fact that GATT was established way back in 1947, the textile industry, till 1994, remained largely out of its liberalisation agreements. In fact, trade in this sector, until the Uruguay Round, evolved in the opposite direction. Consequently, since 1974 global trade in the textiles and clothing sector had been governed by the Multi-Fibre Agreement (MFA), which was the sequel to an increasingly pervasive quota regime that began with the Short-Term arrangement on cotton products in 1962 and followed by the Long-Term arrangement. After the successful conclusion of the Uruguay Round in 1994, the MFA was replaced by the Agreement on Textiles and Clothing (ATC), which had the same MFA framework in the context of an agreed, ten year phasing out of all quotas by the year 2005. The section that follows takes a brief look at the history of these protectionist regimes as also a more detailed look at the MFA and the ATC.

Quantitative restrictions to limit international trade in certain goods have existed for a long time already, but in no sector have they been as common and broadly applied as in the textile and clothing industries. Likewise, no other sector has seen such a rigid institutionalization of quantitative restrictions, which in turn have had very wide reaching intended and unintended consequences. In fact, quotas in this sector have been the common denominator that has shaped the development path of this industry, and—many would argue—have been the single most important factor contributing to its worldwide diffusion in recent decades. International trade policy has for many decades utilized quantitative restrictions on imports as a means of achieving specific developmental outcomes. This form of protection provides a limited shield to local industry against foreign competition, competition which would have been the case if foreign goods were to compete freely on the domestic market. Quotas differ fundamentally from other policy tools, such as tariffs, in that they restrict competition from imports irrespective of any direct price considerations (Shetty, 2013).

The lackluster growth of manufacturing can also be traced to the low technological depth of the Indian manufacturing sector. In India Research and Development (R&D) has not been sufficiently exploited and needs an overhaul in terms of its focus and its organization. Most Indian manufacturing firms appear to be stuck at the basic or intermediate level of technological capabilities. Creating conducive environments to increase business expenditure on R&D complemented by institutional measures around skill development, regulation and standardisation need to be key areas of emphasis

To ensure sustained growth and expansion of the Indian textile industry, it is necessary to maintain healthy export growth momentum, increase production and productivity in cotton yarn, enhance value addition in garmenting and apparel sectors, promote the rich heritage of handlooms and handicrafts, institutional strengthening in the jute sector, and enhance acreages under mulberry production and safeguard employment opportunities. More concerted efforts need to be taken to bridge the skill gap in the textiles industry. Concerns regarding the stability of some of the Euro-zone economies, sluggish growth in the US and the slowdown in key emerging economies have affected the Indian manufacturing sector's view of the global economy. Given this background, a majority of companies participating in our survey saw the world economy as being in a decline. Looking forward over the next 12 months, the outlook does not seem to improve much, with more companies describing it as uncertain or mildly pessimistic (FICCI, 2013).

Despite numerous plans on paper, manufacturing never took off in a meaningful way. The contribution of the sector to the country's output has remained stagnant at around 15 per cent for about 30 years now. In China, the sector contributes about 34 per cent to that country's GDP. It implies that there is need for strong policy initiatives to boost the growth of the manufacturing sector.

Clearly, not much has been achieved since then as the contribution of manufacturing still stands at 15.2 per cent of GDP (Financial Year 2012-13). Not to be left behind, the Planning Commission now has an ambitious target of ramping up manufacturing output to 25 per cent of GDP by 2025 and creating 100 million additional jobs. These targets are unlikely to be realized any time soon. India lacks the ecosystem for developing a robust manufacturing sector. There are a number of issues—ranging from lack of adequate infrastructure, financing, land acquisition and rigid labour laws—that make business in the sector intensely difficult. While infrastructure bottlenecks are well known, the Land Acquisition, Rehabilitation and Resettlement Bill—cleared by Parliament—is certain to make land acquisition even more difficult. This will further affect the prospects of creating a manufacturing base in the country.

The other big impediment in the development of manufacturing is the nation's rigid labour laws. As highlighted in the Economic Survey (2012-13), rigid regulation in the labour market does not allow small and medium size manufacturing units to grow and attain the economies of scale. If anything, after clearing the new land acquisition law, it makes great sense to relax labour laws to enable the easy establishment of small manufacturing units. If large projects seem unviable, rationality demands that smaller ones, which, in fact, have greater employment potential, be encouraged. In India, 84 per cent of the workforce in manufacturing works for micro and small enterprises. The comparable figure is 27.5 per cent in Malaysia and 24.8 per cent in China. There is plenty of room for growth here if only political parties give up their addiction to inflexible labour laws.

There are solutions, of course. In the short-run, industrial production can be spurred if the government gets the ban in the mining sector lifted and removes hurdles in the power sector. The depreciation of the rupee and better prospects of exports will also help manufacturing. However, in the medium term, a different measure is required. While the development of infrastructure will take its own time, relaxation in labour laws will be a major boost for the sector. It is true that the issue of labour reforms is politically sensitive, but it is also true that forming consensus on economic issues is relatively easier in difficult economic conditions. In order to contain opposition from labour unions, the reforms can be carried out prospectively, which will not affect existing contracts. A robust manufacturing sector will not only help economic growth in a sustainable way, but also create much needed jobs and contain the trade deficit (live mint 2013).

Recent Initiatives

To be sure, the government has stressed the need to increase manufacturing output on a number of occasions. In 2004, the United Progressive Alliance (UPA) Government set up a National Manufacturing Competitiveness Council (NMCC) with the objective, among others, to suggest ways to increase manufacturing competitiveness. The immediate objective of the proposed council was to increase contribution of manufacturing and pressed for a growth rate of 12-14 per cent in the sector over a decade, so that manufacturing output can reach the range of 25-35 per cent of GDP.

With the special care to textile sector the Government of India has promoted a number of export promotion policies for the sector. It has also allowed 100 per cent FDI in the Indian textiles sector under automatic route.

- The government has taken a lot of initiatives for the welfare and development of the weavers and the handloom sector. Under revival, reform and restructuring (RRR) package, financial assistance to the tune of Rs. 1,019 crore has been approved.
- Encouraged by turnaround in textiles exports, the Government of India plans to set up a US$ 60 billion target for the current financial year, a jump of over 30 per cent from the previous financial year.

- The Cabinet Committee on Economic Affairs (CCEA) has approved an Integrated Processing Development Scheme (IPDS) with a corpus of Rs. 500 crore to make textiles processing units more environment-friendly and globally competitive.
- The Government of India plans to set up a Rs. 100 crore venture capital fund to provide equity support to start-ups in the textiles sector, in order to encourage innovative ideas in this export intensive sector.
- The Government of India has allotted Rs. 700 crore in the 12th Five Year Plan for the development of technical textiles. In 2012-13, the technical textiles industry reached Rs. 7.48 trillion at an annual growth rate of 3.5 per cent.

In addition to the above, Government of India is taking initiatives to attract foreign investments in the textile sector through promotional visits to countries such as Japan, Germany, Italy and France. It has also allocated US$ 10.4 million for apparel parks under Scheme for Integrated Textile Parks (SITP). The Indian textiles industry is set for strong growth, buoyed by both strong domestic consumption as well as export demand. For the textiles industry, the proposed hike in FDI limit in multi-brand retail will bring in more players, thereby providing more options to consumers. It will also bring in greater investments along the entire value chain—from agricultural production to final manufactured goods. The organised apparel segment is expected to grow at a compound annual growth rate (CAGR) of more than 13 per cent over a 10-year period.

With the removal of quotas, exports of textiles have now to cope with new challenges in the form of growing non-tariff/non-trade barriers such as growing regionalisation of trade between blocks of nations, child labour, anti-dumping duties, etc. (Naumann, 2006).

Nevertheless, it must be realised that the picture is not all rosy. It is now being admitted universally and even officially that the present global scenario is more of a challenge than opportunity. If the industry does not pay attention to the very vital needs of modernisation, quality control, technology upgradation, etc. it is likely to be left behind. Already, its comparative advantage of cheap labour is being nullified by the use of outmoded machinery.

With the dismantling of the MFA, it becomes imperative for the textile industry to take on competitors like China, Pakistan, etc., which enjoy lower labour costs. In fact, the seriousness of the situation becomes even more apparent when it is realised that the non-quota exports have not really risen dramatically over the past few years. The continued dominance of yarn in exports of cotton, synthetics, and blends, is another cause for worry while exports of fabrics are not growing. The lack of value added products in textile exports do not augur well for India in a non-MFA world. Another disconcerting aspect that reflects the declining international competitiveness of Indian textile industry is the surge in imports in the last two years. Imports grew by 12 per cent in dollar terms in 1997-98, against an average of 5.8 per cent for all imports into India. Imports from China went up by 50 per cent while those from Hong Kong jumped by 23 per cent (Verma, 2000).

Government of India has taken various initiatives to boost growth of the sector. Schemes and supportive measures were taken to help the textile sector to overcome from the slowdown. The following are the some of the schemes which widely covered.

- Technology Fund Upgradation Scheme (TUFS).
- Scheme for Integrated Textile Parks (SITP).
- Group Workshed Scheme (GWS).
- Group Insurance Scheme for Development of Power Loom Sector.
- Integrated Scheme for Power loom Cluster Development.
- Marketing Development Programme for Power loom Sector etc.

Concluding Remarks

Textiles and clothing retail comprise 40 per cent of organised retailing in India. Share of organised retailing to increase from about 5 per cent currently to about 24 per cent by the year 2020. The per capita income of the masses has been increasing regularly and is estimated at US$ 1200 per annum leading to consumption of Textiles increasing at 11 per cent compound annual growth rate. Propensity to spend in the case of working women is higher by around 1.3 times as compared to a housewife. It is estimated that the population of working women has increased to around 32 per cent in the year 2010 from 26 per cent in 2001. Increase in nuclear families: The average household size has decreased to about 5.0 in financial year 2009-10 from 5.36 in 2001. As a result per household consumption is increasing.

Favourable demographic profile: The percentage of earning population (15-60 years) in the total population is rising. This group is about 60 per cent of the total population. Higher growth in urban population—The urban population is growing gradually in 1991 Census the percentage of urban population was 25.7 per cent which increased to 28.6 per cent in 2001 census and further increased to 37.7 per cent in 2011 (Census of India). The favourable demography coupled with rising urban population and income levels will act as a key growth factor for the Indian textile and apparel Industry. Similarly, increasing GDP, industrial outputs and vibrant construction activity may also to boost the demand for home textiles. High growth in service sector especially in hospitality may also expect to boost the home textiles.

(i) Rising Urbanisation
(ii) Favourable demographics
(iii) Expansion of Ready-to-wear market
(iv) Increasing disposable income
(v) Changing consumer preferences and lifestyle
(vi) Increase in overall employment

Government policies have largely been favourable to the textiles industry. The policies aim to ensure that the industry is internationally competitive in terms of manufacturing and exports. Besides, providing various schemes, the rear various other statutes, including fiscal policies (governing customs, excise, sales tax, etc.), rules, initiatives, incentives, etc through which government extends support to the industry. The textile sector in the country is in nascent stage and has potential for higher growth in future. There is a rapidly increasing demand by rising urbanization and income levels. The textile sector has been declared a priority sector by the government. However, the sector as a whole turned out to be a job loosing sector. The growth in the textile sector is due to the contribution of industries in organized sector.

References

Chavan, R.B. (2001), "Indian Textile Industry: Environmental Issues" *Indian Journal of Fibre and Textile Research*, Vol. 26.

CII (2012), "Quarterly Survey on Manufacturing Sector" by ASCON and Confederation of Indian Industries, New Delhi.

Devajit (2012), "Impact of Foreign Direct Investment on Indian Economy", Research *Journal of Management Science*. Vol. 1, No. 2, pp. 29-31.

D&B (2010), "D&B Union Bank of India Industry Overview: Textile Industry" Dun & Bradstreet Information Services India Pvt. Ltd., Mumbai.

FICCI (2013), "India Manufacturing Barometer: Taking the pulse" Federation of Indian Chamber of Commerce and Industry (FICCI) and PwC, New Delhi.

GoI (2011), "Strategic Plan 2011-2016 of the Textile Ministry" Ministry of Textiles, Government of India, New Delhi.

GoI (2012), "The Manufacturing Plan Strategies for Accelerating Growth of Manufacturing in India in the 12th Five Year Plan and Beyond", Planning Commission, Government of India.

GoI (2013), "Note on the Textile and Clothing Exports of India" International Trade Section, Ministry of Textiles Government of India, New Delhi.

GoI (2013), "Data Book for the Use of Deputy Chairman Planning Commission", Planning Commission, Government of India, New Delhi.

GoI (2014), "India in Business, Investment and Technology Promotion (ITP) Division", Ministry of External Affairs, Government of India, New Delhi.

IBEF (2014), "Sectoral Report—Textile Sector: 2014" India Brand Equity Foundation, Gurgaon.

Kasi, S. (2012), "India's Textile Industry in the Liberalised Economic Regime an Appraisal of Growth Productivity and Technology" Department of Economics, University of Kerala, Trivandrum.

Mathiyazhagan, *et al.* (2005), "Impact of the Foreign Direct Investment on Indian Economy: A Sectoral Level Analysis", Working Paper No. 6. *Institute of South Asian Studies, National University of Singapore,* Singapore.

Naumann, Eckart (2006), "The Multifibre Agreement—WTO Agreement on Textiles and Clothing" Tralac Working Paper No. 4, Tralac, Western Cape, South Africa. Accessed the article from the website: http://www.fibre2fashion.com/industry-article/pdffiles/the-multifibre-agreement.pdf

Nayak, Shibananda *et at.*, (2013), "India's Manufacturing Exports Dynamics: An Analysis of Technology Intensity Transition" Working Paper No. 200/6. *Centre for WTO Studies*, Indian Institute of Foreign Trade, New Delhi.

Register General of India (1991), Census of India—Primary Census Abstract for 1991, 2001 and 2011 Register General of India, Government of India, New Delhi.

RBI (2013), "Data Base of the Indian Economy—Statistical Tables" Reserve Bank of India.

Shetty, Ramanna *et al.,* (2013), "A Study on the Impact of Quota Removal on the Textile and Clothing Industry in Karnataka State" *International Journal of Economy, Management and Social Sciences*, Vol. 2, No. 6.

Simpson, Vern (2001) "India's Textile and Apparel Industry: Growth Potential and Trade and Investment Opportunities" Staff Research Study No. 27, US International Trade Commission, Washington DC.

Singh, Jitender (2013) "Analysis of Trends in the Manufacturing Growth in Last Five Years (2006-07 to 2011-12)", Ministry of Commerce and Industry, New Delhi.

Verma, Samar (2000) "Restructuring the Indian Textile Industry" Paper for Eldis Programme Institute of Development Studies, University of Sussex, Brighton, United Kingdom.

_______ (2012), Technopak's, "Textile and Apparel Compendium 2012" Technopak Consultancy Pvt. Limited, Gurgaon (Haryana).

_______live mint (2013), "India's continuing manufacturing drought: Despite numerous plans on paper, manufacturing never took off in a meaningful Way", published in Livemint on 9th September, 2013.

Annexure Tables

A 1. Textile Employment and its share

Sectors	Employment in 1999-2000			Employment in 2004-05			Employment in 2009-10		
	Organized	Unorganized	Total	Organized	Unorganized	Total	Organized	Unorganized	Total
Textile sector (millions)	1.58	9.94	11.52	1.71	17.31	19.02	2.25	14.43	16.68
Manufacturing (millions)	13.13	30.92	44.05	16.06	39.71	55.77	16.04	34.70	50.74
Total employment (in millions)	54.12	342.64	396.76	62.57	394.90	457.47	72.87	387.34	460.22
% share of textile in Mfg.	12.03	32.15	26.15	10.65	43.59	34.10	14.03	41.59	32.87
% share of textile in Total	2.92	2.90	2.90	2.73	4.38	4.16	3.09	3.73	3.62

Source: NSSO data for 1999-2000, 2004-05, and 2009-10 and ASI date for organised employment respective years.

A.2 Distribution of Organised and Unorganised Employment in Textile and Overall Manufacturing

Employment Category	*Textile Sector*	*Overall Mfg.*	*% of Ogr. employment in Textile*	*% of Org. employment in Overall Mfg.*	*Growth Rate (CAGR)*	
					Textile	*Overall Mfg.*
1994-95					1994-95 to 1999-2000	
Organised	1195417	9227097	10.59	21.78		
Unorganised	10096583	33134003			5.73	–2.40
Total	11292000	42361100				
1999-2000					1999-2000 - 2004-05	
Organised	1579682	8172836	**13.72**	18.55		
Unorganised	9936619	35788164			1.65	0.68
Total	11516301	44051000				
2004-05					2004-05 to 2009-10	
Organised	1714602	8453624	9.02	15.16		
Unorganised	17304496	47321018			5.58	6.88
Total	19019098	55774642				
2009-10					Decadal Growth rate (1999-2000 to 2009-10	
Organised	2249950	11792055	13.48	23.24		
Unorganised	14433308	38949784				
Total	16693258	50741839			3.60	3.73

Source: Computed from Annexure Table A.1 (Respective Years Data from NSSO for Total and Unorganised and ASO for Organised Employments).

A.3 Major Indicators of the Organised Segment of Textile and Overall Manufacturing

Economic Indicators	*1994-95*		*1999-2000*		*2004-05*		*2009-10*	
	Textile	*Overall Mfg.*	*Textile*	*Overall Mfg.*	*Textile*	*Overall Mfg.*	*Textile*	*Overall Mfg.*
1. No. of factories	12633	123010	17025	131558	16918	136353	19459	158877
2. Employment								
(a) Workers	1011328	6970116	1335702	6280659	1464086	6599298	1921781	9157802
(b) Total persons engaged	1195417	9227097	1579682	8172836	1714602	8453624	2249950	11792055
3. Fixed Capital	1255096	27764512	4772534	40186473	5099685	51306925	11243957	135218367
4. Invested Capital	2227126	38753459	7051852	56663430	7588415	75941770	16245312	193305395
5. Inputs	3278191	39079472	14070529	70936465	11022303	136294133	21273271	303585334
6. Output	4201830	51798701	16395197	89793835	13483116	167256142	26131556	373303593
7. Gross Value Added	923640	12719229	2324668	18857371	2460814	30962010	4858285	69718259
8. Wages to Workers	273800	2201946	364596	2630427	619480	3363505	1114933	6894071
9. Total Emoluments	350405	3534151	641217	4784351	937683	6440594	1806148	14700696

Source: Annual Survey of Industries for different years.

A.4 GDP at Current Price (Current Price and Values are in Rs. Crores)

Industry	*Year/Industrial Category*							
	1994-95		*1999-2000*		*2004-05*		*2009-10*	
	Registered	*Unregistered*	*Registered*	*Unregistered*	*Registered*	*Unregistered*	*Registered*	*Unregistered*
Textile	13843	17007	17538	27915	25355	41291	51501	55525
Over all Mfg.	96606	58924	158535	112719	292344	160881	626452	280578
Price Index at 1993-94 base price	112.6		145.3		187.3		242.9	

GDP at constant price (1993-94 base)

Industry	*Year/Industrial Category (value in Rs. Crore)*							
	1994-95		*1999-2000*		*2004-05*		*2009-10*	
	Registered	*Unregistered*	*Registered*	*Unregistered*	*Registered*	*Unregistered*	*Registered*	*Unregistered*
Textile	12293.96	15103.91	12070.20	19211.98	13537.11	22045.38	21202.55	22859.20
Total (Registered+ Unregistered)	27397.87		31282.17		35582.49		44061.75	
Over all Mfg.	85795.74	52330.37	109108.74	77576.74	156083.29	85894.82	257905.31	115511.73

Source: National Account Statistics, Back Volume Series, 2012.

17

Rural Empowerment through Eco-Tourisim

A Case Study on Darap Village in Sikkim

T.G. Ramaiah

Introduction

Travel and tourism is the biggest industry in the world which makes up 11 per cent of the total GDP of the world and 8 per cent of total employed population in this world and has emerged as a powerful source of income and wealth creation and to some extent helps in fueling tolerance in the world among different communities (Vikash Rikhye, 2008). In other words it shows the importance of tourism as such in the economy of a country. India, with a vast stretch of land possessing different geographical conditions, communities and cultures has immense potential to explore in this regard. However, not much importance is provided to the sector in real terms. Since, most of the tourism attractions were still dominated by ancient structures and buildings that have historical importance. In this context, the very concept of rural tourism sweeping through most of the countries has made little impact in India.

Ministry of Tourism, Government of India has laid top importance to the concept of rural tourism. The government document in this regard emphasizes the importance of rural tourism (Ministry of Tourism, 2010) in the following manner:

> "Tourism growth potential can be harnessed as a strategy for Rural Development. The development of a strong platform around the

> concept of Rural Tourism is definitely useful for a country like India, where almost 74 per cent of the population resides in its 7 million villages. Across the world the trends of industrialization and development have had an urban centric approach. Alongside, the stresses of urban lifestyles have led to a "counter-urbanization" syndrome. This has led to growing interest in the rural areas. At the same time this trend of urbanization has led to falling income levels, lesser job opportunities in the rural areas leading to an urbanization syndrome in the rural areas. Rural Tourism is one of the few activities which can provide a solution to these problems. Besides, there are other factors which are shifting the trend towards rural tourism like increasing levels of awareness, growing interest in heritage and culture and improved accessibility, and environmental consciousness. In the developed countries, this has resulted in a new style of tourism of visiting village settings to experience and live a relaxed and healthy lifestyle. This concept has taken the shape of a formal kind of Rural Tourism. Under this Scheme, thrust is to promote village tourism as the primary tourism product to spread tourism and its socio-economic benefits to rural and its new geographic regions. Key geographic regions are identified for development and promotion of Rural Tourism. The implementation is done through a Convergence Committee headed by the District Collector. Activities like improving the environment, hygiene, infrastructure, etc. are covered for assistance. Apart from providing financial assistance, the focus is to tap the resources available under different schemes of Department. of Rural Development, State Governments and other concerned Departments of the Government of India."

In fact, given the Indian context, the concept of rural tourism is defined (Ministry of Tourism and Culture, Government of India) in the following manner:

> "Any form of tourism that showcases the rural life, art, culture and heritage at rural locations, thereby benefiting the local community economically and socially as well as enabling interaction between the tourists and the locals for a more enriching tourism experience can be termed as rural tourism. Rural Tourism is essentially an activity which takes place in the countryside. It is multi-faceted and may entail farm/agricultural

> tourism, cultural tourism, nature tourism, adventure tourism, and eco-tourism. As against conventional tourism, rural tourism has certain typical characteristics like; it is experience oriented, the locations are sparsely populated, it is predominantly in natural environment, it meshes with seasonality and local events and is based on preservation of culture, heritage and traditions."

This in context, the Himalayan region is a big boon to promote Rural Tourism as an economic activity and at the same time promoting rural tourism. The Himalayan range possesses distinct geographical conditions and pattern of culture. The distinct nature of these two resulted in specific economic activities derived through geographical conditions, raw material available, specific skills possessed by the people inhabiting in the vicinity etc. Thus, the Himalayan region has distinct place for promoting 'Rural Tourism.'

Though, the Himalayan region has been attracting tourism from all over the world, the region's capacity to attract tourists on the basis of 'Rural Tourism' has not been widely practiced. Only a few such experiments were in vogue. One such experiment which has been considered as one of the successful 'Rural Tourism Initiative' is observed in Darap village in Sikkim State.

Darap Experiment on Rural Tourism

Darap Village is situated 16 kilometer away from the West Sikkim district headquarter. Educated unemployed Youths of-Darap Village has initiated Rural/Village Tourism realizing the potential of the nearby situated villages like—Ipsing, Sidibung, Seingpheng, Lagey and Rimbi under Yangthang Assembly constituency, West Sikkim. As these villages are rich in natural resources, bio-diversity and particularly very rich in cultures and customs of local tribes called 'Limboo's' and is inhibited by 95 per cent of Limboo population with their fascinating village lifestyle. Realizing the immense potential-natural beauty, rich biodiversity and culture of various communities living in our state and to provide mechanism to boost up the village economy, the villagers, group of likeminded people and the senior citizens constituted 'Darap Eco-Tourism Committee' with Hon. Area M.L.A. Shri P.L. Subba as its Patron in Chief and shri Sushil Tamang residence of Darap as president and organized ourselves into 'Darap Eco-Tourism Committee' and had decided to promote and develop Rural/ Village Tourism believing that it could be one sustainable sources of livelihood for the villagers. The involvement of educated unemployed youths in Tourism sector at the very grassroot level are making serious attempts to pursue tourism business as a means of bringing about affective economic development for the community as a whole.

Darap Eco-Tourism Committee

'Darap Eco-Tourism Committee' is a full-fledged non-profit making, secular and non-governmental organization. From its initial establishment the committee has been working towards providing livelihood especially to the villagers on sustainable basis by catering Tourist in the village. In order to support village tourism, construction of Tourism Centric Infrastructures or assets like—Ethnic Houses of three different communities of Sikkim i.e., Bhutia, Lepcha and Nepali, Traditional Limboo House is felt very necessary to attract Tourist. To demonstrate local culture to the Tourist, construction of combined Ampi-Theatre and Museum at the heart of the village is also felt very necessary. Darap Eco-Tourism Committee is the local community based organization which is leading the village community for tourism development. It brings the village youth under one roof to sensitize them and other members towards the development of sustainable form of tourism in the village. It has its own tourism office at Darap. Formed in 200 our objectives are to build awareness about natural and cultural resources and to mobilize the villagers on tourism and conservation activities. Their vision is to develop Darap as vibrant village society that is self-reliant and empowered its tourism activities.

The Vision of Darap Rural Tourism is "to accomplish sustainable development the organization has dedicated itself in nature conservation and promotional activities for the well-being of the people through sound eco-practice. Ultimately, the goal of the Committee is to to strengthen the Village home stays and establish links and promotion and cooperation between local communities and tourism stakeholders to benefit from tourism. As per the records available, the Mission statement of the Committee is as follows:

- To build capacity of Darap village community to cater tourist in home stay.
- To promote rural areas/village as eco-tourism and village tourist destination.
- To increase socio-economic status of rural areas/village through eco-tourism/village tourism.

- To raise the community participation level and to develop sense of ownership and belongingness.
- To conserve the environment this is main biodiversity capital of our State.
- To conserve the culture and tradition of the communities living in the area.
- To make the development process of the village a sustainable one for the local people."

How does Darap Eco-Tourism Committee Work

Home Stay for the tourist is being organized by the 'Darap Eco-Tourism Committee' at different houses of the members of the committee at Darap village. So far, the society has identified *thirty houses for Home stay, out of which 10 are the operators and one village resort and one village retreat under Darap Eco-Tourism Committee*. Beside this, the maintenance of other houses is also under way giving sanitation the topmost priority. Furthermore, in order to ensure the equitable benefits to the community, operational guidelines have been framed for equal opportunity for income and also the tourist gets good service.

Strategies for Promoting Rural Tourism

The rural tourism cluster has enough growth potential provided strategic intervention is made in certain "Key Areas."

The "Key Areas" in which the strategic interventions are as follows:

- Improvement in the interpretation of the site for better visitor satisfaction.
- Village beautification, waste management and hygiene issues.
- Skill Development Practical trainings for Diversification of product.
- Capacity building to sustain the product and provide better tourist satisfaction.
- Telecommunication facilities for the cluster for enhanced communication.
- Publishing promotional and publicity materials.
- Networking among tourism operators and other key stakeholders.
- Developing and strengthening the vertical and horizontal linkages.

- Awareness and tourism quality consciousness by conducting seminars, workshops and exposure visits.
- Orientation programmes for conservation and responsible practices.
- Product diversification and enhancement.

Darap Eco-tourism Project

The enterpreneuring village youth, driven by the urge to conserve their culture and at the same time equipped with entrepreneurial skills. approached the government with a comprehensive project plan with an outlay of Rs. 34 lakhs, out of which Rs. 17 lakhs is the committee's investment. SABCOO Bank Gangtok offered them a loan of Rs. 17 lakhs.

The broad activities of the project includes in Table 17.1.

Results from the Project

The systematic approach, attention on culture, care for environment and the strategy adopted resulted in successful implementation of the project. For instance, the project attracted 500 visitors in the initial year i.e., 2005, and it rose to already 1070 visitors in the year 2010. The following Table 17.2 depicts the economy of the project from its inception year to till date.

As observed from the information provided, the following important aspects can be derived:

- Dramatic progress in attracting domestic visitors.
- Consistency in attracting foreign visitors.
- Over 100 per cent increase in turn-over within a span of six years.
- Consistency in maintaining 100 per cent net profit against the expenditure incurred.

In other words, the novel idea of village/Rural/Eco-tourism project in Darap village is increasing its strength and viability since its inception. Since the project is built on exposure on traditional culture, the tourist traffic is not disturbing their culture as well and this has been the bastion of the project.

Table 17.1: BUDGET: Proposed Budget for Rural Tourism at Darap Nambu

Sl. No.	*Activities*	*Cost*
1.	**Feasibility Study and Planning Framework**	
1.1	Planning and Feasibility assessments	10,000
1.2	Initial sensitization of Stakeholder	10,000
2.	**Product Development and Site Enhancement**	
2.1	Identification home stay operators	10,000
2.2	Village beautification - garbage / solid-waste management	15,000
2.3	Interpretation and signage in village and trails	20,000
3.	**Trainig Capacity Building of Service Providers**	
3.1	Spoken English	10,000
3.2	Organizational development training	12,000
3.3	Lodge and Home stay operator training	15,000
3.4	Guides training	16,000
3.5	Porters training and cooks training	12,000
3.6	Ecotourism Awareness Training	10,000
3.7	Computer operation and training	10,000
4.	**Marketing and Promotion**	
4.1	Market Survey	10,000
4.2	Development of promotional material	30,000
4.3	Exposure Visit	30,000
5.	**Monitoring and Evaluation**	
5.1	Mid-term evaluation	10,000
5.2	Final evaluation	20,000
6.	**Human Resource Cost**	
6.1	Project Coordinator	5,000
6.2	Project Assistant	2,500
7.	**Administrative Cost**	
7.1	Stationery	2,000
7.2	Communication	1,000
8.	**Local Travel and Conveyance**	
8.1	Travel cost	4,000
9.	**Infrastructure Cost**	
9.1	Village Marketing Centre	
10.	**Equipments**	
10.1	Village Telecommunication Centre	

Source: Darap ECO-Tourism Committee.

Table 17.2: Investment on ECO Tourism

Sl. No.	*Loan from the SABCOO Bank*	*Individual contribution*	*Total Investment*
1.	17,000,00 lakhs	17,000,00 lakhs	34,000,00 lakhs

Source: Darap ECO-Tourism Committee.

Table 17.3: Expenditure particulars ECO-Tourism Resorts

Sl. No.	*Year*	*Total no. of Visitors*	*Domestic*	*Foreigners*	*Income*	*Expenditure*	*Net Profit*
1.	2005	500	150	350	5,00,000	2,50,000	2,50,000
2.	2006	651	300	351	6,51,000	3,25,000	3,26,000
3.	2007	781	381	400	7,81,000	3,90,000	3,91,000
4.	2008	821	500	321	8,21,000	4,00,000	4,21,000
5.	2009	930	600	330	9,30,000	4,50,000	4,80,000
6.	2010 till date	1070	686	384	10,00,000	5,00,000	5,00,000

Source: Darap ECO-Tourism Committee.

Observations on Scope and Threats to the Project in Darap

The village has rich bio-diversity and located adjacent to the Khanchendzonga National Park. Though the village has a mixed community, the social cohesion among the different ethnic groups is very strong. The villagers are very excited to have rural tourism development and the newly formed Darap Eco-Tourism Committee is spearheading the movement. The village is rich in agricultural produce with strong Animal husbandry practices. The site is accessible and had remarkable forests and water falls. However, due to lack of exposure and remoteness the villagers have been slightly marginalized. Though the village has many government schools, they all are mostly primary and JHS with only one senior secondary school. Much of the State developmental packages have not reached the village due to its remote location. The young educated youth of the village feel deprived and have a great sense of economic backwardness. However, the village has an opportunity to become self-reliant and develop more employment opportunities for the youngsters. Farming and animal husbandry being the main occupation of the people can be incorporated in the tourism activities, by means of which people can earn the a supplementary income. Developing tourism, would also give them a chance to develop their skills required for hospitality and conservation of their culture and environment. Improvement in sanitation facilities can benefit to improve overall standard of living in the village. Exposure with the outside world will give them a chance to improve their knowledge and awareness. With the presence of the Darap Eco-Tourism Committee, the organization can systematically monitor the tourism activities empower the local people to be involved in innovative mechanisms. Being the tourism representative of the village cluster, infringement of outsiders in the village can be checked. The village has a strong potential to become a successful rural tourism destination, on working to their fullest strength and building upon their opportunities and addressing the threats.

Summary and Conclusion

Darap, a remote village in Sikkim, has shown the world the immense potential of rural tourism and its role in generating employment and economic development in the region. It has also excelled in how a enterprising and enlightened local people can turn the opportunities group of great strength in terms of preservation of culture and at the same time utilizing the same for promoting economic development. The project as well as earned enough attraction from the visiting tourism just by virtue of show-casing the local 'culture' and 'culture products' to the visiting tourists like pattern of agriculture, local artifacts etc. as an attractive elements in promoting rural tourism.

The local Eco-Tourism Committee too displayed enough entrepreneurship skills by dovetailing its efforts with other business organizations. The novel feature of the project is it has been a successful rural tourism venture without disturbing the local culture and geographical terrain. This has been a rare success in the rural tourism sector which was backed by local wisdom, culture, entrepreneurial skills and the local leadership. If these issues are taken care of elsewhere, rural tourism ventures can be promoted in a quicker manner and provide immense employment opportunities to the local youth.

References

Darap Eco-Tourism Committee.

Ministry of Tourism and Culture, Government of India, Website.http://tourism.gov.in/policy/schrural.htm

Vikas Rikhiye, (2008) http://www.vikasrikhye.com/2008/11/24/rural-tourism-in-india/

SITE PHOTOS

Traditional Cottage Cherry Village Resort

Yuma Meditation Centre

DARAP Cherry Village

Traditional Nepali Dance

Chabrung Dance

Farmer Ploughing The Field

Homestay

Tourist Enjoying Food at Cherry Village Resort

Mountain Seen from Upper DARAP

Index